Before the Age of Prejudice

"Today, when individual acts of terror by fanatic Muslims throw up a pall of prejudice against all of Islam, Shirin Tahir-Kheli's story stands out in stirring contrast. George H. W. Bush deeply admired Shirin, and as vice president took her with him to difficult countries like Yemen where she, as a brilliant American Muslim, came up with contacts and insights of great value to Washington. I was on such trips, and saw Shirin in action. Hers is a unique book, full of lessons for all who seek clearer understanding of Islam."
—Donald P. Gregg, *National Security Advisor to Vice President Bush, 1982–88*

Shirin Tahir-Kheli

Before the Age of Prejudice

A Muslim Woman's National Security Work with Three American Presidents

A Memoir

Shirin Tahir-Kheli
Philadelphia, PA, USA

Additional material to this book can be downloaded from http://extras.springer.com.

ISBN 978-981-10-8550-5   ISBN 978-981-10-8551-2 (eBook)
https://doi.org/10.1007/978-981-10-8551-2

Library of Congress Control Number: 2018936581

© The Editor(s) (if applicable) and The Author(s) 2018
This work is subject to copyright. All rights are solely and exclusively licensed by the Publisher, whether the whole or part of the material is concerned, specifically the rights of translation, reprinting, reuse of illustrations, recitation, broadcasting, reproduction on microfilms or in any other physical way, and transmission or information storage and retrieval, electronic adaptation, computer software, or by similar or dissimilar methodology now known or hereafter developed.
The use of general descriptive names, registered names, trademarks, service marks, etc. in this publication does not imply, even in the absence of a specific statement, that such names are exempt from the relevant protective laws and regulations and therefore free for general use.
The publisher, the authors and the editors are safe to assume that the advice and information in this book are believed to be true and accurate at the date of publication. Neither the publisher nor the authors or the editors give a warranty, express or implied, with respect to the material contained herein or for any errors or omissions that may have been made. The publisher remains neutral with regard to jurisdictional claims in published maps and institutional affiliations.

Cover image: Author with President George W. Bush on Air Force One, April 2003

Printed on acid-free paper

This Palgrave Macmillan imprint is published by the registered company Springer Nature Singapore Pte Ltd. part of Springer Nature
The registered company address is: 152 Beach Road, #21-01/04 Gateway East, Singapore 189721, Singapore

Dedicated to
The American Dream

Acknowledgements

My American Dream became reality. So many individuals helped in that journey. I wish to thank a few of those individuals here. I served on the national security staff of Presidents Ronald Reagan, George H. W. Bush, and George W. Bush at a time when the National Security Council was very small and collegial. Access to the Oval Office allowed me to get to know the presidents and to offer my views on issues in my portfolio. I was always treated with kindness and professional courtesy by these leaders who occupied the most powerful office in the world.

The National Security Advisors I served—Bud McFarlane, John Poindexter, Frank Carlucci, Colin Powell, Brent Scowcroft, and Condoleezza Rice—took my views seriously and always allowed me a fair hearing.

It was a privilege to work for Secretaries of State George Shultz, James Baker, Lawrence Eagleburger, Colin Powell, and Condoleezza Rice. My participation in the American foreign policy process was enhanced due to their support.

Condoleezza Rice first suggested in 2003 that I tell my story. Vartan Gregorian convinced me to finish the tale. I am grateful to both.

Years in Washington allowed me to develop links with so many talented individuals in the US government and beyond. Ruth Whiteside and Jim Shelhammer made Washington home for me. Donald Fortier and Donald Gregg shared the enthusiasm and the hard work of promoting better ties between India and Pakistan. John Howe, Anne Heligenstein, and Donald Silberberg were critical to the public—private partnership led by the USA that built the first pediatric cancer hospital in Iraq.

Work on improved USA—India relations and India—Pakistan normalized ties would not have been possible without the support of Prime Ministers Rajiv Gandhi, Narisimha Rao, and Atal Bihari Vajpayee. Their senior advisors, Ronen Sen, Mani Shankar Aiyar, Pratap Kaul, S. K. Kaul, Girish Saxena, S. Jaishankar, Salman Haidar, Brajesh Mishra, Jaswant Singh as well as some outside government, Bharat Bhushan, Shekhar Gupta, Malini Parthasarathy, and R. K. Mishra were all critical to helping build a better future. Jaswant Singh supported joint work on energy and environment which remains a blue print for future progress between India and Pakistan. While the subcontinent remains unsettled, I am hopeful that permanent peace is possible.

Pakistan's Prime Ministers Benazir Bhutto and Nawaz Sharif supported improved Indo-Pak ties, and I am grateful for their vision of a better future in Indo-Pakistan relations. President Pervez Musharraf supported back channel talks that broke some new ground toward rapprochement. Senior members of Pakistan's establishment, Sahabzada Yaqub Khan, Syed Babar Ali, Shaharyar Khan, Mahmud Ali Durrani, Shahid Khaqan Abbasi, and Shah Mehmood Qureshi were indispensable to changing the mindset. I will forever be grateful for their contribution. Their vision for Pakistan made an enormous difference to stability and peace.

Sadia and Hafeez Pirzada were always consummate hosts and tutors through years of discourse on Pakistani politics.

Robert Strausz-Hupe took a chance giving me entry to the graduate program at the age of eighteen. When I received my M.A. in International Relations a year later, he made me a junior fellow at the Foreign Policy Research Institute, then part of the University of Pennsylvania. My Ph.D. dissertation supervisor, Alvin Rubinstein, mentored me for the rough and tumble of a professional career.

The production of a book is a complicated affair. The search for declassified official documents from the Reagan presidency took me to the Ronald Reagan Presidential Museum and Library set in picturesque Simi Valley, California. Chief Archivist Ray Wilson and his staff were incredibly helpful and welcoming.

Mark Ramee at the Department of State oversaw the clearance of the manuscript through various parts of the US government with efficiency and thoroughness.

Alan Luxenberg, who replaced my friend Harvey Sicherman as President of the Foreign Policy Research Institute, cheerfully guided me through various issues of scholarship and editing of the manuscript. Darryl Hart made the lengthy manuscript readable while keeping my voice. Eli Gilman, Tatiana Cunningham, Ash Khayami, Thomas Shattuck, and Payton Windell helped with the critical final work of pulling it all together.

Robert Intemann gave generously of his time and talent in helping incorporate some of the images of my life into the manuscript. He and his wife Marguerite were always hospitable despite the time my requests took away from their other commitments.

My dear friend Mary Ann Weems badgered me through summers in New Mexico to finish the story. She suffered through my discussions of various parts of the manuscript with humor and sound advice. Her suggestion to title this book "Lifting the Veil" was tempting.

I want to thank the Dean of Johns Hopkins University School of Advanced International Studies, Vali Nasr, and Director of the Foreign Policy Institute, Carla Freeman, for their support of my work. The late Donna Dejban, my longtime colleague and friend, was an important and creative presence in Washington in all of the institutions I have served.

Palgrave Macmillan Senior Editor Jacob Dryer and Editorial Assistant Anushangi Weekaroon helped immensely in the publication of the manuscript. I am indebted to them for their sound advice.

My parents, Khurshid, and Raziuddin Siddiqi were exceptional people. Their example of public service and strong support for education shaped my life. Their pride in my record of public service in my adopted land, America, was total. They imparted a sense of adventure and a trust in performance that made it possible to move alone half a world away from them to go to Ohio Wesleyan University at the age of fifteen.

Toufiq Siddiqi, always the most brilliant, thoughtful, handsome, and kind big brother a girl could have, helped push for the work of a collaborative South Asia. An energy and environment expert, his path-breaking work produced joint efforts on water and energy. He and his wife, Ulrike, remain a source of support and love.

Leaving home early means distances between siblings. I was very fortunate to remain close to my sisters, Farida and Sayeeda. While work kept moving me in different directions, sisters provide a key link for memories and great reunions.

I married early and Raza, my husband, a physicist, changed my life in so many ways. His quip in response to my comment shortly after we married in 1962: "I am going to be a housewife" with "We live in an apartment, you need to get a Ph.D." launched my professional life. A young mother needs the help of her children in order to juggle a variety of roles. My daughter Shehra and son Kazim always made my life worthwhile with their love, even as an absentee mother who commuted home to Pennsylvania on weekends from Washington. I am so very proud of who they are and what they have achieved and celebrate their respective choice of a perfect life partner: Ethan Boldt for Shehra and Victoria Bogdanova for Kazim.

Grandchildren make the later years extremely special. Blessed with Gadia and Cyrus Boldt and twins Alexander and Taisiya Tahir-Kheli, I have so much to be grateful for.

A special thanks to Carnegie Corporation of New York for supporting the work of looking back at my life and experiences with major grants.

Philadelphia, PA, USA
November 2017

Contents

Part I Cradle of Civilization

1	The Times: Celebrating Hyderabadi Style	3
2	The Old and the New	11
3	Education and Romance	23

Part II Milestones

4	Return to the USA	41
5	Back to Pakistan	53

Part III Call to Duty

6	Home Is Where You End Up	63
7	Monitoring Pakistan as a Scholar	69
8	US Army War College (USAWC)	75

9	Joining the Secretary of State's Staff	79
10	The Zia Visit	83
11	Returning to the Land of My Ancestors	91
12	The Burden of Being First	97
13	Diplomacy with India	105
14	Adding Pakistan to the Equation	111
15	Failed Statecraft?	119
16	Ambassador from Where?	129
17	The First Gulf War	135
18	The Last Trust Territory: Palau	141
19	The Muslim Ambassador from the USA	145
20	"Name and Shame"	151
21	Return to the University	157
22	The BALUSA Group	163
23	Family Life	171

Part IV Taking Stock

| 24 | Washington Return | 191 |
| 25 | George W. Bush Years | 197 |

26	9/11	203
27	White House Redux	213
28	A Changed Model	229
29	Democracy Promotion	237
30	Ongoing Diplomacy in South Asia	253
31	Return to Democracy	279
32	The Freedom Agenda: What Went Wrong?	285
33	GTMO	303
34	Forum for the Future	321
35	Vice President Cheney	333
36	The American Legacy of the Basrah Children's Hospital	343
37	Trip to Iraq	359
38	Rallying Support	375
39	The Big Picture	387
40	Women's Empowerment	399
41	Reflections	403
Appendix		431
Index		437

About the Author

Ambassador Shirin Tahir-Kheli is a Senior Fellow, Foreign Policy Institute, Johns Hopkins University School of Advanced International Studies, and an Adjunct Scholar and Member of the Board of Advisors at the Foreign Policy Research Institute in Philadelphia.

As a senior member of the US government in three stints during the 1982–2009 years, she worked with key foreign and domestic policy advisers around the world in her conduct of US foreign policy issues. As Special Assistant to the President and Senior Director for Democracy, Human Rights, and International Operations, she oversaw the work of the National Security Council in these areas and chaired meetings of other agencies of the US government in matters related to her portfolio.

As Senior Adviser to the Secretary of State, Tahir-Kheli played a key role in policy formulation toward UN Reform during a critical year for reform efforts and has been central to the effort to support women's empowerment. She has worked with the international community and has spearheaded the establishment and the work of the Women Leaders' Working Group, which consists of twenty foreign ministers and five heads of state/government.

Throughout the course of her stint in the US government and in her academic career, Tahir-Kheli has been active in outreach efforts and worked to mentor students around the globe.

Ambassador Tahir-Kheli has dedicated more than ten years to finding areas of agreement between India and Pakistan that could change their relationship to one of productive peace. Toward that end, she has been chair of the 12-member BALUSA Group comprising senior Indian and Pakistani and US participants that is geared to influencing policy toward cooperation. She has co-chaired an important study on "Water and Security in South Asia" and has been co-chair of an effort to promote India–Pakistan cooperation in the fields of energy and the environment.

She is the author and editor of several monographs, including: *Pakistan Today: The Case for U.S. – Pakistan Relations* (FPI SAIS, 2017), *India, Pakistan and the United States: Breaking with the Past* (Council on Foreign Relations, 1997), *The United States and Pakistan: The Evolution of an Influence Relationship* (Praeger, 1982), and numerous journal articles, including *Manipulating Religion for Political Gain in Pakistan: Consequences for the U.S. and the Region* (Johns Hopkins SAIS, 2015).

Shirin Tahir-Kheli has a Ph.D. in International Relations from the University of Pennsylvania and a B.A. from Ohio Wesleyan University. She has been a member of the Council on Foreign Relations since 1990 and a past member of the International Institute for Strategic Studies.

Prologue

The Boeing 707 is cruising at an altitude of 36,000 feet. It is a hot summer day in May. The sky is clear. Suddenly, several people on the aircraft point outside at the appearance of six fighter jets flying in close proximity, three on either side. Someone inside the plane explains that the fighter jets represent an honor guard to escort the aircraft, which carries special markings. The honored visitor and the five accompanying officials inside the aircraft all watch. The official photographer takes a beautiful photo of the escort. As I watch along with the few other colleagues present, I ponder this special landing in a place of great familiarity. The circumstances of my return are indeed unusual, but so much of what I will be privy to upon landing is genuinely familiar.

As the plane starts its descent, a hushed announcement indicates five minutes to "wheels down," official parlance for landing. This is Air Force Two with USA blazoned on its fuselage. It is taking Vice President George H. W. Bush to Islamabad on the second leg of his May 1984 journey to the Indian subcontinent. I am there as an advisor on the visit as a member of the White House National Security Council Staff.

PART I

Cradle of Civilization

CHAPTER 1

The Times: Celebrating Hyderabadi Style

Born in Hyderabad Deccan, in pre-partition India, I was aware of my religion from earliest childhood. Hyderabad was a Muslim-ruled state, though the population was largely Hindu. Hyderabad's nobility was Muslim and lived an elegant and lavish life based on old traditions. Hyderabad was a wealthy state where the ruler, called the Nizam, wanted reasonable education and health access for all his subjects, an uncommon practice in the day. The gold and precious stone mines of the state allowed for spending on public well-being.

My maternal grandfather was the "peshi" (first) minister to the Nizam. He was an important man in the state's government. My paternal grandfather had lands in Aurangabad in central Hyderabad. When my parents married, my father, Dr. Raziuddin Siddiqi, returned to India after completing his education in the UK and Europe. He did his Tripos in mathematics at Cambridge University in England. He then went on to do a master's in Paris and a Ph.D. in physics in Germany. He had studied in the 1930s with the stars of the day: Heisenberg, Dirac and Einstein. His entire education, from first grade to the Ph.D., had been paid for by the Nizam's government. Merit was universally rewarded, he used to say, whenever I marveled at the "socialist" bent of the state!

These were neither the best of times nor the worst of times, to quote a cliché. Born just prior to the partition of the subcontinent in 1947, I was lucky to be in the south, Hyderabad. We were spared the turmoil of partition but the partition of the Indian subcontinent by Great Britain into India and Pakistan left no one untouched.

My mother was my best friend.

Her name was Khurshid, which means the sun in Persian. She was a favorite daughter of a nobleman. She lost her mother when the youngest of her siblings, her brother, was born. She was very close to her sister and brother all of whom were brought up by their paternal grandmother. There were many cousins, and all of them enjoyed vacations together in wonderful hill stations of India. They swam, went boating and hiked. Family became an important component, and these ties sustained our family even after many moved to Pakistan while others remained Indian.

The family was liberal by subcontinental standards. Girls were education, with most of them completing high school and on rare occasion receiving a graduate degree. Girls in the family married young, in keeping with the tradition of the time. My mother followed in the tradition, marrying when she was not yet fifteen. It was an arranged marriage. My father was a dozen years older, already a rising star in the Indian scientific community. They were devoted to each other for the nearly seventy years they remained married.

I called her Mama, which was somewhat unusual in Hyderabad. She wanted me to call her that since my older siblings called her Apa. She was a stylish and elegant woman. She was 5 feet 4 inches with soft brown eyes. In her circle of friends and relatives in Hyderabad, India, clothes and jewels were designed for wear but nothing was worn frequently. My mother and aunt were leaders in fashion. I loved flopping around the house in her lovely high-heeled evening shoes, some bought in Europe. She never scolded me.

One of my first impressions of my mother was of her "ittar," perfume. Specially created for her, she wore it all the time. As a young child, I would climb on to her bed and lie next to Mama. I would sniff and tell her I like her smell. She would laugh and say it was the ittar. However, not realizing that the perfume gave her the wonderful aroma, I just thought this was how a mother smelled.

My father would recount the many trunks and cases of clothes and jewels my mother travelled with when he took her for her first European tour in April 1936. They set sail from Colombo, Ceylon, on "Victoria" for Marseilles, France. Travel took them to France, Germany, Norway, England, and Austria. Seeing the great cities of Europe and visiting old colleagues in Europe's major universities my father attended, he recalled that my mother was most fashionable. In Paris, she "caused a sensation" he remembered, in a yellow Sari with matching accessories. She would tell tales of the fashionable ladies of the era and compare it to the general sloppiness of attire on much later visits to Paris or London. "Where did the sense of style go?" she would lament.

She was a devoted daughter. When my grandfather suffered a stroke which left him partially paralyzed, she was always at his side. She told us that he was both her father and her mother and his loss would be difficult to bear. When he did pass away, she was already living in Pakistan, making frequent trips to India to be with him. Unfortunately, she was not with him when he died. I remember waking up in the middle of the night to the deep sorrowful crying of my mother for months.

Although we each had our respective nanny, we were disciplined as children by our mother. The nannies sometimes would fight with the cook to make sure that "their" child was served first at meals. This was often in the evenings if our parents were dining out.

Mama was a wonderful hostess, enjoying extensive entertaining. She would tell us that her cook, a Goan, would get upset if there were not at least a dozen additional people at dinner each night. She had a great sense of family and kept us close despite the continents that separated us as we grew up.

My mother was a firm believer in education for all her children, including her three daughters. She made sure that we were focused early on toward that goal. She said that especially with her husband being an education leader in the country, their children would serve as models for others. She regretted that she had not been formally educated beyond high school as she was married young. She felt educating us all was a sacred duty. When the best schooling meant boarding school, she agreed to send us away.

By the time of my birth, the academic bent of family existence was set. My brother, Toufiq, the first born, was the first grandson and was feted as such. My older sister was a tomboy. It fell on me to carry the fussy dressing traditions. I was delighted and happily indulged my mother's desire to supply me with a steady stream of outfits befitting a little princess. When I entered school at age four, I thought this was the school uniform and recall painful conversations with my parents stressing that gold lame outfits and pearl necklaces belonged in parlors, not at school.

A Muslim Upbringing

Religion was my father's arena. I called him Baba for father. He had the most amazing gentle eyes. He never scolded me. He was tutored at the famous Darul Uloom in Hyderabad starting at the age of five to learn Persian and Arabic where he studied the Quran along with mathematics, science, history, and geography. He became a learned scholar of religious thought and knew the Quran through detailed study. He was a scientist, a mathematician whose education, life, and work spanned the East and the West.

My mother was a "Syed," descended from the Prophet Mohammed. She had studied the Quran and learned religion from her grandmother and her aunt, both enlightened women for their time. Her aunt went to England to study the Montessori system of education and started an institution to promote children's education in that system in the 1920s Hyderabad. But it was Mama who helped me get started with my religious tradition. As customary in Muslim families, my religious education began at the age of four with the reading of the Quran.

Hyderabad was ceremony-prone. Elaborate ceremonies sprang up around all sorts of things, complete with lavish foods. At the age of four years, four months, and four days, I had my *Bismillah*, my initiation ceremony into Islam. I would recite *"Bism illah ir-rahman ir-rahim..."* (In the name of Allah, the compassionate, the merciful...).

On the day of my *Bismillah*, I had a *tika* on my little forehead, of diamonds and rubies. I had matching earrings. Life was perfect, I thought at the time. But beyond the ceremony, Bismillah meant that henceforth that was the religion you subscribed to.

There are a couple more milestones in religious education of children besides the "Bismillah." For me, the keeping of my first fast in Ramadan was an important occasion. I was seven years old, and the fast from dawn to dusk was an exciting prospect. I was told by my mother that the fast involved abstaining from water along with any other food. Nothing must pass your mouth, she stressed. Since Ramadan that year fell during the summer, the period of dawn to dusk fasting would be more than 15 hours.

Friday is the Muslim special day for prayers. I was to keep my first fast on a Friday. The Muslim calendar is a lunar one so the start of the month of Ramadan varies each year. The fasts occur in winter months when the days are short. There are months of Ramadan where the fast is eighteen hours. I was awakened at 3 a.m. for my meal before first light appears. When there is sufficient light to see a hair, the time for fasting begins.

The day went relatively quickly. I slept a bit more than was normal. The prospect of a celebratory meal at sunset encompassing the special foods common to Ramadan was something to look forward to. Late in the afternoon, my mother came into my bedroom. She asked how I felt and if I was glad to have embarked on a new experience central to Islam. I remember asking her "what is the purpose of the fast." She replied, "It is a time for reflection, prayer, simplification of needs." I then asked could I learn to say the prayer, another tenet of my religion.

My paternal grandfather, my Dada, taught me the "namaz." Muslims pray five times a day facing Mecca. The prayer is recited in Arabic and the format is set. I learned what to say in what sequence for each prayer. I was taught that religion is a private affair. Public displays of religiosity beyond the celebration days of Eid where Muslims pray in large congregations are not mandatory.

As a child, I accompanied my father when he went to the mosque for Eid prayers occurring two times a year, celebrating the end of Ramadan and the Haj, respectively. As an adolescent, I prayed at home. Much later, whenever I traveled to Islam's holy places or to beautiful mosques, I make it a tradition to pray outside my home. I have been fortunate in having prayed in the mosques of Mecca, Jerusalem, Istanbul, and Muscat, besides the exquisite mosques of the subcontinent.

Like much of India, Hyderabad was a multireligious state. While the ruler and the elite were Muslim, non-Muslims were an important part of the culture. Many non-Muslims, Hindus and Christians, served in the government and educational institutions. Many of my childhood friends were the children of these individuals who were family friends. Thus, my first sense of being a Muslim in a Muslim-ruled state with a Hindu majority did not mean the exclusion of others who were different from my circle of religion. The Hindu–Muslim divide which became the basis for the splitting of India and Pakistan did not touch me in my early years. Ours was an inclusive household. I was not taught that being "Muslim" meant cutting out or disrespecting those who were different.

That was the core of beliefs I carried as a child and it stayed with me long after Hyderabad…well into my journey and citizenship in America.

The year 1948 was a critical year in Hyderabad when police action by the newly independent Indian government led to the absorption of Hyderabad state into India. Under the British partition plan of the subcontinent in 1947, Hindu-majority areas became part of India and Muslim-majority areas went to Pakistan. The two notable exceptions were: Kashmir (Hindu ruler and Muslim-majority population, where the ruler opted for India—a decision still not accepted in Pakistan) and Hyderabad (Muslim ruler and Hindu-majority population whose ruler opted for Pakistan—similarly, a decision not accepted by India). The Indian Army occupied Hyderabad in September 1948, known locally as a "police action."

My life was eventually changed dramatically due to these developments.

I was about 6 years old when I recall my father (who traveled internationally a great deal along with extensive Indian travel) went on an annual journey to Lahore to lecture on mathematics and on poetry; he was a scholar of both. But in 1949, his normal travel to Lahore meant a journey to the newly established Pakistan. While he was there, the founders of Pakistan asked him to stay and help establish science and education in the new country. He agreed, which meant that in terms of Indian law, he surrendered his Indian citizenship and all of his property, including the house we lived in Hyderabad, and bank accounts and items stored in bank safety deposit boxes were then confiscated by the government of India.

This was in 1949 and my first memory of Muslim–Hindu International Relations. It is embedded in the shadow of the aftermath of my father's sudden move to Pakistan and the arrival of "custodian" officials in our house to remove all things that belonged to him, including his research papers. Even at the age of six, I felt the vindictiveness of the act and its pain. Was I ever going to see my father again? My mother assured me I would, and we waited for a few months as my grandfather was ailing and then moved to Pakistan in 1950.

Early in my life, I learned from my parents that you live with decisions you make. You spend no time lamenting loss of material possessions, even large estates and fabulous jewels. You follow your principles and adhere to your path of choice. Integrity is worth maintaining, and rewards for that come in time.

I saw how that ethic served to make my parents respected citizens of the country of their birth, India, and of their adoption, Pakistan.

The only person to have been a founding member of both the respective Indian and the Pakistan Academies of Science, even after his move to

Pakistan, my father went to India for meetings as a guest of the Indian government until the mid-1990s, when he became too frail to travel. That mattered to him and, by extension, to the rest of the family.

CHAPTER 2

The Old and the New

We have family in India. There are also childhood friends. Moving to Pakistan did not sever Indian family connections that took us there for weddings, funerals, and travel home.

I never heard any bitterness on the part of my parents that they had surrendered a gold mine of real estate in 1949–1950. Apart from my parent's residence, my grandfather's house in Banjara Hills, Hyderabad, was confiscated by the Indian government and is the Administrative Staff College of India today. My parents moved on to revive their relations with India. In a telling aside, my father, who was a Nehru Gold Medal for Science winner in India, talked of how in 1952 he returned from Pakistan to Delhi for a science meeting at which he again met Prime Minister Jawaharlal Nehru. "Why on earth did you go to Pakistan" Nehru asked? My father said he explained the circumstances that led to his lecture tour and the Pakistani Prime Minister asking him to stay and help with education. "Well then, now I'll ask you to come back," Nehru said with a twinkle.

"What did you say," I asked my father. He replied that he told Prime Minister Nehru "Sir, I shall become a stateless person if this continues!"

There was a sense that we were in Pakistan by choice. India was still a place of closeness for us even as we made Pakistan our new home. This was an early lesson for me as I chose the USA as my home decades later. It was a great way to grow up and a wonderful initiation of my global compass.

The Frontier

Even to a girl of six, the contrast between Hyderabad, India, and Peshawar, Pakistan, was dramatic. Where verdant gardens shaded clean organized boulevards in the former, one found chaotic dusty cluttered streets of the latter. There was openness to the terrain with the Khyber Mountain looming over the city of Peshawar.

The most distinctive part of Peshawar was its old city with the fort and the fabled "Qissa Qani," a collection of narrow streets with shops selling all manner of things from gold to copper and silver to spices and carpets and with the ubiquitous tea stalls that carried an aura of ancient secrets and modern danger. Even the animals on the road were different.

There was a preponderance of men in the bazaars. The scents of food cooking in the old city areas were tempting, even as they appeared foreign to tastes developed in the south of India. Hyderabadi cuisine, noted for its elaborate presentations and complex tastes, might as well have been from Mars! Peshawar with its open Tandoors, meat kababs, and huge plates of food seemed beyond belief! Restraint and delicacy were not the hallmarks of the new frontier.

Life was lived heartily. People ate with gusto. As they subscribed to extraordinary seclusion for their women, life was lived behind boundary walls. People dressed differently. Women were shielded head to toe in burqas or wore the white chadors they draped over their clothes.

For those who were invited into the inner sanctum, it was a different view. As I was a young child of six and part of the social network where my parents fast became friends with a new set of people, I was granted entrée.

While I spoke Urdu, the girls in Peshawar spoke Pashto. But to some extent Urdu provided communication links. I was soon to be dispatched to a boarding school in the hills of Murree, the Convent of Jesus and Mary. There, only English was allowed and the idea was to become conversant in this universally useful language. Urdu was not permitted at the school. My English proficiency was nonexistent. But I was unwilling to risk the wrath of the Nuns by communicating in my mother tongue. Instead, I rapidly focused in on the school's motto which could be loosely translated as: "speak English or die" and caught on fast as is likely at a young age in total immersion in any language.

From that moment, Urdu became my second language. I found myself as a child in the peculiar situation of using English as a primary language for communicating ideas. It did not strike me as strange even though we were in a culture where the proverbial "cloak of colonialism" had then only recently been thrown off. The British had left. They left in place language and customs developed over two centuries of occupation. The best private schools continued the English-only traditions. The parents did not object.

Immersion in English had a negative impact on learning the finer points of Urdu, beyond reading, writing, and speaking. I did not get exposed to the Persian influenced literature that was so important to my parents. My childhood English language focus meant that as an adult, I had no capacity to interact with the vibrant gatherings where poets gathered to share their own and recite verses written by noted poets of earlier times. As a child, when I was home from boarding school for vacations, I recall my father reciting in Persian and Arabic and regretting the total Western orientation of my own education. Some fifty years later, my father brought up the subject chastising himself for not insisting on some balance.

There was no heating in the buildings of the Convent of Jesus and Mary even though the school is set at an altitude of 7500 ft. in Murree which was established by the Governor of Punjab, Sir Henry Lawrence, as a sanatorium, or "hill station" for British troops in 1851. The school vacation period extended through the harshest winter months, December–March, when the worst of the snow came. The school provided for a Spartan existence.

On the simple diet of lentils, and brown bread for breakfast, the daily lessons began.

Beyond language proficiency, the Murree Convent had a massive influence. There was little hot water and we had to make our own beds, dress ourselves, and complete the morning chores regardless of age rather than being waited upon by maids. We were in charge of our own uniforms. Keeping to the strict school program and timetable was also left to students. There were heavy penalties for breaking discipline so most went along.

We arose at six in the morning in the snowbound cold hills. After cold-water cleansing and dressing, we marched off through the snow-cleared passage of the school courtyard to the Chapel for early Catholic Mass, recited in Latin. We were watched like hawks so no fidgeting, even for the youngest.

I recall once asking the supervising Belgian nun why chapel was a requirement. "You want to succeed, don't you?" "Of course," I replied. "Then," she said, "You must go to Chapel and pray!"

A month went by and the excruciatingly early visit began to make a dent in my appreciation for this center of excellence.

The early morning routine in winter months had me searching for a solution. Finally, I asked to go see Mother Superior, a highly unusual move in the best of circumstances. The day of the appointment arrived and I nervously made my way to the office where the tall, broad shouldered senior most Nun in her habit awaited me. She looked down a ways at me and asked in a dulcet tone: "What do you want to say, child?"

Here was my opening. "Mother Superior, you know that I am a Muslim?" "Yes" came the reply. "You know that Muslims do not go to Mass in a Catholic Church?" "What are you saying?" she asked. "Only that that if you excuse me from attending the 6 a.m. service, I will never mention it to anyone, including my father (whom the Nun knew was important in education in Pakistan) that I am forced to go." After a shocked moment, Mother Superior said with a twinkle in her eye "It will be our secret." Thereafter, I never went to Mass and I never told anyone why I did not. A first negotiation ended amicably.

Only at the end of the term as we headed in the gaily painted school-rented buses from the hill station toward the plains of Rawalpindi from whence we would all travel to our respective homes, did the mood change. Then, all students would chant favorite songs, e.g., "No more English, no more French; No more sitting on a hard hard bench; if the teacher interferes: knock her down and box her ears ......"

But the school taught me independence and self-sufficiency. It meant going to a place where you knew no one and making it work. At the age of six that early lesson did not seem necessary. However, when I came to the USA at the age of fifteen, the philosophy was critically helpful.

Growing Up in the Shadow of the Khyber Pass

Even in the frontier town atmosphere of Peshawar, bordering on the famous Khyber Pass providing passage to Afghanistan, there were traditions based on a different culture than that of my background. Peshawar was proudly Pathan. There was a visceral tribal connection between people, and the rules of engagement were very different from the hierarchical interactions between the rulers and the ruled that was Hyderabad. There was more of an egalitarian atmosphere in Peshawar.

A "Khan" or landowner chief always shook hands with his land tenants or his male household staff members. He spoke to them with respect, and he was careful to ensure hospitality was extended to all who visited, of rank high or low.

In 1950, my mother was the only woman in Peshawar who wore a sari (recognized as an Indian form of dress) rather than Pakistan's shalwar kameez (trousers and shirt). She did not wear a chador or a burqa. She did not seem self-conscious although it might have been difficult to be so visible in her Hyderabad roots. Looking back, it was an adventurous time and we all approached it as such.

Family and friends had been left behind in India. New ones had to be made. My youngest sister, Sayeeda, was an infant. I was six years old and at an age when it was easy to make new friends. The first circle comprised the daughters of other senior officials in the small town that was Peshawar. Some twenty-plus families interacted regularly in casual as well as more formal settings. The tradition of "calling" on friends and families meant there was a good amount of daily interaction.

Within the circle of friendship, "purdah," i.e., the separation of sexes was unenforced. Girls tended to gravitate to a different place in the house although as children we met the males of another household and family.

Another ring of friends came from school. In the Convent of Jesus and Mary, most of the girls I got to know and the senior class members, who were prominent, were mostly from the Northwest Frontier Province, Peshawar being its capital.

Women were publicly sidelined but wielded considerable influence within the family. My mother connected with these mothers/wives. Discussions in the informal atmosphere of their get-togethers focused on the need for girls' education. There was considerable emphasis on how to make sure their daughters had every opportunity. One such formidable woman was Bajigul (older sister flower) Safdar, a hookah-smoking matriarch with several extremely talented children of both genders. She struck awe as she held forth with emphasis on why it mattered to all that girls get ahead.

My mother would take me on her visits to Bajigul. I learned a lot from the women gathered there. At a young age, I assumed that these gatherings represented the norm beyond the two dozen influential families of Peshawar. At the time, I was not old enough to understand that girls around the world did not grow up with assurances that they would go on to college and professional careers.

Bajigul remained a force, and her two daughters went on to college in Pakistan and university in the UK (Cambridge University) to respectively become a scholar in English and a member of Pakistan's Foreign Service. Her son also joined the Foreign Service and rose to the rank of Foreign Secretary.

My mother, normally a lot less strident on the matter, was equally forceful in pushing for the need for fund-raising for less fortunate girls to go to school in Peshawar. She headed up the Peshawar Chapter of the All Pakistan Women's Association and spearheaded fund-raisers that helped support education, women's shelters, and employment.

This was the 1950s. There was a great deal of excitement about what Pakistan meant and how progress could be made in a nation where independence had been hard won. The Northwest Frontier Province was ambivalent about the Muslim League which spearheaded partition from India. The Pathans disliked Punjabis a great deal more than they did the Hindus and were sorry to see familiar people leave.

In 1954, I transferred from the boarding school in Murree to the Saint Xavier Presentation Convent in Peshawar. Going as a day student was so much better. Life at home was bliss, and the boarding school had already instilled the discipline for self-sufficiency and hard work that my mother oversaw. There were no more nannies to look after every need. Yet, it was a privileged upbringing.

The reason for our move to Peshawar was the desire of the government to build new major universities to kickstart higher education in Pakistan. The area that separated from India was far less developed. The balance needed correction, and my father was a crucial man in that effort.

Building a large university in Peshawar in an area where the Islamia College campus existed made sense. It was outside the military cantonment area where the gates were locked from sunset to sunrise. For several miles after the gates, there was a single lane asphalt road built by the British as part of the Grand Trunk Road system. That road traversed past Islamia College and continued onto the fabled Khyber Pass. Alongside were verdant fields around which clustered mud hut villages. The area was pretty much considered as a "no man's land" in the early 1950s.

But land was available and belonged to the government. This was where Peshawar University with its planned professional medical, engineering, law and humanities and science faculties would rise. Making the decision was the easy part.

As I heard told around the dinner table, the need for education was huge. Resources in a new country were extremely limited. Any area of study requiring equipment for training was in particular jeopardy. When I queried my father why he had to travel outside the country so much, he replied that it was because he was a known person in Europe from his extensive stay there during 1926 to 1936 period and after 1951. His friends and colleagues, who studied mathematics and physics with him or were his tutors, occupied important positions in the scientific recovery of various countries.

As Europe pulled itself out of WWII, my father's friends understood the special hardship of building science in resource-starved Pakistan. In 1951, they came to the rescue and offered help in the development of Peshawar and Karachi universities.

Witness to History and Participating in Diplomacy

These were heady times. My parent's generation was the pioneer sacrificing for and building Pakistan. Listening to conversations, around our dinner table or others, one got caught up with the dreams of a new nation. Peshawar was a quiet place. But here too there was a sense of urgency and plans for lifting the entire province and the nation into a new era of prosperity. India and Pakistan became independent of colonial rule decades before many other nations did. Progress was often difficult. As the lesser known and developed country compared to newly independent India, Pakistan worked hard to put itself on the map.

In March 1952, an important Science Conference was held at the rapidly rising Peshawar University campus. I was present as the boarding school term was out. There were eminent foreign scientists present, including Dr. Lea Dubridge who was President of Caltech; Professor G. P. Thompson from the UK; Dr. Harold Hartley of the Royal Society. As the local host, my father oversaw their stay and I got to meet these amazing men with a sense of history in the making in Peshawar. Protocol was stepped up as the Governor General of Pakistan Ghulam Mohammad came to Peshawar from the capital in Karachi in order to inaugurate the conference.

Among those who visited at other times in that period, received an honorary degree, and often dined at our residence were: Eleanor Roosevelt in 1952, Prime Minister Laurent of Canada in 1954, King Faisal of Iraq in 1954, and Ambassador Hildreth of the USA in 1955.

I remember meeting President Sukarno of Indonesia in 1950, a very young King Hussein of Jordan who came with his mother, Queen Zein in 1953, King Saud of Saudi Arabia in 1955, and Premier Chou En-lai of China who came on an eight-day visit of Pakistan in 1956.

Pakistan was the first Muslim state to recognize the People's Republic of China in 1950.

Even as children, daughters and son in our family were taught the protocol of high-level visits. We got to meet the distinguished guests, often at home over a meal or tea. The most memorable in my mind was tea for the Chinese premier.

It was December 1956, and my mother was out of country. My father asked if I would act as hostess when Premier Chou En-lai came to tea. I happily agreed, giving no thought to what the duties involved. I had watched on innumerable occasions as foreign leaders were entertained. "How hard can it be to pour tea for a Prime Minister?" Well it turned out to be nerve-wracking.

For one thing, lifting a large boiling hot teapot and pouring tea in a small steady stream into a delicate porcelain cup when you are a child is not easy. On top of that, a bevy of butlers hovering nearby in the sure knowledge that you are bound to mess up is another distraction. There was plenty of advice before the event and a great deal during. However, a hushed silence descended on the gathering once the chief guest, the Prime Minister of China, was seated. I was formally introduced by my father who had earlier prepped me a bit on the significance of the visit and the visitor.

I was immediately struck by Chou En-lai as an unusual VIP. He looked at me directly and inquired in English about my school and interests. There was a bit of banter about girls my age in China, a very different land, certainly in the mid-1950s. I was able to hold my own in the conversation which led to a huge sigh of relief from all the nearby grownups. Tough moment, but it passed without incident as the premier calmly talked to me in quiet tones. Tea was poured and the conversation continued. I sat in silence after my brief interaction with Chou, thinking that he had a very kind demeanor. He spoke to my father about the challenge of creating a unified country after a long civil war in China. My father mentioned similar sentiments in terms of Pakistan's newly won independence after a bloody partition from India. I found the discussion fascinating, even at the young unsophisticated age that I was.

Beside cursory parts of conversations witnessed between the grownups, I did not know much about the nature of China, its Communist system, its victory and control in 1949 over the mainland. What I did gather quickly from my conversation with the Chinese premier was that he was an educated erudite man. He was proud of his country and wanted to help Pakistan develop, particularly in the fields of higher education as represented by his presence at the seminal moment in the development of the first major university in the shadow of the Khyber Pass.

Chou asked me what I planned to study. I responded with all the seriousness I could muster something which had only then occurred to me. "I will travel and study about the world." He seemed pleased with my response. My father smiled and noted that given how much I liked to talk, my mother had thought I should be a lawyer!

Moments like my encounter with the Chinese premier have stayed with me. Beyond his capacity to make a young girl feel worldly was the image of an international statesman and what that meant to my future career in International Relations. I realized there was a huge world out there and it was important to be involved in its understanding. Years later when I focused on International Relations as my field of study, I saw that my experiences as a child naturally led me toward that field of specialization.

By mid-1950s, Peshawar University was gaining support from the international community as a modern progressive institution. Visitors to Pakistan were welcomed and progress in education garnered economic and institutional support for the young university. The steady stream of foreign leaders who visited was one indication. On the ground, even our family's children were swept up in the change that accompanied the development of Peshawar University. A quiet dusty town on the road to a famous pass became a "must go" destination for the powerful and the learned. Being exposed to so much from around the world in the backwater that was Peshawar helped make me comfortable with engaging leaders. It was an early lesson that one need not be awestruck by rank. That was another lesson that served me well in later years of service at the White House, a world away in Washington.

Moving On

The tide of new experiences has its own swift momentum and spares none. At thirteen, there was a moment of great sadness when I was told that we were moving from Peshawar. I had grown up there, made lifelong friends there, and felt in sync with the rhythms of the frontier. The so-called wild frontier had given us a second home and a real sense of belonging. But at thirteen, I could not hold on to that sense and understood that other experiences lay ahead. I finished high school. College beckoned.

But Peshawar was also changing. Its integration into the political "one unit" comprising all of what was then West Pakistan meant a diminution of the uniqueness that characterized the province. Politics was prominently based more than a thousand miles away, in the sand dunes of Karachi, Pakistan's only coastal metropolis. A population of less than 50 million at that time made for less stress on Pakistan's resources. A "transfer" involved moving family and possessions from one official residence to another. Air travel was yet distant. The journey commenced on the aptly named "Khyber Mail" which chugged out of Peshawar railway station with a fabulous nostalgic send off. Although I had always wanted to spend time in Karachi, I was unsure how life in the big city would actually be. "You have cousins your age there" my mother reminded me. "Yes, but they have their own friends," I replied.

The 1,100-mile distance from Peshawar to Karachi via Khyber Mail took more than eighteen hours. We had a compartment with beds made up with bedding carried in "hold-alls" from home. The food for the journey was carefully prepared in order to resist spoilage. I always loved the menu which included specialty breads and preserved meats. At many of the large stations en route, the tea hawkers ("chai wallas" or tea sellers) plied their trade and offered up tempting cakes.

I loved these travel days. One could watch the countryside float by. The terrain changed dramatically from the hills of the north to the lush fields of the Punjab, bright yellow with mustard in the spring, green, and then gold with wheat in other seasons. Lahore was always a major stop. We were met by family who brought fresh supplies of food and new reading materials. As an aficionado of "Little Lulu" comics, I traded my stash with that my cousins in Lahore brought.

The heat and dust of Sind always came as a shock to the system after the verdant rolling scenery I was more used to. The names of successive stations, Khairpur, Rahim Yar Khan, Bahawalpur, Multan, Hyderabad, Kotri, rolled off the tongue of the conductor who kept track of designated disembarkation points for various passengers.

"Why are so many people always on the move?" I asked my mother. It seemed amazing that Pakistanis of all economic backgrounds found it necessary to travel. They did not have the urgency of travelling for work/business. Pakistan was not yet a culture of mass movement for meetings. "Mostly to visit families, or when they are going after a transfer of job just as we are doing" was my Mama's response. Yes, that made sense. The tribal and familial patterns required people to attend weddings, funerals, and all celebrations in between, including two Eid celebrations. Attendance was required, not just discretionary. One needed a very good reason to be excused from participation.

It was indeed unfortunate that as air travel became available in the 1970s to most, the railway system, a great legacy of the British Raj, was allowed to fall apart. In the late 1990s, Prime Ministers pushed for super highways as a contribution toward modernity. The burgeoning population of Pakistan needed all forms of reasonably priced transport. In simpler earlier times, we all relied on the trains for comfortable, safe travel.

Arrival in Karachi required dressing for the occasion, not simply falling out of bed. Dusty and wrinkled we may have been en route but we did our best to look smart for the big city. Coming from provincial Peshawar, Karachi was a metropolis with wide roads, fancy shops and restaurants, taller buildings, and a nightlife unthinkable in the northern part of the country. "There are two Pakistans," I would venture to my siblings each time we came to the port city.

"Tomorrow, we will go to Hawk's Bay for a day-long picnic. It will be a full moon and we can come back late," my Aunt told us. "Wow the seashore!" Although my family had gone to Bombay in India for annual vacations, the seaside in Karachi seemed more exotic, perhaps in sharp contrast to the mountainous scenery of the north. There would be camel rides on the beach, cookouts, and games. It was always a happy time.

Pakistan of the early years was, as my cousin Samina Ahmed recalls, an "extremely open place. Relaxed and safe with an attitude that everything is possible and that things would work out well in the end. A nation with a hodgepodge of nationalities with hierarchies of ethnic background, it was not a polarized country." And women were involved, including in the National Guard.

The pattern of my life was to change dramatically in 1959. The time had come to think about the future. Education was a requirement and my family set great store by it—for girls and boys. "I'm going to America" was a reminder by me just in case the family had forgotten an earlier conversation.

CHAPTER 3

Education and Romance

As President of the University of Peshawar, my father established the first exchange program between Pakistan and the USA, between Peshawar University and Colorado State University. Education thus provided my initial link to the USA. I would never have come to this great country if I had not in my school years made friends with American children whose parents were living in the Peshawar University campus having signed on to teach there for one to two years. Interacting with them made me aware of the USA and I liked these new friends. I recall teaching them the Pakistani national anthem, and they taught me "America the Beautiful."

Though a small town, Peshawar of the 1950s was a broad-minded place. Add to that the traditional Pathan hospitality code, Americans were welcomed. The guest professors were understood to be helping raise Pakistan's educational standards. They brought credentials and experience. They were dedicated. They were feted and a newly formed Rotary Club showcased USA–Pakistan relations through an American night where there was American food and music. The children of the American professors at the university were pressed into performing American musical numbers. They needed Pakistani reinforcement. I was asked to join in.

We sang various well-known American songs, including "God Bless America" and "America the Beautiful." These conjured up images of vast spaces and falling waters. I was smitten. On the ride home to the university campus some eight miles away, I announced to my surprised parents that when it came time for me to go abroad for higher education, I was going to America, not the "stuffy" Cambridge in England where I was expected to go.

My parents agreed, to everyone's, surprise, including my own. Pakistani girls did not go to the USA in 1959. It was highly unusual and several relatives warned my mother that she would be very sorry to let a daughter go to America to study at such a young age. My mother was my staunchest supporter and she did not waver from the pledge that I would be educated to the highest degree to which I aspired. But to actually get to the USA meant enrollment in a university and the fact that I was less than fifteen might present a problem.

Friends from the Colorado contingent counseled that my parents not apply to Columbia University, under discussion at the time, because Manhattan might be too much of a difference from Peshawar. Instead, one friend, Mildred Rausch, wisely offered the choice of a small mid-western university where I would not feel so lost. As the family set out for the USA on my first trip abroad, we made a two-day stop in London. The pre-jet flight from London to New York in September 1959 took more than fourteen hours and involved an emergency landing at Gander in Newfoundland. While pretending to be very mature, I was struck by the long road we traveled from Pakistan to New York. Commenting on that to my mother as we were landing in New York, lamenting the distance from home, she asked if I had not previously been aware of that fact. "Not really," was my sad response.

What 15 year old is not mesmerized by Manhattan? It was a place full of sound and movement. Everything was vertical and so different from anything I had ever seen. Its energy was palpable. As my parents settled into Columbia University for three months where my father was a distinguished professor on leave from his cabinet position in Pakistan, I was soon to be escorted to Ohio. I vowed to return and work in New York City one day.

Baba loved to recount the story of how I had told him en route to Delaware, Ohio, that I would only stay in the USA if I was allowed into college, which my age might preclude. Should Ohio Wesleyan after the day's testing ask me to undertake high school study prior to admission into university, I would return to Pakistan with him. "Fair enough, let us see what happens" was his reply.

We flew to Columbus, Ohio, and took a Greyhound bus to Delaware, Ohio. As a University President, he was given the courtesy of waiting with the Ohio Wesleyan President while I was going through a series of interviews. At last, these were over and I joined my father and his host while awaiting the verdict on my entrance to the university. Finally, in came one of the professors and after initial banter noted that: "We can't take Shirin in as a freshman, but we will take her as a junior!"

Demonstrating my lack of sophistication, I panicked as I assumed being a junior meant going back to high school! What a blow. Noting my sadness, the University President quickly said, "That is a third year student in university." I rejoiced that I would after all be able to study in the USA. But accompanying my happiness was a huge sense of sadness as I bade farewell to my father who headed back to Columbus and then New York and finally to Pakistan.

My college years were US focused. I entered college as a junior at age 15 and graduated two years later from Ohio Wesleyan University, not quite 17. My time in Delaware, Ohio, covered an era where the only possible contact with my family back in Pakistan was through the weekly letter. Yet surprisingly, I did not feel isolated in Middle America. Friendship and understanding seemed to soften any loneliness that might have been natural in a very young Muslim girl's transplantation from the frontier town of Peshawar in Pakistan to the bucolic meadows circled by the Olentangy and Scioto Rivers in Delaware, Ohio. Obviously one of the very few female "foreign" students in the Delaware, Ohio, of the day, I found my fellow students, teachers, and the townspeople curious about me. However, their curiosity contained no hostility; instead, it aimed at the novelty of a different religion or culture that I clearly represented. In retrospect, I wish I had stayed in college the full four years. I loved my college years.

As graduation in June 1961 loomed closer, I was summoned to meet with my student advisor to go through the checklist of requirements. "Humanities, check, economics, check, arts, check" went the list my advisor rolled off. "Swimming, check" she said. With true panic, I stopped her with my "I don't swim" comment. There was genuine surprise coupled with a sense of frustration as I was told that one of the requisite qualifications for graduating from college in the USA was swimming.

While I argued that my ability to swim had little to do with my future, I realized we were at an impasse. Six weeks to go but I had to become sufficiently proficient in order to pass the test and graduate. With the advisor's help, we found a potential solution. One of the few foreign students at the university was a German girl, Bettina. She was a natural athlete and did some work with the physical education program at the university. She agreed to coach me and was extremely understanding of the dread with which I entered water above my knees. She would walk alongside with a long pole with which, she assured me, she could hoist me out of the pool should I start to go under. My faith in her ability to teach me how to swim and to save me should I start to drown made it possible to learn enough to pass the test and graduate.

My mid-west experience stayed with me as I returned to Pakistan upon graduation in 1961. Based on my understanding of life ahead, I assumed the journey back to Pakistan would absolutely end my interaction and experiences in the West. "Why not try something different?" I asked myself. One option for the return journey by sea offered just such a chance. I had traveled all across the USA in the vacation periods and had experienced the USA sufficiently to understand its unique history, geography, and ethos.

I went to a travel agent and asked for advice on ships sailing for England. I was helped in reserving for the Holland America Line ship "SS Rotterdam" to sail from New York to Southampton, UK, in June 1961.

Only in Hollywood movies had I seen departure of famous ships setting sail from Manhattan past the Statue of Liberty. Now I found myself on one, waving from the deck to no one in particular as I knew none. Finding my way to the lower deck where my interior room was booked, I was delighted to find as my roommate, Dana, a female student who had just graduated from Duke University. She was a Southerner and extremely kind.

First night out on the ocean, my roommate suggested we go check out what evening programs were offered. She talked me into signing up for the Cha Cha Cha dance contest. Mastering this new fad had been one of the "new experiences" I enjoyed at Ohio Wesleyan. I did not date but there were group events so I got to practice. Dana and I showed up dressed for the occasion. We were each assigned a partner. Mine was a young man from Columbia. We knew nothing about each other's country which made for no conversation. But he could dance!

After many rounds, my partner and I were declared winners. I started to leave but my roommate, Dana, who had participated in the competition with another young partner, came to tell me I had to stay for the prize distribution, which was handed to the female partner. I was excited wondering what treasure or trinket would be bestowed as a memory of my nimble footedness on the high seas! When I saw the award, I was crestfallen! It was a magnum of Champagne! But I did not drink so I thought it best to offer it to my Colombian partner who in turn was delighted to claim it for his group of friends.

Love and Marriage

I arrived at Southampton feeling extremely worldly. I was heading home and I could not wait to see my family and recount to my friends in Pakistan all of the experiences my American sojourn had offered. Life was exciting and I was nearly seventeen!

To scout for possible candidates for tenure-track research and teaching positions at Pakistani Universities, every few years my father would visit Harvard and Yale, in the USA, and Oxford and Cambridge, in the UK. My arrival in the UK in June 1961, after my graduation from Ohio Wesleyan University, coincided with one such visit.

Baba and I traveled together, en route to Pakistan, and stopped for a few days in London so that at both Oxford and Cambridge my father could interview some possible candidates and cajole a few others who were not actually offering themselves for consideration. Cambridge, which had been both my father's and my brother's alma mater, was familiar but Oxford was not. Interested in visiting the "other place," I requested to tag along.

There were several young men: some who had come for their scheduled interview, and a few others who seemed to be there just to scout the scene and possibly get a feel for the "lay of the land." And then there was one who claimed to have come only to say "Hello" to my father. He nonchalantly stepped into the large waiting room, acting as one who was there not in need of anything but as one only interested in proffering a friendly hello to the head of a university where he had once been a student.

And indeed, there must also have been a tiny thought in his mind those six years earlier my father had been one of those responsible for the award of a prestigious fellowship that brought him to Oxford to read for a B.A. (Hons) in Physics. The British government, during its waning days in British India, had endowed a triennial fellowship, tenable at Oxford University, to be awarded to a resident of the Northwest Frontier

Province and its unruly neighboring territories—e.g., Waziristan—that had given the British everlasting grief. (And, unfortunately, continue to do so to "us" these days. History never teaches anybody anything!)

He sat in a chair, not far from mine, with eyes half open, fixated firmly at the ceiling. Suddenly, he seemed to wake up and shot at me in an imperious tone: "Where did you pick up this bizarre accent?" I was completely taken aback. Nonplussed, I replied: "if you must know I have just got my B.A. in America and that is of no interest to you." "Yes, it is," said he, "because, I am a friend of your brother and my name is Raza."

Unused as I was to this sort of pseudo-British upper classicism, I had an instant thought: "Be wary of this man." Turning my attention away, I returned to my conversation with another about subjects that seemed not of much interest at Oxford.

Interviews completed, my father emerged. Raza got up and in a very deferential tone said: "Welcome back to Oxford, sir." My father giving a sign of recognition said: "Thank you very much. It is fortunate that for a change the weather is friendly. Would you join us for lunch?" "Yes, I should love to: except, I just had some." "Maybe, a cup of tea, then?" We marched across St. Giles to the restaurant. It was past two o'clock. Oxford lunch hours generally lasted till 2. But arrangements had been made in advance.

At lunch, Raza seemed to listen and talk only to my father. After inquiring which train we were planning to take, he got up, thanked my father for his hospitality, walked over and shook my hand and said: "Charmed!" And with a general remark that he had another appointment, left the restaurant. My thoughts: what a curious character! He certainly stood apart from anyone I knew.

The following day my father picked up the phone. He handed it over to me. "For you," he said. I was amazed. It was Raza. He spun a long sorry tale of woe: how after finishing with his appointment, he had bicycled furiously to reach us at the station, only to arrive just as the train started to move. And because he had failed to say "Bye" at the station, he had been trying to reach us by telephone. And how, finally, the Pakistani Ambassador's Secretary had provided the number, etc. The upshot of it all was that he had tickets to the world famous Kirov Ballet that was performing at Covent Garden in London and he was wondering whether I would be interested in joining him at the performance.

Would going to the ballet, which I very much wanted to see at the famous Covent Garden, constitute a date? Not really I decided as Raza was a friend of my brother and my father knew him. I thought: "We are not leaving for Pakistan for three days. Perhaps I shall join him."

He had done his homework and suggested the train I might catch, and promised to meet upon arrival at the platform. Raza mentioned that we would get lunch near Covent Garden. Also, because the ballet was in the evening we could catch Ingmar Bergman's "Seventh Seal" being rerun, and because "Max von Sydow is such a great actor, it might be interesting."

I was being polite when I had said: "Sounds good." Weaned on Bollywood and Hollywood productions, I was not sure about a Swedish movie. I figured that as I was headed back to Pakistan that might well be the only chance I had of seeing a Bergman film. He was as good as his word. As planned, we met at the station. Right on time. He was holding a fancy umbrella. In my ever-present desire to converse, I said: "Great umbrella." Pleased, he responded: "An Oxonian, and his umbrella, stay together."

We wandered around for an hour trying to find the restaurant on foot. Failing, we finally caught a cab. Destination? Raza's directions were vague. The objective was to arrive somewhere close to the intended restaurant. He thought he knew where the place was, but clearly didn't. Finally, we settled down in another small place that offered British lunch fare. I ordered an omelet.

The omelet was inedible. Food at the time in British restaurants could be mediocre at best. Good conversation was more available. Raza talked about how he had "won" the fellowship that had brought him here. In the interview, that my father headed, he was declared tops. But there were other candidates with considerable influence on the system and one, who was both extremely well qualified and had a father high-up in the provincial government. Quite obviously, he was the winner. This was early July 1955. And the Michaelmas Term at Oxford began October 7.

I asked how then did Raza manage to get to Oxford. It turned out that a cousin of Raza's mother, Sardar Bahadur Khan—younger brother of the Army Chief—became the Chief Minister of the Northwest Frontier as its Chief Minister and Governor on July 29, 1955. Raza continued: "My father, who owned and edited a newspaper, was already aware of the news. Unlike their (late) father, General Ayub's, and the new Governor's, mother is not a descendant of the Tareen tribe. Rather, she is a Tahir-Kheli. But most importantly, she is a cousin of my mother."

Physics was a difficult subject and Raza was clearly brilliant. He "went up to Oxford" in October 1955 though he recalled: "All in all, my first week at Oriel was a memorable disaster."

Raza continued his amazing tale:

> In Pakistan, we were taught to memorize things. But real understanding of what was memorized was not required. Martin Aitken, a very polite man, my physics tutor, was absolutely horrified to find one who could not discern the top from the bottom. He advised: "Rather than Physics, best to read Engineering."

The Provost (head of Oriel College), Sir George Clarkalso said as much: "We encourage those who cannot read and write to read Engineering!" Apparently, in Oxford, one "Reads" a discipline, rather than "Study" it, as one does in the USA.

> Somehow, Sir George's feelings about me got rapidly transmitted to the education attaché and the Pakistani Ambassador. The attaché called, commanding me to appear at the embassy. Before his diplomatic assignment, he had been a university Professor in the Punjab, teaching literature and other esoteric subjects. He told me: "It pains me to say that you Pathans, though admirable as fighters, are very poor as scholars." And, for relevant emphasis, he added:

> Your predecessor, at Balliol, is being sent down. He has failed to qualify for any degree. Perhaps, you should talk to him before he leaves the next two days. Also, you will surely agree with the Ambassador that, you must return home, post-haste. Pakistan would not want another holder of this important fellowship, that your predecessor and now you have been awarded, experience such disgrace.

He added: "Your airline tickets, as well as the money assigned to the embassy for your three year fellowship—a sizeable sum, indeed!—will also be provided." I was struck by Raza's ability to surmount all the challenges, especially given his limited ability at the time to speak Oxonian English at the time of his arrival at Oxford in 1955.

> "Persisting with Physics, I continued to perform abysmally poorly. The tutorials were painful. But I kept working hard, most days, twelve hours. It all paid off, however. Nine months later, in the first 'Public Examinations'—the so called 'Honour Moderations'—I took a first class.

All the national dailies, including the times of London, published the Honour Moderations results. There were about 210 of us taking that exam and approximately only six percent were placed in the First Class. And my name was right at the top!"

What an impressive performance I thought, one that must have made his parents and the family proud.

Next, we went to the movie: the Seventh Seal. As noted, I had not yet learned to appreciate heavyweight studies of human frailty and other such scholarly musings. It was a "dark" film, shot appropriately in black and white. And for me it was a total loss. "Still, there is the ballet." And that turned out as good as I had thought. Indeed, many times better.

A couple of days later, my father and I flew back to Pakistan. En route we went to Paris my first French experience and onto Vienna. Given Baba was on the Board of the International Atomic Energy Agency headquartered in Vienna, he went to meetings and I went sightseeing in historic Vienna. The last evening, he took me with him to the official dinner and ball. I waltzed at the Schonbrunn Palace with elegant gentleman friends of my father. For a sixteen-year-old girl, it was heady business! We landed in Karachi and I was on home turf.

Soon I forgot about the two unusual days in England. Used to being a student, I toyed with the idea of studying for a master's. But, after two years away from Pakistan, there were many friends, cousins, and acquaintances to visit. I was extremely busy just settling in. But, of course, my seventeenth birthday was fast approaching. Friends wanted to hold a big party, especially to celebrate my graduation from Ohio Wesleyan earlier this summer.

Some came from distant places, others from places close by. As the guests arrived, so did a letter from Oxford! With some amusement, I opened it. Ah! Raza has remembered and is wishing me many happy returns of the day, I thought. What a nice thing to do and he was clearly a decent guy. Couple of weeks later, I thought he deserved a reply. I did finally get down to writing a chatty letter: interesting and happy things about the party. And wondered whether he still looked at the ceiling a lot?

In those days, the mail system worked. I received a rapid-fire response. Raza was very pleased to hear from me. But it's clear: he would be even more so, if my letter were free of misspelling! He had gone to the trouble of returning my letter, with the misspellings corrected. Brilliance does not preclude eccentricity.

A week later a long epistle arrived: "Shirin! Sorry. I probably did not tell you that the Department—meaning, the Theoretical Physics Department—etc., etc." I was updated on Raza finally being willing to give up his cushy arrangements at Oxford and claim his D.Phil.

> Dr. ter Haar keeps pushing for the dissertation to be written up. He has even finagled a Lectureship for me at the University of Aberdeen. You see, usually it is only an Assistant Lectureship. But, at Oxford, my British Commonwealth Graduate Fellowship is very comfy. And it is good for another six months. So, don't want to finish just yet. But really, when I do finish, am likely to accept the offer from Robert Brout at Brussels whom I met him here a year ago. He is brilliant, but very abrupt. If one can bear it, should be great to work for him. But, to make things more confusing, Prof. Herbert Callen has just called and is wondering whether I would join him at the University of Pennsylvania, in the U.S. His wife and he were here. We met during a summer school in Scotland. They are a fun couple. And he is overtly friendly. An American trait, perhaps? Bye, now! And do tell me what keeps you in such great fun? Raza

That was a long letter. In response, I wanted to say something clever about the Europe versus USA options that Raza faced. "As you must well realize, after eons of warfare, Europe is old and expired," I responded. "The, USA, on the other hand, is young, welcoming, and vibrant. Who in his sound mind wants to go to Brussels instead of "somewhere" in the USA?" My prejudice for America was evident. But I was simply lightly offering my opinion. I was not aiming to really influence Raza's choice of post-D. Phil fellowship. I hoped he understood that.

Shortly after, he wrote on March 23, 1962:

> Been extremely busy. And, sorry! I have been incommunicado. Much to ter Haar's displeasure, I decided against Aberdeen. Also, because the University of Pennsylvania added teaching to the postdoctoral position, it resulted in a substantial increase in their offer. It is much more than I could possibly get at Brussels. So I decided to accept Pennsylvania. But, the really Good News is: Today, the Pakistan Day, I successfully defended my 'D.Phil. Thesis'. Received a call from London. The head of Pakistan Atomic Energy Commission wants to see me in Professor Salam's offices in Imperial College tomorrow". And finally: "Now that I have my D.Phil., will You Marry Me??? Raza

Whoa!!

I always knew that my path to love and marriage would be different from the arranged marriages so typical for most girls at the time. Whenever Mama reminded me that there was a list of "vetted" bachelors with proposals for my hand, I would laugh it off with: "I doubt it will be anyone from that list!" I had watched my cousins and friends marry in this fashion and they seemed happy enough. But I always knew that arranged marriage of the traditional type was not for me. I always thought love would not strike one as a bolt of lightning as in the movies. Based on shared values and respect and of course a spark, love had to form the basis of a relationship and marriage. By choosing my own mate, I felt "the spark" could be identified and nurtured.

But Raza's proposal threw me off as being too soon and far from expected. But I had begun to know him through our conversations, mostly via letters. That alone set him apart from other eligible bachelors I knew who seemed less intellectual in things that mattered, such as mastery of complicated mathematics and science. He was handsome and charming. I suspected that despite his brazen push for us to marry, he was likely to be understated in his dealings.

My years in Peshawar and friendships with Pathans gave me a sense of familiarity with Raza. We had both grown up in the same neighborhood, though under different situations. Was that enough? I remained unsure of my feelings at the time and thus wrote off a quick response once my mother said marriage was out of the question: "No! Don't think it is possible! Shirin."

Undeterred, another letter informed me of his arrival in Karachi on April 12 and hopes to meet up soon thereafter. Clearly, I realized my "No. Not possible" response that I had been proud of penning was still airborne: undelivered. But definitely, it will reach him well before his planned flight? Good, I thought!

Weeks passed. I heard nothing. My feeling was that as a clever man he is purposely not acknowledging the note. It's one sure way not to have to take No for an answer!

My family had many relatives and friends in Karachi. Thus, I had numerous "cousins." During the seven to eight years that I had been in Pakistan, my family would visit Karachi at least once every year. And this year was to be no exception.

In addition to being Vice Chancellor of a university, my father was also the Chairman of The National Academy of Sciences. The academy had an office in a wonderful residential neighborhood in Karachi and staff that generally responded to phone calls and written questions. Raza called and found my father's office and home telephone numbers.

One evening in April 1962, I received a phone call in the evening from Raza. "Am in Karachi. Not far from the Atomic Energy Commission offices, where he had joined as a senior scientist. Am staying as a guest at a cousin's: a certain Wing Commander in the Air Force. The National Academy offices tell me that you chaps are coming here next week? If so, I should much like to say hello to the family." I consulted my father. He did not have any overt objection to receiving a visitor, especially one who is both civil and possibly a future candidate for a university position. But he suggested my mother will decide.

Having had to welcome visitors of all shades and persuasion for years in Peshawar, my mother was reluctant to receive yet another whom she did not know. Sensing her squeamishness, I phoned Raza back. "You are right. We are planning to be in Karachi for a month. But will be fully booked up with visitors and the like. Sorry! Perhaps, some other time." "Yes, yes. But I should like to ask also your parents for us to get married." I could not believe that he had not given up his idea. My mother, who had always known how best to help whenever I needed it, should come to the rescue, I thought, especially since she knows dozens of Pathan families. I was close to Mama and always shared my thoughts, so I took her into confidence. My mother reminded me of those on the "list" who had fortunes.

Much as I had expected, my mother also responded: "Pathans marry multiple times. Therefore, a Pathan, by definition, is an unsuitable partner." I understood that argument but asked that she invite him to lunch in any case. That decided in the affirmative, I telephoned to offer him the invitation.

Lunch was an elaborate affair. Raza arrived. He was very friendly. I had expected tension. And was greatly relieved when there was none as the meal was simply a social affair.

Before leaving for a dinner party, my father would always eat at home. This way he was served on time. Traditionally, in Hyderabad in India, in somewhat similar fashion, people arrived for dinner after already having eaten a bit at their place. At the party dinner, they would generally eat a tiny amount, declare themselves satiated, and spend the evening conversing. The hostess' task, however, was always to keep urging the guests to try some of the untouched but tasty dishes. Baba had continued the practice in Pakistan.

Raza, as is the Pathan custom, ate heartily—especially the meat dishes. The rest of us—my mother, my sister, and I—kept him apparent company by using our knives and forks gently, only for pushing the food around the plate. Lunch finished. Before leaving, Raza told us about his job at the Atomic Energy Commission, and that he was taking up a Summer Visiting Fellowship at Harwell—a research institute run by the British Atomic Energy establishment.

Raza arrived in Oxford to spend the summer at Harwell. By this time, I had had many conversations with my parents about Raza and told them that, with their approval, I would like to marry him because I had developed strong feelings for him. My parent's reaction questioned what a girl of seventeen knew about love. They understood that I would not marry without their blessings so the matter rested with them.

The next letter from Raza included the good news about a Fulbright fellowship for travel to the USA in the fall. But, he noted, the fellowship required that he return to Karachi for his US visa, fill out some forms to receive the travel expenses, etc. Then, there was the bombshell: "Now that I am going to the US—a country that YOU love—we must get married before we leave Karachi in August. And, I am telling my parents of my plans."

Unbeknownst to any of us, Raza's wishful thinking rapidly metastasized into "There's going to be a wedding!" Thus distorted, the news spread to the Tahir-Khelis all over and soon thereafter, also to the Tareen clan, and the Pakistan President's family.

My father took the question of Raza's proposal under advisement. He was a man given to serious consideration of all issues presented and did not make decisions without full analysis. And he was very busy. The President of Pakistan, indeed the Dictator of Pakistan, General Muhammad Ayub Khan—who by decree was the Chancellor of the university—was coming to inspect the university in a month or so and much needed to be done before his arrival, etc.

The President arrived to much ceremony. Normally, my mother would skip all university functions. However, Ayub Khan, personally visiting, was different. As per the protocol, my parents were first among the receiving line. Before my father could conduct the President around to introduce each of the gathered dignitaries, the President stopped for a moment to chat with my mother, whom he knew from early days in Peshawar. "Congratulations! I gather a wedding is being planned? The lucky groom, I am told, is a cousin of ours." My mother was stunned!

We all sat together for breakfast the following morning. Baba had always thought very highly of President Ayub Khan because of the support he had given for improving education in the country. As such, it was no wonder his casual remark to my mother the previous day had left an impression.

Baba began after noting that he himself liked Raza and thought he was a brilliant physicist who would do well. His promise is in the future he noted, but: "It behooves us to take note. Without our noticing, the cat has wandered out of the bag. And the news has spread. But that is not the issue." And looking me squarely in the eye asked: "Clearly, you are interested in this man? You know that you have another suitor: who is both moneyed, and is known to the family."

Uncharacteristically, I was tongue tied. Baba interpreted that as tantamount to a positive response regarding Raza as he knew me well. "Then it is good that even the President thinks well of him. Of course, I have known for several years that the President's younger brother also does the same." My mother finally joined the conversation: "Getting a mention from the President! He must, probably, not be all bad? But I wish they wouldn't marry multiple wives!"

Clearly, all that my father needed was a "non-negative" reaction from my mother. "But," he said, "no child should marry before the age of 18. And you are not yet that age. Fullstop."

I was impressed: particularly with myself, for having held my tongue and not mentioning my strong feelings for Raza by that point! But 18? That would happen in five weeks. I decided to immediately send a very brief note: "My father thinks one may marry at the age of eighteen. And the eighteenth arrives soon. However, are you planning to marry more than once? Your traditions reflect many wives!"

"No," he answered. "I have lived with the consequences of a multiple wife family so rest assured this is it!" I asked him if he was sure he loved me and his immediate response: "Too much" quieted any anxiety on that score I might have had. I said: "Likewise." He reminded me that he would be headed back to Pakistan return well in time. "But you need to contact the U.S. embassy for the visa. Mine is all set: thanks to the Fulbright. Raza"

And so was made one of the most important unplanned decisions of my life.

3 EDUCATION AND ROMANCE

Weddings in Pakistan are no fun for the brides to be. While everybody else engages in doing fun things, the central character stays seated in a room. All cooped up, looking demure. And this rigmarole begins days before the final ceremony. We got married on my 18th birthday in Hyderabad, Sind. The ceremony went for days. Once concluded, we left for Karachi. Following morning we went to the US Consulate for the visas. Raza filled out the needed Fulbright forms and was handed a note authorizing the purchase of airline ticket through one of the embassy travel agents. And we were both requested to wait because the Consul General himself wished to see us. The wait was short. And the Consul was extremely welcoming. Fortunately, my father had invited him to a post-wedding reception to be held in Karachi that evening. Our visas arrived moments later and we headed to pick up the airline tickets.

Early next morning, after another exhausting day of partying and acting our appointed roles during the evening reception, we boarded the Pakistan International Airlines flight headed to Geneva for a week's honeymoon. As always, the government's foreign currency reserves were depleted. There was very limited availability of foreign exchange. Those traveling out of the country were limited to a maximum annual amount of only 50 Pounds Sterling per person. And Raza had already used up his allowance for the year. That left us pretty short of funds for visiting Switzerland for a week.

Fortunately, as a theoretical physicist, Raza was used to handling, if not real money, at least "real numbers" and had anticipated the need for additional funds in Switzerland. To that purpose, before leaving Oxford, he had borrowed 250 Pounds from Martin Aitken, his friend and former tutor. And transferred them to a Bank in Geneva, to be collected on our arrival there.

We landed in Geneva absolutely deadbeat. Exhausted to delirium, we struggled into a cab and asked for the hotel in town Raza had booked. Minutes after a quick check-in, we placed the "Please, Do Not Disturb!" sign and fell into deathly sound sleep. Some forty hours later, came a very loud knock on the door. Hotel officials were concerned. "Something serious must have happened?"

The knock was welcome. We were famished. As an apology for the disturbance, the hotel manager offered to send up breakfast although it was well past the hour for the morning meal. We were touched by the normally rule following Swiss to bend one. Soon thereafter, we opened the door to the wonderful smell of coffee, eggs, and fresh croissants.

Satiated, Raza wanted us to look for the bank he had sent money to. Compared with banks at home, I found the Swiss one here focused, to the point, and efficient. Raza's passport was carefully inspected, his signature triple checked, and we received the funds. At the rate of 11.20 Swiss francs to a Pound Sterling, it was quite a packet.

Raza had learned to drive in the UK where the test is rigorous. I had learned in Pakistan on a stick-shift Ford that my brother had brought back when he returned from Cambridge University after his Tripos. Raza had the rules down. I had practice in the heavy unruly traffic of Hyderabad Sind. We rented a small car and found that we got around safely and saw a bit of Switzerland. We also had quite a lot of fun listening to Ernest Ansermet conducting Orchestre de la Suisse Romande in Montreux. Also, with borrowed cash in our pocket, we ate well.

PART II

Milestones

CHAPTER 4

Return to the USA

Early morning, the fifth of September 1962, after a week's stay in Switzerland, we took a taxi to the Aeroport de Geneve. Changing our few remaining Swiss francs to US dollars, boarded a two engine, ear shatteringly loud, Caravelle jetliner, that was being flown by Swiss Air to London. In London we transferred to Trans World Airlines' much quieter, much sleeker, much larger Super Constellation turbo prop, and flew slowly to the USA.

We were met by Herb Callen at the arrivals gate in Philadelphia. He drove us to a Sheraton, near the University of Pennsylvania campus in West Philadelphia. The weather was hot and steamy. Air-conditioning in the hotel was extremely welcome. Tired after a long day of travel, we soon went to bed. Early next morning, Raza started to worry about our finances. Immediately after breakfast, he approached the checkout counter and inquired as to the cost of staying in the hotel. Whatever the numbers were, they were far too much for us to afford. Raza decided that we have to leave the hotel that day. But where to stay was the question.

First, we located the Physics building. Next, we started to scout the neighborhood for available apartments within walking distance of campus. Given that the semester had started, our options were very limited. Fortunately, we found an apartment, on Baring Street, less than ten minutes brisk walk from the Physics building. The landlord wanted a month's rent in advance. We told him we had just arrived: in fact only about 15 hours ago, and will not be able to access our funds for a week or two. He inspected us warily. Spying the fancy sari I was wearing as a new bride, he decided to take a chance on us.

We returned to the hotel, packed our things, paid the bill, and checked out. Raza told me he had only two US currency notes left: a twenty dollar bill and a one dollar bill. We took a taxi. It was a short ride and the cost was only 52 cents. Raza handed the driver one of the two bills in his wallet. The guy thought for a moment and said he does not have the change, Raza, believing that he had given only a one dollar bill, said: "Hold the change. All we need is for you to carry these suit cases to the second floor." The taxi driver was full of gratitude. He thanked us profusely, and with great alacrity carried the two suitcases to the top floor.

The very next morning, Raza asked me another question that changed my life, yet again. "Beginning tomorrow, you know, I will be very busy trying to get some Physics done. And, there won't be much time for us to get together during the day. So you really should take a course, or register for a degree, or something." "What do you want to do?" "Oh, I am going to be a 'housewife'" I replied instantaneously with a great deal of conviction. "Housewife! But we have no house! Just a small apartment," responded Raza.

Well, I thought that meant a plan B. Given that we were on our way to the campus for lunch, I decided to reflect on the issue for a while. Soon we entered the cafeteria. Raza opened his wallet. "Just to check," he said. We were aghast. Raza had given away his 20 dollar note to the taxi driver and had allowed him to hold the change! All we had left now was a dollar. But, fortunately, it was enough for one double-burger that we shared. The completely empty pockets had focused my mind! Somewhere in my luggage, I thought, there is a 40 dollar check from Ohio Wesleyan. Apparently, I had overpaid a university bill there. And a year later, the university business office had noticed the over-payment and just before our wedding, this check had arrived. At that time, I had no idea that this tiny amount of money would be needed so desperately one day.

Immediately after the burger, we walked a block down to the Physics building and arrived at Herb's office. He was busy talking to a student but invited us in as soon as he finished. Raza conveyed the embarrassing news. We checked out of the hotel early this morning and found a place to stay on Baring Street. And we said that we are dead broke, and desperately need his help in expediting an advance from Raza's salary.

In Herb's view, our choice of the apartment was unsatisfactory. And he was not pleased because he thought the area was dicey, especially since I will be walking there mostly by myself. I said that we were unused to the concept of a "ghetto," his term. The area looked fine for a student place. Regarding the money, Herb added that he could loan us $500. "Hopefully that will be enough until the end of the month when Raza receives his first paycheck," he said.

With Herb's check safely in his pocket, Raza decided to broach a controversial subject. "Herb: You are right. Mostly Shirin will be walking by herself. In addition, there is the problem that because she has nothing much to do, she will demand my attention. And I am going to be busy trying to do some Physics. So, we have decided that Shirin should seek admission to a graduate program that keeps her fully engaged." "Oh, that is a great idea," Herb said. "And she is well on time. Usually, after choosing the program people are interested in, they apply for admission in late January or early February. And your wife seems bright enough. There is a chance she will make it." "Oh. That won't do," replied Raza. "This way, for a whole year, she will be footlose and fancy free. And being a very active person," Raza looked at me and continued: "Shirin needs to be occupied." Herb was un-impressed, and we felt we had got about as far as we could go with him.

Back in the apartment, I asked Raza: "How does anybody, paying one dollar, possibly hand over a twenty dollar bill?" Raza had an explanation: "You see, in all the countries I have visited, I have never come across notes that are all the same size. But here in Philadelphia, except for a not very noticeable mention of the denomination, to an untutored eye they all look the same. In particular, I am used to Britain and Pakistan and both have currency notes that have different colors and different sizes for different denominations. And besides," Raza said, "whatever the subject, if a mistake can be made, I will make it."

I started searching my luggage for the Wesleyan check and after some looking found it. We now had two checks but no cash. And the banks closed at three. The nearest bank, we had observed, was not far. We practically ran and arrived there in time.

At the bank, Herb's $500 check was quickly honored. But the $40 Wesleyan check was a problem. It's not easy to cash an Ohio check, especially if you have not lived in the USA recently. But after some coaxing, the bank contacted Ohio Wesleyan—it was still 2 p.m. there—and the teller got an OK for the payment. Wallet thus replenished, we went to eat a better-lunch-cum-early dinner. And Raza gave a solemn promise (that he has broken many times since): "I shall always double-check the currency bill before I hand it over."

Raza and I had agreed to meet outside the Physics building at 10.30. He was late but had an explanation. "Associate Dean William M. Protheroe, who also deals with admissions, is from the Department of Astronomy that is closely associated with Physics. So we are going to visit him to see whether he can help." It seemed a long shot, but Raza wanted to try. Protheroe's office was not far but it took a while before he could see us. His response to our request that I be admitted was essentially identical to that of Herb's. But he noted in passing that the Department Chairmen generally have an important say in such matters.

We thanked the Dean and hurried off to the Department of International Relations—the subject I wanted to study. The Chairman there was extremely unwelcoming. Even though we mentioned that Raza was in the Department of Physics, he paid no attention to Raza, and practically none to me. We left dejected after a short visit. As we were leaving we saw a couple of graduate students who clearly were taking a course in International Relations. Seeing a young woman looking lost, they came over and said hello. I asked them how they felt about this Chairman guy whose office we had just left? We talked a bit and soon they started to express less than warm feelings for him. They suggested that the person who really mattered was not this Chairman but rather Robert Strausz-Hupe who was also the head of the Foreign Policy Research Institute. "Where is the Institute located?" asked Raza. The institute was nearby and we arrived there within minutes.

Strausz-Hupe was famous. And, as could be anticipated, he was very busy. We spoke to his Senior Secretary. She was reluctant, indeed unwilling, to give us an appointment. But after we started to talk to her the lady agreed to check whether we could see him sometime the following month. Strausz-Hupe clearly heard some words of that conversation. And as he came out to say good-bye to the visitor he was hosting, he walked over to say hello. I started a conversation. Strausz-Hupe, very gallantly, asked me to come in. Though uninvited, Raza also joined in. Strausz-Hupe and I conversed for a half hour or longer. He said that he was impressed. And as I began telling the story about the International Relations Department Chair, Strausz-Hupe started to shake his head. Visibly annoyed, he asked his Secretary to get the Chairman online. Their conversation was brief and to the point. Strausz-Hupe told the Chairman he was sending over "a brilliant young lady, named Shirin Tahir-Kheli, who would be a great addition to the department. And she needs to be admitted right away so that she can start attending all the lectures beginning Monday the 10th." To my amusement in response to a question the Chairman must have asked, Strausz-Hupe added in a somewhat annoyed tone: "Yes, she speaks excellent English."

We walked back to the department and I went in to see the Chairman, who was no more welcoming than he had been earlier. He asked me to fill out a couple of lengthy forms wrote a short note, and handed it over to me saying: "Give this to the Dean of Admissions and he will admit you to the General Studies program. But, remember, few students in this program ever make it to full-fledged, University admission. To be allowed proper admission, they must take a minimum of two courses every semester and achieve a 3.5 point average." I walked out with the note. Raza studied it and decided: "If you are a serious student, this admission should do alright."

The Dean's office asked that I choose the courses I wanted to register for, fill out a couple of forms, and walk over to another Secretary who would accept the required payment. I chose a couple of courses—the minimum number required for those who would later be admitted to the masters program—and was told that the total cost for the year would amount to about two thousand dollars. Raza double-checked and discovered something interesting. Because for a graduate program, a two-course load was treated as full load, the cost of taking four courses per semester would be about the same as that for taking two courses. Always willing to oblige, I chose two more courses from the list of those available for the masters program in International Relations. "But we do not have the money?" Raza decided to call it a day, saying: "We wait till Monday when I see Herb."

Monday morning, we both saw Herb. He said: "I have never heard anybody registering in the College of General Studies with the hope of becoming a full-fledged student later. And, expecting to achieve such lofty grades! It's nothing but wishful dreaming." Still, he was willing to help with the tuition. "First, because Raza has a research and teaching appointment, as his wife you are entitled to half tuition remission. That makes it only a thousand a year. You need to go to the bank for the loan. And I know the manager there." He wrote a note for the bank manager.

The bank manager clearly knew Herb. And Herb's note did the trick. We headed back to pay the tuition. But we were told: "Dean Protheroe's signature, testifying that you are indeed entitled to the 50% tuition discount, is required." We were off again to see the Dean. His signature appended, we paid the tuition, and I received the documentation needed for taking the four courses I had chosen. Classes had started that morning. I spent a couple of hours scouting the relevant classrooms, met Raza for lunch, and asked him to conduct me to the main library.

Raza, as teaching faculty, could use any library he wished. Having just become a tuition paying student, I too expected to be able to do the same. In order to enter the Van Pelt—the main library at Penn—all were required to show identification. While Raza was OK'd, I was told in heavy Balkan accent (with an attitude to match): "Islamic female-dress is not allowed in the library." I was confused. I was wearing a Sari. And that had nothing to do with any religion. It is worn in India by women of all religious persuasion: millions of them.

Raza decided not to argue with the burly attendant. Because he wanted to get back to work, he suggested we quickly walk back home, and I change into some "more appropriate clothing" and come back to the library. I wore a very non-Islamic pair of western trousers, and returned to the entrance to the Van Pelt. The burly guy was still there. I was again refused admission, this time on the grounds that: "Women wearing trousers are not permitted in the library. If you want to be admitted you have to wear skirts and show your legs." "God! I never had any such problem at Ohio Wesleyan," and I walked away almost ready to cry and arrived once again at Raza's office.

Raza was perplexed. His thoughts were that there cannot be any such rule. This is a university after all and libraries are central to its existence. He decided it must be due to some cultural hang-up that the attendant had. So we walked over to see our savior: Herb Callen.

Herb had not heard any such thing before. He started to think that I was trouble and tended to manufacture stories. But as a gentleman, he decided to investigate the matter. He called the head of the libraries. The libraries head professed ignorance of the rule and promised he will double-check and get back. Minutes later he did. "There may have been such a rule. But as far as I am aware, it has never come up. Perhaps it's never been used?" Herb was unhappy with that response: "But the rule is being enforced on this young woman. Perhaps you should call and ask that she be admitted." The boss of the libraries preferred not to make a fuss. I thought: "Sad how administrators actually administer." Disgusted, Herb turned around and decided to get back to his physics. I was aware that my stay in Philadelphia would be indeed be a brief one if I was unable to enter the library and was not to simply be a housewife.

Raza was perplexed and angry. "This is shameful behavior on the part of a self-important University. Let us push the matter further up the administrative ladder. But how to do that because that has to be the University President?" said Raza.

The mention of the university President suddenly rang a bell. When we were leaving Karachi, my father had given me a letter for Gaylord Harnwell—whom he knew possibly from their student days reading physics at Cambridge but more likely through meetings they had attended together as university Presidents. "We must go deliver my father's letter to President Harnwell and possibly also talk to him. Maybe he will allow me to use the library," I said.

It was nearly 4 p.m. We gave Baba's letter to the President's Secretary, and she suggested we wait just in case he should want to see us for a few moments. The President, presumably after reading Baba's letter, called us in. Much like my father, Dr. Harnwell had been a student at Cambridge, was a physicist, and roughly the same age as he. The President welcomed us warmly. I told him I was taking courses. He was pleased that I was now a member of the university. The story about the library seemed to surprise him. He couldn't possibly imagine his university would have such an arcane policy. He called the chief of Libraries and suggested he immediately inform the library administrators that there was no hindrance to women wearing trousers or indeed even saris if they chose. He instructed his Secretary to also call Herb Callen to say the President had appreciated his efforts to encourage the chief of libraries to do the right thing. And tell Dr. Callen that henceforth there will be no confusion that women may wear trousers while using the libraries.

This was really astounding! I was making waves that were not planned.

Very grateful to the President, and pleased with ourselves, we walked slowly to the library. Entrance was granted and at the time the victory seemed consequential. When the official letter from the head of the library came assuring me entrance, I noted that the letter asked that I carry the apology at all times in case of future trouble!

The following morning, I went back to Van Pelt. The same, "No Islamic Dress-No Trousers," guy was manning the doors. But he had clearly been instructed not to repeat his performance of the days past. And I walked in, wearing trousers! That was 1962 and it felt like an immense step forward. I had never had any such problem in the midwest in my 1959–1961 college stay.

We lived a simple life and worked six day weeks. Occasionally we went to the movies and sometimes to the Philadelphia orchestra with Eugene Ormandy conducting. Early next year, I was told that I had done well in the exams: two B's and two A's. According to the requirement imposed, that qualified me for admission to the MA program. To that purpose we went to see the Dean again. He examined the transcript and OK'd the admission. And for the spring semester, I again took the equivalent of four courses, which included the writing of a thesis. The subject I chose for the thesis was the United Nations. The thesis was well received. Also, again I got very good grades for the course work. This completed the eight course requirement for the MA program in International Relations and in early June 1963, I was awarded the MA degree.

Herb Callen was impressed. He kept telling people: "Here is a woman who receives her bachelors at age sixteen and takes a year off for fun. Then arrives here un-announced; gets the University to allow women to wear trousers in the libraries; forces her way into the masters program; and receives the MA: all within eight months. And she is only eighteen!"

After a brief celebration, I decided to go visit Strausz-Hupe: mostly to thank him for his help with the admissions process and to give him the good news that I had qualified for the masters program. He was kind as usual and wondered whether I would be interested in working for the Foreign Policy Institute that he led. "Of course, I would. But my visa does not allow me to work full time. Also, any work I do has to be related to my studies." He saw the point and recommended that I may do an internship related to the United Nations: a subject I had worked hard learning for my thesis. Raza had been invited by the Aspen Institute for the summer. So I suggested I start working in September as the fall semester began.

Travel West

To images of "purple mountain majesty" conjured up in my early foray into American national songs learned in Peshawar, I prepared for our time in the Colorado Rockies. Raza had taken driving lessons in a Morris Minor, a small car built by Morris Motors near Oxford. When he saw that a friend in Philadelphia wanted to get rid of a Morris, he jumped at the opportunity to own it and pay to get it rehabbed. The car was in a state of dismal repair and needed, among other things, a new engine. Undeterred, Raza spent four hundred dollars and got the mechanic to fix the car. It had no air-conditioning and drove at a snail's pace. But it was a type of car that Raza had learned to drive! I was excited because I knew how to drive a stickshift, which the car was. I got my American driver's license and felt very grown up.

Soon after my M.A. commencement, we took to the road on a long trek from Philadelphia, Pennsylvania to Aspen, Colorado. Because the car barely functioned beyond 50 miles per hour, days were spent traveling. Going up the Independence Pass in Colorado, height in excess of 12,000 feet, the car almost completely gave up. Water kept boiling over, requiring us to stop for the engine to cool down. Occasionally, water needed replenishing. Fortunately, we had kept some in the trunk for just that eventuality. When we finally made it to the top of the pass, we were greeting with loud cheers by an assembled crowd consisting of drivers who had passed us earlier, who treated us to lunch. Going down the mountain the other side was a breeze. The Minor acted as a Major and we arrived in Aspen in great spirits.

Raza went to work most days, and I walked around and enjoyed the scenery in what was then a simple and beautiful small town. We went on weekly hikes with Michael and Regina Cohen and generally had a good time. The Aspen Institute and the Music Festival each offered interesting evenings with varied guest lecturers and performers. At one dinner I sat next to Buckminster Fuller, creator of the geodesic dome. He talked of Sufi spiritualism of the Indian subcontinent and was a charming dinner companion. I felt that was a perfect summer in so many ways with the physical beauty of Colorado offering the backdrop for intellectual improvement and enjoyment.

After a couple of months in Aspen, because we were already most of the way to California, we decided we might as well drive there. With a sense of adventure we got started. The drive was slow and stiflingly hot in a car with no air-conditioning. We entered Nevada headed for Las Vegas, which seemed hotter even than areas in the Sind, in Pakistan. As we coasted on the last hill into that city, it was a truly mesmerizing scene. Brilliant lights of "the strip" set amidst desert desolation: hotels with no doors, cool breezes of the air-conditioning and names of famous entertainers blazing on billboards. One could have a good time for not much money if one did not gamble.

We drove from Las Vegas to much pleasanter southern clime and arrived in La Jolla, California. Raza had a friend from Oxford, a Rhodes

Scholar, working at the University of California San Diego. We went out to dinner with him and his Swiss wife. At dinner, no alcohol could be served to anybody less than twenty-one years of age. So the restaurant demanded identification. But the person serving asked that only the Swiss lady show her ID. The rest of us passed muster simply because we looked old enough. The Swiss lady grudgingly produced her driver's license: She was twenty seven. I was still only eighteen, and the waiter offered to serve me a glass!

Driving safely on crowded California highways requires both experience and skill. To be on the safe side, we stayed mostly in the extreme right lane. But that was clearly not enough. And on our way early the next day, while Raza was driving as we were approaching Los Angeles, a truck hit and pushed us off the road toward a ditch some fifty feet below. We hurtled down, over heavy stones and small trees and my life flashed before my eyes. But Raza had the presence of mind to break hard. And mercifully, the car stopped before falling into the ditch.

Raza felt negative about all truck drivers. We got out of the car and walked up to the road. Raza stayed in the background and said: "You try to seek help because people are friendlier to women and especially to those who are wearing a Sari." While Raza was wrong about all truck drivers being nasty, he was right on the button about people willing to help those wearing a Sari. Soon a small truck, with a couple of young men in it, stopped and offered help. The truck used a rope, while Raza pushed hard on the accelerator. Soon the Morris was up and on the road again. Its bottom was badly damaged while the side where it had been hit was quite serviceable. We drove slowly till we saw a phone booth. I called and discovered that Morris Minors were serviced by Rolls Royce dealers in nearby Long Beach.

We arrived at the dealer's. It was a super fancy place. "Won't get to it today," we were told. Raza and I pleaded: "Perhaps you will and hoping that you do, we shall wait. And, is there a place nearby where we can get a sandwich?" Raza walked out looking for something to eat. There was a very elegantly dressed, superbly coiffed woman sitting next to me and we started to converse. She liked my Sari and was interested in whether the requisite blouse could be stitched in California, etc. I said I knew nothing about California, having spent only a few days in San Francisco as a student. "Then how come you are here today?" I answered the question by telling the lady of the accident an hour ago. Also that given that at a Rolls Royce dealership, our beat up Morris was unlikely to get attention.

Upon hearing that she called the manager. He came over and speaking very deferentially said that her car—a brand new Rolls Royce—was almost ready. She responded: "I am waiting for you to also finish fixing my friend's car—and as she said that, she pointed to me—because she is to follow me to our home." That was a powerful signal and apparently two men immediately started to work on our Morris. An hour or two later, Raza was trying hard barely able to keep track of the nifty Rolls. Finally we arrived at our hosts' estate. We eyed the Olympic sized pool but I was impressed by their extraordinary bar with Brazilian jacaranda tables.

Raza and I were both exhausted. The accident and its aftermath had been traumatizing. Sensing our fatigue, our hostess conducted us to our bedroom and suggested we rest a while because she was planning to invite a few of her friends for a party that evening. "The party is to celebrate your presence here." A little while later, I heard her on the phone saying to a friend: "You have to come to dinner and meet these two exotic people who are our guests." We went up to retire for a couple of hours. I kept thinking: "What extra-ordinary hospitality! And it's being offered to total strangers! In the western world, this can happen only in the USA!" At the party we met our hostess's husband: a famous thoracic surgeon. After the party, everybody wanted to swim. Even Raza joined in. But I kept my distance: swimming in a pool that large, I thought, was dangerous given my inbred fear of water.

The following morning we started to drive north eventually arriving in San Francisco along the famous Pacific Coast Highway. Monterrey, Carmel and San Francisco offered a wonderful stay. The Morris worked in the cooler temperatures of northern California and we headed to Reno, Nevada. From there, we drove to Salt Lake City and then further northeast, arriving days later in Yellowstone and the Teton National Park.

It had been a long trek in a rudimentary vehicle, and we wanted to rest a while at the camp ground. Hotels nearby were expensive but we had a pair of sleeping bags in the trunk. Lying down in the open, a moonlit night, and whispers from trees nearby were breathtakingly lovely and I was glad of our decision to stay at the campsite. But early next morning was a different story. Both of us had practically frozen solid during the night as had the radiator of the car. Despite the excitement watching the Old Faithful, and the beauteous splendor of nature, clearly we could not afford to stay there. However, once again other people who were more proficient in the art of camping came to our rescue, inviting us to sit alongside others around a camp fire until we all warmed up and offering us hot coffee.

Late that afternoon, we set out on the long journey back home to Philadelphia via Colorado to visit Mildred Rausch who years earlier had been in Peshawar and recommended that I go to Ohio Wesleyan. The fall semester was due to begin in ten days and the rate at which the car moved required that we drive 12 hours a day. En route one late evening, not having found a satisfactory motel, we lay down in our sleeping bags in an open area near the highway to rest for a while. We felt no fear. There was basically no traffic and we went off to sleep. A few hours later I woke up screaming. Raza was confused. I had seen a real, live ghost and Raza insisted none existed. To settle the controversy, Raza said let us get moving because ghosts stay in areas of choice and do not follow Morris Minors slowly moving away.

Eventually, we arrived home in Philadelphia and I started my internship at the Foreign Policy Research Institute. The work was undemanding but intellectually rewarding. But most importantly for Raza, the job kept me occupied and allowed him time to do his physics.

Those two years of early marriage were memorable in so many ways. We made lifelong friends even as we prepared to leave for Pakistan after a few choice stops in Madrid, Geneva, Venice, Stockholm, and Frankfurt and the UK.

CHAPTER 5

Back to Pakistan

August 1, 1964, we flew to London after the planned two-year stay in the USA. I felt lucky to be going home and appreciated immensely the fact that Raza kept his promise that we would live in Pakistan. I knew from Herb Callen that Raza was offered a tenure-track position as an Assistant Professor of Physics at the University of Pennsylvania, which he declined due to his promise to me. "True love" I told both Raza and Herb. En route in the UK, Raza again had been invited to spend two months at Harwell. We stayed in Oxford, while Raza commuted. October took us back to Karachi where Raza registered at the Atomic Energy Commission offices and began waiting to have an audience with the Chairman.

Again a week passed before Raza could see him. The Chairman instructed Raza to go to Lahore where the Atomic Energy had a large establishment. And with a view to taking over its administration, advise the Chairman as to how its performance could be improved.

Raza arrived in Lahore. He was given a big office and spacious living quarters, in fact one of a newly built, four bedroom homes in newly built Gulberg. Raza studied the lay of the land in the Atomic Energy establishment and decided within a few months that he did not want to be the administrator there. The Chairman was very displeased. Raza was told in no uncertain terms that he was at best useless if he could not appreciate the golden opportunity handed him to be the big boss in Lahore. "Instead, you really want to do Physics?" asked the Chairman said in true horror.

Although I knew Lahore well, it was new for Raza. Also, I had several relatives there. The head of the Pakistan Board of Revenue—a powerful position because it controls the country's economic sector—and the head of the Pakistani Naval Forces (retired) were two of those. And it was good that they were there because we needed a lot of help. And in Pakistan, help is provided best by top government officials. Telephone connection, which was trivially easy to secure in the USA, was about impossible to arrange in Lahore. Raza's colleagues at work told him it normally takes a year or longer to get a telephone connection and even so one has to pay a hefty bribe. Undeterred, we decided to try. But after two weeks of getting nowhere, especially when asked for extra-legal payments amounting variously to three to five thousand dollars (measured in today's currency values), I decided to seek help from my uncle, the head of the Board of Revenue. Within a couple of days, and after paying only the official cost that amounted to about ten dollars, we received the telephone connection!

Though we had the connections, it always bothered me that nothing could ever get done without them. Not an ideal way to live in a country that had been established with so many dreams of good people like my father.

When leaving the USA, we had only about a thousand dollars to spare which we parked with a friend for safekeeping. We bought a new Chevrolet Impala which we took to Pakistan. The car was too huge for existing roads so we sold it and bought a brand new Mercedes-Benz—a desirable status symbol! One day, while driving from Islamabad to Lahore with Dilys and Saul Winegrad, close friends visiting us from the USA in late July 1965, we found ourselves stuck behind a slow-moving truck. The road was not wide enough to safely overtake the truck. And, as is often the case in Pakistan, the truck, rather than keeping left, stayed in the middle of the road: thus making the overtaking both unsafe and difficult. The air-conditioning in the car was a survival tool that boiling hot summer afternoon. Suddenly, a stone was thrown up by one of the back tires of the truck. It instantly struck the windshield and completely shattered it. Saved by the special security features of the Mercedes-Benz windshields, neither of us was injured. But hundreds of pieces of shattered glass needed clearing from within the car. Once that was done, we restarted on the drive to Lahore, but now in utter discomfort, both because of the steaming hot wind that was hitting straight into our faces and the resultant ineffectiveness of the air-conditioning.

The next morning, Raza went to the Mercedes-Benz dealers. He had expected to have to wait for a couple of hours while the windshield was being installed but not the response that he received. "There are no Mercedes windshields to be had any where in Pakistan," he was told, "and with the country on a war footing, none can be expected for the next year as no ships are arriving into Karachi port to discharge parts." I thought this was still another instance of where massive amounts of bribe would be required, so I brought the matter to my uncle's attention. The car was resubmitted to the dealers. A day later, we heard they had removed a windshield from a new vehicle and installed it in ours: and all of that for the standard price!

Sometime in August, Raza's physicist friend Michael Wortis and his wife Ruth arrived. They had driven from Europe in their impressive new Land Rover through Afghanistan—where Michael had gone mountain climbing. They recounted wonderful stories about the hospitality along the way. This was mid-1960s, and the roads through Afghanistan into Pakistan were hospitable to foreigners. Hippie culture made Kabul popular, and road traffic to Peshawar was the transit route to Nepal and beyond.

We had plenty of room to accommodate them and Raza, who was bored with the Atomic Energy job, was happy to have his friend there. He told me: "It is great to have somebody nearby who can actually write, read, and calculate and think Physics." Michael pointed out to me that Raza's talent was going to waste. Given that his Physics doctoral dissertation had been a pathbreaker, he was wasting his time in Pakistan. Also, medical issues began to surface. Raza was diagnosed with a stomach ulcer, and follow-up treatment was rendered. I understood that ulcers are a recurring phenomenon.

I was expecting our first child and needed my mother to help with various matters that only mothers can help with. To that purpose, I left Lahore to stay with my parents in Rawalpindi to await delivery not far from a new town to be called Islamabad that was under construction. My father was establishing a new University in Islamabad under the tutelage of then President Ayub Khan.

Soon thereafter, on September 6 to be precise, the continuing hostilities burst into full-fledged war between India and Pakistan. They were off again on an incalculably dangerous but oft-traveled trek. Our Lahore home was not far from the Indo-Pak border. When I heard that the war had broken out and India had attacked the border near Lahore plus the news of reported dogfights between Indian and Pakistani fighter aircraft over Lahore, I immediately called my favorite Aunt, Malika, who lived in one of the official residences in a grand compound built in the days of the British Raj in Lahore. Malika picked up the phone and when I rushed my urgent message to find Raza, whom I had not located via the phone, and ask him to come to Rawalpindi, Malika asked: "Why?" "There's a war on," I replied, noting that I needed him with me before the baby's arrival.

My aunt calmly asked me to hold for a moment, opened the front door of her residence, looked out, returning to the phone said: "No love, there is no war on. All is quiet here." We finally found Raza. He said: "The rumble of the heavy weapons is eerily audible." I started to worry and with dread in my voice asked Raza to immediately return to my parent's place and also bring the Wortis' along. Indeed, all three of you can drive here in their Land Rover. Raza transmitted my suggestions to the Wortis'. Completely unconcerned about any possible danger, they decided to stay put. They wanted to complete their stay in Pakistan and go by road as planned into India some six weeks later.

Raza left early the next morning on a 160-mile train ride to Rawalpindi that normally should take about three and a half hours. But soon after starting, sirens blared and the train slowed to a halt. Loudspeakers screamed that an Indian bomber was approaching, and the train was a likely target as military hardware was generally transported via rail between different military commands. Therefore, everybody had to get out and lie down somewhere at least 50 yards away. Announcement will be made to re-board, when it became safe to do so.

Hours seemed to pass. No bombers were heard or seen overhead, and no announcements were made. Passengers became very restive. Some started to walk back with a mind to re-board but found the train locked. Noisy agitation ensued. That must have awakened the engineer-driver from his restful sojourn because he started to blow both his horn and the train siren and used the loudspeaker to instruct everybody to come back in.

All seemed to forgive the driver for the inconvenience he had caused: and were happy that the train was moving again. But the happiness was short-lived. The train could not have traveled more than a dozen miles before the sirens sounded and the loudspeaker warned of an imminent air attack. The previous drill was repeated. And a hundred minutes or more must have passed before everybody was back in their seat, and the train was in motion again. But now the mood was belligerent and nobody was in a forgiving mood.

Unbelievably, the whole process was repeated two more times, and the train arrived at its destination more than twelve hours late, at 1 a.m. the following morning. I was haunted by the nightmarish scenario that Raza was lost even before his child was born. Upon arrival, Raza found a telephone booth in the railway station and placed a collect call. Deliriously happy, I accompanied the driver and we picked Raza up, all in one piece!

My parents lived in close proximity to Rawalpindi Airport and not far from the Catholic hospital where my obstetrician worked. There was a perceived threat that the airport will be bombed and the possibility that inaccurate bombing will affect the neighboring areas. As a safety measure, all were asked to have trenches dug and at the sounding of an appropriate siren lie in them, a difficult task for anyone nine-months pregnant! We followed those instructions for three days. I was huge. My father pressed me to check into the hospital, which was not an option in a war situation where medical facilities are in high demand. Every night to the sirens wail, we were aroused from sleep and ran to the newly dug trenches in the garden. These had been dug haphazardly in a hurry. Defense planning for the general population had never been a priority.

Running through one trench was the main water pipe into the house. On September 13, the nightly raid warning got me out faster. I thus was the first one in line to get into the trench. Shortly after stepping down the ladder, I realized that there was a pipe I would need to go under in order to move forward and allow other members of the family to enter the trench. Given the late stage of my pregnancy, that task was impossible. On the other hand, I did not want the family standing outside in full view of air activity and be hit. I fell on all fours and navigated myself under the pipe. My water broke!

I went into the Holy Family Hospital which not far from the airfield. Labor was long, and we were moved into an unprepared for such contingencies basement, when the sirens sounded which prolonged labor. Two friends, Rehana (Nano) Hayat and Shahida Saigol, were in the same hospital at the same time and delivered babies on the same day. Despite the stress, we laughed our way through the situation with them teasing me "you did all this family planning while away in America to find the perfect time to have a child. And here you are delivering in the middle of the war."

On the evening of September 15, my daughter was born. All mothers find their baby exceptionally lovely. My Shehra, described in the Quran as "the brightest star in the heavens," really was beautiful, long at 21 inches, with big eyes, long eyelashes, and a lot of hair. The hospital's nursery was set at a distance because of the war. Shehra stayed in my room, and my mother and I looked after her. She was a happy baby who seemed most observant.

The war had been a disaster for both countries, especially so for Pakistan. At the urging of the articulate and very savvy the then foreign minister Zulfiqar Ali Bhutto, President Ayub Khan had been coaxed into "encouraging volunteer helpers"—meaning, sending Commandos from the Pakistani Army, including as it happened, Raza's brother—into Kashmir, a contested area, to inspire a spontaneous uprising against Indian rule there. Not only did this ill-advised attempt fail to achieve its objective, it irked the Indian Government enough to start a full-fledged war across the international border. India ordered its Army to attack Pakistan proper and its Air Force to pound the military establishments in Pakistan. Ayub, an erstwhile military commander, was sensible enough to realize that the war was being lost and clever enough to arrange a cease-fire. Bhutto was irate. He started to attack Ayub from within the government. He charged him with being both a loser, who lacked courage, and a President who had handcuffed his brave military. These charges were cleverly circumscribed but had two effects: one, they made Ayub lose his footing on the pedestal of grace that he had occupied since he took over the presidency in 1958; and two, they made Bhutto a new political force to be reckoned with. Bhutto seemed to enjoy his position in the Government as well as his ability to work against it. But that would not last and he noisily resigned on June 21, 1966.

I continued staying with my parents as Raza decided to move from Lahore where he felt he was unable to pursue research in theoretical physics. I sensed we would not be long in Pakistan and wanted to spend time with my parents who doted on their first grandchild. Because Raza had already lost the Chairman's confidence, he decided to self-transfer to the Pakistan Institute of Nuclear Science and Technology (called PINSTECH, for short). PINSTECH was housed in a magnificent modern building. Built by a world famous architect, Edward Durrell Stone, it sketched shadows of past Islamic history. Located in Nilore, a twenty-minute Pakistan Atomic Energy bus ride, Raza found it a congenial place. Indeed, when in June 1966, Herb Callen stopped by on his way to India, Raza took him to PINSTECH. We also drove Herb to Murree and Nathia Gali. Raza had long conversations with Herb, and both became convinced that if Raza wanted to do any Physics, he would have to return to the USA. Two days later, Herb left Pakistan. When leaving, he remarked: "What a magnificent land, where the 20th century commingles with the 18th!"

Few weeks after Herb returned home, he cabled saying: "There is a position at Penn for you. As is usual, it is an Assistant Professorship with an initial appointment for three years. I trust you are interested? Phone me back, ASAP."

Raza was overjoyed, but I was of two minds. Living far away from my parents was not my idea of a good life. Besides, before our wedding, Raza had promised we shall not live abroad. Long conversations ensued. Finally, Baba emphatically declared: "A young brilliant scientist needs an appropriate environment for his work and it would be very sad if Raza were denied that opportunity." Mama was sad that we would leave and take Shehra away from them. But, she reminded me that I had wanted to marry Raza because he was a scholar and a handsome one at that. "You cannot stay back if he decides he cannot work in Pakistan," she noted.

Raza called Herb and expressed strong interest in the job. Tickets for travel abroad were priced in hard currencies. In order to purchase airline tickets, one needed authorization from the National Bank of Pakistan for the appropriate amount of foreign exchange. There were three of us who would need tickets. It was now August, and the universities started within a month. And the National Bank was always slow making foreign exchange commitments. Raza mentioned this array of impending difficulties to Herb.

Temple University in Philadelphia had very recently been added to the duo of public universities: namely the Pennsylvania State University and the University of Pittsburgh. Formalizing the partnership with the State, added millions of dollars to what previously had been meager State funding. The upshot of it all was that now the Temple University Physics department had adequate funds for additional hiring. To this purpose, the Chairman of the department asked Herb Callen for advice and help. Herb was happy to advise that Raza would be a suitable choice. "But Dr. Tahir-Kheli already has an offer from Penn.," Herb added. "Therefore, if Temple is interested, it will have to up the ante. In particular, if Temple would pay about 10% more in salary than that being offered by Penn., and also buy him airline tickets for three, then I (Herbert Callen) would try to convince him to accept the offer," said Herb. This was a clever ploy. Within a week, Raza received a telegram, with the offer fully spelled out exactly as Herb had proposed. All it asked for was a proper copy of the Oxford University document that certified having received the Ph.D. degree.

Raza was astounded, not only with the offer, but also with the airline tickets. Also, not least because the offer had been occasioned, sight unseen, without Raza even asking for it. Raza called Herb and informed him of this surprising turn of events. Herb laughed and told Raza the story and strongly recommended Raza to respond immediately and accept the offer.

Here was another unplanned change.

Reflecting on life as we pondered a major permanent move, I felt that I was extremely lucky. I had a great childhood full of love spanning two continents, had been fortunate in parents who believed in a daughter's education, married the man I loved, and had a beautiful baby girl. Thus, in late August 1966, we left for the USA with all of the visa formalities completed for immigration in advance of travel. With Raza's scientific background, he and we qualified to be admitted as immigrants on a special visa. As we left Pakistan with an eleven-month baby to head to the USA, I decided that if we are destined to live in America, I would not live as an immigrant but become an integrated citizen of the country in which we chose to live, holding only one nationality, American. Henceforth, the USA would be home.

PART III

Call to Duty

CHAPTER 6

Home Is Where You End Up

I was married at 18. I became a mother at 21. By Pakistani standards, I already had delayed motherhood by not having a child right after marriage. I remember my mother telling me that my sweet mother-in-law had quietly asked if there was something wrong with me because I had not yet produced a child two years after the marriage. It was a different era and a different culture.

Our permanent return to the USA in 1966 meant that our baby daughter would leave also. There was a lot of heartache as family ties were stretched. Back in Philadelphia, it was very satisfying to stay home with the baby and to look after her. To do so on my own without help for the first time was enjoyable. I wanted to go on with that as the central theme of my life.

Yet, I was extremely aware that I was brought up with the clear expectation of public service. It was the familiar "to whom much is given, from them much is expected." At twenty-two, I was not sure which direction seemed more suitable.

Academia was my background. My father exemplified public service. It was also a way of "giving back" even in my newly adopted country through service. I had my M.A. The next step in order to move to a teaching career at the University level was attainment of a Ph.D. I wanted the flexibility of a University teaching career. With small children and a husband as an academic, my joining the ranks of academe made sense. I would return to my alma mater, the University of Pennsylvania, to join the doctoral program.

I was admitted to the program, and the requirements for a Ph.D. were carefully explained to me. Everyone noted that it was most important to sign on with a doctoral advisor quickly. Full of trepidation, I showed up outside the office door of Professor Alvin Z. Rubinstein. A brilliant scholar and teacher, he had a tough reputation for grading and for being a no-nonsense guy. I had earlier taken a course on Soviet Foreign Policy with him and had earned an A. I hoped that grade made me acceptable for a doctoral student under his supervision for my dissertation. The professor was probing in his questions regarding my interest in working with him. Why "Soviet foreign policy"? I replied that my interest focused on the making of foreign policy and its implications as it applied to the Pakistan, Afghanistan, and Iran region. I wanted to focus on these three countries of the newly termed "Southwest Asia" region and how they related to the superpower to the north. With a bit of a twinkle in his eye, Professor Rubinstein (as I deferentially called him) said: "Remember, you're entering a man's world. I make no exceptions for requirements for female household responsibilities!"

"None will be asked for" I promised. Through the seminars full of cigarette smoke indicative of "a man's world," I kept my promise and asked no dispensation for my being a female. Through the Ph.D. preliminary exams, the two language requirements and the dissertation, my mother offered critical moral support and even came to spend time with her granddaughter while I studied for the exams. "You must finish the degree," Mama always said. "You'll be the first girl in our family to get a Ph.D." She always noted with appreciation Raza's encouragement in my continued pursuit of higher education. Whenever he came on work-related visits to the USA, Baba came to visit in Philadelphia and noted the importance of finishing my degree.

I was not sure that a full-blown career was what I wanted. There were expectations, sure. Here, I was with husband and child 12,000 miles away from the subcontinent where I was born. But here in America I expected to be judged for myself, not as someone's granddaughter or someone's daughter. This was the proverbial "land of the free," which also meant freedom of choice.

Most women are familiar with the hard choices they face even as options are considered. Economic need or professional expectations or family pressure may launch a career or necessitate a job. But everyday, at some level, women live with the consequences of choices we make. The way most of us dealt with the issue is to try and do everything, that way, no one gets shortchanged. We work, shop, cook, clean, give parties, go to parties, travel, organize the kids' activities and play dates, carpool and do the myriad chores that form the daily ritual.

My generation of women entered the professional world having had their kids early. My second child, my son, Kazim, was born when I was twenty-six. He was born in Philadelphia but a world away, another India–Pakistan war was being fought in 1971. I remember my brother, Toufiq, calling to congratulate and noting that I had produced two kids born the same respective years as the two India–Pakistan wars. "Don't have any more. South Asia can't afford it!"

I had a tough second pregnancy. My Ph.D. dissertation, which I hoped to finish before Kazim was born, had to be put aside as I was confined to bed for months. In that state, the last thing I wanted to do was write on Soviet Foreign Policy, the chosen subject. As I lay in bed and the season's turned from fall to spring, I was very worried about the baby. I was also guilty about not writing and kept justifying that I could be thinking of what I would write once I was well enough.

Kazim was born on April 16, 1971, in Philadelphia. When the baby was old enough to take naps and also to sit up, I thought hard about where I could set up my work headquarters with all of the baby paraphernalia and my research spread out. The dining room was the obvious choice. There, for almost a year, I pounded my two finger typing (never having learned it the proper way in school) effort. Shehra was five when her brother was born so she was starting kindergarten.

Finally, the draft was sufficiently ready to go to my supervisor, Professor Alvin Z. Rubinstein who had wisely counseled that I stop doing a half-hearted job the previous year while in France with Raza for his sabbatical. "Just enjoy Paris in the spring. Work when you return to the U.S." he wrote. I happily put it out of my mind until my return in September. Then I found out I was expecting and the pregnancy complicated the schedule.

All of my graduate studies were undertaken after marriage. I was serious about being a housewife but domestic responsibilities allowed time for other pursuits. Thus began my M.A., which I received from the University of Pennsylvania in one year. I was not yet nineteen. I became a research assistant at the Foreign Policy Research Institute at the University for the second year of our stay in the USA. When we returned to Philadelphia in 1966, I started work on my Ph.D.

In those days, the prevailing attitude was that women were not serious about graduate work. I recall many a colleague, male naturally, would questions the need for me to get a Ph.D. International Relations was man's territory and I along with very few other female students in the program were simply wasting everyone's time. "You are wasting your time in a man's world," I often heard. My response that a woman had to be twice as serious given my full life and the fact that for every class I attended, I drove twenty miles in the opposite direction to leave my baby with a trusted baby sitter. Then picked her up, came home, made dinner, etc. "Why do you bother?" was the rejoinder.

In the three decades plus that I worked, the professional world of women changed. No longer is there any need for a handful of women to be knocking for entry into professions that in the 1970s were solely a man's domain. The growth of job options and fields of expertise are now dazzling. Women believe that it is up to them to make it, acknowledging only in passing that good fortune and a handy mentor can indeed smooth the way.

The late 1970s and 1980s were about freedom of opportunity and breaking down previously held taboos about women in the workplace. It was a heady time because that freedom had been hard won. For women who chose the national security policy path, the chance to become professionals without the hassle of being constantly reminded that it was "a man's world" was both refreshing and empowering.

Women chose to do everything in my time and not only because we were "super moms." Some, like me, were lucky in having a very supportive husband whose professorship allowed him to work from home when not teaching and get the summers off for research. I remember in the midst of a particularly hectic week in Washington years later when I said over the phone to my husband: "I need a wife." Without missing a beat, he responded: "Me too!" I assumed it was humorously said. I did not seek clarification.

Professional women of my era carried a sense of guilt when we were away from the children. When I left for Carlisle Barracks in Pennsylvania, I made it a practice to have breakfast with my 9-year-old son while we chatted on the phone before he left for school. It was only a few minutes but we connected. Shehra was in High School so moving the kids made no sense, especially since my jobs away from home involved very long hours. But I missed something. The small things that make up the life of a family and do not necessarily happen only on weekends when I was home.

Women are marrying later now, having children later and tend to focus on their professions much earlier. Whenever I speak to young audiences, which I make every effort to as often as is possible for me, the questions from young women all relate to how is it possible to combine the demands of work, home, marriage, and children. They want to know if I had a life other than working and whether I enjoyed it. When I respond that for me a full life included my husband, children, entertaining, travel, parents, and that while frantic, it was a very full and mostly enjoyable life.

In August 1971, I received my Ph.D. My neighbor took care of my son while I went to the graduation ceremony with my daughter, Shehra and great friend Ruth Gales. Raza was away in Brazil helping in the setting up of a Physics department in Recife in the northeast. When the family and friends of graduates were asked to stand to receive thanks for their help in the process, Shehra and Ruth stood up. We held hands and grinned madly.

Raza, Shehra, and I became US citizens in 1971, as soon as eligible. We gave up Pakistani citizenship just as my parents and thus I had done years earlier with Indian citizenship when we went to Peshawar in Pakistan from Hyderabad, India.

It was thus in December 1971 that we were asked to come to the Federal Courthouse on Market and Eight Street in Philadelphia to become US citizens. There were only a handful of immigrants in the courthouse all waiting to take the solemn oath. I remember over preparing for the test that preceded granting of citizenship. Ruth Gales was again the one who vouched for me. It was a small ceremony held in courthouse. The District Attorney for Philadelphia, Arlen Specter, swore us in. (Arlen Specter became a Senator from Pennsylvania and introduced me when I went up for my confirmation hearing to be a US Ambassador in 1990.) As we stood up to take the oath, I felt proud of us for integrating fully into a new country. I felt proud that the USA was welcoming. The future looked bright and we pledged to do our best.

Credentials in place, I started job hunting. Over and over again I was told that the possibilities in the years it took me to have my kids and get my Ph.D. the market for International Relations degrees had turned markedly negative. There were few full-time tenure-track teaching jobs. I had taken a chance but it would have been virtually impossible to add a full-time job at a lower rank without the degree to the full mix that was my life.

So I prepared to compromise and look for a part-time job to start with. Time and again in various interviews I was told that a woman with a husband was lower in terms of hiring preferences, "because you have a husband to pay the bills." By definition then, the man who paid the bills got the job. When I asked about single men or women and preferences there, I met with an awkward silence.

Contributing fully and developing professionally required a career. I wanted to work and not be a "sponge" simply living off my husband. My female cousins all told me this was a crazy plan and I noted that none of them worked. My siblings did and I did not want to break with that family tradition, especially since a fair amount of effort had gone into my education. I continued to hunt for alternatives to teaching. But my whole life had centered on universities, as a daughter and then as a student plus now as a wife. My preference remained an academic position.

Then one day I got a call that the Dean of the College of Arts and Sciences, George Johnson (who went on to lead George Mason University in Virginia in a spectacular manner) wanted to see me. I knew George and respected him. Ushered into his office, he said he heard I had finished my doctorate and wanted to know if I was willing to take a job as an Academic Advisor in the college. He explained the duties which involved mentoring incoming undergraduates at Temple University. I enquired about teaching. The dean noted that while I would not be assigned teaching, I might be able to do some as a part-time faculty member at one of the campuses in suburban Ambler. "Sounds like a plan," I noted.

Two things worked in favor of the offer beyond the fact that it was a job. First, it was at the same campus where Raza was a professor of Physics. Our little son, Kazim, could go to child care in the same building where I would be working. Second, it was a University job. Administration rather than faculty but I could get started. I accepted the position and felt very pleased to be launched.

Temple University is a state-related institution and has a 40,000-plus student body. As I secured a full-time faculty position in 1973 and started to teach there I realized that while the admission requirements were less stringent than the ivy leagues, we had some superb students who were in other jobs but wanted a college degree in order to move ahead. Their desire to succeed made teaching exciting. I over prepared but it was better that than being caught shorthanded. Teaching gave me the fall to summer work schedule that Raza and Shehra were on. Kazim was still a toddler. I enjoyed teaching; so it was far more than simply a job.

CHAPTER 7

Monitoring Pakistan as a Scholar

Research on South Asia and relations with the USA continued to take up my summer months when I was free of my teaching and administrative work. We traveled for summers either to various places Raza was doing his research in solid-state physics or visiting my parents in Islamabad.

In April 1977, I traveled to Islamabad and was pleased to find all my family in good health. For a couple of years, Raza had wanted to visit his Oxford buddy, Pradeep Sahgal, in Delhi. As Raza completed his teaching responsibilities for the spring semester at the end of May, I suggested he join me in Islamabad and if he were interested we would go visit Pradeep.

Political winds in Pakistan had started to flow in yet another direction. While Bhutto himself had absolutely no interest in religion, in order to curry favors with the Saudis, and to broaden his political base at home, he started toying with the idea of Islamization. A cheap shot was to declare: "In keeping with the Islamic traditions, sale of liquor is henceforth illegal." While this change of law won plaudits among the majority—meaning the lower- and the middle-classes—the well-to-do minority were irate. They needed their evening inspiration. Also, the political elite who often invited foreign diplomats, and sometime non-foreign imbibers, needed access to their bottle of premium Scotch whiskey. One of my friends, a close associate of Bhutto and a powerful Minister in his Government, suggested that when Raza flies to Pakistan he should carry as much Black Label in his luggage as could be accommodated. Realizing that a bottle would often be a very desirable gift, I urged Raza to carry as many as he could manage. And while changing flights at Heathrow, Raza purchased twelve bottles of one liter each.

Raza's flight arrived in Karachi at about 2 a.m. In London, as was customary, the whiskey had been delivered directly to the aircraft by the duty-free shop. Therefore, in Karachi, it was placed in full view of a youthful customs inspector next to Raza's suitcases. The inspector instantly focused on the booze and declared (in Urdu) "It is absolute contraband for a Muslim. Only non-Muslims may carry liquor as luggage and they have to pay duty for it." I had failed to tell Raza anything about this brand-new law and he was confused. He declared solemnly: "No problem. Yes, I should be happy to pay the duty." The inspector became agitated. "No. You may not pay any duty. You are a Muslim. You cannot bring liquor. Full stop." Raza thought for a moment and took out his American passport. "See. This is a Christian passport. And it does not say anywhere that I am a Muslim."

This commotion clearly woke up the senior guy, and he came out of an inner office. First, he opened one of the liquor cases and started to handle a bottle. Seeing that, the agitated young guy also did the same. Finally, the senior guy spoke: "You shame your father. I know him well. He is a good Muslim." At this, Raza repeated: "Please look at my passport. It is a Christian passport. It allows me to carry some liquor as my baggage." As the conversation continued, the young inspector started handling the bottle and moved his body with ever greater feverishness: as if he were in a trance. No wonder that the bottle dropped on the hard cement floor, shattered into pieces, and spread its telling aroma all through the large room. Hundreds were waiting for their baggage to be cleared and many believed themselves besmirched and befouled by the smell which they viewed as Haram.[1] Raza saw his moment and demanded the bottle be restored so that he could, without entering Pakistan, return on the next flight out. Realizing the spot he was in, the senior guy commanded Raza to disappear forthwith and take his stuff with him. It was thus that Raza arrived safely in Bhutto's new Islamized Pakistan with eleven liters of Black Label Scotch Whiskey: all cleared through the customs duty-free.

Early June, Raza and I flew to Delhi and stayed with Pradeep Sahgal's family. Raza had told me that Pradeep's mother is closely related to the Nehrus. After arrival, we discovered that Pradeep's sister Anjali and her husband, Commander Shamu Varma, were good friends with Rajiv Gandhi. All that encouraged me to ask Pradeep's mother if she could get me an appointment with Mrs. Gandhi. I wanted to talk to her about India's relations with the USA and with neighboring Pakistan.

After serving three consecutive terms as Prime Minister, Mrs. Gandhi had recently—that is, March 20, 1977—lost election for the fourth term. An appointment with the ex-Prime Minister was secured for the third day that we were to be there. But I was told they could get an appointment right away with their relative Vijaya Lakshmi Pandit. And she was a figure of great prominence in International Relations. A sister of Jawaharlal Nehru, Mrs. Pandit had served as India's Ambassador to the USA, the Soviet Union, Ireland, and also as High Commissioner to the UK. But even more interesting to me, she had been the first female President of the UN General Assembly. As such, she was a woman of great stature, not-unequal to Prime Minister Gandhi. And to top it all, my father was a friend of hers and each had represented their respective countries at various international fora.

We all went to Mrs. Pandit's place. She was gracious: sharp of mind and spirit. We were served tea. And altogether it was a great experience. An additional thing that impressed me was that unlike what one might find in the home of a similar personage in Pakistan, her accommodations did not reek of exorbitant riches or political nobility.

Two days later, we drove to meet Prime Minister Gandhi. She had been informed about me, my background from Hyderabad Deccan, and my interest in International Relations. But Raza's presence was a surprise. Being gracious, she inquired about Raza's background. Raza mentioned he was born in a small village, bred in two towns: a small one and a somewhat larger one. And all these places are close to each other. For simplicity, Raza mentioned only the larger town: Abbottabad. Greatly surprised, she repeated: "Abbottabad! Really?" The mention of the word Abbottabad seemed to ring a bell, energizing Mrs. Gandhi. She raised a finger and instantly a servant ran forward. She made another gesture and the servant ran out. Moments later a handsome man named Yunus Khan, magnificently dressed in a Churidar Pajama, entered and said "Namaste." Apparently he was a close associate of Mrs. Gandhi and had been working in the room next door. Raza and I had not known that he was a distinguished Foreign Service member who had been India's Ambassador to several countries including Turkey, Indonesia, Iraq, and Spain. And after retiring as Secretary Commerce in 1974, he had been serving as Special envoy and Advisor to Prime Minister Gandhi.

Mrs. Gandhi introduced Yunus Khan and joked that two men from Abbottabad were better than one! Yunus was effusive. He talked about his childhood in Abbottabad and mentioned that, sadly, he was later imprisoned there. But when he fell very ill, "they" decided to release him. "They" of course were the British Government. Raza was curious: Why were you imprisoned? "You see, I was an active member of the 'Khudai Khidmatgar' movement. ('Khudai Khidmatgar', meaning God's Servants, was a movement initiated in the North West Frontier Province. Its objective was both social, meaning to educate the masses, and political, meaning non-violently struggle to oust the British Raj.) And for many years, I worked closely with Khan Abdul Ghaffar Khan. And, as you know, Khudai Khidmatgar was anathema to the British."

Raza was enthused and responded: "My father too had a similar experience. He had graduated as a civil engineer and worked as a government employee managing the building of roads. That is usually a very lucrative occupation. But, strongly motivated by the Khudai Khidmatgar movement, he became also a political activist. His downfall, however, was that he did not keep his activities secret, nor did he keep 'his mouth shut'. That got him into hot water. He was fired from his government job. And to teach him a real lesson, 'they' also imprisoned him for about three months. Out of prison and without a government job, he started actively to work with Ghaffar Khan's older brother, Abdul Jabbar Khan who was better known as Dr. Khan Sahib. Dr. Khan was a Physician who took care of the poor. But more importantly, he was a savvy, successful politician. As you know he was thrice chief minister of the North West Frontier Province."

"My father joined Dr. Khan's version of the Congress Party and provided it meaningful political support through his newspaper." Ambassador Yunus, who had seemed mesmerized by Raza's recollections of his father, suddenly looked askance: "What do you mean by Dr. Khan's version of the Congress party? There is only one Congress Party. And alone through its efforts did India achieve its independence?" Raza tensed up but kept his cool: "As everybody knows, Dr. Khan was ambivalent about his allegiance. Was it to be the new India or was it a separate country to be called Pakistan, he could not decide. A year before partition, while Dr. Khan still held the chief minister-ship of the N.W.F.P., my father, at Sardar Bahadur Khan's urging, went to see Dr. Khan and told him that he (my father) was now joining the Muslim League and suggested that Dr. Khan do the same. But even though Dr. Khan started to move closer to the Muslim League, he retained his congress party membership till the end, meaning until the Partition. After the Partition when Dr. Khan and his brother were imprisoned in Pakistan, it was Sardar Bahadur Khan who, as the new Chief Minister of N.W.F.P., released them both. But as you know, while Ghaffar Khan was jailed and released many times, Dr. Khan, with Sardar Bahadur's support, was spared additional bad treatment. And indeed, in October 1955 at the introduction of the 'One Unit' scheme in Pakistan, Dr. Khan, with much applause by my father, became the first Chief Minister of the newly enlarged single province of West Pakistan."

Ambassador Yunus and Raza continued their conversation. I was feeling restive. It was at my urging that an appointment with Mrs. Gandhi had been arranged, I thought. And the subject at hand does not interest me much. Rather, I am focused on learning Mrs. Gandhi's views about current issues both in India and the world at large. Raza noticed my impatience and suggested that it was my turn to talk. Mrs. Gandhi quickly sidestepped that suggestion and said: "Well, we are all enjoying the conversation and I am sure that Shirin is also very interested."

Our visit was scheduled only for a half-hour but had lasted twice as long. In order to conclude the proceedings, Sanjay—Mrs. Gandhi's younger son, and in many peoples' view, the heir apparent—appeared and mentioned that a Chief Minister was waiting. We all got up, bid our thanks, and parted.

We returned to Islamabad at the end of June. Raza and I went up to Nathia Gali in the mountains above Islamabad and stayed with our friend Sadia and Hafeez Pirzada who was the senior most minister in Bhutto's cabinet. There was palpable foreboding in the air. And only a few days later, on July 5, 1977, in yet another bloodless coup d'etat led by the Military, the Prime Minister was arrested. Early days, it was clear that General Zia-ul-Haq, the leader of the coup, was hesitant and was trying to measure the country's response to his misdoings. The wind appeared not all blowing his way and Zia released Bhutto on July 28.

Pressure on the civil government as well as propaganda against it continued and General Zia-ul-Haq felt safe enough to re-arrest Bhutto on September 17. In order to make things really stick this time, the military police also arrested Bhutto's chief lieutenant, and the best lawyer in the country, Hafeez Pirzada. Pirzada was released the following year. But Bhutto was charged with what many thought were trumped-up charges. And despite Pirzada's pleading, Bhutto was hanged on April 4, 1979.[2]

As a full-time faculty member at Temple University, I got my tenure on time despite a painful period of harassment from a senior male colleague. Then came another unplanned event that took me in a different direction and which led me to a decision to resign my tenure in order to stay on at the National Security Council in the Reagan administration.

Notes

1. "Haram" is the word in Islamic law that refers to something sinful or forbidden.
2. Abdul Hafeez Pirzada wrote the 1973 Constitution of Pakistan. He was Pakistan's most eminent constitutional lawyer. He died in September 2015.

CHAPTER 8

US Army War College (USAWC)

The college for mid-career Army officers sits 116 miles from my home outside Philadelphia. Set in Carlisle in beautiful countryside near Gettysburg Pennsylvania, the war college is an important milestone in my life. I went there on a one-year fellowship in 1980 to work with Colonel William Staudenmeier at the Strategic Studies Institute.

My husband was a fellow at Oxford, and we spent many a summer there. I was a tenured associate professor at Temple University and spent my summers on research and writing. I had chosen strategic studies as my area of interest.

I was offered the fellowship by chance in the course of a conference I was attending at Oxford University in the summer of 1979. I was presenting a paper and during a break sat next to an American professor to continue our discussion on the Persian Gulf region.

A couple of major events occurring in 1979 focused US attention on the Persian Gulf and South Asia region, referred to as Southwest Asia, a region I knew. The first, the Iranian revolution, overthrew the US-friendly Shah Reza Pahlavi and replaced him with a US-hating Islamic theocracy in January 1979. The second event was the invasion of Afghanistan by the former Soviet Union in December 1979. Washington worried that these events bracketed a foreign policy reversal in an area where US interests were vitally engaged.

The Carter administration looked at existing American military assets in the Gulf region and decided to create a Rapid Deployment Joint Task

Force (RDJTF) in March 1980. The goal was to create a US presence in the region in order to make facilities and forces available for use in theater should the need arise. Marrying up regional expertise with military planning meant bringing in regional experts to interact with the military side. I was one of those who went to Carlisle to help with the overall effort.

Colonel Staudenmeier was deeply involved in working with the Chairman Joints Chief (JCS) office on the contours of the newly proposed RDJTF. The J-5 was the liaison office, and Bill Staudenmeier informed me that due to the classified nature of the work, I would promptly need to apply for a Top Secret security clearance. As it was a new experience for me, I struggled with the multiple questionnaires. Having been born in India and growing up there in my early years, living six years in Pakistan and then in the USA for my studies, and acquiring citizenship in 1971, the forms required checks in multiple locations. In addition, my research work and Raza took us all over the world, including a summer in Ljubljana (then Yugoslavia), where Raza was a US Academy of Science professor at the university. All the travel we undertook meant time for the clearance process. Eventually, the Pentagon granted me clearance and I began my fellowship.

Carlisle Barracks offered a chance to get engaged with the practice of foreign policy, always of interest to me. The War College student body consisted of colonels destined for leadership positions in the Army. There were a few Air Force officers. Some two dozen officers from a variety of countries also came for the year-long course. These were coveted competitive positions, and the foreign officers had been selected by their respective countries based on their expected rise in service. Most of the foreign officers came with their wives, as did all American colonels. The year I was there, the college had a prince from the Saudi Arabian Air Force and a two-star general from India who, in 1984, went on to command the brigade that attacked the Golden Temple, the Sikh's most holy shrine in Amritsar, under Mrs. Indira Gandhi. Gandhi was in turn assassinated by one of her own guards, a Sikh.

I had never lived alone until Carlisle. Yes, I had gone away to boarding school and then had lived in a dorm at college, but there were always others around. I married at 18 and moved from my father's house to my husband's. When time came to go to Carlisle and rent a place in 1980, I was worried. It is a small town certainly. But, it is a place where I would be at home alone at the end of the day. I would commute home to Philadelphia on the weekends. But there were five nights alone.

My nine-year-old son, Kazim, went with me one weekend as we scouted apartments in Carlisle. Finally, I settled on one that was "running distance" from the War College gate, where a guard stood at duty around the clock. It was a functional place but it would do. I furnished it sparsely and was set for my year of teaching and research in a different academic setting than was my usual habitat. In any case, I had to finish my study of US Foreign Policy toward Pakistan for a series on "Influence" commissioned by a major publisher.

There were only a handful of professional women at the barracks. It was a macho culture, but it was an elegant place with a great deal of camraderie. The very first day, as I went for my faculty badge (for identification purposes), I was told not ever to wander the halls without proper identification. This being an Army outfit, I recognized the seriousness of the order.

Assignment of an office followed. I was to share one with Keith Dunn, a Sovietologist who was also in the Army reserves. Bill Staudenmeier had better digs as a senior officer. A wonderful smart and knowledgeable man, Bill also coached little league and invited Kazim to join in if he was in Carlisle. Bill and his wife Betty knew that my family was staying on in Philadelphia. They were wonderfully hospitable to me during my time at USAWC.

The dearth of faculty females meant that everywhere I went I was asked: "And whose secretary are you?" I would explain what I was doing, and that would suffice until the next time. The War College was bustling with activity, as a great number of senior officials from Washington, military and civilian, would come by to give talks. These were senior Pentagon brass and cabinet and subcabinet civilians. They came down by helicopter for a few hours, and their lectures were eagerly attended by all. When a talk was classified, a US Marine was posted outside the door of the auditorium, a large hall with plush red seats that the officers dubbed "the bedroom" since so many fell asleep there.

One such talk on Afghanistan brought me to the auditorium. I noted that the Marine carefully checked my identification badge to ensure that I had the requisite security clearance for the level of the talk. There were few people inside. That reflected the non-sexy nature of the topic and that it required a higher security clearance level. I found a seat, avoiding the first row. I noted that I was the only woman in the room. Shortly, the general from Washington and his staff walked in and sat nearby. Just as the lights were dimming, he looked around nervously at me. Looked away.... then looked again. He coughed, leaned closer, and said in a harsh whisper: "do you have a security clearance?"

Carlisle being a chivalrous place, my colleagues shifted in discomfort while the general looked directly at me. "Yes" I replied, wondering how he thought I could have got past the Marine guard. "Oh," said the general. "I thought you were somebody's wife"!

"I am," I responded, to hoots of laughter now in the auditorium!

When the talk was over, the apologetic general making the error and General Jack Merritt, commandant of the college, both came up to me to say sorry. I decided that I could make a fuss or let it go. I said "honest mistake" because there were wives who came to some of the lectures and one may have slept in the red bedroom and forgot to go home. Anyway, the general was very grateful and we became friends, a friendship that came in handy when I went on to the White House to work at the National Security Council staff.

CHAPTER 9

Joining the Secretary of State's Staff

Opportunities often came by sheer chance. Mine have almost always followed such a path.

My monograph on USA–Pakistan relations published in 1982 was well received. It was part of a series on influence in foreign policy, a term used rather loosely, focused on precise relationships between superpowers and less developed countries. There were some six books examining US relations with various countries and another six looking at Soviet relations with a similar number. This Praeger-published series was edited by Alvin Z. Rubinstein.

The book in the series that I authored, "U.S. and Pakistan: The Evolution of an Influence Relationship," focused on two issues where there had been an assumption of American influence over Pakistani policy: the Pakistani nuclear weapons program and arms sales from the USA to Pakistan. The study concluded that in neither case did the long history of relations indicate any US influence in Pakistan.

In June 1982, I received a call from Francis (Frank) Fukuyama, a colleague serving at the Policy Planning Staff of the Department of State, inviting me to a meeting with the Director of Policy Planning Paul Wolfowitz. Pakistan was a hot topic of discussion within the administration and that my book had ideas that were not conventional wisdom, and thus, Frank asked if I would come down to Washington to discuss them with the Director. I agreed and a mutually suitable date was found. I took the train down, went to the State Department, got cleared into the building, and was ushered into Wolfowitz's office on the seventh floor.

I knew that it was the Secretary of State's Policy Planning Staff. I had been a part of the State Department's scholar diplomat program in 1979 just as the Soviets were invading Afghanistanand soon after the Iranian revolution. Those watershed moments had made the time at State extremely interesting as the assembled academic experts were also drawn into policy debate and formulation.

Never having met Paul Wolfowitz, I did not know what to expect. My good friend Harvey Sicherman, with whom I had been in graduate school at the University of Pennsylvania, was the Special Assistant to the Secretary of State George Shultz. Harvey had said to let him know when my appointment was done so we could meet up. My appointment with Wolfowitz went late as we talked of Pakistan and US issues. Pakistan's President Zia was scheduled to come for a State Visit in October 1982, and the Director of policy planning had many questions. Two of the more urgent issues were those detailed in my book, the nuclear program and arms sales. Finally, Harvey came to Wolfowitz's office and we talked together for a while and Harvey and I then left.

After my State Department meetings, I headed to the White House. I was to see Geoffrey Kemp, then Senior Director for Near East and South Asia. After some thirty minutes of discussion, we discovered that both were scheduled to attend the reception for departing Defense Attaché General Mahmud Durrani being hosted by the Pakistani Ambassador to the USA Sahabzada Yaqub Khan that evening.

En route to the reception, Geoff's White House beeper went off—cell phones and Blackberry's were not yet ubiquitous. Kemp murmured that there never was a moment off and said he would call when we reached the reception at the Ambassador's residence. Geoff went off to find a phone in those pre-cell phone days, and I went upstairs to the reception, crowded with Durrani's friends and colleagues. I had met him in 1979 at a conference on South Asia held in Rosslyn, Virginia. While still in conversation with Durrani, Geoff came up and said to me "Call Wolfowitz. He wants to speak to you today before you leave Washington for Philadelphia."

Not atypically for a woman and a mother, my first thought was that something had happened to my husband or children. Why else would I be tracked down by the office of a man I met for the first time that day? Quickly finding a nearby phone I called the given number, which was answered by Wolfowitz's assistant Lee Ann. Is there a problem, I asked hurriedly? Lee Ann assured me that there had been no call from my home and that it was Paul Wolfowitz himself who wanted to talk to me. She asked me to hold and put her boss through. Wolfowitz began with how much he appreciated the meeting and my returning his call. I told him that I was calling from a noisy reception and could barely hear him. He said he would not take long, but he wanted to find me before I left Washington to offer me a job on the Policy Planning Staff. He said my knowledge of issues that were urgently under consideration would be very helpful to the Secretary of State and as the Director of his planning staff, Wolfowitz, wanted to make the offer.

I replied that my family and life are in Philadelphia. Moreover, I held a tenured faculty position and my career path was set. Further, that I was leaving in a week for the summer for various meetings where my just-published book was a topic of discussion. Paul gave me his various phone numbers. He asked me to think about the offer and to let him know, if possible before I left for Europe.

On the train back to Philadelphia that evening, I realized that the offer could potentially change my life. It was a bit scary. Yet, I knew that it was an extraordinary milestone in my life and one that I could not have foreseen even that morning as I took the train to Washington. The two hours en route gave me some time for thinking. I decided that the first thing I would do was to speak to my family. I had just returned to teaching after my year at the Army War College in Carlisle. The thought of setting out again, this time for Washington, was more complicated even if exciting.

The following day, after the kids came home from school, Raza and I sat down with Shehra and Kazim and I mentioned the events of the previous day in Washington and the unexpected job offer. I noted that I had already been away in Carlisle and that going away again made no sense. I pointed out that I had pretty much said no in my reply to the verbal offer over the phone from Wolfowitz.

"What did he say?" asked my eleven-year-old son, Kazim. "He asked that I think about it, take a leave of absence from the university and join the Department of State," I replied.

I was amazed by the grown-up conversation my children were having. They noted that I had always been interested in the "making of foreign policy" which they deduced from my extensive travels and many interviews with US and foreign leaders. I wrote about policy making. So, they asked: "Why would you pass up a chance to be involved in the *making* of U.S. foreign policy?" Reminding the kids that the job meant my moving to Washington and coming home only on weekends, Shehra responded that she was finishing High School in January 1983 and moving on to Magdalen College at Oxford University in the UK. Shehra was admitted straight from American high school rather than after a B.A. as is the case usually and was going up to Oxford as a scholar. We were immensely proud.

Kazim said he would enjoy coming to Washington during the vacations but hoped he could remain in Bala Cynwyd with Raza. We discussed the option of all of us moving, but the family preferred to stay in familiar surroundings.

As we went to Manhattan to attend the wedding of Peter Heeger whose parents Ruth and Alan are two of our earliest and closest friends, Raza and I continued the discussion. I was leaving for Europe following the elaborate and wonderfully festive two-day celebration. Decision time was upon me.

On a stormy evening in June 1982, as I waited to board the British Airways flight from JFK for London, en route to Milan and Rockefeller Foundation Villa in Bellagio on Lake Como, I finally called Paul Wolfowitz and accepted his offer. It was a somber evening with dark clouds and pelting rain. The weather matched my mood as along with the excitement of a new challenge was a sense of foreboding that my life's pattern of the unexpected continued.

There is a ton of paperwork that must be completed, forwarded, and followed up on if one is to enter US government service. The requisite high-level clearances mean more paperwork detailing one's life from the age of 18. Once again, in my case, with all the travel attached, pages of detail were required in order to process the security clearance. I had already done so once before when the Top Secret clearance was granted to work at the Army War College in 1980. However, I was told that the Pentagon and Defense Department had granted the previous clearance. The new one would come from the Department of State, a separate process. A bit redundant I thought but later in 1984 when I was going to the National Security Council, the White House did yet another check all over again.

Going from academia to the State Department in October 1982 turned out to be less of a shock than might have been expected. My new home, the Policy Planning Staff, serves as a sort of "Think Tank" for the Secretary of State. You spend time thinking "big thoughts," and out of the box thinking is tolerated simply because the problems loom large, and fresh ideas may actually move solutions forward.

CHAPTER 10

The Zia Visit

I had been hired to focus on the Indian subcontinent in the aftermath of the Soviet invasion of Afghanistan. The immediate issue was the impending state visit of General Zia-ul-Haq of Pakistan to Washington. The Pakistani nuclear weapons program loomed large, and the USA wanted to find a way to get the Pakistani leader to pledge that he would cap the program. Zia wanted more US military assistance as he noted his worry about Soviet expansion to Pakistan and beyond. These were not matching goals and the visit aimed to find some common ground through the scheduled talks between President Ronald Reagan and General Zia-ul-Haq.

Being the new kid on the block does not endear one to those who have long held themselves as bureaucratic experts on South Asia in the US government. The turf wars that are legend in the bureaucracy do not help matters. Further, regional bureaus tend to view Policy Planning Staff members as stepchildren of the foreign policy-making process. Then, to top it, I was advocating a different approach to US policy in South Asia.

Conventional wisdom had it that India and Pakistan, having fought two major wars, were destined to remain enemies. The USA could do nothing to change that reality even as it worked hard to challenge the Russian takeover of neutral Afghanistan in 1979. I felt that given the new Pakistani sense of vulnerability to the Soviets and their perceived status as a front-line state, Zia might welcome US support, even if it came with some caveats.

Because Washington needed Pakistani help in defeating the Soviets in Afghanistan, an essential element of the strategy had to be finding a way to defuse the two-front threat possibility that was the nightmare of Pakistani military leaders. If the USA could help India and Pakistan move toward some measure of normalization, Pakistani cooperation would be more likely and effective along the border with its other main neighbor, Afghanistan.

The Zia visit provided an opportunity. Discussions within the State Department were on going and often heated. Bureaucratic inertia dictated many meetings scheduled by those pushing for a fresh look at age old rivalries in the subcontinent. I was one of those and the Director of policy planning pushed for a hearing of these views. Eventually, the matter was set to move to a decision point in terms of the US approach to the powerful Undersecretary of State for Policy, Larry Eagleburger, the third highest position in the system.

Eagleburger was a legend. He intimidated the timid with relentless questioning ensuring that anyone appearing before him to promote a view point had better do all his homework or be torn apart. Wolfowitz told me that we had secured a meeting with Eagleburger and asked if I was prepared to argue why the Zia visit could serve as a much needed opening for a new direction toward South Asia.

The day of the scheduled afternoon meeting on the 7th floor office of the Undersecretary, I was having lunch in the cafeteria with my former classmate from Penn, Harvey Sicherman, a special assistant to the Secretary of State. I was discussing my ideas for the meeting and why I thought the USA could be actively promoting India–Pakistan normalization in order to defuse tension and make it possible for Pakistan to concentrate on the Afghan war, when none other than Larry Eagleburger walked up to our table and sat down. He knew Harvey but had never met me.

My immediate thought was "only in America" would such a powerful man be eating a quick lunch in the cafeteria downstairs. Harvey did the introductions and said that we were discussing his upcoming meeting on the Zia visit. "Oh and what were you saying?" asked Eagleburger. That was my cue to chime in with my proposals for a different focus. He pulled out a small pad from a pocket and a pen and took the points down. Eagleburger then asked if I was coming with Wolfowitz to the meeting. I answered that I was attending. Saying "See You" the Undersecretary departed. Harvey and I were laughing over how the lunch had turned out and parted with my promise to report back to him how the meeting on the 7th floor went.

As we gathered in the Eagleburger office, I noted the heavy cast of characters I was arrayed against from the regional South Asia bureau. Howard (Howie) Schaeffer was the Deputy Assistant Secretary of State (DAS) dealing with India and Pakistan. Even before I said anything, Howie made disparaging comments about my "strange thinking about India and Pakistan" which he felt would not go anywhere. The meeting went on for the scheduled time and concluded with plans for smaller group follow-on in a few days when the schedule allowed. Eagleburger asked all tough questions and wanted some answers to be provided expeditiously.

I felt encouraged by the line of thinking the Undersecretary had shared. He was dissatisfied with the status quo and seemed very willing to look at the Zia visit in a different light. He asked me to send him a memo on the matter we had discussed earlier in the cafeteria. It became clear to Howie et al. that there had been a chance meeting between the Undersecretary and me but no one asked where, nor did we supply the information. I did mention the cafeteria meeting to Wolfowitz. In the end, Secretary Shultz undertook to pursue the policy of pledging support for Pakistan's request for assistance provided breaks were put on the nuclear weapons program and a genuine opening for normalization with India in talks with President Zia.

The Zia visit included a reception by the President to which those involved with Pakistan in the foreign policy establishment of Washington were invited. I had known Zia as my father was one of his early education advisors. The summer before joining the Policy Planning Staff, I had a long meeting with Zia at the presidency in Rawalpindi where we discussed my then newly published work on USA–Pakistan relations. I was invited to the Zia reception in Washington during the official visit.

Upon going through the receiving line, when my turn came to greet the Pakistani leader, Zia recognized me and kept me in conversation with him for a few minutes, which was captured on film by the staff photographer from the *Washington Post*. The next day's style section had the photo on the front page with my name even spelled correctly. I did not then know that in Washington the style section was always read with interest.

When I got to the office that morning, not yet having seen the paper, Jim Roach who was the deputy to Wolfowitz called me into his office. He asked if I had seen the day's *Washington Post*. "No," I replied. He pulled out his copy and berated me saying: "Why was your photo in the paper when the boss Wolfowitz was also there but not photographed?" "Ask the photographer," I suggested and mentioned that as an academic I knew Zia, had interviewed him and that he wanted to discuss my book, the very one which led Wolfowitz to get me to join his Policy Planning Staff. When I walked out looking annoyed, Ruth Whiteside, the senior staff assistant asked me what was going on. I told her and she joked, "You are in the photograph maybe because you look better than Paul."

This early interaction with Roach was a good thing as he had a reputation for bullying female members of the staff. He watched himself with me thereafter rather than try what he did with another female colleague whom he regularly drove to tears.

Soon thereafter, Paul Wolfowitz left to become Assistant Secretary for East Asia and the Pacific, and Ambassador Steve Bosworth became the new Director, Policy Planning. Bosworth, a former member of the Foreign Service, had a different style, and he made policy planning better able to access the rest of the State Department. His relationship with the Secretary of State, George Shultz, was close and thus things worked more smoothly for his staff.

One of the earliest things Steve mentioned to me was that Moshe Arens, the Israeli Ambassador to the USA had come into see him and noted that a Muslim had been hired for the Policy Planning Staff. I do not know the reply but the Ambassador's comment seemed strange to me, especially as it seemed to imply that the deluge was sure to follow. I simply put the event down to one of the costs of my being a first.

My eighteen months at the State Department were great training for the career in government that followed my policy planning stint. I used to think that if one survived in policy planning, one learned to survive in the US government system.

Discussions on South Asia had brought me into contact with Donald Fortier who had left as deputy at policy planning and gone over to the White House National Security Council (NSC). Following my work for Eagleburger, I followed up with Don Fortier, who became the Deputy Assistant to President Reagan for policy development at the NSC.

Don's links to the world of policy went deep. He had served as senior staff at the House and had been an Albert Wohlstetter student at Chicago. He thought that the Soviet invasion of Afghanistan was reversible and that the role of Pakistan was crucial. He understood the need to offer relief in the form of improved India–Pakistan relations. Only then could Zia be made to focus his energies on the threat from the Afghan front then under Soviet control.

I met Fortier in December 1982 in the course of a meeting in Eagleburger's office at State. After the meeting, Don said he liked my proposals and asked me to come to talk to him at the White House. He gave me the number for his assistant Sally and when I called to make an appointment, Sally noted that Don had instructed an early meeting.

The meeting with Don took me into the White House complex again. Once cleared in, I went to Don's third floor suite in the Old Executive Office building. He had just returned from an Oval Office meeting with President Reagan. There was talk of some impending travel, and we settled down to looking at Pakistan-related issues and the possibility of forging better relations between arch enemies India and Pakistan. It was a detailed discussion on my perceptions and Don's impressions, including his astute feel for the interagency problems that hampered creative thinking and execution of policy. Towards the end of that meeting, Don suddenly looked at me and said: "Shirin, how would you like to work here at the NSC?"

Taken aback, I told him that I was obviously flattered. The NSC sat at the apex of foreign policy making. Serving the President directly, it was a dream job. Yet, I realized that I had been at the Department of State for only a few months. Given that State had paid to get my Top Secret clearance and I was just beginning to understand the system and make progress on the policy proposal front, for the moment, I needed to stay on at State. I added that hopefully in the near future I might be able to come over, if Don still wanted me to move.

On my way back to the State department, I felt that it was an embarrassment of riches. I was on leave from a tenured job, had just started one in the US government and had been offered a chance to switch to the NSC, and work on the President's staff. I hoped desperately that I had made the right decision in telling Fortier to wait. It was a calculated risk. I did not share news of the offer with anyone other than family and went to work.

During my early tenure at State, I recall saying to my colleague Ruth Whiteside that it seemed that "if one did not care who got the credit, the sky was the limit" in policymaking circles at the State Department and indeed in Washington. I lived by that belief and found that even without taking credit, I became involved with policy with some of the senior most people in Washington's policy community.

In early May 1984, I was called to a meeting with Eagleburger when he was focusing on the upcoming visit of Vice President (VP) George H. W. Bush to India and to Pakistan. He asked if I had thought further on the types of India–Pakistan confidence building measures (CBMs) the USA could help promote in order to help stabilize the relationship in the subcontinent. I had done that and went through the list. Eagleburger told me that the reason he had called me in was to say that the VP was headed for India and Pakistan mid-May. Fresh ideas were needed in addition to the more traditional briefing books being prepared by Howie and his group. I was then told to go to the White House to see Donald Gregg, who was the National Security Advisor to George H. W. Bush, then the VP.

Returning to my office, I called Phyllis, assistant to Don Gregg. Mentioning the purpose of the call as a follow-up to the Eagleburger conversation with me, I asked Phyllis to check with her boss and let me know if and when he wanted to meet. She called back within the hour and said Don Gregg would like to see me later in the afternoon and asked for my information so that she could clear me in. I let my boss Steve Bosworth know that I was reaching out to the Office of the Vice President (OVP) at the express direction of the Undersecretary. I also spoke to Don Fortier and updated him. He said to stop by his office, just one floor above that of Don Gregg in the Old Executive Office Building after my meeting in OVP.

I set upon preparing for what I felt was a game-changing meeting for me. Having been born in India and caring about its welfare and having lived equally long in Pakistan which I feel is an amazing country with much talent but little leadership, I watched the subcontinent spend its blood and treasure on useless wars. The USA was a friend of both countries but historically had not played a constructive role in promoting a productive peace between India and Pakistan. Yes, it helped terminate the wars between these two nations in 1965 and in 1971, respectively, but then disengaged allowing them to, at best, go back to a state of cold peace.

With President Ronald Reagan's interest in peeling India away from the former Soviet Union and Mrs. Indira Gandhi's desire for better economic relations with Washington, the USA had a golden opportunity to try actively to promote India–Pakistan normalization on a broad front. The payoff would be a more stable and secure South Asia and enhance

Pakistani cooperation in the flight alongside the USA to defeat the Soviets in Afghanistan.

With the above in mind, I went to the Gregg meeting. Don had one of his colleagues there and the VP's chief of staff Admiral Daniel Murphy dropped by for a while. Don Gregg asked how I saw the upcoming visit of the VP to India and to Pakistan. I responded that in my view the visit could either be a great public relations exercise since the countries are interesting and the hospitality legendary. Or, the visit could build on the vast interest and experience of the VP in international diplomacy (China, the CIA, and the UN) and try and do some real good. I then outlined the various CBMs that I firmly believed could be put on the table in each of the two stops after some discussion, leaving the host leaders to think about them for a while before the USA reached back for their reaction. I noted that in my experience, both countries wanted to change direction but each was trapped in the past.

Don Gregg asked a very critical question: What is the downside of undertaking such an approach for the first time with Gandhi and Zia? After some soul-searching, I responded that the exercise I proposed would not lead to a war between India and Pakistan. At best, the leaders would be intrigued by the detailed ideas developed in the proposal on lessening political tensions, building in some agreement on nuclear safety and notification of accidents, trade enhancement, and people to people travel. I added that knowing both leaders, I felt they would be intrigued by US willingness to actively underwrite India–Pakistan normalization in a time of peace rather than in simply assisting termination of wars in the subcontinent as in the past.

Don said he would brief the VP. I thought: Wow, he is talking about the Vice President of the United States! What a chance to help change the direction of policy on a small yet critical issue. As I was leaving, Don Gregg asked if details could be worked out, whether I would be willing to travel with the small team accompanying the VP. I said personally it would be a tremendous honor.

My next stop in the White House was to see Don Fortier. I briefed him on the morning Eagleburger meeting, the subsequent discussion with the VP's national security advisor and the query about my possible travel to South Asia. I detailed the CBM menu and why it made sense to engage Gandhi and Zia on the matter. Don Fortier asked if I knew them and I replied in the affirmative. Fortier then said: "Shirin, this may be the time for you to switch from the State Department to the NSC. That way you could also travel in the small entourage, difficult to keep small, that is the norm for travel with the VP."

On the way back to my office, I deliberated the issue of leaving State for the NSC. It seemed a good time for the work I might help guide but I would need to talk to Steve Bosworth. When I did, Steve was very gracious and said he would be sorry to see me go but it made sense. He said he would tell Eagleburger who he thought would understand given that it was he directing me to the White House.

Word spread fast. Howie Schaeffer was incensed that he was not on the visit to India and Pakistan but I was. The model for the official party was usually one from State, one from the NSC, one from DOD, the VP's chief of staff, his national security advisor and his press spokesman. Mrs. Barbara Bush was also going. Thus in the entourage were Richard Murphy Assistant Secretary of State for Near East and South Asia (Howie's boss), Geoffrey Kemp from the NSC, Richard Armitage from DOD, myself as leaving State and joining the NSC upon the visit's conclusion, Don Gregg, Admiral Murphy, and Marlin Fitzwater the VP's press spokesman.

On the day of departure, I headed up to the Executive Secretary's office. Jerry Bremer was the Executive Secretary for George Shultz. He asked if the rumor that I was leaving State and heading to the White House was true. I responded it was and that I hoped to build on my friendships at State for the work we would do together. The speed with which the word had got around was surprising since I did not consider myself to be a longtime member of the establishment at State. I concluded that my relentless questioning of options for South Asia and challenging the traditional way of doing things had left a mark. It also gave me my two big breaks: Lawrence Eagleburger and George H. W. Bush.

CHAPTER 11

Returning to the Land of My Ancestors

Touching down at the New Delhi airport on Air Force Two with the Vice President (VP) was a very evocative experience for me. A daughter of the soil taking a circuitous route for a return in May 1984 meant a great deal. Indira Gandhi was the Prime Minister. I recalled some of the stories my father, whom I called Baba, had told me about his friendship with the Nehrus and how her father had personally presented a gold medal for achievement in science to my father. He had not fled India for Pakistan. He had gone to help educate a new nation. When Baba went to India for a conference in 1953, Jawaharlal Nehru, then Prime Minister, had asked him to stay on in India since he was a son of the nation and was also needed there. After some bantering, they agreed that while a return was not feasible, Baba would remain a founding member of India's Academy of Science and other institutions in an advisory role. His unique links to both India and Pakistan could be helpful in bringing the two countries together.

Vice President Bush and Mrs. Bush came down the stairs of Air Force Two to a red-carpet welcome. The official party accompanying him followed. It was a clear very hot day in mid-May. The welcome was even warmer. As the motorcade lined up, the VP limousine was headed for Rashtrapati Bhavan, the residence of the President of India. It was a singular honor as, generally, the VP would be expected to stay at the residence of the US Ambassador, a complex building designed by Edward Durrell Stone, also the architect of the Kennedy Center in Washington.

The rest of the entourage broke off as we were to stay nearby at the Maurya Sheraton. Security was tight but nothing compared to what it would be like today. A Marine guard stood at the entrance to the floors of the tower where the American delegation was ensconced. We were to change and move for the briefing at the US embassy where the VP was to be updated on the state of USA–India relations.

After the very long flight which included refueling stops for the Boeing 707, all, including Bush, were exhausted. The Ambassador, Harry Barnes, held forth in his conference room where the hum of the air conditioners added to the soporific voice of the Ambassador. The Washington group recognized immediately that the briefing was not illuminating any responses to questions the VP had. He was looking impatient as he asked about the nature of Indira Gandhi's government, the tough issues she faced, the prospects for improved closer relations with the USA. Clearly, the VP and President Reagan had talked of the latter's hope to get India out of the Soviet orbit. Bush wanted specifics to work with. Unlike some other VP's, Bush had come to the job with vast knowledge of the world. He did not need a very basic introduction to India.

In the course of the long flight from Andrews AFB to Delhi, when I was asked to brief the VP, I had mentioned that I felt it likely that Prime Minister Gandhi had made a decision to strengthen relations with the USA, and the Bush visit was the first important milestone in that endeavor. I indicated that my personal view was that Mrs. Gandhi would reach out to the VP with a private dinner at her modest official residence with only Sanjay Gandhi present. It would be a family evening giving both leaders a chance to meet and talk without officials, notetakers, etc. Thus, when at the end of the briefing, the American Ambassador looked at the VP and said: "The Prime Minister has invited you and Mrs. Bush to a family dinner at her residence on Safdar Jung Road," Bush looked at me. I smiled back. On the way out of the briefing, Don Gregg turned to me and said: "Good call." I was thrilled; the private dinner without officials present offered the best opportunity to start the discussion on an India–Pakistan rapprochement and the role the USA could play.[1]

India was a great visit. Official talks were good. The showing-the-American-flag aspects were also full of warmth. The Indian President Zail Singh gave a formal dinner in honor of George and Barbara Bush on a magical full moon night. We were all exhausted, and jet-lagged but upbeat that the visit was going well.

11 RETURNING TO THE LAND OF MY ANCESTORS

No official goes to India without a visit to the fabled Taj Mahal, built by Mogul Emperor Shah Jahan as a monument of love upon the death of his wife Empress Mumtaz Mahal in the course of the birth of their 14th child. Started in the year of her death in 1631, the monument was completed in 1645. It was the first time that I was to see the Taj, even though I was born in India. As the motorcade drove from Agra airport to the monument, I noted the cramped bazaar that surrounds the Taj. We alighted from the motorcade and stepped into the portal right behind the VP and Mrs. Bush. I held my breath. Would it be as amazing as the world said?

The Taj Mahal's sighting took my breath away. It was even more spectacular than I imagined. Familiar in its design from all the photographs seen, the Taj held a unique majesty in its scale and its sense of history. Walking into the gardens after the obligatory wearing of covers for my shoes, I was pleasantly stunned to see this monument of Muslim rule surviving the religious purges that are a part of the subcontinent's sad history.

The government of India and foreign office protocol had closed the monument to other visitors as the American leader and his party toured the historic site. A special guide accompanied the visit and gave its relevant history and a sense of the romance and sadness of a love-struck king's tribute to his departed wife, his queen.

At the end of the tour, everyone lined up for the photo op sitting on the bench that has the Taj Mahal at its back alongside with George H. W. Bush. I stood to the side, with Barbara Bush watching. Finally, she said to me: "Shirin, go get your photo taken with the VP." I replied that he had probably had enough of it. She persisted, and no one ignored a command from Barbara Bush. I went and sat on the bench and had my photograph taken and was forever glad that I did. Coming back to the country of my birth with the American Vice President after I had moved to the USA and become a citizen of my adopted country in 1971, here I was visiting the Taj Mahal for the first time having flown in on Air Force Two. Later upon our return to the White House, I got a signed copy of the photograph taken at the Taj with the VP along with an inscription that read: "To Shirin, Thanks for your terrific support on this special trip." I have treasured that photograph and its message all these years and more than many of the other presidential messages that I received from the three Presidents I served.

Prime Minister Gandhi gave a formal lunch for the VP at Hyderabad House. The venue served as a poignant reminder to me that Hyderabad House had once belonged to the State of Hyderabad where my grandfather Nawab Kazim Yar Jung was the Peshi (First) Minister to the last Nizam, the ruler.

With the heat of India had come the mango season. The Alphonso, an incredible flavored sweet mango, had come on the market. A friend, Prem Shnkar Jha who was a classmate of Raza's at Oxford and whose father had served as the Indian Foreign Secretary, brought me five and given there was no time to eat, I have a photograph of myself running to get on Air Force Two holding onto five mangoes before the VP said his farewells and boarded. One knew once he boarded, the door would close and the plane took off, or "wheels up."

On board, we assessed the visit and all seemed to agree that an opening for closer relations existed. Gauging President Zia's interest in normalization with India was the next step. We were to land in less than an hour. When Air Force Two entered Pakistani airspace, six fighter aircraft provided an honor guard and escorted the VP's plane into landing at Islamabad airport.

Following the VP and Mrs. Bush down the stairs to the welcome, I noted that President Zia had himself come to the airport. His entire cabinet and senior officials were in the receiving line, including my father who looked very proud. It was soon clear to the US delegation that I knew most of the Pakistani officials. The VP seemed pleased at the thought, but I recall thinking that some colleagues back in Washington would make me pay.

Pakistani hospitality is legendary. The full welcome mat was laid out for the visit of the US Vice President. Talks were held in Islamabad, where an elaborate official lunch was given. There was the helicopter ride to Murree in the hills for official talks and private time for the two leaders to discuss sensitive issues such as the Pakistani nuclear weapons program and confidence-building with India. The helicopter landed near my old Convent of Jesus and Mary School where I had gone as a young child. There was a great deal of interest from the US delegation when I pointed out the fact.

The 1984 visit by the VP was a productive opening. The conversations on the need for better relations between the subcontinents largest two countries offered much needed impetus for the follow-on work.

Between May 1984 and October 1989, several presidential missions were dispatched. I was heavily involved in the substance and preparation for each visit and traveled on the fast-moving missions.

I was not wrong about discontented colleagues. Soon after my return, I got word from White House Deputy Press Secretary Larry Speakes' office that the following day the *Washington Post* was to run a column by Dan Van Atta about my unusual selection for the visit of the VP to India and Pakistan. That evening, I heard loud banging on my front door. I lived in an apartment building in Georgetown, and the front desk was to screen visitors and call before allowing anyone to go up in the elevator. No such call had come.

I looked through the peephole, not recognizing the man on the other side, asked who it was. He identified himself as a reporter and asked to come in. I said no and told him to call the White House press office. He would not go away and kept banging. I finally got in touch with Larry Speakes who told me he would take care of it. He called back to say he had asked the *Post* to stop harassing White House staff.

The next morning, right next to the comics, there was an article by Van Atta in the column that Jack Anderson nominally wrote but had deferred to others once he was ill in 1986. The story line covered my multiple acquaintances in India and Pakistan and questioned my appointment in the US government and at the National Security Council.[2]

Robert Oakley told me that the National Security Advisor had been asked by President Reagan if there had been any problems with my knowing so many officials in India and Pakistan. After careful checking, which was then unbeknownst to me, none were found. My own response to the article was that it was a low blow, fed by people who resented my access in three countries. They should remember that I had been hired because of my knowledge and connections in South Asia. I had a life before the White House and was proud of it. After this incident, whenever issues of my friends or my parents living in Pakistan came up, people like Eagleburger said: "They have to live somewhere!" I was honored to have the confidence of the President, the National Security Advisor, The Secretary of State and others. I had always said that if I was the sort of person who asked her elderly parents to move continents so that I could hold on to a job, I should be let go.

Notes

1. For a detailed study of US Relations with India and Pakistan from 1984–1990, see Shirin Tahir-Kheli, *The USA, India and Pakistan: Breaking With the Past* (New York: Council on Foreign Relations Press, 1995).
2. See Walter Pincus, "FBI's Interests in Columnist's Files Detailed," *Washington Post*, April 25, 2006.

CHAPTER 12

The Burden of Being First

In my first months at the White House, I used to joke that the President thinks that I was left behind by a visiting foreign delegation. That was because in 1984 there were few females and certainly none who looked like me at the National Security Council (NSC). I was Director in a very small NSC so I got to brief the President on my issues. At the end of one of these, President Reagan asked me to stay for a second. He said with a twinkle: "Shirin, I know that you work for me and have not been left behind by a visiting delegation!" I wondered who had mentioned that to him. I mumbled something and stumbled out of the Oval Office.

There were several state visits that I was in charge of including that of the President Jayawardene of Sri Lanka in 1984, Pakistani Prime Minister Junejo in 1986, and the two visits of Prime Minister Rajiv Gandhi of India in 1985 and 1987, respectively. The Reagan presidency focused a good deal of energy in creating better relations between India and Pakistan as a corollary of the effort to defeat the Soviets in Afghanistan.

President Reagan's vision went beyond tactical shifts. Moving India away from the Soviet Union and closer to the USA intrigued him. He thought that India, the world's largest democracy, would want a seat at the table of the world's democratic developed nations. The Soviet Union was collapsing anyway, and the President wanted better relations with India and worked to charm Prime Minister Indira Gandhi and, upon her assassination, the next Prime Minister, Rajiv Gandhi. The effort to reach out to India had already begun when the President met Prime Minister,

Indira Gandhi in the fall of 1981 in Cancun as part of the 22-nation North–South meeting on Cooperation and Development. In that meeting, Reagan had been impressed with the possibility of strengthening US relations with India. As I heard him say in the Oval Office, India was primed for an improvement with the USA. He found Gandhi engaging, despite a history of "being a special friend of the Soviets."

At the NSC my task was to put together an interagency process to map the Indo-USA relationship. This effort was to coincide with the cooperation in bilateral ties with Pakistan in the aftermath of the Soviet invasion of Afghanistan. My years in policy planning had given me a perspective on the workings of the US government: one needed buy-in from other agencies for presidential policies in order to get implementation. As the coordinating mechanism for foreign policy, being on the President's staff meant close collaboration, particularly with the Defense and State Departments. The months-long process led to a presidential directive which provided the framework for the outreach to India. On October 11, 1984, President Reagan signed the National Security Decision Directive (NSDD) 147.

Indira Gandhi with whom I had already had such an interesting meeting in Delhi in 1977 was assassinated by her Sikh bodyguard on October 31, 1984. We were all in shock. The President wanted to go to the Indian embassy to sign the condolence book. I drafted the remarks. There was turmoil as days of rioting followed in India. The appointment of Rajiv Gandhi to the prime ministership later the same day brought continuity even in the midst of tragedy. The forty-year-old surviving son of Indira had made a positive impression on VP Bush during his visit to India. It was natural for President Reagan to invite Rajiv Gandhi for an official visit to the USA.

Nothing focuses the US bureaucracy like a presidential visit abroad or a visit by a foreign head of government to the Oval Office. The interagency process mentioned earlier took on added urgency. 1984 was not a time of universal support for tightening US relations with India. Defense department officials were particularly unwilling to look at new ways of engagement. Consultations with senior officials from India including Rajiv Gandhi's advisor Ronen Sen made it clear that India wanted a new chapter and that the young Prime Minister was desirous of acquiring cutting-edgetechnology from the USA to jump-start Indian progress on multiple fronts, particularly defense.

Donald Fortier, as the deputy national security advisor for policy development, oversaw the effort to better relations with India.[1] As I worked directly for Fortier, on numerous occasions I heard him speak of the need for expelling the Soviets from Afghanistan and the fact that as a close friend of Moscow, India mattered. The key to better relations involved issues of trade and technology. Both required a framework and thus was launched the negotiation of a memorandum of understanding (MOU) with India to oversee technology transfer provision for items sought by Gandhi.

I put together my thoughts on what it would take for India to be enticed for Fortier. He shared these with the President, and sometimes I was called in to the Oval Office. The small size of the NSC at the time enabled a good deal of interaction between the President and his NSC staff members. I noted that it would not be easy, but the USA could and should reach out with concrete proposals for improving trade, technology cooperation, and eventually defense sales. India would not want the basic items, given its own capacity for development and production. India would seek high-end items which up to that time the USA sold only to NATO allies.

Based on the go-ahead from the boss, I set up an interagency group to look at ways in which concrete positive movement could be made. I undertook the writing of a decision memorandum that the President signed laying out the new focus for South Asia. All key agencies participated, and some who were intimately involved in the procedure and the product continue to tell me that it was one of the best such documents they saw in their time in government. It was succinct and goal oriented with a decision milestone that was adhered to.

Early conversations with Gandhi indicated his understanding of the US desire to develop meaningful relations with India even while cultivating assistance to Pakistan to counter the Soviet occupation of Afghanistan. For Reagan, Soviet withdrawal was a must and Pakistan's role as a frontline state in the effort was critical. Beyond Soviet withdrawal from Afghanistan was the challenge of a peaceful and prosperous South Asia. Unplugging that animosity carried a challenge, but the rewards would be significant to the USA. At that time, Washington was prepared to use its opening to India to help promote peace with Pakistan, rebutting the age-old argument that the USA could not be simultaneously friendly with both countries. The President knew that a two-front war was not something Pakistan could stand and without better relations with India would not play the role against the Soviets in Afghanistan that Washington desired. Moving toward better understanding with India was now the goal of the Reagan White House with India. Official visits, going back to that of India's first Prime Minister, Jawaharlal Nehru, Rajiv Gandhi's grandfather, in 1949 were scrutinized for openings missed for better relations.

The five-day Rajiv Gandhi visit to the USA began on June 13, 1985. From the outset, it was clear that the chemistry between Reagan and Gandhi was exceptional. The forty-year-old Prime Minister seemed to connect with the seventy-four-year-old President. The White House geared up for a state visit of significance in substance of meetings and in protocol for the Prime Minister of India. Under discussion was the export of US high-technology items and the defense production cooperation. USA aid to Pakistan against the Soviets and the need for stability in the South Asian major relationships were also on the agenda.

In his private moments and in expanded meetings, Gandhi noted his desire for rapid development and modernizing of India. As a member of India's younger generation and one fascinated by newly emerging technology, Gandhi's outlook and his outreach to Reagan were different from preceding interactions. He noted that Moscow supplied nearly eighty percent of military hardware imported from abroad. He wanted to look to the USA for alternative sources of supply.

Gandhi's address to a joint session of Congress was applauded for its vision. His meetings with Defense Secretary Caspar Weinberger and Treasury Secretary James Baker resulted in better understanding on both sides. His lunch at the Department of State hosted by George Shultz preceded the glittering White House State dinner in which first lady Nancy Reagan was personally involved to an extent that I did not see replicated in my service to three presidents at the White House by any subsequent first lady.

The combination of Mrs. Reagan's involvement and following the State dinner protocol of limiting guests to 200 put huge pressure on me. The growing Indian Diaspora and some major Indian industrialists all wanted a seat at this major event. After checking with the first lady's protocol person, Linda Faulkner, I was able to say that the limited gathering was under Mrs. Reagan's strict control. In any case, I was the NSC officer in charge of the meetings with the President and the dinner was beyond my range of responsibility.

On the third day of the visit, VP George H. W. Bush flew Gandhi down to Houston for a special tour of the Johnson Space Center. Gandhi, a commercial pilot before his induction into his mother's position, was known to be fascinated by space and technology. In the planning for his visit and as follow-on to the VP's meeting him in Delhi in May 1984, the Texas visit was conceptualized. I was the NSC coordinating officer for the visit and as Director for South Asia and thus on Air Force Two as it took off from Andrews air base for Houston. We went in a small group as Bush wished to keep the Texas meetings informal. Retired Admiral Daniel Murphy, the VP's chief of staff, and Donald Gregg his national security advisor were the other staff accompanying Bush. We stayed at the Houstonian, the Bush's Texas abode at the time.

The tour of the Space Center captivated Rajiv Gandhi. He was thoroughly involved, and the officials of the center were delighted. After a limited amount of "down time," we left for the dinner hosted by the VP and Barbara Bush in honor of Rajiv and Sonia Gandhi. There were a total of thirty guests and after the obligatory receiving line, came the interaction with the guests. These were the Texas friends of the Bush family, and I found myself seated between the head of what was then Conoco, Archie Dunham, and his lovely wife. Discussion of the visit was paramount and Mani Shankar Aiyar, Rajiv Gandhi's advisor, accompanying the Prime Minister, and I engaged with other guests at the table on respective US and Indian hopes for the visit and its follow-up efforts.

Sometime early in the course of the elegant dinner, Mrs. Dunham turned to me and said: "Your Prime Minister is so handsome!" I smiled happily and replied: "He is indeed handsome, but I am here with the handsome US Vice President as a US delegation member." After a couple more times, Mani kept saying to me in Hindi "This is what happens when you are a First!" Finally, I explained to Mrs. Dunham that I was at the Bush-hosted dinner as the White House officer in charge of the visit as the Director for South Asia at the NSC. "Oh my dear! Then I must ask George and Barbara to bring you with them to our Ranch so we can extend Texas style hospitality," noted the gracious lady. I mentioned the conversation on the plane ride back to the amusement of all.

Once back in Washington, agendas for the White House included a private thirty-minute meeting between Reagan and Gandhi. A larger group from both sides assembled for discussions with their respective leaders in the Cabinet room. The US President laid out the consequences for the region stemming from the Soviet invasion of Afghanistan some five years earlier. He noted that India as a friend of the Soviet Union was important in pressing for Afghanistan free of foreign occupation. Gandhi was more in a listening mode on the issue and was far more animated in pressing his case for a different India where technology and trade would make his generation more modern.

There was greater rapport on the issue of Pakistan which continued to receive major military and economic assistance to the tune of $3.2 billion for a six-year period starting in 1982. At the same time, especially after the Rajiv Gandhi 1985 visit, the USA entertained and often approved a growing list of Indian requests for technology, including the Cray XMP-14 supercomputer, once US concerns for protection of the technology through a MOU were finally painfully but successfully negotiated.

Technology transfer requests from India proceeded even as the USA recognized Pakistan's role in defeating the Soviet Union in Afghanistan loomed large. President Reagan and VP Bush were involved in helping guide India and Pakistan toward normalization and some level of rapprochement. The effort was based on the cold calculation that a two-front war for Pakistan was untenable. Further, that Rajiv Gandhi's vision for India's future required a peaceful neighborhood, which meant an opening for promoting Indo-Pak confidence-building measures (CBMs).

The White House encouraged meetings between Prime Minister Gandhi and President Zia of Pakistan, which actually took place on three different occasions. Some of these were held on the margins of the UN General Assembly, where they each had the follow-up meeting with President Reagan. The USA appreciated that in December 1985 Gandhi and Zia agreed on a "non-attack on nuclear facilities agreement," which meant that the two agreed to focus on the most dangerous aspects of their relationship, their respective nuclear weapons program. This CBM had first been suggested to both leaders by the USA in September 1985.[2] It was clear that any attack on the other's nuclear facility would lead to war. Thus, an agreement that pledged against such an attack was worthwhile. Other CBMs were also encouraged by the White House, and Indian and Pakistani leaders turned their attention to probing withdrawal of soldiers on the Siachen Glacier, examining a possible "no war pact" and increasing trade and travel.

Throughout, my job was a diplomatic high-wire act. The thrill of the work and the ability to reach out to the highest levels of government to make the case for a certain policy option were beyond compare. But I also understood that some watched for me to fail and fall off the wire.

I was a first as the highest serving and closest to power Muslim. As a woman, the challenge was further multiplied because the workplace was still very much a man's world. As a South Asian woman, there were all the naysayers who felt my academic credentials and personal relationships in India, Pakistan, as well as the USA gave me an unfair advantage. They sought to make life difficult.

One such obstruction surfaced early in my tenure at the White House NSC. All the talk about my parents living in Pakistan, my many contacts, made an impact on the agency which needs to give top-level security clearance, a must if you work for the President. During this discussion, I stayed away from all highly classified material to ensure no problems down the road and because I wanted always to do the right thing. The firewall thus created enabled me to do my think pieces, which was what was needed in order to provide a framework for the work I was brought on to do for the President.

One morning, Sally from Don Fortier's office called and asked that I come by to see him. Don said that he had been in touch with the relevant government people regarding my upgraded security clearance. He had noted to them that I had already had a record with similar clearance from the Defense Department and later from the State Department. Of course, the White House required special procedures and so he shared his conversation with me. Adding that, he recognized that I was a first and thus the system was still tougher on me for that fact.

I thought for a bit and then responded. My first reaction was that indeed I was a new type of person showing up to work in the halls of the White House. However, my two years at policy planning at State taught me that some people are never satisfied and I could not change them. Further, it was exactly my life and work which had intrigued the system in the first place to ask me to join the US government.

I also felt the burden of being a first and did not want it to be said that all Muslims, women, South Asians were suspect. Therefore, I was willing to play by the rules the clearance-granting agencies set up. However, I would go through the process only once, that the system could set the bar high but that I would only work with the very best people the agencies had (so that later they did not rejoinder that a rookie had goofed up), and once I passed the tests, which I knew I would if the system was fair, the requisite clearances would be given. As an aside, I told Don Fortier that this was an important job and I did not want to let him down. However, it was only a job. I was on leave from my tenured university position. I would jump through the hoops only once but then resign and return to academia. Don replied: "Not so fast!"

The night before the agreed test, I was told that the best person in the business would be administering the procedure, the same official who had caught the Walkers spying on the USA. I thought it good news because at least there would be no issue of incompetence. Don Gregg noted to me the seriousness of what I had agreed to undertake and pointed out that George Shultz, Secretary of State, had been firm in opposition to polygraphs and would not subject his officers to it. I told him that on the one hand was my deep sense of insult at the upcoming procedure being the person I am, where I had been born and into the rank and the privilege that was mine at birth. Yet, I chose to come to the USA and chose to stand on my own. Being a first carried responsibility and I never shied away from doing the right thing.

On the requisite day, I took a day-long test, at the end of which the officer said to his colleague in obvious jest: "Guess we won't have to send for her clothes and tooth brush." I went back to my old executive building office and saw a note to come see Don Fortier upon my return. Going to the West Wing where he now sat as the deputy national security advisor, Don said he had got the news. Per rules set prior to my taking the test, I would be granted all of the requisite clearances. He told me that he had briefed the President and the national security advisor and told them what I had said about being a first. In response, they asked that I be dissuaded from resigning and be offered a promotion in rank. The rest, as they say, is history.

NOTES

1. Donald Fortier died at the age of 39 in August 1986.
2. For an account of the US effort, see John Walcott, "The South Asia Two-Step," *Newsweek*, November 4, 1985.

CHAPTER 13

Diplomacy with India

Despite some of the challenges of being a Muslim woman from Pakistan, it was an exciting time and as I worked on a daily basis with the countries involved and oversaw the interagency process, I was fortunate in having colleagues at the Departments of State and Defense who were partners in implementing the President's directives. Peter Tomsen Director in the Near East and South Asia Bureau for India and Robert Peck for Pakistan were colleagues who made the long hours each day in the office productive.

The interagency process focused on key elements of moving US relations forward with India. The dialogue with the Pentagon led to the first-ever visit to India by a Secretary of Defense, when Caspar Weinberger traveled to Delhi and Bangalore in October 1986. By that time, the approval of the GE F-404 engine, the first by the USA to a non-NATO ally, for the Indian light combat aircraft had changed the conversation between Delhi and Washington.

As the NSC Director for South Asia, I accompanied Weinberger on his visit. Conversations en route on his military aircraft reflected a willingness to engage productively with Rajiv Gandhi on the growing and complicated list of defense and technology items India sought from the USA. The supercomputer sale depended on a robust protection regime and part of the high technology city Bangalore visit for Weinberger was to demonstrate the seriousness with which the Indians separated technology from Moscow from that requested from the USA. Technology transfer for defense depended on a clear understanding between the two states.

Previously having accompanied the Vice President and Barbara Bush on their Indian visit in 1984, I was struck by the pomp and ceremony the Indians accorded to the Defense Secretary, almost to the point of being a State visit minus the twenty-one gun salute. The meetings were extensive and the protocol events lavish. When I asked my Indian friends, including the Prime Minister's advisor Ronen Sen and Defense Minister Arun Singh the reason, they said that Rajiv Gandhi understood the importance of opening up defense cooperation for the future of India's relationship. Hence, he noted, the emphasis on pulling out the stops.

We flew in the Secretary's aircraft to Bangalore. One of the Indians pointed out that we were flying over Hyderabad, where I was born. It was a poignant moment as I recalled my childhood in the elegant places I had called home a lifetime earlier! At the Bangalore aerospace center, we were given an extensive tour and briefings. I got to fly the simulator for the light combat aircraft for which GE 404 US engines were approved. A new experience for me, I managed to crash the aircraft early in flight trying to land. "Not a good omen," mumbled someone as I climbed out of the machine.

Jaipur in Rajasthan was the only touristic stop on the visit. Arnie Raphel, a Deputy Assistant Secretary of State at the time,[1] was also a member of the US team with Weinberger. We shared the obligatory elephant ride from the palace in Jaipur to the hilltop fort. Secretary and Mrs. Weinberger had their own elephant, and there was much amused conversation about those of us Republicans getting faster service from the elephants! The weather was hot and the sights beautiful as we sped through a sightseeing tour in an hour that most would take at least over a full day. It was an unlikely mode for a US Secretary and his entourage!

Upon conclusion of the successful secretary of defense visit, I moved forward the memorandum of understanding on pending and future technology requests from India, I wanted to make sure that the entire interagency process was on board. Otherwise, future complications seemed likely. Given my own South Asian roots, I made sure that the final paper went to the President to avoid any question of circumvention of the process. I drafted it meticulously being an honest broker between Defense Department worries and the President's desire for a breakthrough moment, which seemed possible with Rajiv Gandhi. In any case, Weinberger had regularly scheduled meetings with the President where he could make his own case. It was important I felt to carry the interagency process in a positive direction, recognizing that not all detractors of the opening to India (for example, DoD's Frank Gaffney) could ever be brought around. The President signed the decision memorandum and set the stage for the flow of US defense technology to India.

At the same time, we walked the delicate line of reaching out with assistance to Pakistan to counteract the Soviet presence in Afghanistan. Close coordination showed demonstrable effect on Soviet capabilities for the control of the state. Costs were high in Afghanistan and in Pakistan where more than three million Afghan refugees took refuge and thoroughly and permanently changed Pakistan. But Pakistan remained a firm partner of the USA in expelling Russian troops from Afghanistan, thus helping with the demise of the Soviet Union.

Rajiv Gandhi would eventually come back for a working visit to the White House in October 1987. This time the visit was less ceremonial but the friendship with President Reagan was evident. They were relaxed over the lunch served in the family dining room as an indication of the change and comfort level. Colin Powell was then the National Security Advisor and was aware of the hundreds of hours of preparation that had been put in by the US team and the effort that I had devoted to making the second Gandhi visit a substantive one. Rajiv Gandhi and I shared a birthday, and clearly, his staff had so informed him. Upon his arrival into the Cabinet Room for talks, he came straight to me to say that and to thank me for the hard work of promoting USA–India relations.

As part of White House events, a photographer captured the moment with Gandhi's hand stretched in front of Powell as he reached out to me and I quickly extended my arm into a long reach for the handshake. After the visit, Powell sent me a signed copy of the photograph with the line "Sorry about my quizzical look and one closed eye! CL Powell."

However, the lunch agenda went extremely well and, as the notetaker, I was frantic in trying to take down as much of the conversation as I possibly could, knowing later it would be needed for follow-up work. The food was served and cleared, and I did not touch it. Finally, President Reagan, always thoughtful, looked at me and indicated I should eat as the dessert, date ice cream, was served. The President then launched into telling jokes, which gave me a respite.

The joke involved Soviet leader Gorbachev. As told beautifully by the President, one day, the Soviet leader was being driven out of the Kremlin in a fancy new car. He asked his driver to go faster. The driver demurred citing his instructions from the security detail. Upon hearing this, Gorbachev asked the driver to stop the car and exchanged seats with the driver. Then, he speeded up to well past the speed limit in central Moscow. From the side street came two motorcycle police who put on their sirens and stopped Gorbachev's car. One policeman went up to the car and then came back to join his comrade indicating that he had not given a speeding violation ticket to the driver. "Why is that, who was in the car?" asked the comrade. Replied the first policeman: "I don't know. He must be extremely important because Gorbachev was his driver!!" Rajiv Gandhi roared with laughter and I got to eat my dessert! It was the best ice cream ever, even by White House standards!

The US opening to India accelerated contact between senior officials, increased trade and created an understanding for protection of US technology sought by New Delhi. By mid-1987, the USA was already India's largest trade partner. The USA–India Science and Technology Initiative (STI) of 1987 dovetailed with the Reagan–Rajiv Gandhi meeting that year. The accord signaled strong joint commitment to a variety of areas including health, agriculture, material sciences, and meteorology for which Gandhi had sought and acquired the Cray XMP-14 supercomputer. The STI maximized funding and reduced bureaucratic delays in evaluating projects for bilateral cooperation. With the signed MOU on technology transfer in place, the number of Indian high technology requests approved by the USA went up dramatically with fifty percent of bilateral trade going toward high technology items.

The NSC continued its work in support of the expanded India–USA relationship. Senior officials were easy to convince to make public remarks which helped in the interagency process. As I worked with colleagues to lay the foundation for a strong relationship with India because that mattered to US interests, the American business community was particularly helpful. This enthusiasm as reflected in the remarks of National Security Advisor, Frank Carlucci who was a first at that level in addressing the growing India–USA Business Council. Carlucci noted the US desire to reinforce strong ties to

India. These ties would encompass research establishments, including scientists and engineers; as well the private sector reflected also in greater cultural contact and increased tourism. Announcing the eight new agreements, President Reagan noted in public what I had seen in the internal agenda that in his talks with Rajiv Gandhi, he had urged India and Pakistan to "intensify their dialog to build greater mutual confidence, to resolve outstanding issues and to deal with the threat of nuclear proliferation in the region."[2]

The growing friendship between the US President and the Indian Prime Minister led to their regularly corresponding on bilateral issues along with the need for normalization between India and Pakistan. With Soviet withdrawal from Afghanistan, the Soviet Union involvement in the region declined. At the same time, the interaction between the USA and India grew rapidly.

Even after the change in administrations from the Reagan to the Bush presidency in January 1989, US engagement continued. While some later traced the opening to India with the George H. W. Bush White House,[3] the actual opening occurred in the Reagan administration and with George H. W. Bush as Vice President. On the Indian side, those such as Ronen Sen and current Foreign Secretary Jaishankar, who were closely associated with the relationship as it was energized in the mid-1980s, recall that time.

But those improved relations took a different character after the assassination of Rajiv Gandhi on May 21, 1991, while campaigning for reelection. My interaction with him as the NSC officer in charge of the White House meetings and several visits on presidential missions to Delhi had given me access and empathy for this young leader. In addition, one of his cousins was a very close friend of my husband from Raza's Oxford days and his son, Rahul, was a friend of my son Kazim at Harvard.

I was at home recovering from massive emergency surgery in May rather than in my office as Ambassador at the US Mission to the UN when I received the call from the operations center telling me that Gandhi had died. I immediately found my son and asked him if he knew. Kazim told me that he and Rahul were scheduled to play squash later that day. "Go find him and be with him as he is likely to hear very soon," I said. With a profound sense of loss and sadness, I recalled the leader Gandhi had been and how much he had moved the Indo-USA relationship.

Notes

1. Arnold L. Raphel also served as US Ambassador to Pakistan and died in the plane crash that also killed President Zia-ul-Haq of Pakistan in August 1988.
2. Joint Press Conference, President Reagan & Prime Minister Gandhi, The White House, October 20, 1987, text available at https://www.c-span.org/video/?189556-1/white-house-news-conference, accessioned October 18, 2017.
3. For example, Council on Foreign Relations Task Force Report No. 73, *Working with a Rising India: A Joint Venture for the New Century* (November 2015).

CHAPTER 14

Adding Pakistan to the Equation

After the tragic death of Rajiv Gandhi, the USA carried on its diplomacy with the new Indian Prime Minister Narisimha Rao, who, as foreign minister in the Gandhi government, was already a familiar leader at the White House. As we negotiated last-minute hitches in the joint statement at the end of the 1987 Rajiv Gandhi visit, the President's National Security Advisor Frank Carlucci called upon Gandhi. Indian Foreign Minister Narisimha Rao was from Hyderabad and knew my father which always made for a good side conversation in Hyderabadi when he was foreign minister and we were awaiting the arrival of our respective leaders into meeting venues.

I later devoted part of my academic research to these developments while working on the monograph published by the Council on Foreign Relations, but for now, my portfolio for NSC continued to be Indo-Pak relations. The USA continued to push on several fronts: pressing for full Soviet withdrawal from Afghanistan; rapprochement between India and Pakistan; strengthening of USA–India ties through the development of trade and defense cooperation; pressure on Pakistan not to cross the nuclear weapons grade fuel enrichment threshold; and a follow-on assistance package for economic and military support for Pakistan. In addition, the USA gave more than any other to help Pakistan shoulder the burden of some 3 million Afghan refugees living in Pakistan after the 1979 invasion by Moscow. It was hoped that the settlement of Afghan conflict following withdrawal of Russian troops would lead to the return of refugees to their homeland.

US pressure on Pakistan to restrain its nuclear weapons program required constant vigilance and bilateral discussions, often at the highest levels.[1] Some of these were notable in the sense of urgency demonstrated, but there were also moments of humor. One such event occurred during the visit of Prime Minister Muhammad Khan Junejo's official visit to the USA in mid-July 1986.

US legislation required the cutoff of American assistance to Pakistan should the latter cross the nuclear weapons threshold. All were aware that given the general state of hostility between India and Pakistan, Pakistanis saw nuclear weapons capability as the key guarantor of their security, even existence. By trying to help normalize relations between these two neighbors, the White House hoped that the race to nuclear weapons could be slowed if not eliminated.

With the growingly tense relationship between the Pakistani President General Zia and his appointed Prime Minister Junejo on all manner of things especially the desire to settle the end of the war in Afghanistan, it appeared that as always, the Army with its control over the nuclear weapons program was not keeping the civilian Prime Minister in the loop. The President also wanted to ensure that Junejo understood the practical ramifications of Pakistan crossing the nuclear threshold in terms of the congressionally mandated US assistance termination.

On a blisteringly hot and humid July morning, the official Junejo visit to the USA began. Matching rising temperatures mid-morning, he received a warm ceremonial welcome with the gun salute and the resplendent Fife and Drum Corps providing a festive atmosphere on the South Lawn of the White House.

Meetings between the two leaders followed. Junejo arrived with a large official delegation so that the Cabinet Room was going to be stretched to accommodate all around the table. Even as members were gathering, the NSC and State Department planned for a one-on-one meeting between the two leaders. In order to have notes for the follow-up, one notetaker (me) was included in the Oval Office meeting. Given that I spoke Urdu, it was assumed that I could act as translator if necessary. At the appointed hour, President Reagan and Prime Minister Junejo convened in the Oval Office. I accompanied the President and, en route, Secretary of State George Shultz offered some clarification. Once inside, the Secret Service closed the door and, as ever, stood guard outside.

Thousands of photographs of multiple Presidents sitting in front of the fireplace with the honored guest to his right have been flashed around the world for decades. This was the same arrangement and I sat myself on the sofa nearest President Reagan, pen poised for note-taking. Both men were polite and friendly enquiring about family and events in the subcontinent. Then, President Reagan started his discussion on the Pakistani nuclear weapons program and the need to curtail its development toward a bomb option. I saw that Junejo was listening intently and I hoped that presaged his own support for putting brakes on the program in order to prevent severance of US assistance.

Then, came Junejo's turn to offer his thoughts on what the US President had said. I could practically see him thinking in Urdu and translating into English as he spoke. He was a quiet man and this tete-a-tete with Reagan was not scripted so he had no pre-planned response in hand. After an initial period of silence, the Pakistani Prime Minister launched an expose of his country's tense relationships with key neighbors. Thus, in his mind having laid the foundation of Pakistan's need for nuclear weapons as a deterrent, he noted that the USA ought not to worry so much given that "your bums (the Urdu word for Bomb) are bigger than our bums"!

I saw President Reagan look puzzled and turn up his hearing aid a couple of notches. He noted that he missed the last sentence. Junejo feeling relieved that Reagan had caught on, happily repeated "your bums are bigger than our bums." The President continued to look perplexed and so I thought I should interject and point out that the Prime Minister was talking about the relative size of the USA and potential Pakistani nuclear bombs. "Ah!" was the remark made by a relieved President. I realized that Junejo was using the Urdu word correctly but in the American lexicon, the result was bizarre. As the meeting broke for the two leaders to go into the larger meeting in the Cabinet Room, Reagan said "Thank you for saving that one" with his usual twinkle. All in a day's work at the White House, I thought but did not say.

Most of the decade of the 1980s found Pakistan in alliance with the USA. The Soviet invasion of Afghanistan in December 1979 brought the two countries into close collaboration in fashioning and executing the response. The Reagan administration pledged strong support for Pakistan's economic well-being and military upgrading, always a key goal of Pakistan's military leadership. From my perch in the Reagan White

House, I saw the interaction firsthand. Finally, there seemed to be a shared goal uniting American and Pakistani foreign policy. By upping the Carter offer of $400 million to a $3.2 billion five-year program, Reagan found immediate resonance with Zia. Yet, even at that time, there were voices in Pakistan who cautioned the President, as had occurred in the mid-1950s that responding to events in neighboring Afghanistan with the vehemence required by American policy would not serve Pakistan in the long run.[2] However, Zia was the ultimate decider and he touted the fact that two "God-fearing" countries had come together to expel the "Godless Communists."

As American funds began to flow into Pakistan, Afghan resistance leaders were headquartered there, and the Pakistani intelligence agency played favorites in dispensing the funds. Intelligence coordination remained close between the USA and Pakistan. The US goal was to expel the Soviets and Pakistan willingly became the "front-line" state.[3] Zia held to the goals set by the USA: the preservation of Afghan sovereignty, territorial integrity, political independence, and non-aligned character; the right of the Afghan people to select their own form of government, political, and social system; immediate withdrawal of foreign troops; and return of Afghan refugees (over 3 million of whom were in Pakistan).

In private and official conversations with US officials, Zia would talk of the duty of every Muslim to support the jihad in Afghanistan. He welcomed numerous leaders from the Muslim world and others and proudly spoke of Pakistan's responsibility to be a part of the Umma in support of Muslims. He felt Pakistan would weather the crisis and, even as he took assistance from the West, in the process cleanse itself of the Western culture. The Arab "Mujahideen" were welcomed as brothers in arms. Their integration into the culture of the northern areas of Pakistan sowed the seeds for the havoc that was to follow in terms of the Pakistani body politic. Countries providing assistance, especially Saudi Arabia with its strict Wahhabi Islam, began to increase their presence and influence in Pakistan.[4]

Because of their shared goals, American motives were not really under fire in Pakistan at the time. Friday sermons in mosques did not stray into anti-American rhetoric. After all, the Mujahideen were Muslims and America their benefactor. Given that US assistance started as a covert affair, the ISI Directorate was the funnel for the assistance. Zia kept the ISI profile low and focused on the Afghan effort. His Director General of ISI, General Akhtar Abdur Rahman, was a favored colleague who completely towed the President's line. Zia directed Rahman to remain in close contact with the CIA Director, William Casey. During those years when I accompanied White House and senior US government visitors on visits to Pakistan, General Rahman was always present in Zia's meetings with American interlocutors.[5]

Coordination between the USA and Pakistan on Afghan policy continued throughout the 1980s. High-level talks were a frequent occurrence and collaboration on a range of issues beyond the war in Afghanistan brought a new dynamism into the relationship. This was a time, however, when the Pakistani intelligentsia was questioning Pakistan's involvement in what was considered to be the American agenda. As millions of Afghan refugees streamed into Pakistan, many in areas where the Afghans settled found it to be a great annoyance. They began to bristle at what they considered to be the high cost to Pakistan of the war. Within the province bordering Afghanistan, there was recognition of the shared ethnic background with the refugees. The money that was being pumped into Peshawar (which became the headquarters for many of the Mujahideen leaders and related international efforts) forever changed that gregarious but sleepy town where I had grown up.

President Zia maintained tight control over the political system. He attempted to bring political players into government after the 1985 elections but the result was anemic at best. He appointed Mohammad Khan Junejo as titular Prime Minister in 1985 but dismissed him in 1988 when the latter, finally realizing that he was there only as a showpiece, began to act independently of his patron, Zia. The war against the Soviets intensified. As a result, the ISI became more powerful. Zia kept tight control over the ISI and its funding, weapons distribution to the "freedom fighters," and their training in Pakistani military camps. Billions were poured in by the USA and by friends in the Arab world. Transparency and accountability seemed out of the question.

One of the direct consequences of this period of USA–Pakistan relations was the development of a "Kalashnikov" culture in Pakistan. Weapons and drugs moved freely into the country from the porous tribal areas. A percentage of items destined for Afghanistan's war ended up in local arms bazaars. Even more lethal was the slow conversion of Pakistan's northern areas into a Wahhabi version of Islam. The Arab fighters extolled by Reagan as brave "freedom fighters" when he met with some of them in Washington were beginning to seize control of the mosques and those who prayed there. Always socially conservative, Pathans were facing even more control under the new emerging culture of jihad. In the vast refugee camps where Afghans lived in Pakistan, the women often spoke of suffocating restrictions under the newly acquired Wahhabi culture. Before the onset of this culture, in Afghanistan where they lived in their own villages, they had felt less constrained.

The Reagan administration was extremely focused on the expulsion of the Soviet Union from Afghanistan and Pakistan's help toward that goal. Domestic impact within Pakistan of the war machine created to fight communism was an afterthought, if that. Disruption in neighboring Afghanistan had occurred at Soviet hands. Defeating Moscow meant changing the great game and altering the boundaries of the Soviet empire.

The Pakistani Army, and perhaps even more the ISI, knowingly created a fighting machine using illiterate fighters and trained them to use modern weapons such as the Stinger missiles. Pakistan coordinated with the USA in talks, through the UN as an intermediary, for total withdrawal of the Soviet troops. These talks accelerated in 1986 as the offensive against the Soviet occupation of Afghanistan began to pay off. Reagan reached out to the Soviet leader Mikhail Gorbachev.[6] I was on the National Security Council staff at the time and recall the genuine excitement that the December 1987 visit of Gorbachev to the White House would change east–west relations on a broad range of issues, including Soviet occupation of Afghanistan. It was in the course of this visit that Gorbachev hinted at Soviet withdrawal from Afghanistan, removing one of the most contentious items on the agenda.

American policy makers worried that Pakistan might make a separate deal with the Soviets before the USA was ready to lessen the pressure. The Saudis were important interlocutors for American goals in Afghanistan at the time. Zia, who had allowed unparalleled access to Pakistan by Arab "freedom fighters," was pressed by Saudi leaders to keep a united front. As pressure on the occupiers increased and the American sponsored fighters began to exact a heavy toll on Soviet forces, a degree of independence began to creep into Mujahideen leader's lexicon. On one occasion, the White House wanted the visiting Afghan resistance leader Gulbuddin Hekmatyar to come to the White House for a meeting and photo op with the President. Multiple calls by Pakistani leaders did not shake Hekmatyar's resolve to stay away from being branded an American ally. In the end, he did not come to the White House to meet with Reagan because he felt that in his world, closeness to the American leader would not be a plus. While, at the time when Hekmatyar was literally living off American largesse, this was a surprise, it really was a harbinger of things to come.

Zia felt that the strong support of Pakistan along with American funding had been a key to Soviet defeat in Afghanistan: "A miracle of the twentieth century." Even as he worked hard to revamp Pakistan as a committed Islamic country, in his private conversations, he sounded optimistic about continued good relations with the USA long into the future. All through the Zia years, a great deal of US military assistance to Pakistan was sought and delivered. Despite delays and concerns caused by the Pakistani nuclear program and the "litmus test" hardware such as the F-16s, American leaders honored their pledge and worked hard to deliver on the $3.2 billion economic assistance and military sales package for the 1982–1987 period. In making the case for Congressional approval of the package, US Undersecretary of State James Buckley noted in his testimony on November 25, 1981, before the Senate Foreign Relations Committee that assistance was pledged because "Pakistan had elected to condemn the occupation of Afghanistan....and found itself thrust into the unwelcome status of a front-line state." Buckley went on to note a commitment that has gone on to become a permanent pledge by the USA "a strong, stable and independent Pakistan is an essential anchor to the entire South West Asian region." There was no mention of a "democratic" Pakistan in this equation. A military leader with parallel policies was worthy of American arms and material, especially since he was willing to act as a conduit into Afghanistan.

Pakistani military leaders would proudly claim that they would not offer nor accept American bases in Pakistan. However, this was an unnecessary claim since at the time the USA was not looking for a base. Working indirectly through the Pakistani intelligence service was easier and the pressure on the Soviets was considerable without the risk of a direct confrontation between the two mega powers. In the course of one of my conversations with President Zia, I asked him why the constant refrain that Pakistan will not give a base to America when none was being asked for. In response, Zia noted that he wanted to forestall the possibility of a request because "the people" would not stand for it and that he did not want the "U.S. to go from a perception in Pakistan as an ally for the eviction of foreign troops from Muslim Afghanistan to one seen as an occupier itself."

Notes

1. Recent US Government declassified documents for this period detail specific efforts and exchanges. Some of these are included in the Appendix.
2. General K. M. Arif, *Working With Zia: Pakistan's Power Politics 1977–1988* (New York: Oxford University Press, 1995), 314.
3. Shirin Tahir-Kheli, *India, Pakistan, and the USA: Breaking with the Past* (New York: Council on Foreign Relations Press, 1997).
4. Arif, *Working with Zia*, 317.
5. General Akhtar Rahman was also killed in the air crash that took Zia's life. It was said in Pakistan that upon his death, his family found cupboards full of cash from American sources in his house. His son has entered Pakistani politics.
6. After complicated negotiations lasting six years, the Geneva Accord was signed on April 14, 1988. Soviet troops left Afghanistan shortly thereafter and no interim government was ready to take charge in Kabul. Various estimates put the cost of the Afghan invasion and occupation at over $70 billion and Soviet military leaders noted that the war had cost nearly 14,000 soldiers dead and some 35,500 wounded. The war cost nearly 200,000 Afghan and Arab supporter's death and another 80,000 wounded. Afghanistan suffered enormous physical damage as well with its elementary infrastructure in tatters. Arable land was destroyed, lives uprooted and nearly a third of the Afghan population at the time ended up as refugees mostly in Pakistan and Iran. See Arif, *Working with Zia*, 325–327.

CHAPTER 15

Failed Statecraft?

The end of the Zia regime came in a catastrophic fashion via a plane crash on August 19, 1988. Zia's death in an air crash which also took the life of a popular American Ambassador created a sense of camaraderie in the loss on both sides. From my NSC perch, I worked on arrangements for Secretary of State George Shultz to attend Zia's funeral and for the return, on his aircraft, of the body of my friend, the American Ambassador to Pakistan, Arnold Raphel. At the time, Shultz noted that "United States relations with Pakistan are based on long standing shared purposes and common goals." At Pakistan's request, a team of experts was dispatched from the USA and worked alongside the Pakistani team investigating the crash of the usually very reliable C-130. The inquiry did not point to any sabotage, but it also did not completely rule it out. As a result, conspiracy theories became rampant. The end of Zia's rule meant a chance for an American focus on a new democratic Pakistan.

Following US elections on November 8, 1988, George H. W. Bush became the 41st President. Shortly after, on November 10, Bush noted "I would like to reaffirm my commitment to a stable Pakistan. The USA and Pakistan have a historic relationship" which he pledged to further strengthen. There was no overt mention of democracy. But Bush had begun to evaluate a new course whereby "stability" in Pakistan meant a return to democracy.

Elections in Pakistan on November 16, 1988, offered an opportunity to put that hope into practice. Bush became personally focused on the affair even as he waited to assume the office of President. Benazir

Bhutto, leader of the Pakistan People's Party (PPP) founded by her father, led an energetic campaign. Her party won 92 out of the 217 seats in the National assembly. Her closest opponent was Nawaz Sharif with his Islamic Democratic Alliance (IJI), which ran in support of the Islamization efforts launched by Zia and won 55 seats. As the White House focused on these results, it appeared that the former finance minister and later President of Pakistan Ghulam Ishaq Khan was less than eager to allow the majority winner to put together a government. Ishaq Khan was nervous at Bhutto's lineage and the policies enacted by her father under the first PPP control. As a bureaucrat par excellence, Ishaq Khan felt that Zulfikar Ali Bhutto had systematically destroyed Pakistan's institutions in the name of socialism. The daughter's popularity with the same base that had supported the father was of concern to both the military and the civilian President.

President-elect Bush focused on ways the USA might be able to nudge to action the reluctant Pakistani President whose duties included asking an elected leader to form the government. To this end, in November 1988, he held a discussion with the White House. In his mind, approving the appointment of a duly elected Prime Minister was necessary to restoring democracy. I made the case to President-elect Bush that if Pakistan is at all to succeed in its effort to establish democracy, Bush should seize the moment and send a direct personal letter to President Ishaq. Bush agreed and two letters were carefully drafted. One was for Benazir Bhutto. It congratulated her on her party's win. The second, to be delivered to President Ghulam Ishaq, lauded the election in Pakistan and noted that the USA looked forward to working with the leader who had garnered the most seats in the National Assembly. We went to Pakistan as a Presidential Mission that consisted of Richard Murphy, Assistant Secretary of State for the Near East and South Asia, and Richard Armitage, Assistant Secretary of Defense for International Security Affairs. We traveled to Islamabad in late November 1988. As the NSC officer in charge of South Asia, I accompanied the duo as part of the delegation.[1]

Upon our arrival in Pakistan, we were met by the American Ambassador and stayed at the residence. Our call on the President was already set up, and the delegation was received at the Presidency by President Ghulam Ishaq Khan. Murphy did the introductions, and the Pakistani President noted (as he always did whenever I accompanied American officials in the course of my White House work) "I have known

Shirin since the time when she was a little girl with pigtails"! He never explained, and it was always left to me to point out later that when I was growing up in Pakistan, my parents and Ghulam Ishaq were neighbors in Nathia Gali, the hill station to which senior officials from Peshawar retreated in the hot summer months. When discussion got underway, Murphy and Armitage went on to extol the management—presumably by the President—of a successful fair election and how it had set the stage for democracy to flower. Given the tragic death of Zia, they noted that the USA had lost one of its own Ambassador Arnold Raphel, a close friend of all three of us in the American delegation. The return to civilian government via a peaceful election was a tremendous achievement. The Pakistani President did not say much, but he carefully read the letter from President-elect Bush handed to him and bade us farewell.

I was in Islamabad for less than twenty-four hours. Though ensconced with the rest of the delegation in the embassy compound, after the arrival day's work was done, I made a couple of hours visit to see my aging parents in nearby Islamabad. They were sorry not to see me for longer but reinforced their message of pride in my commitment to my chosen country and public service path of my career. It was one of my life's proudest moments.

Before departing for Washington the next morning, the delegation met with the PPP leader, Benazir Bhutto, at the American Ambassador's residence. Murphy noted that we had met with Pakistan's President and delivered a letter from the American President-elect. He shared the sentiments in the letter just delivered and also passed a letter to Bhutto. It was an important meeting, and Bhutto was well aware that her chance to form a government would finally come with the express support of the incoming American President. She had become a savvy politician but was yet untested as a national leader. She noted that she would stay in close touch with newly appointed American Ambassador Robert Oakley, who had replaced Raphel. A few days after the departure of the American delegation from Pakistan, Benazir Bhutto was invited by Ghulam Ishaq Khan to form the government. She put together a coalition with smaller parties and independents and was sworn in as the first female Prime Minister of a Muslim country on December 4, 1988. It was a heady moment that both Pakistan and the USA celebrated.

From the outset, Bhutto felt a sense of siege in terms of key issues, especially the nuclear issue. I had known her for a time before she became Prime Minister, and she would invite me over for a meeting or a lunch when I was in Pakistan. Over the years, even as she granted patronage to ever-increasing numbers, both leaders and the rank and file of the party, she always claimed that she was not in charge of many things, including security and military matters. In 1988, she was undoubtedly aware of the presence of Arab fighters in the midst and the rising role of the Mullahs in the establishment of madrassas both inside country and especially along the northwestern borders. The ISI was now without the close scrutiny that was possible under Zia. Ishaq Khan had become President at Zia's death, and he was under no illusion that in reality the Army Chief and the head of ISI were the key figures in Pakistan. These institutions were less than complimentary about Bhutto and her lack of experience when, as her first ever job, she assumed the office of Prime Minister at age 35. Additionally, her marriage in 1987 to Asif Zardari openly added to their disdain.

It was often said in Pakistan at the time that Bhutto was less interested in the welfare of Pakistan than she was in avenging her father's death. Of course, she was the modern face of Pakistan, especially to the West. But the West was losing out in Pakistan as the Mullahs and the intelligence services pulled the country in the opposite direction. Pakistan was becoming conservative as the former Mujahideen remained in situ in Pakistan after the Soviet withdrawal from Afghanistan. The initially hoped for promise of a democratic, educated, female Prime Minister was not fulfilled as controversy swirled around her and others in her orbit with open talk of corruption enriching personal coffers circulated at all levels of Pakistani society. Bhutto denied that either she or her husband was making illegal money and charged her opponents with maligning her name in order to destroy democracy. The Army and bureaucratic leadership remained disdainful, citing instances of political patronage that was collapsing Pakistani institutions. I was often struck by Bhutto's statements to me reflecting a certain sense of siege. In response to my noting that the Pakistan–USA relationship could fall apart over the growing belief in Washington that the known nuclear redline, i.e., no uranium enrichment beyond 5%, was being violated, Bhutto claimed that she was out of the loop on the nuclear program because that remained in the exclusive hands of the military.

Bhutto wanted close relations with Washington. She consulted openly and frequently with the American Ambassador which won Oakley the nickname "Viceroy." USA hopes for stability included expectation of accountability and transparency, including with respect to the nuclear program. Congressional pressure for sanctions accelerated in the face of mounting evidence of Pakistan having crossed the nuclear weapons threshold. This was a time of escalating tensions with the USA. Within the White House, President George H. W. Bush remembered that in the course of his visit to Pakistan in 1984 as Vice President, he had directly questioned Zia regarding the weaponization of Pakistan's nuclear program. Zia denied the charge assuring him that Pakistan's uranium enrichment capability was destined to be used for energy purposes only. Later, when Bush was President, it became clear that nuclear weapons capability was the real intent, Bush felt personally insulted because as he recalled of his 1984 conversation with Zia: "I asked him for his word as an officer, and he looked me in the eye and lied!" This comment, made to me by President Bush, is hard to forget.

It fell to the USA to brief Prime Minister Bhutto on Pakistan's nuclear program. The briefing by senior administration officials preceded the October 1990 cut-off, required under the Pressler amendment, of US assistance to Pakistan. Delivery of Pakistani-purchased F-16 aircraft was halted, and it appeared clear to American senior officials that Bhutto was not in the loop on nuclear preparedness in her country and that the more hawkish President Ghulam Ishaq Khan and the Army Chief Aslam Beg were calling the shots in the escalating tensions with India over Kashmir.[2] Of course, in Pakistan, neither the President nor the Army Chief faulted Pakistani nuclear policy. Given that Pakistan was no longer needed to fight Soviet policy in Afghanistan, American aid termination was always seen as reflecting Washington's preferred option. Also, General Beg and President Khan were both more comfortable with an anti-Indian bent. In particular, Beg cultivated Pakistan's Islamic credentials in and out of office. He established a special relationship with Pakistan's Shia Islamic neighbor: Iran.

Despite decades of contact, Pakistan and the USA never managed to cultivate a lasting relationship. Anyone who assumed that assistance and support, irregularly given, would result in American influence in Pakistan was likely to be mistaken.[3] Even with a democratically elected Benazir Bhutto in office and despite the $5.7 billion in economic and military assistance doled out by the USA during the Zia years, the focus of Pakistani policy remained India. The Reagan White House worked hard to promote confidence building between India and Pakistan resulting in some success, including the agreement to refrain from attacking each other's nuclear facilities and bringing Zia and Rajiv Gandhi into meaningful talks in December 1985. After 1988, with Gandhi and Bhutto as Prime Ministers, many in Washington hoped that the new generation of political leaders would usher in a new era of good relations. While notable movement did take place—for example, Bhutto ended support for Sikh extremists who plotted against India from Pakistani soil, and the two countries brought military delegations into talks on a settlement of the contested 20,000 foot-high Siachin Glacier—long-term benefit proved elusive.

However, changed conditions in Afghanistan and the seeming uprising in Indian Kashmir proved too tempting for the military and the ISI not to exploit. Thus, doors to genuine normalization in the subcontinent remained closed.

Hard-liners in the military, intelligence, and politics including the President were unhappy with Bhutto's outreach to Gandhi. The most contentious issues have always been related to defense, and final progress was not possible by either side without the support of the hard-liners. Both intelligence agencies, India's Research and Analysis Wing (RAW) and its Pakistani counterpart, the ISI, were loathe to go along with rapprochement. Conservative religious elements (there were few Pakistani extremists at the time and the resident Arabs who had fought in Afghanistan were still celebrating the expulsion of Soviet forces) had always disapproved of westernized Bhutto. The Prime Minister was mindful of these negative sentiments, and in order to establish some Islamic credentials, her first foreign trip was to Saudi Arabia. There she traveled to Mecca and performed Umrah and met King Fahd.

After demonstrating due reverence to the Wahhabi Saudi state, where a Muslim female Prime Minister was an aberration, Bhutto thought it is safe to visit the far more welcoming USA. Addressing a joint session of Congress, Bhutto stated that Pakistan had not and would not develop nuclear weapons. In order to make the military happy, she asked for an additional 70 F-16 fighters and arranged to put down half the requisite amount, $658 million, in cash towards the purchase. Feted as a star in the USA, she went home with a sense of having secured a long-term relationship with the USA.

But then, the President of Pakistan dismissed Bhutto, only 24 months into her tenure, based on charges of incontrovertible evidence of corruption and incompetence. In addition, her foreign policy with its very obvious American tilt was not popular with the President and the military that had control of the nuclear program; both knew that thresholds were being crossed. As Kashmir burst into rebellion against high-handed tactics of the Indian security services, Benazir Bhutto's attempts at normalizing relations with India were perceived as being out of touch by the Pakistani defense establishment. In addition, there was great public disillusionment with her government's performance on the socioeconomic front. These issues were considered sufficient grounds for her ouster.

In August 1990, Bhutto was dismissed from office by the President. In response, on October 1, 1990, the USA cut off all assistance to Pakistan. Bhutto had been ushered into office as Prime Minister with the explicit support of the USA. Her dismissal and then the severance of assistance reflected a sad chapter in her failure primarily to deliver good governance and stability to Pakistan's democratic experiment. Secondarily, as always, it represented her inability to safely ride the tiger that is the Pakistani military.

In Pakistan, however, the dismissal was a domestic matter and the break with the USA, after the 1990 aid cut-off, was seen by most, especially the Army Chief, as a natural outcome of the Soviet collapse rendering Pakistan "useless" to Washington. Critics of American policy were many and included Aslam Beg, the Army Chief, and President Ishaq Khan. None were willing to accept the assistance termination as a consequence of the congressionally mandated legislation on nuclear proliferation. Instead, in Pakistani minds, Pakistan had remained a reliable ally but one that the USA no longer needed to do its dirty work because for all intents and purposes the Soviets were now dead and gone. According to the Army Chief: "With the end of the Cold War, and (its) economic interests in the new world order, the USA has been hasty in downgrading its relationship with Pakistan."[4] Beg and other critics of American policy were unconvinced that the break was really the result of deliberate double dealing by Pakistan on the nuclear weapons issue. Rather, they preferred to believe that the program was where it was, but the need to overlook the transgression had disappeared with Soviet defeat in Afghanistan.

Beg argued internally for closer relations with Iran and against Pakistani support for the Gulf War. He stressed the need to turn towards the Islamic world which had routinely come to Pakistan's rescue in tough times. The alliance between the military and the mosque was further cemented after the breakdown of Pakistan–American relations.[5] Bhutto continued to say she was unaware of ISI support against India in Kashmir after 1989. Pakistan's military, openly supported by Pakistan's

Islamists, pushed Gulbuddin Hekmatyar in the power struggle in Kabul. There was deep suspicion within the Pakistani establishment that India would use Afghan proxies to put Pakistan in an impossible two-front situation, especially since the ISI knew what it was trying to do against India in Kashmir.

From my perch at the National Security Council and in subsequent meetings, I had observed Bhutto's interest in ending the Afghan war and getting on with other priorities. She was first to admit that she was out of the loop and the military and the ISI controlled all strategic and Afghanistan issues. Given the hidden nature of that enterprise, the ISI used religious extremists and their activists to help carry out its policy in Afghanistan. More moderate Afghan leaders were appealing to Washington to stop ISI interference. In their journeys to Washington and meetings elsewhere, they pleaded for ISI exclusion from supporting conservative elements from the previous Jihad. In conversations with reporters, they kept voicing their frustration that no one was listening![6] In the post-Bhutto period, checks against ISI actions were further reduced.[7] By 1990, Pakistani institutions had weakened to the point that political oversight and accountability over strategic issues were not even a facade. The Army's direct involvement after the 1958 martial law had left a long-lasting legacy of opaqueness in all policies deemed by the military and intelligence elite and their operatives to constitute the national interest. Citing fear of Indian control in Kabul, the Taliban were nurtured to bend to Pakistani preferences in their battle for control of Afghanistan.

Around the time that the USA was considering a military operation in the Persian Gulf, public opinion in Pakistan had turned decisively against US policies directed toward the Muslim world. A Chief of Army Staff (COAS) Beg carefully nurtured the view that American policy aimed at weakening the Islamic Umma, and Pakistan needed to be mindful of American designs. Ignoring the new Prime Minister, Nawaz Sharif, Beg went on to declare sympathy for Saddam Hussein's venture into Kuwait and even criticized Saudi Arabia for toeing the American line. Beg noted no Pakistani troops needed to be dispatched for the anti-Saddam coalition headed by the USA. While Sharif disagreed, he did not dismiss Beg, cognizant of the fact that a Pakistani opinion poll taken in January 1991 showed dislike for the US and "overwhelming" support for Saddam Hussein.[8]

By the mid-1990s, Pakistan political culture had changed. Ever-increasing number of Afghan refugees, meddling by ISI inside

Afghanistan, the destruction of Afghanistan in the continuing civil war, an insurgent Taliban with control in Kabul and recognized as the government in power only by Saudi Arabia, the United Arab Emirates, and Pakistan—had all begun to isolate Pakistan and side-line its image as a Muslim country with a serious educated elite and a rising middle class. Democracy had returned, but the leaders were mired in bickering and the nation's business was left to drift. Economic crisis brought bankruptcy even as corruption siphoned out what there was left of the treasury. Internal politics were once again consuming a lot of attention inside Pakistan. In Washington, Pakistan was often referred to as a "failed state." Except for the pressure on the security and safety of nuclear weapons, American preoccupations in Pakistan were muted and limited to the half-unspoken desire to bring back better governance and stability. Only a half-hearted mention of the need for normalization with India continued.

Despite the obvious discomfort of Pakistani leaders whenever the USA asked the ISI be reined in, most Pakistanis openly talked of the support given to Taliban in their training and equipping as "hundreds of Afghan mullahs began to descend on Kandahar in the cool spring weather of 1996."[9] It was clear that Kabul was their goal, and other warlords who had come together to form the government would not surrender without a fight. Taliban invoked Islam freely and noted that their rule constituted serious implementation of the Shariah as interpreted by basically illiterate Afghans. Pakistan's President Farooq Leghari, its COAS General Jehangir Karamat, and the ISI chief met with other former Mujahideen leaders in Islamabad in order to coax cooperation from the Taliban.

NOTES

1. The trip was mentioned by Peter Galbraith, then a senior staffer on the senate Foreign Relations Committee to Elisabeth Bumiller, "How Bhutto Won Washington," *New York Times*, December 30, 2007.
2. Seymour M. Hersh, "On the Nuclear Edge," *The New Yorker*, March 29, 1993.
3. The disconnect between US access to Pakistan and its leaders and Washington's ability to influence Pakistani policy is detailed in Shirin Tahir-Kheli, *The United States and Pakistan: The Evolution of an Influence Relationship* (New York: Praeger, 1982).

4. Paper delivered by Robert Oakley, "Conflict Prevention and Confidence-Building in South Asia: The 1990 Crisis," Washington, DC, The Henry L. Stimson Center, April 1994.
5. Husain Haqani, *Pakistan: Between Mosque and Military* (Washington, DC: Carnegie Endowment for International Peace, 2006).
6. See for example, comments by Hamid Karzai to Ahmed Rashid, *Descent into Chaos: The U.S. and the Disaster in Pakistan, Afghanistan and Central Asia* (New York: Penguin, 2009), 12.
7. Assistant Secretary of State Richard Murphy and Assistant Secretary of Defense Richard Armitage, both crucial actors on Pakistan, subsequently noted that the USA had been too sanguine on the Taliban's developing threat against American interest.
8. Barbara Crosette, "War in the Gulf: The Muslims, Islamic Asians Solidly Back Hussein," *New York Times*, January 27, 1991.
9. Ahmed Rashid, *Taliban: Islam, Oil and the New Great Game in Central Asia* (London: I.B. Tauris, 2000), 41. Rashid details the rise of the Taliban and Pakistan's role in the effort.

CHAPTER 16

Ambassador from Where?

Two days after November 8, 1988, when he was elected President of the USA, I met with George H. W. Bush in his West Wing office. After completing the scheduled policy discussion, he asked what I had planned to do next. I responded light-heartedly, saying that having come in for one year, I had been in government for six years already; I was tired and would simply go back to Pennsylvania. "No" said the 41st President of the USA. "You should go to the UN for me." As I always found respectful repartee was appreciated even at the very top, I replied: "Why Mr. President? Because I look like I should go to the UN?" Not missing a beat, Bush '41 said: "That too but it is the best job and you have done well here at the White House and we need to promote you."

At the same time, John Bolton, Assistant Secretary of State for International Organization, asked for my detailed biography which I provided him. He told me that he would like to offer me the position as one of his deputy assistant secretaries. When I demurred saying that the new President had himself asked me to go to the UN, Bolton was unhappy. In a petulant tone, he said: "Shirin, I am offering you the world, and you want the UN?" At the time, I did not know the extent to which he disliked the UN or the US permanent representative Thomas Pickering. But I was firm in declining the offer, saying I could not bypass the President's summons especially as he had kindly offered the ambassadorship. I also reminded Bolton that I had worked closely with then Vice President George H. W. Bush on India and Pakistan. And that in any case, given that I was headed to the U.S. Mission to the UN, Bolton would be a colleague with whom I would interact a great deal.

Thus, I was nominated to become a US Ambassador, a presidential appointment. Once again, all manner of papers had to be filled. The various security clearances plus the additional financial and medical clearances had to be secured as an ambassadorship comes as a presidential appointment. Again, some of the old business about "does she look American, Is she American?" surfaced among the Senate staffers for Senators Gordon Humphrey and Jesse Helms. When I made the traditional rounds with members and staff, I was asked that by Tom Kline, one very junior white male staff member. My rejoinder: "have you looked around lately? There are more Americans who look like me than are those who look like you." He was taken aback, but I pointed out that the President felt I was worthy of the job. I had academic and government credentials that led to my nomination. I had been holding a high security clearance for six years at the National Security Council doing work for the President of the USA. I could not have done that without being a US citizen. I pointed out that unlike some, I did not carry dual citizenship. I chose solely to be an American.

Being a first again made it harder, but it was worth it. As several noted, "You are the very first Muslim, male or female, to be nominated to an Ambassadorship." I had not set out to make history, but I was delighted. This being America, I always believed, good things happen.

In order to become an Ambassador, one must first be nominated by the President and then be given all the requisite security and other clearances. Then, one must go before the Senate Foreign Relations Committee for confirmation hearings as required by law. Only when the full Senate agrees, can one take the oath of office. One then serves at the pleasure of the President. I met some of the Senators in advance of the hearing. Senator Nancy Kassenbaum was most gracious in her remarks when I called on her prior to my hearing. Senators Pell and Moynihan said my credentials were strong. Senior Staff member Peter Galbraith was most encouraging in terms of my nomination. He also responded to the Helms/Humphrey staffer who kept asking about my having been born elsewhere that his own illustrious father John Kenneth Galbraith sent by President John F. Kennedy to India was born in Canada.

Appearing before the Senate Foreign Relations Committee on one's own behalf is a very special feeling, and I prepared as I had for my Ph.D. preliminary exams. My M.A. dissertation was on the UN. My Ph.D.

dissertation had elements of overlap with the UN. I prepped on all manner of issues relating to US policy, current and past, so that I would be cogent and knowledgeable in my responses. I had an opening statement that was entered into the record. The floor was then open to Senators questions.

The night before the hearing, I ran into Senator Arlen Specter in the basement garage of my apartment building in Georgetown in which he also lived. I mentioned the hearing the next morning to the Senator who was from my home state of Pennsylvania and who as District Attorney of Philadelphia had sworn me into citizenship in 1971. The Senator immediately said that he would introduce me at the hearing, which he did with gracious comments mostly about how young I was when I graduated from college. Later, I was informed that I had been voted out unanimously from the Foreign Relations Committee.

Immediately after the committee's unanimous vote, to my utter surprise, I was informed that "a hold" had been placed on my confirmation due to questions regarding the US-led effort against the Soviet occupation of Afghanistan. Given my unfamiliarity with the complicated world of senatorial processes, it took a great of effort to get any further information. Eventually, I found out that two junior staff of Senator Gordon Humphrey had managed to put a hold in his name despite the unanimous approval of my nomination by the Senate Committee itself. A "hold," which any Senator could invoke, meant that my nomination could not go before the full Senate for approval until such a "hold" was removed by the Senator.

Janet Mullins served as Assistant Secretary of the Bureau of Legislative Affairs in 1990. Her office oversaw the confirmation process for ambassadorial appointments. She was considered an insider on Senate matters. I met with Mullins to seek clarification regarding my nomination. She urged patience and asked that I respond to the hundreds of written questions, based apparently on my bio which I suspect they had received from Bolton. The two men staffers requested written responses, though the matter could have been sorted out faster in person. Thus, it went for a few weeks while I repeatedly answered the same line of questioning: "why were you not as a member of the NSC staff, sending more covert assistance to the Mujahidin in Afghanistan?" No amount of repetition to the effect that I did not oversee covert programs and that Congress itself had imposed restrictions on lone wolf action by NSC staff after the Oliver North Contra

Affair seemed to satisfy. After a while, the matter appeared more of a matter of personal dislike of me by the two staffers than a policy position.

I decided to use the intervening time to strengthen my French given that it could come in handy at the UN. Thus, days were spent walking across the river from Georgetown to Roslyn to attend classes in conversational French. The Foreign Service Institute is top notch for language training, and I felt fortunate that I could join. It was worth the wait, and the learning served me well.

One of the saddest days of my Washington career was to learn from people in the know that individuals I thought of as friends, for example, Zalmay Khalilzad, were actually helping the two staffers in blocking my ambassadorship. The fact that at the same time Khalilzad would call me for information on how the confirmation process was going seemed galling. So it went for a couple of months.

Then one day when I was at the White House for a meeting, the President saw me as he was moving to his motorcade. He stopped and asked how the confirmation was going. I was somewhat surprised as I did not know that he was aware of all the hold-up. I told him the state of play in a shortened version. He was clearly distressed to hear that I was being taunted for my looks and my heritage. We said goodbye with his words "hang in there!" ringing in my ears. At times, I had wondered if all the fuss was worth it but knew that the President himself had wanted me to serve at the UN. A life in public service meant that you do not say "no" to the President when asked to serve. So I was caught in the middle.

The very next day, I received a call from a senior colleague saying that I should know that the full Senate would vote on my ambassadorship that afternoon. Senator Humphrey had removed the hold but had asked that his own staff not be told! Apparently shortly after he saw me, the President spoke to the Secretary of State, James Baker, who spoke to the Senate leader Senator Robert Dole, who asked for the hold to be removed so that the full Senate could vote on my nomination. I was specially asked to keep all this to myself given the rapidly unfolding events.

Two minutes later, Khalilzad called and tried a sympathetic query regarding what was happening to my case. It sounded like a fishing expedition on behalf of all those who tried to block me but found the grounds shifting from right under them. My response was "you would know better than me. I live all the way out in Pennsylvania!"

Thus, the nomination was approved by the full Senate, just as it had been unanimously by the Senate Foreign Relations Committee. I was approved to start my new assignment as Ambassador to the UN for Special Political Affairs. My confirmation by the US Senate had come in early July 1990. I was sworn in by Deputy Secretary of State Larry Eagleburger, who had given me my first break in government, on July 5, 1990. It was extremely gracious of the Deputy Secretary to agree to swear me in. After all, I was a political appointee and Eagleburger was a keen Foreign Service supporter.

Held on the eighth floor of the State Department, the ceremony was elegant. My family was there. Referring to the work on India and Pakistan that I had done for him, Eagleburger who had a reputation of being tough and demanding said in his remarks: "Shirin is one of the best I have ever worked with" something he apparently seldom said of non-foreign service personnel at the State Department and a remark that truly touched me to the core. The swearing in was well attended by former bosses, colleagues, and friends, including General Colin Powell, for whom I had worked at the NSC when he was the National Security Advisor for President Reagan. He was in July 1990 the Chairman of the Joint Chiefs. Typical of Powell, he came, stayed the entire time, and lined up with everyone to say hello in the 8th floor Benjamin Franklin room of the State Department.

Following the swearing in, there was much to attend to now that I was officially in the title. Finally, the movers came to pack my belongings and take them to New York. Once my household effects were packed and shipped, I got a call to await the truck at my new residence in Manhattan, a short walk to the US Mission on First Avenue on August 2, 1990.

The USA has four Ambassadors to the UN. All require confirmation by the Senate. The Permanent Representative of the USA to the UN is the senior most. Tom Pickering was a particularly senior Foreign Service officer with extensive experience. Alex Watson, another career officer, was his immediate deputy. My portfolio was a very interesting mix of Security Council, General Assembly, and Trusteeship Council. I also headed up the US Host Committee, overseeing liaison with all other missions to the UN, then numbering 184.

Tom Pickering told me to join my assignment in August, "A slow month at the UN." I planned to arrive on August 2 in order to get settled into New York before the annual UN General Assembly high-level segment begins in the third week of September. "You are the Ambassador and the wife, so get here in August and settle in" had been Pickering's advice. "Sounds good," was my response.

I took the train from Philadelphia on August 2, 1990. I met a close friend, Pappu Aziz Khan's son, Ali Khan, who was visiting the USA at the empty apartment and we stood looking at the spectacular view of East River and beyond while we drank our coffee and ate bagels ... this was New York after all. Ali said upon his arrival that something big was afoot in the Persian Gulf region. I had been on the move, and there was nothing in the news that gave me a clue. I assured Ali that all was supposed to be calm. However, I called the US Mission and asked to speak to Pickering. I was put through to his office, and his assistant said that the permanent representative was away at a meeting and had left a message for me in case I called asking that I come to the office soonest possible.

The moving van arrived and I asked the movers to just unpack, put the furniture in the right places and leave all boxes unpacked since I had to go to work. They were happy to oblige, saving themselves hours. The box's pretty much stayed unpacked for more than six weeks. So much for a planned smooth settling in period! I was "both the Ambassador and the wife."

CHAPTER 17

The First Gulf War

August 2, 1990, was the day Iraq's Saddam Hussein invaded Kuwait. My life and work as a US Ambassador to the UN changed dramatically from what I had assumed would be one of endless diplomatic receptions and meetings for routine issues. Instead, the three years of my US service in New York was crowded with meaningful work. President Bush '41 had himself served as the US Ambassador to the UN and understood the potential of finding support for US positions from 184 member countries, the 1990 total, in one place and at a common institution. The period after August 2 saw a huge amount of effort by everyone at the US Mission to the UN (USUN). In the period between August 1990 and January 1993, 137 UN Security Council Resolutions (UNSCR) were passed, the majority having to do with threats to international peace and security.

President H. W. Bush's firm determination that Iraq's invasion of Kuwait would not stand meant that an international coalition supporting US policy had to be put in place. While the President and the NSC and the Department of State went into high gear, the task of condemning Iraq's invasion of a smaller neighbor entailed passage of an immediate resolution in the Security Council deploring Iraqi action. The USA rightly wanted unanimous action which meant getting all five permanent members (USA, Soviet Union, France, UK, and China) as well as ten countries elected for a two-year membership (Malaysia, Canada, Finland, Ethiopia, Zaire, Ivory Coast, Yemen, Cuba, Columbia, and Romania) on board.

The diplomatic model adopted required heavy lifting in New York by USUN and in Washington at the White House and the State Department. The President himself was on the phone and in meetings soliciting support for joint action to defeat Iraq's move into Kuwait. Secretary of State James Baker was also a diplomat par excellence who knew the value of diplomacy. Baker came to the UN on several occasions, including for meetings with his Soviet counterpart, Eduard Shevardnadze.

My initial calls on Ambassadors' of other member states became more substantive because of the specific actions the USA was proposing at the UN to censure and defeat Iraq. Tom Pickering was the senior-most Ambassador, referred to as the Permanent Representative, and each of the Ambassadors had a specific list of countries to work with. Each morning began with a small Ambassadors meeting in Pickering's office. Then, we moved to the larger "delegation" meeting comprising heads of various sections, such as Political, Economic, and Host Committee. That session often included innumerable US diplomats who came up from Washington for specific meetings. This was a crucial meeting for senior diplomats to get a sense of the order of the day across the street at the UN headquarters. Pending issues of policy and coordination, always a quagmire given the desire of Washington to control what the US Mission to the UN was doing in New York, were also the subject of the gathering. John Bolton's testy relationship with Tom Pickering quickly became apparent even to those unfamiliar with either one.

Each of the US Ambassadors posted to the US Mission in New York had designated portfolios. In addition, there was a division of countries that each was assigned to coordinate with. The sexy stuff of Security Council's five permanent members (the P-5) was handled by the senior-most diplomat, Tom Pickering, as he was the Permanent Representative. Yet, there was so much work and so many issues to cover, that all four Ambassadors were heavily involved in one aspect or another with the P-5. The Iraqi invasion of Kuwait and the US President's desire to make the UN front and center of the American response meant that diplomacy at the UN went into high gear.

My multifaceted portfolio overlapped with the Security Council and included the Sanctions Committee on Iraq, the Trusteeship Council (the USA was the last remaining trustee with Palau in the South Pacific as the last remaining Trusteeship), The Third Committee of the General Assembly with a host of issues including Human Rights, The Fourth

Committee of the General Assembly, which covered decolonization issues and where the USA had to spend a lot of energy in order to nurture friendships that helped in the overall votes garnered for other American initiatives and priorities. I also served as the head of the Host Country Committee, where many vexing issues from parking violations, VIP arrivals in the USA for the annual September gatherings, visa problems to misbehavior by diplomats, such as harassment of hotel maids by officials (often Arab), came up. The last portfolio was referred to by Raza, my husband, as my being the "policeman for the U.S." If the telephone rang in the early hours, the likely cause was a diplomat being caught up in undiplomatic behavior with all of the attendant complications, including dealing with the Manhattan prosecutors.

The Host Committee portfolio also meant protocol duties, such as receiving the then-Emir of Kuwait who arrived in his personal Boeing 747 at JFK to show the flag as the USA-led effort to throw Saddam Hussein out from Kuwait was shaping up. As the Emir descended the stairs and I was introduced to him, I will never forget the look of utter astonishment on the ruler's face! An American Ambassador with a Muslim name, and a woman to boot, was not what he expected.

These were the lighter moments in my life. Most of the work was utterly serious. The USA worked hard to get every single vote on every one of the UN resolutions, especially those dealing with expelling Iraq from Kuwait as well as others impinging on additional matters of importance to the USA's national interest.

August 2, 1990, the day of the Iraqi invasion of Kuwait, was followed immediately by the UN Security Council adoption of Resolution 660 (1990) the same day condemning the invasion and demanding the immediate and unconditional withdrawal of all of Iraq's forces to positions that they occupied the previous day.

The UN structure for the Security Council, the premiere institution where questions of use of force were debated and authorized, consists of the Permanent Five (P5) USA, Russia (Soviet Union in 1990), the UK, France, and China and the non-permanent members mentioned above. Non-permanent members are elected on the basis of complicated geographical groupings. They matter because in order to pass, each Security Council Resolution (UNSCR) needs nine affirmative votes, including all P5 countries. A negative vote by a P5 member constitutes a "veto," killing the resolution. An abstention, on the other hand, does not but simply allows the resolution to move forward with the abstention recorded.

The US Mission to the UN is an instructed delegation, a forward post of the US foreign policy agenda. We carried out instructions sent from Washington. Given close proximity, there was a constant flow from the headquarters on issues of note. With George H. W. Bush as President, it was well known that the President himself stayed abreast of UN actions on Iraq. He had served as the US Permanent Representative to the UN under Richard Nixon. His network and his memory of global leaders were legend. But even more importantly than his familiarity with the world's leadership and the UN's work, he believed that US-led diplomacy was indispensable and coalition building in support of common goals critical to the conduct of American foreign policy.

As he recalled in his diary after learning that Iraqi Army had gone across the border into Kuwait, Bush '41 asked his National Security Advisor, Brent Scowcroft, to call a meeting of the National Security Council the next morning, August 2, 1990. The President at the same time also called Pickering instructing him to call for an emergency meeting of the UN Security Council. He instinctively reached out to the UN as *the* key Forum in which to seek and gain global support against the Iraqi invasion.[1] The President's declaration that "This will not stand, this aggression against Kuwait" in reference to the invasion made the work of his officials at the US Mission to the UN keenly focused on helping make that declaration a reality.

Coalition diplomacy meant a great deal to the President. As James Baker recalled in his oral history of the times, the President's view was: "I do not want history to judge that I had acted precipitously or impetuously. I want people to see that we've left no stone unturned in search of a peaceful resolution of this, albeit an unconditional withdrawal" from Kuwait.[2] As Baker noted, the President wanted to ensure that the USA worked under UN authority in form of a Security Council Resolution authorizing the use of force. The President wanted that and the State Department legal opinion endorsed the view that UNSCR 687 authorized force if Saddam did not fully and unconditionally withdraw from Kuwait.

From the USUN perspective, building coalitions against the Iraqi occupation of Kuwait in 1990 meant garnering the support of members, in particular, Security Council members of the UN. We understood that some members would be harder to bring on board, mostly because they often held negative perceptions of US policy. Some would be crucial as their representative Ambassadors carried weight of additional votes beyond their own. One such was Ambassador Razali Ismail of Malaysia.

Tom Pickering had many a round with Razali Ismail but found him unconvinced to come along in support of the rapidly multiplying resolutions of the Security Council against Iraq. For example, in the short period between the invasion on August 2, 1990, and November 29, 1990, the Security Council (with US leadership) adopted twelve resolutions dealing with a variety of key issues stemming from the Iraqi invasion of Kuwait. The November 29 adoption of Resolution 678 specified that if, by January 15, 1991, Iraq had not complied with all resolutions adopted subsequent to its invasion of Kuwait, member states of the UN, in concert with the legitimate government of Kuwait, were authorized to use "all necessary means" to compel Iraq to do so in order to restore peace and security in the region.

There was a great deal at stake. Invasion of small countries by more powerful neighbors is a nightmare scenario for many a member state. Unanimous votes meant unity. That required bringing the recalcitrant Razali Ismail, the Malaysian Ambassador on board early after August 2 invasion of Kuwait by Iraq. Probably in frustration after his own attempts and preoccupied with numerous concerns, Pickering decided that he was going to pass on to me the task of engaging with Ambassador Razali on partnering with the USA on votes against Iraq in the Security Council.

Protocol is essential to diplomacy. The initial call on an Ambassador dubbed "a courtesy call" a requirement of making a new acquaintance. One called on the Ambassador at his Mission, his office. Subsequent meetings usually occurred on the margins of scheduled meetings on UN premises.

Keeping such matters in mind, my office made a request for my call, which was quickly set up. I went to the Malaysian mission to the UN and was received and taken to the office of the Ambassador. Razali Ismail was gracious in his welcome and being the suave diplomat that he was which won him strong support among his colleagues from the non-western world, made some comment to the effect: "Always good when the Americans come to see you, unless it's not for good reasons"! I joked back that I was always in the category of "wanting to do good." Coffee was served, and it was time to make my point.

Turning to look directly at the Ambassador, I noted that he was undoubtedly aware of how important it was that the international community receives Malaysian support for the effort to expel Iraq from Kuwait. I noted that while I had just arrived in my position as the newest of the US Ambassadors, I already knew that Razali was considered to be one of those who could bring significant support to a resolution before the UN. I then added that above all this, there was yet another and more significant reason where I needed his support for the US-led effort. "What is that?" he queried. I quickly responded: "No one named Razali could possibly not agree with my request since my husband's name is Razali and you will be setting an awful precedent."

With a loud chuckle, Razali agreed to be supportive. We parted amicably with his saying, "I'm going to ask Ambassador Pickering not to send in his big guns next time." He would on occasion make a big show of groaning on seeing me saying: "Oh no! What now?" But when UNSCR 678 was adopted, Malaysia did not vote against, only Cuba and Yemen did.

Secretary Baker was an active presence in New York for key UN votes. He used UNGA to meet his counterparts, especially Soviet Foreign Minister, Eduard Shevardnadze, whom he met at the US Mission for longer meetings as it was just across the street from the UN. Timelines were drawn to give the Iraqi leader sufficient time to withdraw and prevent forcible expulsion from Kuwait. Offering a deadline some weeks away, as Baker notes: "also helped us get the Soviets on board, it helped us bring other nations into the coalition because it was an imminently reasonable period of time and it helped us particularly with domestic opinion in the United States. Which was at the beginning of all this very, very much opposed to the idea of going to war in the Persian Gulf."[3]

Notes

1. Jon Meacham, *Destiny and Power: The American Odyssey of George Herbert Walker Bush* (New York: Random House, 2015), 423.
2. James Baker, Secretary of State, Oral History, *PBS, Frontline, The Gulf War: An In Depth Analysis of the 1990–1991 Persian Gulf Crisis*, January 9, 1996.
3. Ibid.

CHAPTER 18

The Last Trust Territory: Palau

Even as the Gulf War occupied US diplomacy, I needed to attend to other responsibilities at the United Nations. One of those involved US oversight of the work of the Trusteeship Council of the UN, a body once in great demand as decolonization picked up pace after WW II. In 1990, Palau was the only remaining trust territory, and it was part of the US delegation's charter.

In December 1990, the Security Council considered the status of the Trust Territory of the Pacific Islands and adopted, by 14 votes to 1, resolution 683 (1990). By that resolution, the Council determined the objectives of the Trusteeship Agreement had been fully attained with respect to those three entities and that therefore the applicability of the Trusteeship Agreement to them had been terminated. Palau, therefore, remained the only entity under the 1947 Trusteeship Agreement. The Trusteeship Council at its annual regular sessions continued to review the situation in Palau.

Under the UN Charter, the Trusteeship Council is authorized to examine and discuss reports from the Administering Authority (the USA) on the political, economic, social, and educational advancement of the peoples of Trust Territories and, in consultation with the Administering Authority, to examine petitions from and undertake periodic and other special missions to Trust Territories.

Palau wanted a UN Mission to come to the territory and to petition the membership on the economic and social issues prior to the push for independence. There were commercial interests at play as well. Japan, it was said, was offering the construction of a large jet-capable runway in order to promote direct flights from Tokyo. The fact that some of the world's freshest tuna exists in Palauan waters meant a fast route for trade of the sought after tuna. I was told that France was pushing for a Mission to examine the state of affairs and to investigate complaints of US oversight. The Deputy Permanent Representative of France to the UN was to lead the mission, and as the Ambassador of the US overseeing the trust, I would represent American interest. Jokingly, I noted to the French diplomat that I thought it was a long way to go and why was his country pushing so hard. "Don't worry, it is beautiful with the world's best diving," he responded. "Mr. Ambassador," I replied: "It is a long ride, the U.S. is a responsible Trustee and I carry my tan permanently and do not swim!"

Nonetheless, we set out from New York for the long flights to Honolulu and then Guam. There we would connect to Karor, the capital of Palau. My office made the arrangements and told me the delegation was staying at the one existing hotel there.

The Department of the interior oversaw the administration of Palau for the USA. Its Assistant Secretary for Territorial and International Affairs, Stella Guerra, accompanied me. As the senior officer of the US government overseeing Palau, Stella was known in the region and knew Palau and its grievances and politics in detail. She kept up with the issues and the personnel of the territory as well as who stood to gain the most post-independence from financial deals. I hoped that the long flight would enable me to get to know Stella and learn a lot more than materials my official briefing books offered. I realized it was to be a long week.

Complicated travel rules meant that State Department officials had to travel in economy class on airlines while others did not. My colleague, Stella, was in business class so consultations during flight impossible. "Can do it once in Guam" I thought as we had a brief layover before catching the connecting flight to Karor. However, as the longest ocean flight I had ever been on finally ended with us arriving in Guam, I heard my name being called on the plane's intercom. Resigned, I identified myself to a flight attendant. Given my disembarking from the economy side of the plane, I missed Stella who had left with others passengers exiting from the front of the plane.

The airline staff told me that I was invited to dine with the governor of Guam. And that a car was waiting planeside to take me directly to the dinner. Feeling less than appropriately dressed after the flight from Honolulu, I asked if it was possible to get my luggage which had been stored in an overhead bin. This the staff could do, and I rushed to the front area in order to make myself a bit more presentable before going to the dinner.

The governor, Joseph F. Ada, was extremely hospitable and seemed well versed on the issue of Palau and its desire to terminate its trust status. He offered some helpful advice on Palau which came in handy the following few days. Dinner was announced, and Stella Guerra and I were escorted in by the governor. As we were settling down, fighting sleep and fatigue, I overheard him say to Stella, "You know our tradition, after dinner there is dancing and singing. As honored guests, you and the ambassador need to lead." I quickly responded, "given her long experience in the region, I know Assistant Secretary Guerra will do a great job at singing and dancing"! And, so she did. As we parted, Governor Ada said: "my staff and I are impressed that the U.S. officials in charge of the tricky negotiations are both women. One is Hispanic, the other a Muslim from India/Pakistan." I smiled and said that we represented the melting pot that is the strength of the USA.

Karor sits in a breathtakingly beautiful setting. As the plane descended, I could not help but glue my gaze to the approaching scenery. Tiny islands in tranquil turquoise sea and waters so clear and calm that one could literally see the bottom of the ocean. My guidebook noted that this is one of the few surviving habitats for endangered sea tortoises, and the purchase or export of any items made with their shells was strictly forbidden. Stella asked if I went diving as she had never seen such an underwater scene as in Palauan waters. "Alas! I am from South Asia so swimming came late to me and that too just in order to graduate from U.S. College." She sympathized with my predicament but was happy I would get to work even during the few hours off we had when she would certainly go diving.

We went quickly to meet up with the President of Palau Ngiratkel Etpison and the Vice President Sandra Pierantozzi. We asked for, and they agreed to time together before we met the next couple of days with the rest of the UN delegation. Both officials were cordial but tough in what they felt needed doing. They took us out on one of the flatboats present to see a group of nearby islands. The boat was slow and thumped along the shallow waters. The discomfort of the choppy journey was mitigated by the spectacular scenery. We circled many a small island while the officials talked of their plans for development. "What sort of development," I asked, aware of the Japanese offer to build an airstrip over the coral reef. At this, both Palauans offered the need for tourism and noted that their request for development often got turned down by the US Department of the Interior officials. The fact that the destruction of amazing coral reefs in order to build a runway or hotel over them could in the end kill the goose that lays the golden egg analogy was not particularly appreciated. We traveled along islands, and suddenly President Etpison said "ambassador, I want to honor you with the gift of this small island." Taken aback, I quickly responded that I was grateful and honored by his gesture, but I could not accept because of my strict adherence to US government gift rules that prohibited anything above a small amount, just over $100! "Well, then I shall simply name it Shirin island" he responded, and I never asked if that really happened.

The delegation worked in a series of hearings whereby the Mission determined the quality of US actions as a Trustee. The choppy rides through clear waters had the thrill of occasional spotting of large sea turtles. We maneuvered through dozens of tiny and larger islands to meet with civic and political leaders to discuss how the USA administered the trust territory. Grievances were voiced with delays in decisions on economic issues such as the building of a huge runway on coral reefs. Educational matters were highlighted.

Palau and its surroundings saw a great deal of action in the Pacific during WW II. We visited cemeteries and paused to consider the impact of war in its brutality. I had never expected to be a visitor to those shores so took the opportunity to engage with Palauans on the subject. The Vice President, Sandra Pierantozzi, was a dynamic interlocutor. She explained the history of the islands, and why it made sense to end the trust territory status of her country. Stella Guerra and I refereed the discussions with the Mission members. The French, with a history of involvement in Polynesia, were particularly interested. As the visit came to a close, all felt that the distance traveled was worth the engagement on the ground. The report to the Trusteeship Council of the UN would be substantive and fact based. Thereafter, in November 1993, the island in the Pacific, Palau, successfully passed a referendum for a compact of Free Association with the USA. The last trust territory thus became independent upon ratification of the compact on October 1, 1994.

CHAPTER 19

The Muslim Ambassador from the USA

The "Ambassador from Where" aspect of my tenure as US Ambassador to the UN from 1990 to 1993 was a unique moment for me. The feeling was made all the more striking because of the response I received from other delegations. The presence of a Muslim female Ambassador of the USA to the UN was a new experience for colleagues. Mostly they reacted positively. Sometimes, I simply startled a few! Early on in my tenure, I recall being in the US seat in the General Assembly Third Committee getting ready to give the US statement on Human Rights. There was a buzz around the room as the Permanent Representative of Cuba, Ambassador Ricardo Alarcon, entered. I did not know the Ambassador as the USA had no diplomatic ties with Cuba and we generally ignored the Cuban delegation. Alarcon was a popular representative, having already then served at the UN for his country for over two decades. A junior colleague explained quickly to me who he was.

I gave my remarks and at some point so did the Cuban diplomat. We were considering issues of Human Rights, and the Cuban record on the issue was a poor one, even if its diplomacy was smooth. As the meeting adjourned, the Cuban Ambassador came up to me, introduced himself, and added: "You made me change my remarks today." "How is that?" I asked. "Well, I was going to open with a scathing attack on U.S. colonialism and white domination. Then I realized that you were in the chair and certainly did not look the part so I made a change." As I left, I mentioned that the USA is full of good surprises and it is good to keep others on their toes. The Cuban delegation worked hard to garner support against US positions at the UN. The US delegation countered by befriending many of the same colleagues and peeling them off in support of important US resolutions across the multiple parts of the UN in New York and elsewhere.

Sometime around the third week of September each year, the UN General Assembly holds what is termed its general debate for two weeks. During this time, heads of state, governments, or foreign ministers come to New York and address the full General Assembly. As host country, the US Mission was particularly frantic. We had issues relating to visas of visitors not normally welcomes to these shores but who would demand and have to be granted a visa, even with a geographical restriction in movement, for the period. We also had the multiple requests that came from Washington for legions of officials descending given the short hop to New York. Then, there were complicated logistics with diplomatic protection of foreign heads of state. And, of course, there was the perennial issue of gridlock in mid-Manhattan as various motorcades buzzed about.

There was also the detailed planning effort required for a visit of the US President who came on opening day, gave the US statement, met with several counterparts, attended the lunch hosted by the Secretary General of the UN, and hosted a sought after well-attended evening reception. The 1990 meetings were taking place in the shadow of the Iraqi invasion. The 41st President cognizant of all the sidebar work that accompanied the social hoop-la understood the UN venue as a valuable Forum for his leadership.

Quite apart from the official requirements to get ready for the presidential visit and the accompanying opening of the general debate, I was personally excited to be seeing the President again and in a milieu where he felt that I would well represent the USA.

September 18, 1990, brought President George H. W. Bush to the UN. The arrival took place early morning as the USA is the second speaker (after Brazil) on the first day. While the UN session started at 10:30 in the morning, all delegations needed to be in place much earlier. Seating is alphabetical with a randomly pulled country name which gets the first set of seats, followed alphabetically from there. For example, if Ecuador was picked, then following would be Egypt, El Salvador, etc. At times, the USA has been in the front part of the General Assembly hall. Other times, it is way in the back. Nonetheless, regardless of where the US delegation sits, there is always activity nearby. While leaders and diplomats gather and give formal statements, some of the most important work and conversations take place on the sidelines. The US President usually returns to the White House the following day. The US Secretary of State stays longer for a series of meetings since everyone is gathered in one city.

Opening day for the US Mission is fully choreographed prior to the arrival of the President. Each minute is accounted for, and the influx of officials from Washington puts a squeeze on personnel. It is always in my experience an exciting day. It is where we show the world the American foreign policy top brass. Given 1990 was the full effort to expel Iraq from Kuwait peacefully, if possible, we were especially busy given the President and Secretary of State's presence.

The President always meets with officers and staff of the US Mission. This "meet and greet" is an informal affair to hear from the boss and for him to say thanks to those he knew kept long hours during his visit and beyond. Because he himself had served as US Permanent Representative to the UN, Bush '41 understood the requirement for officials in New York. He was thus especially engaged in his interactions with the Mission staff. All of his ambassadors to the UN were also present.

As he spotted me, the President called me over. After exchanging greetings, he leaned over and said in quiet tones: "Wasn't I right, Shirin? Isn't the UN the best job?" Recognizing that this was more of a statement than a question, I happily chimed in with: "Yes, Mr. President, it is the best job." I did not add that my earlier worries stemmed from a perception of unfocused socializing for votes. But that having arrived as Iraq invaded Kuwait, the work of the USA in New York to garner support for the US position had become as critical as the work that I had done at the White House National Security Council in prior years 1984–1990. This ritual affirmation took place at each UNGA during the Bush '41 presidency with the President asking me to confirm my views each year. I looked forward to this connection.

Multiple UN Security Council resolutions on Iraq noted continued occupation and calibrated penalties. One of the most important even before use of force was the establishment of a Sanctions Committee under resolution 661, which acknowledged Kuwait's right of self-defense and mandated compulsory international sanctions against Iraq. UNSCR 661 was a complicated resolution as it required the setting up of a mechanism through which the international community would monitor implementation of the ban against buying from Iraq or Kuwait all products and commodities, especially oil. Iraq was precluded from transfers of funds. Only medical or humanitarian goods, including food, were exempt.

The "Sanctions Committee" as it was called was set up and consisted of representatives at the ambassadorial level of all members of the Security Council at the time. The committee operated by consensus so each item on the agenda, from blocking financial transactions or trade to allowing food and medicines, was a lengthy affair. I was asked to serve as the US Ambassador to the committee and, accompanied by the legal advisor of the US Mission, spent endless hours arguing the US/international case. This was the era before the ubiquitous cell phone, enabling an instantaneous link with the Department of State. Only Pickering had a large cell phone into which he incessantly spoke as he crossed First Avenue from the American Mission to the UN across the street.

As an instructed delegation, USUN is required to pass back controversial issues to Washington for consideration and ask for an adjournment in proceedings of UN committees if issues got tricky. Given that Cuba and Yemen were prone to challenge most US positions, debate was lively. These were serious deliberations. We were dealing with the lives of people under threat from the invasion and Iraqi civilians. When there were no precedents, international law got made so one had to be careful. We also understood that the Iraqi regime would not be the one to suffer deprivation. Balancing needs of the people against the proclivity of Saddam Hussein's regime to garner maximum benefit was an extremely difficult task.

The larger agenda of the UN kept going at the same time that the resolutions against Iraq were growing. But the August 1990 to January 1991 time frame was almost all consumed by attempts to get a peaceful resolution of the crisis, i.e., Iraqi full withdrawal from Kuwait. At the same time, getting the world's representatives focused on "use of force" to expel Saddam Hussein if diplomacy failed meant mustering support from allies, doubters, and antagonist nations to the best of our ability. This was also the time of "eating for Democracy" as Pickering called it when I complained of the constant requirement of meeting with colleagues over a meal to press the US case for a positive vote. All manner of arguments were employed including the key ones that aggression by a larger country against a smaller neighbor is still aggression and Saddam Hussein wants control over the oil resources of Kuwait and other neighboring countries.

The deadline for Iraqi compliance with UNSCRs expired on January 15, 1991. The next day, January 16, the US-led air campaign began followed by ground action by the coalition on February 24, 1991. Ground action was terminated on February 28, 1991, following the liberation of Kuwait and the defeat of Iraqi forces following withdrawal from all Kuwait territory. The exhaustive diplomacy preceding and following military action in Kuwait paused only briefly to celebrate victory. The corridors of the UN are always full of diplomats. Most of the topics under discussion are contentious. There is seldom a pause for celebration. Yet, there was a general sigh of relief when UNSCR 687 of 1991 set a comprehensive plan for a formal ceasefire in Kuwait and established mechanisms for verification and follow-up. Iraqi diplomats finally passed on Saddam's acquiescence in the loss and the formal ceasefire ensued.

Residual and new issues constantly kept us all busy. UNSCR 689 of 1991 established a demilitarized zone between Iraq and Kuwait, which was to become the venue for the UN Iraq-Kuwait Observer Mission (UNIKOM). Because it was established under Chapter 7 of the UN Charter which applies to "use force" measures, UNIKOM had the responsibility to monitor violations of the agreement for further action. Given the devastation inside Kuwait and oil field fires deliberately set by a retreating Iraqi Army, there was a general consensus against Iraq which helped us garner votes for US positions with UN member states. Apart from a full agenda of work, we had to deal with related issues, such as potential threats against US personnel, especially ambassadors. We took some precautions but went about our business as required.

As I represented the USA on the Iraq Sanctions Committee, I recalled my earlier worry that after six years in very active NSC portfolios at the White House, a UN ambassadorship would be a walk in the park! That was far from the reality of my work weeks in New York. The push for US diplomacy in which I was heavily involved made my transition from "ambassador from where?" to a known US Ambassador a reality.

It was during the work of the Sanctions Committee that I personally observed a change in the behavior of the then "Soviet" delegation. The committee worked by consensus so we needed Soviet delegations concurrence on procedures and items cleared for import/export involving the Iraqi regime. I had come to my assignment as ambassador from the White House after Soviet Union leader Mikhail Gorbachev signed the Geneva Agreement in 1987 to withdraw all Soviet troops from Afghanistan. There was growing talk of the problems besetting

Gorbachev. Soviet troop withdrawal and his pledge for more openness with the USA during his historic summit with President Ronald Reagan at the White House on December 8, 1987, was indeed a historic watershed in East–West relations. Even we jaded NSC staffers lined up to witness that visit.

However, it meant that, in the words of James Baker: "Gorbachev was at the time becoming weaker and weaker." His country had not vetoed UN resolutions against Iraq and his detractors pressed for him to act against a US-led coalition war in expelling the Soviet client state, Iraq, from Kuwait. While he did not manage to shake Bush's resolve, it made for incredible theater in New York as various times the Soviet delegation scrambled to hold its leadership position, including in the Sanctions Committee on which I represented the USA.

On a clear morning in early June 1991, I attended the Sanctions Committee meeting along with a colleague from the legal advisor's office. At issue was the approval of the dispatch of food and medicines to Iraq. All shipments to sanctioned Iraq had to get the approval of the committee. The discussion was quite charged as there were reports of the Iraqi regime siphoning off food and medicine for the use of its armed forces and elites. Somewhere in the middle of the meeting, a junior member of the Soviet delegation came to speak to my colleague asking if I could step out for a meeting with the Soviet Mission to the UN Deputy. I went out to meet an agitated official who said he had instructions to tell me that his team would agree with the USA on the issues being debated inside the committee room. The surprise must have shown on my face as the deputy asserted that he had the authority of his boss, Ambassador Yuli Vorontsov, in making the statement. At the end of the consultations, I returned to my office looking for Tom Pickering the US permanent Ambassador who was away at a meeting. I then made calls to State Department and White House colleagues to alert them to the information I was given. "Go about as usual" was the response to my query regarding "what do we do now?"

CHAPTER 20

"Name and Shame"

Work to strengthen human rights and condemn systematic and severe violations of the same receives a great deal of time and effort by the USA and others. These constitute the generally termed "name and shame" resolutions. Work occurs mostly in the General Assembly's Third Committee, the Commission in Geneva, the UN High Commissioner for Human Rights, and Special Rapporteurs. The UN system focuses on these issues most comprehensively during the annual meeting of the Human Rights Commission[1] that meets generally in March in Geneva. The 53-member body consists of elected members representing a wide variety of influential states, some of whom are habitually named violators of human rights.

In March 1992, I went to Geneva as the US New York-based Ambassador to the Third Committee as part of the US delegation to the Commission headed that year by Ken Blackwell.[2] The US agenda required identifying and condemning violations of human rights by several countries but especially Cuba. Given that Cuban diplomats were personally popular and were seasoned at their jobs, the US delegation worked hard to get sufficient votes to pass a resolution condemning Cuba. In return, Cuba led the effort to condemn the US-led sanctions on the country. While the USA garnered sufficient votes against Cuba's human rights record, it generally took a great deal of heavy lifting by senior members of the delegation.

The other resolution that got a great deal of press and required US engagement was the issue of Palestinian rights in Israel and occupied territories. Given the close nature of the US–Israeli relationship, the delegation worked closely with allies to stem the tide against Israel, which was singularly unpopular in Geneva.

When President George H. W. Bush came to the UN in September 1991, he called for the repeal of the General Assembly resolution passed in 1975 which noted that: "Zionism is a form of racism and racial discrimination." At that time, Arab states and Muslim nations working closely with the Soviet Union had succeeded in passage of the resolution. The diplomatic muscle the USA put behind the repeal around the world and in New York finally led to 111 nations voting with the USA for repeal on December 16, 1991. This count was some 11 votes higher than the best US Mission estimate count. Some twenty-five mostly Muslim states along with a few from the Communist bloc voted against. Thirteen states abstained, and seventeen others, including Egypt, Kuwait, and China, did not take part in the deliberations.

The resolution repealing the earlier one simply declared that the Assembly "decides to revoke the determination contained in the resolution 3379 of 10 November 1975." The vote was by roll call and the US delegation, led by Deputy Secretary of State Lawrence S. Eagleburger felt the tension build as the votes were lit one by one as they were cast on the huge vote count board in the General Assembly. All of us in the US delegation, particularly the ambassadors and the political officers, circulated through the chamber to shore up the promised vote in favor of the repeal. We were particularly proud that 85 countries had co-sponsored the repeal resolution giving them a special stake along with the USA in its passage. India was one of those which changed its vote from supporting the 1975 resolution to supporting its repeal in 1991. I had personally worked hard on that one and was pleased. Eagleburger in his statement on the vote noted that repeal could "only help and not hinder efforts currently underway to bring peace to the region,"[3] a hope yet to be realized.

1991 was a promising year for US diplomacy. Action against Iraq in Kuwait had succeeded and US leadership in a post-communist world seemed secure. As the President noted in his address to the nation in January 1991, the world was witnessing the birth of a "New World Order" which involved collective security with multinational cooperation. The expulsion of Iraq from Kuwait and the end of the Cold War offered an opportunity "for us and future generations a world order where the rule of law, and not the law of the jungle, governs the conduct of nations."[4] Critics argued that the USA was fast taking on the role of international policeman. Others complained that without the Cold War, there would not be sufficient justification for US involvement unless the national interest was clearly involved. But 1991 offered myriad opportunities for US leadership in multilateral diplomacy. This was to be the "era in which nations of the world, East and West, North and South, can prosper and live in harmony."[5]

Each year, the US President appointed two or three "public delegates" to the particular session of the General Assembly as part of the delegation accredited to the UN. One year's highlight for me was working with megastar Gloria Estefan, who was an amazing colleague. She wished to work in the Third Committee dealing with Human Rights, and that was part of my portfolio. Gloria worked tirelessly in lobbying for US position both in the committee and in the General Assembly. She stood in line for hours when USUN hosted receptions for other delegates. She signed hundreds of autographs from delegates without complaining. She was so low key that there were times that it was simply her personal security detail that reminded me that a star worked alongside me. Our sons were roughly the same age, and we became friends and remain in touch.

Beyond the issues of the day, there were two others that took up a deal of time and effort. One was the Fourth Committee of the General Assembly, the Decolonization Committee, which in decades past led the charge in promoting independence from colonial rule. While member states acknowledged that there was little colonialism to sling at the USA, they pressed issues of Puerto Rico and its seeming desire for independence. The committee required constant tending to and given that it was part of my portfolio, I oversaw US interest in keeping the hostility down. One of the reasons was that alliances made in the course of the work of the Fourth Committee came in handy when support was needed for US interests across the board. For the same reason, countries with opposing views, such as Cuba, also worked hard to drum up support for anti-US positions.

Tradition and protocol required the hosting of receptions by respective US Ambassadors charged with oversight for delegates to each General Assembly committee. These receptions were held on the eighth floor of the US Mission building with its panoramic view of the UN and East River. My turn came for the Decolonization Committee. Erin Walsh was the protocol officer with many ideas and great energy. I sat down with her to see if we could do something a little different from the typical receiving line and the usual refreshments. Because I had spent time cultivating the ambassadors, we expected that attendance would be large despite the unpopularity of US positions within the committee. As I lined up with key members of my team to receive guests, Erin came by and said all was in place and it should be a success. My colleague leaned across and asked "what was that about?" I answered: "you will see." The flowers and food were elegant, and the theme was Asian Fusion. I noted to my guests that given the huge mix of peoples in what is the USA, we were celebrating one part of our heritage. There was a great deal of buzz with much conversation and a large crowd. As I greeted each of the over two hundred guests, I specifically asked that they not forget to pick up a fortune cookie from the very large glass bowl near the exit door.

As the reception wound down and guests moved to leave, I heard a loud laugh from the general direction of the exiting crowd and Erin and I looked at each other with a smile. Clearly, a fortune cookie had been cracked open and the fortune read. And the message was clear: "You will vote for all U.S. Resolutions in the Fourth Committee," said the fortune and indeed every fortune in the bowl! We collected on that admonition handsomely.

Some thirty-one years prior to my arrival as a US Ambassador to the UN in 1990, I had landed at Idlewild airport in New York. My American journey began in New York, and I always wanted to return. Coming back as a presidential appointee to serve as an Ambassador of the USA was a singular honor. It was a time rich in diplomacy and representation. The US Mission is the outpost of diplomacy but based in New York.

The job required making friends and influencing people. We took the task seriously. As the only woman Ambassador of the USA at the time, I decided to go about the job differently. First, I made it my business to seek out the other women ambassadors serving as heads of mission for their respective countries. We created a "Women's Network" where we cooperated on issues and got votes for each other if the goals were shared, which often was the case. There were only about seven women besides me at the ambassadorial level. These were from Canada,[6] Finland, Liechtenstein, Barbados, Jamaica, and Trinidad and Tobago. On occasion, we inducted male ambassadors, for example, Jan Eliasson of Sweden[7] or Amr Moussa of Egypt[8] into our ranks when key issues were under consideration.

Second, being the wife and Ambassador and without the official residence and staff that Pickering had, I decided I would do my "representational" work by hosting small dinners at my apartment and personally cooking for colleagues from other countries. While that meant doing prep work late into the previous night and cleaning up late into the dinner night, I was able to build a set of relationships with key ambassadors who helped me garner votes for the USA. My husband, Raza, is a wine connoisseur. He would contribute good wines to serve at these small dinners even as he joked that his salary as professor and Chairman of the physics department at Temple University could not sustain his contribution beyond my limited term as US Ambassador!

Friendships have been very much a part of my life. Raza and I had come to the USA right after we married. While I had studied in the USA for my B.A., my married life began in Philadelphia where Raza was a postdoctoral member at the Department of Physics at the University of Pennsylvania. We became close friends with a group there. While we subsequently scattered, we remained in close contact. One fall when Ruth Heeger, whose husband Alan is a Nobel Laureate in Chemistry, was visiting me in New York, we thought it was time to start a New Year's Eve gathering with the first one scheduled for New York City in 1992. We continue the tradition meeting in different cities with this extraordinary group. One time when I was boasting to a New Yorker that the group of four couples had two Noble Prize winners, my friend asked, in typical New York fashion without missing a beat: "What is wrong with the others?"

We went to the Rainbow Room for dinner and dancing, to the UN for lunch and to the Museum of Modern art for a special exhibit of Matisse. There was much laughter and catching up, and it reminded me how much these friends mattered to our assimilation and life in the USA.

NOTES

1. Renamed The Human Rights Council with 47 members in the UN Reform process of 2006.
2. Who later served as Secretary of State of Ohio.
3. Paul Lewis, "U.N. Repeals Its '75 Resolution Equating Zionism With Racism," *New York Times*, December 17, 1991.

4. President George H. W. Bush, "The New World Order," address before a joint session of Congress, September 11, 1990.
5. Ibid.
6. Ambassador Louise Ferchette of Canada went on to become the Defense Minister of Canada and then Deputy Secretary General of the UN.
7. Eliasson served as Deputy Secretary General of the UN.
8. Moussa went on to serve as Foreign Minister of Egypt.

CHAPTER 21

Return to the University

I had started my academic career in 1973 as a professor of Political Science. One of my favorite courses to teach was the American Political System. It was an introductory course and always well subscribed. I not only taught its details but also offered a comparative framework against which one could measure the specific achievements of the American Constitution and the system of government. By 1992, I had been privileged to have witnessed the 1984 and 1988 elections from my perch within the White House at the NSC. I had watched Presidents Reagan and Bush, respectively, campaign for office and prevail in victory. Though I could not participate in election-related activities, as a White House staff member is precluded from such under the US federal law of 1939 known as the Hatch Act, which prohibits employees in the executive branch of the federal government, except the President, the Vice President, and certain other designated high-level officials of the branch, from engaging in political activity.

So while one was caught up watching the swirl of presidential elections and the comings and goings of the President and Vice President to events, one had to be particularly careful to stay well away from anything deemed *political*. My work at the NSC involved not domestic politics but foreign policy so the work part was easy. Because the NSC of the 1980s and 1990s was tiny compared to its size today, the pace was frantic and not much time was left to dabble in political activity in any case. Late at night though, as I would surface from my office in the Old Executive Office Building to go home or to walk across the drive to the West Wing of the White House, I would catch my breath at the lit monuments, including my place of work and note that I worked in a very special place!

The 1992 election was different in that I was no longer inside the White House but serving at the US Mission to the UN in New York. But it was nonetheless personal. I knew the President, and he had been proud to send me as his Ambassador to the UN. Given years of work and travel with him even when he had been Vice President made him a familiar leader, one I respected very highly. I had witnessed his diplomatic outreach, be in small meetings with world leaders half a world away such as with President Saleh in Yemen, or in the corridors of the UN where he seemed to know everyone.

As an American who believes that diplomacy strengthens USA standing for the greater good and is vital to US national security interest, I saw President H. W. Bush reflect the best of leadership. My ambassadorship was a presidential appointment meaning that once confirmed by the US Senate, I served at the pleasure of the President. A change in administrations meant the end of my assignment. I drafted up a letter which reflected tradition and stated how honored I had been to serve and to represent the USA at the UN. As protocol required, I tended my resignation and sent the letter to Presidential Personnel after the Republican loss of the White House in the 1992 election.

As I prepared to leave New York for home in Philadelphia in January 1993, I pondered my years in public service. I had been brought up with the notion of service. Thus, I had joined academia and transitioned to the State Department and then the National Security Council, eventually resigning my tenure at the university in order to continue to serve at the NSC in 1986. During my New York tenure, I had served on the Commission on Public Service appointed by the President.

Earlier, I taught about American government and had ended up being part of the same. I remembered that when I became a US citizen in 1971 I had decided to hold only that citizenship and eschew dual nationality status. I wanted to make my commitment total, and becoming a member of a political party was an important part of the commitment.

I studied the respective platforms of both the Democratic and Republican parties of the time. Given then upcoming 1972 elections, platforms were updated. I found greater empathy with the Republican Party. The platform on foreign policy particularly caught my attention.

21 RETURN TO THE UNIVERSITY 159

The Vietnam era was still with us, and the reaction to the costly engagement and war had left a sense of exhaustion. I was a student during the 1960s and witnessed the rising movement on campuses and elsewhere against the war. The first term of Republican Richard Nixon had ended the Vietnam War but not the deep desire for isolation that lurked just below the surface. I was not yet a citizen and thus could not vote.

When I got the vote, I took it very seriously. 1972 was my first vote ever, and I wanted to understand what that meant. The Republican Party platform noted that: "The nation's frustrations had fostered a dangerous spirit of isolationism" lamenting the loss of American influence around the world. Taking credit for restoring alliances, the platform argued that the Nixon visit to China in 1972 made the world a safer place. The Nixon Doctrine promised US engagement with the world in an era of peace through strength. The party talked of strengthening relationships with allies and extending the "realm of cooperation." There was talk of responsible balanced reduction in military forces in Europe and support for returning soldiers from Vietnam who had offered their life for the country.

I liked what I read about support for a non-discriminatory immigration policy even while looking to halt the entry of illegal entrants. The role of foreign assistance was recognized, and the hope of making that more effective made sense. All in all, it was the America I had chosen as my country where opportunity lay open and rule of law was important and constitutionally guaranteed. I proudly became Republican.

On January 17, 1993, after the movers had already packed the apartment that had been home for three years in New York, I retrieved my car from the UN garage where it was parked and headed through the streets of the city toward home in Pennsylvania. I recall the snowflakes on the windshield which wove a curtain of magic around midtown Manhattan. It softened the noise of this boisterous city. For a moment, I wondered if I had done the right thing in not accepting some of the wonderful offers in the private sector which seemed to be percolating up as my government service ended. My world was one of public service. I felt that while I had been a good diplomat and representative of the USA pushing for votes that mattered to US policy and asking for support in the national interest, I could not in good conscience do the same for any corporation's bottom line. After my eleven years in key positions in government, I had a wonderfully connected global rolodex.

Companies would want to use that access for their profit. That was difficult to accept.

So I deliberately turned away from a lucrative post-ambassadorial career at a time when I knew that to be an American female Muslim Ambassador was unique. Instead, I chose my familiar world of academia. Princeton University was a welcoming place, and I was keen to pen the story of US opening to India and policy toward Pakistan during the Reagan administration. I had been directly involved in this effort for over six years and felt it important enough to resign my university tenure and stay in government in Washington. President Reagan and Vice President Bush had been involved in the subcontinent's affairs and had pushed for peace between them. The confidence-building measures (CBMs) that they espoused were carefully tended and remain to date the only ones adopted by India and Pakistan, respectively, for peace between them.

My perch at Princeton was the Center of International Studies at the Woodrow Wilson School. It was a wonderful place in which to work, learn, and interact with students and faculty. The undergraduate education was paramount there very much like the experiences that my husband Raza and much later daughter Shehra had in their years of study, respectively, at Oriel College and Magdalen College at Oxford University.

Much went on at Princeton University in terms of interesting lectures, seminars, student events, and involvement to keep one busy. The spring term is particularly an active period. The campus is beautiful, and the nearly overnight transformation of the gardens at the faculty club with tulips and daffodils in springtime made for distractions that even years of working in proximity of the Rose Garden at the White House did not. The reason was simple. Finally, I felt that my time was essentially my own. My schedule was not made up for endless meetings and briefings either in terms of the ambassadorship to the UN or the interagency process of consensus building that was such a key to my work for the White House in national security. At Princeton, I was responsible to myself in the task of writing on the US attempt to forge a relationship with India and to help build a better peace between India and Pakistan.

The head of the center, John Waterbury, was a supportive colleague. A scholar of the Middle East, John had early in my tenure at Princeton voiced the hope that in the course of my travels to India and Pakistan I could urge then Prime Minister Benazir Bhutto to come and address the Princeton student body. When I passed the invitation to the Prime Minister during a meeting with her in Islamabad, she said she would honor the invitation, which she did in April 1995 during an official visit to the USA.

Princeton was an ideal institution at which to get down to the hard task of writing. Having spent the 1982–1993 period mastering the art of the one-page memo for the President, I realized that a longer tome on US policy required major readjustment. Fortunately, I had the offer from Ambassador Richard Murphy who held a prestigious chair at the Council on Foreign Relations and with whom I had done a great deal of work in government to co-chair a study group on US policy toward India and Pakistan in the Regan years. This we hoped could become the basis of a manuscript for publication by the Council.

The premise for the study and the subsequent publication was that US relations with India and Pakistan, respectively, had been addressed by a plethora of writers, yet a systematic attempt to trace the interplay between Washington, New Delhi, and Islamabad was needed. What had transpired at the highest levels of the US government in the 1982–1990 years and how had it changed the equation with the subcontinent? Faced with continued Soviet occupation of Afghanistan, how had the Reagan administration dealt with the ongoing animosity between India and Pakistan? How was it possible to alter perceptions of leaders of these two key states and influence them toward an era of building confidence and subsequent peace? These questions informed my 1997 book, *India, Pakistan and the United States: Breaking with the Past*, published by the Council on Foreign Relations. It stemmed from my own work during the Reagan and Bush administrations, and my ongoing research on the possibilities opened by the end of the Cold War for economic opportunities in South Asia and negotiating the difficult issues of Kashmir and nuclear weapons.

CHAPTER 22

The BALUSA Group

The lesson I carried away from my 1982–1993 tenure at the White House and the Department of State was that relationships between nations are not set in stone. The collapse of the Soviet Union meant the end of the Cold War. It opened up the world to new possibilities in political openness and commerce. International boundaries became fluid. The mid-1990s saw the opening chapters of global inter-connectivity. Old enmities could be overcome with new prosperity taking its place.

The Indo-Pak partition legacy of bitterness that led to two major wars did nothing to bring India and Pakistan into a better place. Given the talent of its people, the cultural heritage and many shared experiences might help mitigate the bitterness of religious difference that partitioned the subcontinent in 1947.

Normalization of relations was possible. I saw firsthand the dialogue US Presidents had with Indian and Pakistani leaders, respectively, on the need for a rapprochement. My contacts in both India and Pakistan before and during my White House years gave me a possible list of key individuals who would be willing to use their clout to knock down prejudice and provide for a collaborative platform for economic and political normalization. "What harm would it do to try?" I asked myself. After all other avenues for better relations had failed. At least my efforts would not start a war. I was set.

My academic work required regular travel to India and Pakistan where I focused on starting a Track II, later named BALUSA. Such Track II diplomacy involves meetings that bring together individuals from various professional backgrounds: politicians, retired diplomats, defense personnel, retired intelligence officials as well as academics to explore ways of cooperation and understanding. It differs from Track I diplomacy in that Track II relies on non-governmental and informal contacts in contrast to Track I which features formal diplomacy conducted by government representatives and state officials. Some underlying rules would need to be agreed upon: First, the Track II I launched had to be small with five to six people from India and Pakistan, respectively. Second, the effort required the blessing of the top leadership in each country so that petty issues such as visas did not deter the work and there was an openly acknowledged process. Third, among the small list of potential members, bipartisanship with the political members representing each of the major political parties in India and Pakistan, respectively, was critical. That would help continue the effort beyond the elections and changing fortunes on each side. Fourth, some representation from each side's military would be needed within the group. Fifth, the effort would begin with potential points of convergence, economic progress through collaborative projects on energy, infrastructure, joint investments in the border areas, a joint natural gas pipeline, greater travel, and people-to-people contacts. Divisive issues, such as Kashmir, would be put to the side for future attention in a better climate.

At the outset, I embarked on exhaustive consultations in Delhi and Islamabad on who might join in the effort and what agenda made sense. I found agreement on the need for such an undertaking and a great deal of encouragement for me to spearhead it. "You have credibility," I was told by each side, coming off as I had the exhaustive work on the subject in the Reagan NSC. Wariness of American involvement was not made an issue, presumably given my Indo-Pak roots. I noted that in the effort to move in key new areas such as energy, BALUSA needed Toufiq Siddiqi, a leading expert and subsequent contributor to the Nobel Prize in 2007 awarded for climate change. Based at the East-West Center in Honolulu, Toufiq was well known in the energy and environment field. Many of the participants knew him from his ongoing research collaboration in India and Pakistan. Given that issues relating to energy would figure prominently in the effort, he agreed to join the group, the only other American besides myself.

Nomenclature is important to a Track II effort. I shared various thoughts on this with participants. Finally, the name BALUSA made sense because it was easy and it was mysterious with different interpretations of its meaning. The hard work of pulling the group together and raising funds for the work began in 1995. Trying to build a shared agenda on some key issues was a new concept. As I embarked on rounds with potential funding institutions of note, I found a mostly supportive group who understood the value of the project and that I had the background plus work at the NSC White House along with requisite contacts.

My effort was serious, and I pledged the bulk of my post-government time to it. Resources were needed to underwrite even the minimal travel and housing costs of participants, especially as in the first years I knew the meetings would have to be held outside the subcontinent in appropriate locations.

Institutional support plus housing the effort led me to another in a series of weekly conversations with my friend Harvey Sicherman. Harvey had taught me what I knew about the Middle East in all its complicated machinations. He understood the India–Pakistan tortured history and the need to try for change. Harvey was at the State Department when I started there and knew of my CBM efforts. "Go for it" he encouraged. As President of the Philadelphia-based Foreign Policy Research Institute, he offered to host institutional support for BALUSA.

The very first meeting sponsored by the Rockefeller Foundation was held at its beautiful facility Villa Serbelloni on Lake Como in northern Italy on June 19–23, 1996. A perfect conference center, the villa provided for maximum interaction in an informal setting. The summer long resident writer's program offered some twenty other participants in a variety of fields also present at the villa. Thus, shared formal evening meals meant that BALUSA members did not feel hemmed in by these unusual first contacts with the other side. There were many conversations every evening we were there.

The list of institutions that underwrote the work of BALUSA in the 1996–2002 years is an impressive one including: The Carnegie Corporation of New York, which supported its first ever Track II for India–Pakistan with a major grant for Toufiq and myself on Water Issues in South Asia; The Rockefeller Foundation; The W. Alton Jones foundation; The United Nations Development Programme; Stockholm Environment Institute; and The Starr Foundation. Princeton University and the Cooperative Monitoring Center of the Sandia National Laboratory in New Mexico hosted BALUSA meetings providing resident experts as participants in key issues. Individual countries supportive of peace in the subcontinent were also important hosts, such as former Crown Prince Hassan of Jordan and the National Security Advisor to the Sultan of Oman, Dr. Omar Zawawi.

The first BALUSA meeting already made history by including on the Pakistani side the first-ever serving general of the Army to participate in a Track II effort with Indians. General Mahmud Durrani, Chairman of the Pakistan Ordnance Factories' Board, in 1995 had shared his strong desire to be part of the effort to fashion a peaceful future between India and Pakistan. A decorated soldier from wars with India, his mindset was a refreshing change. The opening his participation provided allowed me to reach across to India, where the then recently retired air force chief Air Marshal S. K. Kaul agreed to join our group. Other Indian participants of the group were, Dr. V. S. Arunachalam, who served as advisor on Defense and Girish Saxena, former head of Indian Intelligence and governor in Kashmir. Besides Durrani, the Pakistani side included General Farrakh Khan[1] and industrialist Yousaf Shirazi. Toufiq Siddiqi and I were the two Americans. The group was expanded in subsequent meetings to add political representatives from the two main political parties. From India, representing the Congress Party, was Mani Shankar Aiyar, member of Indian parliament, advisor to Rajiv Gandhi, Minister for Petroleum in the Manmohan Singh cabinet. From the Bharatiya Janata Party (BJP) was Jaswant Singh, member of Indian parliament, Minister for External Affairs, Finance, and Defense. From the Pakistan side, Shah Mehmood Qureshi represented the Pakistan People's Party (PPP). He was a member of Pakistan's parliament and held a variety of portfolios, including foreign minister and is now Vice Chairman of the Tehrik-e-Insaf Party. There was also Shahid Khaqan Abbasi from the Pakistan Muslim League—Nawaz (PML-N), member of parliament and served as minister for commerce and for petroleum and natural resources and went on to become Prime Minister. Syed Babar Ali, former Finance Minister and educational leader served as host and participant in keeping with his longtime association with senior leadership in India and Pakistan.

Bipartisanship served the group well giving discussion necessary heft and allowing for continuity through changes in party fortunes. Further, with senior members of each political party involved, BALUSA recommendations were widely circulated in the inner sanctums of each government. The mid-1990s were thus a time when we made the case for better relations to skeptical audiences. However, we received a fair hearing and given the stature and the small size of the effort, members found access in each other's capitals and in Washington.

Adding to the effort to create collaboration on energy via a joint natural gas pipeline required bringing in specific technical and legal expertise for these specific meetings hosted by the UNDP and Sweden's

Environment and Policy Institute in a variety of locations including Udaipur, Rajasthan hosted by the Chief Minister and attended by Jaswant Singh among others; Singapore; Muscat, Oman; and Amman, Jordan. Foreign office representatives including Shaharyar Khan of Pakistan (Pakistani Foreign Secretary) and Salman Haidar (Indian Foreign Secretary), Ambassador Pratap Kaul (Indian Ambassador to the USA and Cabinet Secretary) and Vivek Katju (Joint Secretary for Pakistan and later Ambassador to Afghanistan) participated.

Recognizing the importance of changing the mindset from hostility to cooperation, the group expanded to include important members of the Indian media, including Bharat Bhushan, Shekhar Gupta, and Malini Parthasarathy.

The focus was on economic growth, technology, and security. The three days of discussion led to a meeting of minds on substance and process. Given the uniqueness of the effort and the senior ranks of its participants and the desire to build links toward progress, the group wished to record its recommendations but stay away from media dissemination. The goal was to influence policy makers. That was, in the group's view, best achieved at that point, through careful consultations by each member in each country. The report, to be drawn up by the convener, was approved by each side for limited distribution. Briefings on the recommendations were conducted by each participant within his individual network. The report was also disseminated to foreign policy leaders and think tanks in India, Pakistan, and the USA.

Initially, I drafted up the report for each meeting, cleared it with the participants from each side and then sent it for publication. Quickly, each side told me that they had confidence in my fairly representing their respective views and to go straight to publication.

The rapport between the participants was exceptional. Discussing items with shared perceptions or dramatically different ideas were all brought to the table in a total absence of rancor. During one of the breaks in an early meeting, one of the senior Indians said to me "BALUSA may already have made its contribution: demonstrating that serious people from each side can bring up everything without hesitation." This, he assured me, was something that political leaders would hear when he got back to Delhi.

In 1996, BALUSA was the first serious Track II between India and Pakistan that involved senior most ranks of political, military, economic, and intelligence leaders. The *Nimrana* process, named after a town in Rajasthan where the meetings were hosted, was more of a people-to-people effort. I was moved by the number of offers for hosting talks by key countries. The world was fatigued with rancor in the subcontinent. A different era was worth searching for. Offers of help poured in.

For example, our Omani host hosted a BALUSA meeting that was focused on energy. Elaborate arrangements for the comfort of the group were made and our hosts said given senior ranks present, they could do no less. Key officials in the cabinet attended session on economic benefits accruing from Indo-Pak normalization beyond the subcontinent. In his opening address, his excellency Dr. Omar Zawawi noted: "The dividends to be derived from peace and prosperity will benefit India, Pakistan and all their neighbors. We in the Sultanate of Oman particularly feel that we stand to gain much in every aspect be it economically or politically. We firmly believe that peace and amity between India and Pakistan will contribute in a very positive manner to the security and stability of countries in the Persian Gulf and Indian Ocean region."[2]

Each subsequent meeting focused on a different part of the overall agenda. For example, the meeting in the Maldives examined core economic interests that normalization would bring, from granting of most favored nation status to building joint infrastructure projects, a combined energy grid, building of a natural gas pipeline through Pakistan to India, a common electrical grid, water sharing between and among countries of South Asia, the role of technology in monitoring trade between India and Pakistan, building linkages between military and intelligence institutions to mitigate age old suspicion, enhancing the role of the media in reducing prejudice between the countries, and strengthening travel.

The 1996–2002 years of interaction on a broad front was reflected in the specific recommendations years before other Track II efforts multiplied. Beyond building links, BALUSA did pave the way for addressing tough issues in a non-combative manner outside the bureaucratic milieu in which official conversations occurred. In moving discussions from outside the subcontinent in 1996 to Lahore, Pakistan in 2000 and Chennai, India in 2001 and back to Lahore in 2002 the group expanded to allow for senior officials who were not able to travel outside for the meetings. Just getting past the visa regimes in each country was a minor victory, one that I worked on by going directly to the Prime Ministers, knowing that in the end they should be looped into the work we were undertaking.

Beyond the discussions in sessions, there was ample opportunity for intelligence and security officials to meet. Discussion took place even as nuclear tests of June 1998 took place when the group was in Bellagio for a scheduled meeting. Nuclear, political, and security consultations and recommendations over time remained the more sensitive. Economic issues were moved along with in-depth analysis of costs of conflict and benefits of peace.[3] During this period, hostility toward bilateral trade declined markedly.

My life was consumed by working on the Track II. Time differences of nine plus hours in the days before email meant that most nights I would be woken up by phone calls from India or Pakistan. Making sure that this senior group remained connected in addition to making complicated comfortable travel arrangements meant endless conversations. At times I was dubbed "sergeant major" for keeping the talks focused on the agenda at hand in each meeting. Other times I was simply referred to as 'mother hen' for having launched the group effort.

BALUSA provided unexpected openings. At one point, I was asked to work with representatives of each side's Prime Minister in an informal discussion on a key issue to find common ground. At other moments, for example when messages needed to be passed during heightened military tensions between India and Pakistan in the July 1999 Kargil hostilities, BALUSA provided a channel. The group set out to build confidence. I felt grateful that we achieved that even if peace did not descend onto the subcontinent.

Notes

1. Khan died in June 2016.
2. At BALUSA meeting of senior Indian, Pakistani, and US participants held at Al Bustan Palace Hotel, Muscat, Oman, March 20–23, 1998. BALUSA IV Report, Foreign Policy Research Institute, Philadelphia, PA. Available at https://www.fpri.org/wp-content/uploads/2017/08/20170802092849.pdf, accessioned October 15, 2017.
3. BALUSA publications include: Mahmud A. Durrani, *India and Pakistan: The cost of Conflict and the Benefits of Peace* (2000); Toufiq A. Siddiqi, *Natural Gas Pipeline for India and Pakistan* (2003); Toufiq Siddiqi and Shirin Tahir-Kheli, *Water Conflicts in South Asia: Managing Water Disputes Within and Between Countries of the Region; Water Needs in South Asia: Closing the Demand-Supply Gap* (2005).

CHAPTER 23

Family Life

The years 1993–1995 were personally very difficult ones for me. Mama was diagnosed with breast cancer. By the time she had surgery in the USA in May 1994, the surgeon said the cancer had spread, and thus, she did not have long to live. It was painful when I heard her tell the doctors that she would not want any chemotherapy, as it would be fruitless given that the cancer had metastasized. Instead, she wanted to return to Pakistan to live out her days in her own country. So, as soon as she was strong enough to make the long journey, I took her to Islamabad in September 1994.

I spent that September sitting each evening with my father and reading the entire Quran with his interpretation of the Arabic text. A scholar and a modern man, a poet, and a scientist, I wanted to understand how Baba saw the holy text and its application to the modern world. It was in the context of this reading that Baba pointed out the importance of women's empowerment. He noted that according to the Third Surah of the Quran: "I shall not let the work of any worker among you, male or female, to be lost," and the Hadith offers a special place for women through the proclamation that "paradise is under the feet of your mothers."[1]

General practice in the time of Prophet Mohammed and that of the first four Caliphs indicates openness to women's participation. For example, women could participate in the annual pilgrimage, the Hajj; offer prayers in the mosque in Mecca and Medina; and attend community congregations for discussions and consultations. Even the stipulated "proper dress" left the face, head, and hands uncovered. The recent more draconian dress code in certain Islamic societies has emerged under pressures of local influences and cultural traditions. We discussed how this changed in interpretation by mullahs, most of whom were barely educated. Even as we faced Mama's decline, we spent the time talking about the direction Pakistan and the greater world of Islam were heading. Baba was particularly sorry that the learned aspects of Islam, its contributions to science, mathematics, astronomy of centuries were being cast aside for narrow definitions of what constitutes the proper way forward. He felt that only education of the mullahs might save the future and that was becoming ever harder with the external funding of madrassas (primarily from Saudi Arabia and Iran). Through all of these important conversations, we were very aware of a very major influence slipping away from our lives.

My mother was crucially important in my life even beyond childhood. She nurtured in me the desire to be educated and become a professional and to do something useful with my life. She used to joke that given how busy my postacademic government years had become; she would come to visit me after I retired. That was indeed one of the reasons I did not take up a job after my ambassadorial stint. I retired in 1993 thinking there was all the time I could spend with my parents. But there is never enough time.

At the same time in fall of 1994, Raza was diagnosed with a brain tumor after months of headaches and tests. They could not tell if the tumor was malignant, but it sat at a very critical point at the base of the brain where many nerves come together. Microscopic surgery was required, and we set about finding the best surgeon in the Philadelphia area for this particular type of tumor. At last, the surgery took place. I recall sitting waiting in the family area for the surgeon to come and speak to me. There was another spouse waiting for word on her husband, a forty-year-old Canadian who had come for a similar operation because the surgeon was known as an expert in treating meningioma.

Finally, the surgeon came. He took me outside the room and said that Raza was in recovery and that they had drilled a hole in his skull to access the area, but that the skin over the hole would protect the brain. The great news was that his tumor was not malignant which meant no further treatment. The bad news, however, was that in the final moments of surgery, the acoustic nerve to his left ear was severed. Raza lost all hearing in his left ear. In shock, I asked if a hearing aid would make a difference since Raza loved listening to classical music and the tonality would be destroyed with only one ear operational, especially since the remaining ear had always been his weaker one. The surgeon said: "No, as there is no acoustic nerve anymore in the left ear."

Even as I was absorbing all the above, the surgeon told me that I should sit in the waiting area as he was about to tell the other spouse that her husband had been operated on and that sadly his tumor was malignant and given his young age would rapidly end his life.

Instantly I realized how lucky I was. Loss of hearing was nothing compared to a loss of life! When Raza was sufficiently recovered so that we could break the news to him, I tried to lighten his sadness by saying: "These thirty plus years you have always said you did not hear me! So what will change?"

Recovery took a long time, and the winter of 1994 was a severe one in Philadelphia. Ice storms made roads and even getting out of the house on foot impossible. We watched the unfolding scene from the safety of the house and pondered the future. Once Raza was sufficiently recovered, I began the alternate monthly commute to Islamabad to be with my mother. She remained cheerful and brave, but the end seemed near. We worried about our father, Baba, who had been married to her for over sixty-five years. He was older and very frail.

The importance of family and friends in difficult times as these is supreme. My parents were pillars of the community and were widely respected. As I left to come back home to Pennsylvania to care for Raza, my brother Toufiq and sister-in-law Ulrike would arrive in Islamabad from their Honolulu home. Toufiq accepted a senior position as Executive Director of the Energy and Environment Program for UNESCAP, the regional development arm of the UN serving as the main economic and social development sector for Asia and the Pacific. Based in Bangkok, Toufiq hoped he could make his commute to be with our parents a shorter one. My two other siblings, Farida, herself in poor health, and Sayeeda, were also there.

Thus, it went for several months. It was a dark time, but we got through it because of family bonds that kept us all close. I got to say my goodbye to my mother over the time I spent with her in those final months. Given that I had wondered if because of my commute home to Philadelphia to be the caretaker for my husband in his recovery, I would be in the air or some twelve thousand miles away when my mother passed away, I was grateful to have been there with her at the end. She had asked me to delay my departure for the USA from scheduled March 17, 1995, to March 24. I obliged and saw off my family who had come to say goodbye to her and myself stayed behind. She died on March 20, 1995, which at least did not add the additional pain of just having missed being with her for the final moments. The heartache of my loss still stays with me even as the memories of pain have dulled while the happy times shine bright.

My conversations with my father, Baba, were instructive and personally gratifying. He represented the best traditions of both countries and felt that enmity and war had cost both India and Pakistan in terms of a brighter future for the coming generations. Baba was also happy that I was able to visit the region frequently as he was himself in declining health following Mama's passing. He was too fragile to visit us in the USA. He was proud to say that from 1944 to 1994 he visited the USA nearly every year! BALUSA allowed me to see more of him as I shuttled between India and Pakistan. But, to my lasting sadness, I was not there when my older sister Farida died in July 1996. Further, I had just returned home to Philadelphia and was in Charleston, South Carolina, with our New Year's group, when my friend Mahmud Durrani called to say Baba had passed away on January 2, 1997. An era ended. With the death of my parents, I became the older generation for my children. It is a strange feeling not to have my Baba or Mama to call up, write, or visit when anything of note happens. I carried out my professional commitments as needed and also because my parents were always proud of what they felt I achieved in a different land of choice. Failure and sloth were not an option.

23 FAMILY LIFE 175

Author with President George W. Bush on Air Force One, April 2003

Author's grandfather, Nawab Kazim Yar Jung (seated third from left across table), at banquet in Jubilee Hall hosted by the Nizam (Ruler) of Hyderabad (seated tenth from left across) Deccan, India, to bid farewell to the British Resident in Hyderabad, Sir Duncan Mackenzie, 1938

23 FAMILY LIFE 177

White House Residence President and Mrs. George W. Bush's meeting with his holiness the Dalai Lama, September 2003. Author is first on the right

President Ronald Reagan's meeting on Pakistan in the Oval Office with senior US Government officials, July 1986. Author is on the right

Vice President George H. W. Bush at the Taj Mahal in Agra during official visit to India, May 1984. Author represented the National Security Council on the official American delegation

Indian Prime Minister Rajiv Gandhi's official working visit to the White House, October 1987. Cabinet Room handshake with author then serving as National Security Council officer in charge of visit. National Security Advisor Colin Powell is in middle

23 FAMILY LIFE 179

Oval Office meeting of President George W. Bush, Secretary of State Colin Powell, and author, October 2004

Author as bride in
Hyderabadi dress.
Karachi, August 1962

Author's father, Dr. Raziuddin Siddiqi (third from left in second row), with Queen Elizabeth, Duke of Edinburgh, and Princess Margaret at Balmoral Castle, 1958

23 FAMILY LIFE 181

Author's parents Raziuddin and Khurshid Siddiqi with the Ambassador of the USA and Mrs. Walter McConaughy. Karachi, April 1962

Author's brother Toufiq Siddiqi at his college function. Trinity College, Cambridge, England, May 1956

Fatima Jinnah, sister of Pakistan's Founder, Mohammed Ali Jinnah (seated to the left in first row), visiting Peshawar, Pakistan, for a Women's Day event. Author's mother Khurshid is seated third to the right in front row. Peshawar, March 1952

Author's sister-in-law, Ulrike Siddiqi, and Author's sister, Sayeeda Idris, with author. Islamabad, November 1985

23 FAMILY LIFE 183

Author at President
Ronald Reagan's
Second Inaugural Ball,
The Kennedy Center,
Washington, DC,
January 1985

Oval Office meeting with President George W. Bush, Secretary of State Colin Powell, and Ambassador to the UN John Negroponte, January 2004

Author's grandfather and family at his residence in Banjara Hills, Hyderabad, India. Author's mother holding her son Toufiq is fourth from right in second row. Grandfather Nawab Kazim Yar Jung is fifth in second row, and author's father is seventh in second row, March 1939

Author and her husband, Raza, in wedding dress, Karachi, 1962

23 FAMILY LIFE 185

Vice President George H. W. Bush's official visit to Riyadh, Saudi Arabia. Photograph taken at desert picnic following Gazelle Chase hosted by Saudi Royalty, April 1985. Author on left

Author's family photograph (minus younger sister Sayeeda) with parents, Toufiq, and Farida taken upon author's return from her B.A. at Ohio Wesleyan University. Karachi, July 1961

23 FAMILY LIFE 187

President George W. Bush, National Security Advisor Condoleezza Rice, and the author in the Oval Office, May 2003

Note

1. M. Raziuddin Siddiqi, "The Status of Women is Islam," unpublished manuscript (1994).

PART IV

Taking Stock

CHAPTER 24

Washington Return

Paul Wolfowitz, who had offered me my first job in Washington on 1982, became Dean of the Johns Hopkins University School of Advanced International Studies (SAIS) in Washington in 1994. He asked if I would help set up a South Asia program there as none existed at the time. Washington was a familiar milieu, and many colleagues from my government years made the interaction interesting and productive. In addition to meeting with students to gauge interest in courses on South Asia, I wanted to help establish SAIS as a center for research and outreach on South Asia. The Foreign Policy Institute was a wonderful perch for me with its Director, Tom Keaney a very supportive colleague. My office was part of a suite that included the offices of Dr. Zbigniew Brzezinski, former National Security Advisor, and best-selling authors Francis Fukuyama (*The End of History*) and Azar Nafisi (*Reading Lolita in Tehran*).

Work on BALUSA offered immediate opportunities for research seminars. Work with Toufiq on Water Issues in South Asia under the Carnegie grant was ongoing. Beyond that, I reached out to the Indian ambassadors in Washington and in New York to enlist them into a network of all South Asian ambassadors for regular discussions on the eighth floor of the Rome building at 1619 Massachusetts Avenue, NW, the location of SAIS.

Located as it is on the think tank corridor in Washington, it was possible to get colleagues interested in South Asia from Brookings and Carnegie Endowment, as well as others from The Wilson Center and Georgetown and George Washington universities to discussions in our program.

© The Author(s) 2018
S. Tahir-Kheli, *Before the Age of Prejudice*,
https://doi.org/10.1007/978-981-10-8551-2_24

We launched the effort with a well-attended talk by then-Assistant Secretary for South Asia Karl Inderfurth to lay out US priorities for the region and various efforts under way to enhance relations between the countries of the subcontinent.

I continued to commute from my permanent residence in Pennsylvania. This time, though, I was not serving at the White House; so my schedule was more flexible. Raza's health issues were taken care of and he continued to serve as Professor of Physics and Chair of the Department of Physics at Temple University. Both our children had left home: Shehra was married to wonderful Ethan Boldt living at his family farm near Iowa City, Iowa before they returned to New York; Kazim graduated from Harvard and went to work immediately in New York and then onto London for his financial consulting company. Raza and I would marvel that we had hoped to raise citizens of the world in our children and had succeeded. But the problem with that plan was that they went on to work in all parts of the world as evident in Kazim spending considerable periods of time in London, Johannesburg, South Africa, right after that country's independence, and Munich and other parts of Europe, including later in Moscow, and Canada. Home was always the USA.

President Bill Clinton had pledged an official visit to India. The visit was slated for late March 2000. As the time came closer, there was speculation that the President would not go to Pakistan, a departure from traditional practice. As the founding Director of the South Asia Program for the Foreign Policy Institute at the Johns Hopkins School for Advanced International Studies, I was aware of the debate inside the administration on the advisability of bypassing Pakistan. I received a call from the National Security Council, an old work home for me, asking if I would attend a discussion with President Clinton on February 11, 2000, on his upcoming South Asia travel. I said yes and on my way to the White House thought about what would be my two-minute allocated contribution. Upon entering the cabinet room in the West Wing, I realized that there were some nineteen individuals, most of whom I had known for a long time and who had been colleagues on subcontinental matters. In addition, Secretary of State Madeline Albright, National Security Advisor Samuel Berger, and White House Chief of Staff John Podesta were there. As the President entered, introductions were made. Clinton noted to me that he understood that I was "the only Republican in the room" to which I responded that was fine because only one was needed to respond to all the other Democrats! He clearly enjoyed the quip and moved down the greeting line.

Clinton started the discussion, giving his thoughts on South Asia and how much he was looking forward to the upcoming travel. He noted that his advisors were divided on his itinerary. He wanted to hear from the experts assembled around the table about his stops on the visit and substantial issues of importance to American policy. Just as he was making a key point, the phone rang. We all quieted down but no one picked up and the phone would not stop. Clinton looked up and said "It must be Hillary" but still let it ring. Finally, John Podesta answered and said something quietly and hung up! We went back to the matter at hand.

Many of the participants gave good advice on the background of the visit and the main opportunities it represented. Almost all advised against a stop in Pakistan: "As a signal of our displeasure at Pakistan's military's take-over and the poor record of the state." India was the prize, and in order to cultivate a special, exclusive relationship with the world's largest democracy, the President was recommended to focus exclusively on India.

When it came my turn to speak, I made the point that my recommendation was different. There were several critical issues here.

1. Given the important role that President (Clinton) had played in preventing what could possibly have become a nuclear confrontation between India and Pakistan in the mountains of Kashmir in July 1999,
2. Given the fact that a failed Pakistani state would be as dangerous to its contiguous neighbor as it would be to the interests of the USA, and
3. Given the American desire for prosperous and flourishing India, and a stable Pakistan, it was important not to act in a manner that visibly worked against shoring up the (possibly) teetering state of Pakistan. Therefore, on his way back, the President should consider stopping for a short layover in Islamabad.

However, I suggested that the visit should be carefully structured to make the case to Pakistan's military leaders that the USA expected responsible behavior internally as well as externally in the region. A direct address to the people of Pakistan should be crafted which Clinton should give during his brief stay (a first for any American President) that makes the case for America's strong support for a Pakistan that reflected the vision of moderation envisaged by its founder, Mohammad Ali Jinnah. I ended my piece with the suggestion that such a carefully crafted address would be a needed change from just playing guest. Also, it would get the public at large informed of the views of the American President in a fashion that most would consider friendly, positive, and constructive.

At that point, a few of the other participants also indicated support for my suggestions and we talked about what constituted "Jinnah's Pakistan." Clinton then said decisively that he would visit Pakistan and asked if I would be willing to work with his speechwriter, Sam Afridi, to help fashion his speech to Pakistanis. I responded: "Yes, certainly. I should be happy and honored to do so."

The meeting adjourned, and I was asked if I would join Ambassador Frank Wisner in briefing the White House press corps on the President's South Asia visit. Compared to the usual press briefings that I had previously participated in as a White House staffer, this one ended up being a rather lengthy affair. With Pakistan being, so to say, in the doghouse, there were many questions about the rationale. Questions were also asked about the schedule and the mechanics.

Even as Clinton took off for the subcontinent, I pondered how tenuous the link between the USA and Pakistan had become. A series of negatives had reduced the points of cooperation between these two allies. Each side expressed frustration regarding their shrinking conversation. The difference in approach and content was obvious in the warm stories and colorful coverage of the first Clinton stop in India. Clinton's desire to start a new chapter of progress in Indo-USA relations was well received and even beyond that, it was clear that the American President was having a great time in India as he visited Delhi, Agra, Hyderabad, Rajasthan, and Mumbai.

Clinton's arrival in Islamabad was a stark contrast to the festive events in India. He was the first US President to come since Nixon in 1969. Arriving in an unmarked plane on March 25, 2000, driven speedily through strangely empty highways to the capital some fifteen miles away, Clinton did not see the average Pakistani, nor was he seen by them. The people of Pakistan only saw him once he came on the television and radio to make his address to them. Many had followed his visit to India and were startled by the contrast. Even those invited to the presidential palace in Islamabad for the lunch in his honor, felt a strain not evident in the travel across the border in India.

Not appreciating how difficult it had been for the American President to even consider traveling to Pakistan, some Pakistani leaders found it politic to express annoyance for "being treated differently" and said that what I had thought was a very appropriate but respectful speech in Pakistan had been a scolding bordering on rude. In complaints to me during my subsequent travel to Pakistan, several of the leaders noted that they resented the change in treatment by the USA, a country they claimed they had always thought of as an ally. None wanted to hear my response that times had changed and Pakistan had lowered its stock by dismantling a once promising state and to its great detriment focusing only on the past (meaning: Kashmir).

Even long after the Clinton visit, Pakistani President Musharraf recalled his conversation with him, noting that he had pointed out the Pakistani national interest in a stable and just peace with India based on mutual trust and action. Given his role in the Kargil incursion, to some that desire for "mutual trust" would be difficult to comprehend. But, in fact, Musharraf was subsequently supportive of backchannel communications with Indian leaders, even as he eschewed backing down in Kashmir unilaterally.

In his speech to the Pakistani people, Clinton repeated his desire for stability, governance, and nuclear restraint, offering American friendship and (most importantly, in my view) saluting Jinnah's vision for a moderate Pakistan. In closing, Clinton noted his concern that if Pakistan continued on the existing trajectory, it could "grow more isolated, draining even more resources away from the needs of the people, moving even closer to a conflict no one can win." "However," said the President, "if you do meet these challenges, our full economic and political partnership can be restored for the benefit of the people of Pakistan."[1]

As promised, I worked with Clinton's speechwriter, a young American of Pakistani background. Various drafts of the speech had put the basic message in place: There was a clear alternative preferred path to Pakistan's future as a prosperous moderate state. America would support that version and hoped that Pakistan's leaders would make the right choices for the benefit of future generations of an important state. The point was to put the onus for the relationship back on the Pakistanis, noting that while the USA could not give Pakistan a carte blanche, it stood ready to offer friendship and assistance.

In Pakistan, 2000 was still a time when the state writ held sway over a majority of religious elements, both in mosques and on the growing numbers of "jihadists" deployed in Kashmir. Intelligence agencies largely still controlled the jihadists as they took foreign policy into their own hands. But even then, many shopkeepers in Pakistani bazaars openly said in conversation that they would offer money for jihad when asked by groups known to be active in Kashmir. I was told that often the asking was done by a security person on behalf of the fighters. The bazaaris noted that they felt it was their duty to contribute because of "the stressful and difficult lives of the Kashmiri populace who were handcuffed under the tyrannical Indian rule." Indeed, they saw the giving not as charity but an obligation under Zakat, the Islamic requirement to give to the needy. It had been obvious for decades that in order to circumvent sales records, no shopkeeper ever wanted to print a written sales receipt or an invoice. When I would ask why they did not do so, they remarked that sending the regular sales taxes on to the government would be stupid. "The government is full of thieves. Therefore, no sensible person pays tax to the government."

Thus, it was clear by the time the twenty-first century came around that Pakistani state, buttressed by a competing parallel system on all fronts from education to governance to jihad, was in the midst of a perfect storm. Moderate Pakistanis consoled themselves with the belief that the religious elements had little political sway, and if elections were ever held, they would be a small minority in parliament. However, holding of elections, as always, proved elusive, military rule continued, and the street power of the extremists kept growing.

Note

1. President Clinton, "Remarks by the President to the People of Pakistan," The White House, Office of the Press Secretary, Washington, DC, March 25, 2000.

CHAPTER 25

George W. Bush Years

The 2000 US election took place during these SAIS years. I had met George W. Bush in 1987 at a small dinner in his and Laura Bush's honor. Donald L. Evans and his wife were also present. It had been a convivial affair, and Don Evans (who served as Secretary of Commerce in the Bush administration in 2001) actually subsequently mailed me a favorite recipe for making margaritas that he had described during the dinner. In the course of the evening, the future President mentioned my having traveled with his parents in a small group to India and Pakistan and asked: "how did that one go for you?"

I voted in the election and then left on a planned visit to Delhi. I remained in India for a couple of weeks and was startled that the election was still in limbo during my stay in the Indian capital and Mumbai. By the time I returned home, George W. Bush was President. Many of my former colleagues from the White House NSC years were in the process of joining the new administration. Several assumed I would too especially as newspapers in India and Pakistan raised the issue with specific designations in mind. I had transitioned out of government and found a productive niche that I was in no hurry to abandon.

In the meantime, the South Asia program was launched. Paul Wolfowitz left SAIS to become the Deputy Secretary of Defense. Colin Powell who had been National Security Advisor for a part of the Reagan administration and someone I deeply admired became Secretary of State. Condoleezza Rice (who I met when we briefly overlapped in the George H. W. Bush NSC before I left for the UN Mission ambassadorship

© The Author(s) 2018
S. Tahir-Kheli, *Before the Age of Prejudice*,
https://doi.org/10.1007/978-981-10-8551-2_25

and whom I respected) became the National Security Advisor. It was a familiar group of senior officials and I stayed in touch with some of them, including Deputy Secretary of State Richard Armitage in the course of my Indo-Pak BALUSA work, including during buildup of tensions and the Kargil war. Despite familiarity with them, I did not seek or lobby for a position. Armitage said to me: "this is not the administration of George Bush '41" which I assumed was a reference to a more neoconservative bent and a general distaste for multilateral diplomacy.

As the administration got going in early 2001, I received a call from White House Personnel asking me to come by. Stuart Holliday headed up the office and he was gracious in his welcome. He noted that I had not come to express an interest in employment nor sought a position from the "plum book" (which catalogued all senior positions for political appointees in an administration). "And yet here I am" came my rejoinder. "Indeed and I want to talk to you about a way you can help us out even as you remain outside the administration" said Stuart. Continuing, he noted: "The annual meeting of the UN Commission on Human Rights (UNCHR) is scheduled for its six week run in Geneva in March. We are only just beginning to fill the requisite ambassadorial positions which will need to go through proper vetting and then be confirmed by the Senate. However, the UNCHR is important for U.S. interests and we need someone familiar with the UN and with U.S. priorities in the Human Rights arena to head up the U.S. delegation to this year's meeting. We would very much like you to do that and Dr. Rice has asked me to reach out to you," noted Stuart.

Admitting that I had not expected the request I replied that I want to be helpful in the service of my country. I needed to get my academic and track II work organized, be read into the work of the upcoming meeting and get going. As I walked back the short distance from the White House to my SAIS office, I pondered what lay ahead. I had gone as a member of the US delegation for the human rights meetings in Geneva in 1992. However, being the head of delegation was a different matter as it involved managing the delegation in addition to promoting US priorities and garnering votes for key resolutions. In addition, there were the appointed "public delegates" mostly members of Congress keenly interested in certain votes. We would work together to do our best.

Shortly after the cycle of briefings at the State Department was completed and as I administratively signed on for the task ahead in Geneva, I got a call to see the National Security Advisor. Condi was always gracious and she wanted to "touch base" and thank me for taking on the leadership of the US delegation in such a short time frame. She noted that my having once been confirmed by the Senate to an ambassadorial position which involved work on human rights made it easier as the administration was yet filling its main positions. She reiterated some of the US priorities, including the vote on Cuba's violation of human rights. I also learned that Congresswoman Ileana Ross-Lehtinen representing south Florida would be one of the public delegates on the delegation. That meant heavy lifting on Cuba I assumed. "Well, Condi, this will be hard work but interesting and I will report back when it's done" were my parting words. I asked her if I might be in touch with her should the need arise. She answered in the affirmative.

Even though Raza and I honeymooned in Switzerland, Geneva is not one of my favorite cities. But you go where the work takes you and there I was in March 2001 en route on a long flight by way of Frankfurt in coach class which regardless of rank is what the State Department gives its officials. The US Mission based in Geneva representative met me at the airport. "Need to go directly to the Palais (Palais des Nations where UN Geneva is headquartered and meetings occur) in order to get you credentialed," said the officer.

So the mission's car took us to the Palais and as the meetings were getting started later that day, the line for getting the photo identification and a badge in order to access the meetings was a long one. The officer asked if I wanted him to speak to someone and cut ahead as I was head of delegation and that carried priority. "No, not necessary" was my rejoinder. I thought I'd rather use any clout for getting votes rather than to get ahead in a line.

Once the credentials process was completed, I finally got to my abode for six weeks, a comfortable hotel room. We got government-discounted rates, so hotels tended to be more upscale than our limited daily allowance would normally allow. "Pick me up in an hour," I asked the officer after I checked in. Showing up at the US Mission in Geneva meant a protocol call on the US Ambassador to the UN, George Moose, who had been appointed by the previous administration, awaiting an onward assignment. I wanted to get the lay of the land at the Mission where each morning's delegation meeting would take place. I was shown my office and met both the Foreign Service and other staff whose help was indeed crucial to our effort over the following weeks. Finally, I got back to the hotel and decided to settle in as the weeks to come allowed little time for chores like unpacking. And I was right.

In my thirty-seven-year career, I held jobs that required very long hours, a good deal of travel with short advance warning, coordinating of complex issues in the US government, dealing with difficult people and negotiating with impossible requirements and issues. The head of delegation portfolio managed to combine all of the above into one package.

UN Commission on Human Rights (UNCHR) meetings begin in the late morning, but the delegations start early or at least the US delegation did. We began with a "delegation meeting" in which attendance for the full delegation was mandatory. It is a useful hour where the order of business in the commission is examined and the state of play for US priorities discussed. As we are an instructed delegation, meaning all decisions are made in Washington at the Department of State, we have the job of lobbying based on instructions sent by distant colleagues with their own preferences. In reality that meant engaging with Washington way into the night given the time difference and then starting the day very early in order to chair the delegation meeting, get a sense of the day's meeting agenda and engage with other diplomatic missions in order to lobby for the US position.

The 2001 session of the UNCHR opened in the shadow of the US declaration in March that it would veto any one-sided resolutions against Israel. This decision came even as we tried to balance other US priorities requiring support from member countries. Beyond Israel, member delegations criticized the incoming Bush administration's lack of support for the Kyoto Protocol covering climate change; the US negative stance against the International Criminal Court (ICC); opposition to the treaty to abolish land mines and narrower discussion of what constitutes Human Rights beyond political freedoms. One story in the press expressed how US policy came across:

> An administration that thinks that Cuban human rights are an international issue, but that Israeli behavior in the occupied territories is a bilateral affair, to be negotiated between the perpetrator and the victim clearly is overdue for a wakeup call. Capitol Hill may think that consistency is a virtue a Superpower can do without, but in the outside world people notice when the message is "Do as I say, not do as I do!"[1]

Public delegates came with links to the White House or were members of Congress. They felt passionately about certain issues and did not mind pushing the case with member countries in a more confrontational fashion. Sometimes that worked. At other times, it backfired and delegations threatened to block US actions. It took a good amount of the time I had in order to find a common meeting ground within the delegation and to remind everyone that we were an instructed delegation and the decisions were made in Washington.

I got to meet a number of well-known figures in the course of the six weeks and as head of delegation to engage them on Human Rights. Former President of Ireland Mary Robinson was UN High Commissioner for Human Rights at the time, and I had lengthy conversations with her on US priorities for the session under way. The UN High Commissioner for Refugees (UNHCR) was Sadako Ogata of Japan, an impressive spokesman for the plight and protection of refugees worldwide. Discussion with her on the connection between displacement and human rights gave me great insight into the complexity but also the critical need for human rights protection.

We got close to the April 27, 2001, vote. French President Jacques Chirac arrived to address the assembled delegates. He spoke of the special French commitment to human rights and the links his nation shared with so many of the countries whose delegations were present. After his address, as he walked toward the exit, I looked up to see him coming straight at me sitting behind the US placard. He took my hand, raised me, and kissed the hand and kept going! "What on earth was that?" asked my colleague. "It's the French," I replied in my best French accent!

High drama preceded the Cuba vote where the US delegation was keenly focused. The vote was a close 23 "yes" to 21 "no" with 9 abstentions. We manned the exit points to the chamber to ensure supportive delegations did not miss the vote. Other priorities on China (which even the allies would not table); Chechnya (which the Russian delegation fought hard against) ended up with a vote of 15 "yes," including the USA and 16 "no" with 22 abstentions; Iran 19 "yes" and 20 "no" with 22 abstentions. As the vote ended, I made a beeline for the exit to call Condi Rice at the White House. She took the call and as I gave her the result, she said she was headed to the Oval Office for a meeting with the President and would give him the vote. "He will be pleased," noted Condi.

My next immediate call was to Rich Armitage, Deputy Secretary of State whom I had known over decades of joint work. I had stayed in touch with Rich in the course of my BALUSA track II work on India and Pakistan. Rich was pleased and asked if the White House knew? "Yes, I just spoke to Condi who was on her way to tell the President," I replied. What I did not say was that it was the White House that had asked me to go to Geneva in the first place. I would not leave Condi out of the loop.

Note

1. Reuters, CNN, "U.S. Ousted from U.N. Human Rights Commission," May 3, 2001.

CHAPTER 26

9/11

On that crisp blue September 2001 morning, I was on my way to an appointment at the NSC when I came back into my Georgetown apartment to turn off the television which I had mistakenly left on. My morning routine was to watch "Good Morning America" as I got ready for the day. When I unlocked my door, I heard strange sounds on the television. I sat down to watch. Charlie Gibson, co-anchor of the show, was talking about a commercial jetliner going into one of the two towers of the World Trade Center just minutes earlier. Only few years earlier, I had taken my sister to the top observation area and she had bought one of the signature posters of this New York iconic building that noted: "It's Hard to be Down when You are UP!"

"Has to be some awful accident," I, like so many that morning, thought. Even as I watched, the second plane entered the second tower, with great speed and deliberation it seemed. Shocked, I could not move. September 11, 2001 changed many things in the nation's capital and around the world. Immediately, I realized it made no sense to head for the White House appointment. At the time I did not know that another plane had hit the Pentagon and yet another had headed for the White House but had been taken down by the passengers as it flew over Pennsylvania.

In so many ways, I felt the need to do something to help. Many of the individuals in the policy circles were former colleagues and some good friends. I wondered how they were. Phone lines were jammed

© The Author(s) 2018
S. Tahir-Kheli, *Before the Age of Prejudice*,
https://doi.org/10.1007/978-981-10-8551-2_26

I was sure and in any case, tying up the system for information seemed unnecessary. I just got out onto 30th Street NW outside my apartment building, down the main Georgetown thoroughfare, M Street, which turns into Pennsylvania Avenue. My previous six years walking to the White House job from my apartment told me that it was just an eighteen-minute walk.

I walked at a steady pace. As I moved along, others were joining in the procession. I was unaware that an order for evacuation of key government buildings had been given. We all stopped at red lights awaiting the signal to cross. At one such moment, a pedestrian mentioned that the Department of State had been bombed. There was some black smoke visible on the horizon which turned out to be the site of where the aircraft had hit the Pentagon. The government buildings of Washington DC were emptying. All around me were hundreds of people just walking around silently. There was a hush that was deeply moving and very unfamiliar. I reached my daughter in California briefly as I did not want to tie up phone lines. I knew she would be worried. A sense of disconnect prevailed as I wondered where the President was and how the US leadership was coping. After a few hours, I just walked back to Georgetown again noting the total silence of pedestrians and cars clearly headed home from the district.

Then began the marathon television viewing shared that day by so many Americans. We all looked for information on this clearly planned and coordinated attack on the homeland. Details of President Bush's travel from Florida where he had visited an elementary school soon emerged. The image of his chief of staff Andrew Card whispering in his ear that the two towers of the World Trade Center had separately been hit is seared in my memory.

Criticism of the President and his absence from his nation's capital surfaced rapidly. Yet, having served in previous administrations on the staff of the President, I recalled the high-wire balancing act that the leader must undertake in crises. Concern for American safety had to be balanced with outreach to provide empathy in the midst of chaos or tragedy. The Reagan address on January 18, 1986 to the nation as the American orbital shuttle Challenger broke up 73 minutes after liftoff carrying a seven-member crew, including the first civilian woman. Reagan's address: "Nancy and I are pained to the core by the tragedy of the shuttle Challenger. We know we share this pain with all of the people of our country. This is truly a national loss....The crew of the space shuttle

Challenger honored us by the manner in which they lived their lives. We will never forget them, nor the last time we saw them, this morning, as they prepared for their journey and waved goodbye" and "slipped the surly bonds of earth" to "touch the face of God."

The title "mourner in chief" fits the US President. We waited for George W. Bush to explain the tragedy but also the source of the attack and the US reaction to it. The fact that the 9/11 attacks occurred using fully fueled American civilian aircraft bound for known destinations but hijacked for death made the response difficult and complicated. While not yet part of the Bush '43 administration, I could envision the desire for care in drawing conclusions and the desire not to inflame the situation even as protection of the homeland loomed as a priority.

In the evening of September 11, 2001, the President returned to the White House. He addressed the nation:

> Today, our fellow citizens, our way of life, our very freedom came under attack in a series of deliberate and deadly terrorist acts. The victims were in airplanes, or in their offices; secretaries, businessmen and women, military and federal workers; moms and dads, friends and neighbors. Thousands of lives were suddenly ended by evil, despicable acts of terror. The pictures of airplanes flying into buildings, fires burning, huge structures collapsing, have filled us with disbelief, terrible sadness, and a quiet, unyielding anger. These acts of mass murder were intended to frighten our nation into chaos and retreat. But they have failed; our country is strong.
>
> A great people has been moved to defend a great nation. Terrorist attacks can shake the foundations of our biggest buildings, but they cannot touch the foundation of America. These acts shattered steel, but they cannot dent the steel of American resolve.
>
> *America was targeted for attack because we're the brightest beacon for freedom and opportunity in the world* (emphasis added). And no one will keep that light from shining.

There was the call for service, I thought. "A great nation targeted" meant that we must all pitch into do our part. The President noted: "The search is underway for those who are behind these evil acts. I've directed the full resources of our intelligence and law enforcement communities to find those responsible and to bring them to justice. We will make no distinction between the terrorists who committed these acts and those who harbor them."

The Bush presidency was thus inexorably altered. Later there would be time to ponder the "what ifs" had 9/11 not happened? Would the trajectory have been very different? In my mind, I saw the experienced senior people in the administration as being conversant with the issues of the day and sensible leaders. The range included moderates even as the administration tended to be more conservative. The term Neoconservative or *neocon* had not yet in 2001 come to symbolize the strongly interventionist yet staunchly anti-multilateral diplomacy crowd that surfaced after 9/11. In the shock of the moment, not many noted the key sentence emphasized above as the cause of the attack. It set the stage for the invasions that followed.

The following day, President Bush at the urging of his longtime advisor from Texas, Karen Hughes, and against the advice of Karl Rove, went to the Islamic Center in Washington where he talked of the billions of Muslims around the world who were shocked and appalled by the terrorist acts of 9/11. Commenting on Muslims who contribute in a variety of professions, Bush noted they were part of the American fabric and must be allowed to practice their faith without prejudice. It was a powerful message at the time and becomes more so today.

Bush also noted right after 9/11 that America was not at war with Islam but with those who subverted religion toward terrorism. Around the Muslim world, the President received kudos for the statement which was seen as having prevented large-scale attacks on American Muslims in the American homeland. Even as actions against Muslims accelerated in the ongoing war on terror, the celebration of Ramadan at the White House with an Iftar dinner and actions such as the House Resolution 635 commemorating the holy month of fasting and spiritual renewal as a demonstration of solidarity and support for the Muslims in the US and throughout the world were indeed welcomed. This was perceived as America at its best, generous, and inclusive.

Subsequently, I was invited to a meeting of American Muslims in the Roosevelt Room of the White House which the President chaired. Karen Hughes was also present. The twenty or so people in the room had a chance to talk about 9/11 and ways in which all Americans could usefully contribute. The sentiment voiced earlier at the Mosque by the President that "the face of terror is not the true face of Islam" resonated throughout the meeting. There was never a call for collective punishment against all Muslims, including American Muslims.

The message resonated with the group. I was particularly touched that in the midst of what was an incredibly busy schedule, the US President, son of George H. W. Bush for whom it had been my honor to work at the NSC and as his Ambassador to the UN, felt that Muslims were a decent people having nothing in common with the planners hiding in the mountains of Afghanistan and their surrogate executors of evil against the USA.

These were somber times as country after country extended support to the USA. As Condoleezza Rice remarked in private and public so many times, 9/11 changed the focus. In the fight against any future attack, a prime worry, the terrorists "had to be right once. The administration had to be right every single time."

Soon thereafter, Osama bin Laden and his al Qaeda took "credit" for planning and executing this horror. He proudly took credit for the terrorism resulting in the death of some three thousand innocent people, for inflicting billions of dollars in damage, and for causing lasting change in the democratic world. Thus, the "Taliban" in Afghanistan—egregiously mislabeled as the "Students"—whose vision took them back to the fourteenth century had been party to the heinous act and countries such as Pakistan, who had maintained links with them, faced a clear choice. Ignoring the shared responsibility in their creation, American leaders convinced themselves that only the Pakistanis had parented the Taliban. Of course, Pakistan's geographical contiguity had been essential to providing them succor. The US reasoning went as follows: "Without Pakistani support, the Taliban would not have been in power in Kabul. After all, the Taliban had extensive links with the Pashtun areas of Pakistan sharing ethnicity and history of the jihad against the Soviets. Indeed, the Taliban were mostly born in Pakistani refugee camps, were mis-educated in Pakistani madrassas, and learned their fighting skills from the Mujahideen fighters based in Pakistan. Their families often carried Pakistani identity cards."[1] Without Taliban destruction of the Afghan state and its near total isolation (Saudi Arabia, United Arab Emirates, and Pakistan were the only countries that had recognized the Taliban government), Osama bin Laden would not have taken such hold of the country that gave him the space to plan and execute attacks against the American homeland on September 11, 2001.

Thus, within minutes, Pakistan went from its well-honed status as a reluctant ally of the USA to a friend of the perpetrators of terror: it became a potential enemy. President George W. Bush presented Pakistan with a clear choice: "You are either with us or against us." In a bizarre coincidence of fate, the morning of September 11, 2001 found the well-known USA antagonist the Pakistani intelligence chief, Lieutenant General Mehmood Ahmed, Director General of ISI visiting Washington as a guest of CIA Director George Tenet. Summoned for meetings with White House and State Department officials, Mehmood was the first to face the music: the direct ire of American leaders who were beginning to deal with the 9/11 aftermath.

I had met General Mehmood at the Army headquarters in Rawalpindi in 1999 along with a number of the military's high command in a discussion on USA–Pakistan relations. Mehmood came late to the meeting, and I was told that he had just been appointed to head the ISI. This was during my years when I was back in academia. But I had met other chiefs of the ISI in years past when I served in the US government. Mehmood was, in my experience, the single most hostile to the US. It was clear that he did not see much benefit to the Pakistan–USA relationship and was candid in his discussion of the lack of benefit that Pakistan derives from the American relationship. Instead, he thought Pakistan's interest lay elsewhere, the Islamic world in particular. Later, some noted that he was proud of saying that he was a "born-again Muslim" which some felt was more a case of a "born-again Islamic fundamentalist."[2]

It seemed entirely appropriate that it should be Mehmood to whom the American ultimatum was given in 2001. As head of the intelligence agency holding severely anti-American views, it was likely that he would not support his President's move supporting US actions in the aftermath of 9/11. As Bush noted: "This is the time for self-defense....We have made the decision to punish whoever harbors terrorists, not just the perpetrators."[3] The President was noting that the "Deliberate and deadly attacks which were carried out yesterday against our country were more than acts of terror." "They were acts of war." Summing up what lay ahead, Bush said: "This will be a monumental struggle between good and evil. But good will prevail."[4]

Secretary of State Powell was the designated pitcher to Musharraf, officer-to-officer, regarding what specifically was required of Pakistan after 9/11. Several items on the list were deemed "non-negotiable" and conveyed as such to the Pakistani President by Powell and to the ISI chief by the deputy Secretary of State, Richard Armitage. These were: termination of all logistical support for bin Laden; stopping of al Qaeda operatives at the Pakistani border; interception of all arms into Afghanistan via Pakistan;

blanket overflight and landing rights; access to Pakistani naval bases and borders; immediate access to intelligence and immigration information; condemnation of 9/11 attacks and end of all domestic expressions of support for terrorism against the USA, its friends and allies; and cessation of fuel supply to the Taliban and an end to Pakistani volunteers going into Afghanistan to join the Taliban. In the event of the confirmation of the al Qaeda and Osama bin Laden role in Afghanistan and their continued welcome in Afghanistan, we required the termination of Pakistan's recognition of the Taliban government and support for the Taliban and assist the USA as it sought destruction of bin Laden and his al Qaeda network.[5]

President Musharraf agreed to American demands but sought to assert one of his own: namely, that India must not have a role in the Afghan war, or in the follow-on government in Kabul. In a lengthy informal conversation with US Ambassador Wendy Chamberlin, held at the residence of a friend of mine, the Pakistani President said that while he would help in the capture and extradition of al Qaeda, Pakistani citizens, be they from the Lashkar-e-Taiba (LeT) or other Punjabi groups, would be off limits.[6] After the quick rout of the Taliban by the USA, the rapid opening up of Afghanistan to India had caused huge discomfort in Pakistan, which Washington was not willing to recognize or acknowledge. The focus of the Army and intelligence officials was on the dangers of a two-front war.

With Cheney's acquiescence, and possible encouragement, his friend Zalmay Khalilzad, the then-US advisor to Afghanistan, had directed the opening of Indian consulates (read: bases) in Jalalabad and Kandahar, cities bordering Pakistan. Pakistani leadership feared Indian intelligence using these bases for spying and other troublemaking. The perceived linkage of the American goals in Afghanistan to India, and the expanding Indian role there, fed paranoia and suspicion in Pakistan's military and sowed the seeds for continued turmoil in Afghanistan to the detriment of US interest there.

In such a clear demarcation of lines of friendship and good versus evil, Pakistan's choices were stark. Musharraf chose to align Pakistan with the USA, which American officials often felt was the only option available. Yet, Bush himself seemed to understand that there was always another option, even the wrong one. I heard him note many times that: "When I asked, Musharraf decided to stand shoulder to shoulder with the U.S. For that, I give him credit." Often, the less sympathetic in the US administration, complained that "The President himself is the Pakistan desk officer," noting that the case for Pakistan was made more sympathetically by him than by his senior advisors.

The 9/11 attacks on the US created sympathy even as the most extreme challenged the origin of the attacks. The subsequent military action against the Taliban and al Qaeda followed the President's pledge to the nation that henceforth terrorism will be dealt with at its source. In order to help eradicate the Taliban, both in Afghanistan and less ostensibly in Pakistan, the President was now committed to using all means at his disposal, military and diplomatic. While a major military action was required in Afghanistan, weaning Pakistan away from its addiction to extremism turned out to be even harder. After all, in his first speech after the 1999 coup, Musharraf had noted: "Fifty two years ago we started with a beacon of hope and today that beacon is no more and we stand in darkness....the slide down has been gradual but has rapidly accelerated in the last many years." On January 12, 2002, Musharraf noted in a well-received speech that Islamic militants had been allowed to flout the state for far too long but he would confront them. "The day of reckoning" had arrived and asked: "do we want Pakistan to become a theocratic state? Do we believe that religious education alone is enough for governance or do we want Pakistan to emerge as a progressive and dynamic Islamic welfare state?"[7] Most Pakistanis cheered this resolve and wondered if this President, who had crashed in through the backdoor, would break the pattern of weak leaders and undertake bold actions to rein in the growing fundamentalist militancy infecting Pakistan.

In May 2002, Musharraf again appealed to Pakistanis to shun the forces of radicalism citing the existential danger to Pakistan of an unchecked drift to extremism. Noting that the rhetoric and actions coming out of some mosques and madrassas made Pakistan a target for charges of aiding terrorism, the President noted that these charges opened up Pakistan to "serious consequences that Pakistan will be incapable of bearing." He asked that Pakistanis "must condemn and counter any religious personality who is dividing you and fueling hatred and sectarianism and promoting militancy in any form."[8] Again, for a moment, it seemed that under Musharraf's firm leadership, with full support of the Army, militancy would get challenged. There was talk of Musharraf's admiration for the Turkish model and how he just might become the modern-day Ataturk in a nation that, in order successfully to meet the modern menaces of extremism and terrorism, was clamoring for state coherence.

Yet it never quite happened.

Watching the post 9/11 scenario with Pakistan unfold, I felt that there are reasons for the lack of resolve to carry out the lofty mission Musharraf had pledged to undertake. First, and likely the most compelling, was that his base, i.e. the intelligence and military leadership, thought it would be an impossible task with unknown consequences: the domestic situation in Pakistan already being sufficiently tense and tenuous made it difficult to predict the outcome. The anti-American ISI chief, General Mehmood Ahmed, was replaced on October 8, 2001, but undoubtedly there were others of his ilk within the intelligence community. Despite the promise of the January 12 speech, and even though the jihadists were in disarray after 9/11, there was no will either to challenge them and permanently lock away their leaders some of whom had already been picked up, or to enforce the registration of deadline rules for the madrassas. Second, the Army remained focused on India and given that Musharraf was the man behind the Kargil debacle, he understood the need to protect Pakistan in terms of the perennial concern of a two-front problem for Pakistan along its northern and eastern borders. Although the American ultimatum forced a refocus away from the Taliban at the official level, it did not offer any increased hope of a more friendly relationship with India, unlike what had been the case when the US partnered with Pakistan in the expulsion of the Soviets from Afghanistan in the 1980s. Third, after the public pressing of Pakistan to fall in line with American objectives in Afghanistan and the shuttle to Pakistan by CIA Director Tenet to press upon Musharraf the absolute seriousness of the situation, the traditional anti-American sentiment quickly followed the earlier sympathy elicited by the 9/11 attacks.

As one with knowledge of both the US policy establishment and Pakistani politics, I worked on thinking through ways in which a clash between the two could be prevented. Time was of essence, and policy shifts are seldom made in a rush.

My life was about to change, again.

NOTES

1. Ahmed Rashid, *Taliban: Islam, Oil and the New Great Game in Central Asia* (London: I.B. Tauris, 2000), 185.
2. Ahmed Rashid, *Descent into Chaos: The U.S. and the Disaster in Pakistan, Afghanistan and Central Asia* (New York: Viking, 2008), 24.
3. Bob Woodward, *Bush at War* (New York: Simon & Schuster, 2002), 31.

4. Ibid., 45.
5. Ibid., 59. See also Hassan Abbas, *Pakistan's Drift into Extremism: Allah, Then Army and America's War on Terror* (Armonk, NY: East Gate, 2004), 217.
6. Quoted in Bruce Riedel, *Deadly Embrace: Pakistan, America and the Future of the Global Jihad* (Washington, DC: Brookings Institution Press, 2011), 66.
7. Owen Bennett Jones, *Pakistan: Eye of the Storm* (New Haven, CT: Yale University Press, 2002), 282.
8. Reuters, May 25, 2002.

CHAPTER 27

White House Redux

The White House is rife with mystique and legend. No matter who is President, whatever the reason for the invitation to enter, there is always the moment when you feel the weight of history and that of the institution of the presidency. I have been there in Republican times and Democratic. This round in early February 2003 was unexpected as the Bush first term was already in progress for over two years and the policies of the administration in play. I was once more at the northwest gate, checking into see the Assistant to the President for National Security Affairs, Condoleezza Rice. I understood that her schedule was tight, but the staff politely requested flexibility because the National Security Advisor asked them to ensure that we met. I was leaving that afternoon for a six-week stay in Pakistan to undertake research for a study. The window for a meeting was a narrow one.

Sitting in the reception area of the West Wing, I reflected on the unexpected turn of events. The call had come the previous week from Condi's deputy, Steve Hadley. I was in the basement of a fitness center on the main line outside Philadelphia. It was a total surprise to hear an assistant ask me to hold for Hadley. I had never met Hadley but knew him to be the deputy National Security Advisor. The cell connection was terrible so I finally climbed up to street level. There, I heard Hadley say that he was calling on behalf of Dr. Rice. Condi had asked him to convey her hope that I would join her team to work as Senior Director for Democracy, Human Rights, and International Operations, which included the United Nations and multilateral account. My first instinct was to ask "why?" I did not know Hadley sufficiently well in order to do that. Still, I did ask Hadley if he was calling to ask me to come by for an "interview." He said the decision had already been made and that the job was mine and hoped that I would accept it.

I assumed that Hadley knew my record and the fact that I was one of those who had consistently argue for greater American involvement with the United Nations and for gaining support of many countries for US action against Saddam Hussein. This belief surely stood me apart from the neocons in the White House whose disdain for the UN and multilateral diplomacy was already legend. Also, I had a record of service in previous Republican administrations. In particular, during the George H. W. Bush years, I served as one of the American ambassadors to the UN, where I had arrived on August 2, 1990, the day Iraq invaded Kuwait. Robust US activity at the UN had helped cement the coalition in support of the Gulf War and I had come away with respect for what an engaged US foreign policy with the UN could achieve.

With my March 2001 head of delegation appointment to the UN Human Rights Commission as background, I pondered the 2003 offer. While it had come from National Security Advisor Rice, I was sure that there were others in the senior echelons, possibly including Hadley, who would have doubts regarding my credentials for a conservative White House. Yet, this was a call to serve. Further, given the timing of the offer, when the decision to go to war in Iraq had already been made, it seemed positive that the job of senior advisor was being offered to someone whose record would mean reaching out to the UN and the international community. Thus, I felt it important to meet Dr. Rice before making any final decision but an unsolicited offer to take a senior job at the National Security Council (where I had already served in two previous administrations) was obviously flattering. "But clearly," I thought, "to have any real clout, my job would also need the title: Special Assistant to the President."

Waiting in the West Lobby of the White House for my appointment with Condi on February 9, 2003, I ran into a number of individuals with whom I had worked in the past. There was a great deal of activity as visitors were escorted to meetings in the West Wing either into the Oval Office, or into the other offices set beyond the visitors' waiting area leading toward the office of the Vice President, the Chief of Staff, and the National Security Advisor. All of the activity, in hindsight, explained the timing of the plan for the invasion of Iraq and the case for war that Secretary of State Colin Powell had made on February 5, 2003.

Rice had already challenged the UN to live up to the dozen or so resolutions the Security Council had on its books on Iraq. I had served as part of the US team that pressed for and secured some of the key resolutions on Iraq a decade-plus earlier. There was a great deal of frustration apparent by February 2003 at the White House that the UN Security Council was not pressing harder for compliance by Saddam Hussein nor was the American case for action being supported within the chosen US timetable. Rice had been charged with making the statement that the UN had become irrelevant, "a debating society with no teeth."[1] Thus, the timing of my meeting with Dr. Rice was dramatic, coming just weeks before the war to overthrow Saddam Hussein started. I was struck by the reaction of some who passed by that morning, e.g., Scooter Libby, who seemed startled to see me in the West Wing and asked what I was doing there. My response, "just waiting," elicited a quizzical look from him.

When finally ushered into the National Security Advisor's office, Condi met me cordially. She was clearly tightly scheduled but she sat down for a lengthy conversation. She said that she had reached out to offer me the job because she felt I understood how the National Security Council worked. Further, I had experience in multilateral diplomacy and had worked to build support for US policies at the UN. These efforts would be needed in the weeks and months ahead. She also said the fact that I was a Muslim was a plus and I might be helpful in bridge-building to the Islamic world. I understood this last remark to mean that 9/11 had changed everything and the White House wanted to ensure that the War on Terror did not turn into a massive confrontation with Islam. Earliest actions following 9/11 reflected that sentiment as the President had gone to the Islamic center in Washington to say that America's war was with the terrorists and not with their religion, a message that resonated with me personally.

We talked about the duties of the job. The portfolio included Human Rights (where I had already in 2001 served as Head of the US delegation). It also had a Democracy component about which more will be said in the following chapters. The UN account involved all aspects of US policy, including the response to the Iraq war and the potential for support. It was undoubtedly a huge challenge, and I wondered if all in the West Wing would be okay with her choice of me and her agreement to the title Special Assistant to the President and Senior Director.

In the course of our discussion, I mentioned to Condi that as a Republican I had voted for the President and that I had met him in 1987 when his father was Vice President. I had been in India and Pakistan conducting research after the 2000 election and was there during the prolonged election results saga. Subsequently, I had heard from fellow Republicans that this White House applied "litmus tests" to the appointment of individuals to senior positions. I said that it was unlikely that I would meet many litmus tests put in place by neocons so I wanted to be sure that Rice was comfortable in offering me the job. She was dismissive of the idea of litmus tests and asked me to meet with the executive Secretary of the NSC, Greg Schulte, in order to work out the details. At that point, her deputy, Steve Hadley, came in and Condi introduced us. Hadley said he had a few issues to bring to my attention and knew that I had served at the NSC previously. I said that it was a six-year stint during the Reagan and early Bush years (1984–1990). He reflected on the varied styles of those Presidents and the offices set up to serve them. However, in the George W. Bush White House, said Hadley, the NSC setup was "seamless" in involving all constituent parts of the White House.

This specifically meant that "the team" was a larger one and that the office of the Vice President (OVP) was integrally involved in all of the work of the NSC. I thought this was an unusual pitch since in my experience, while all NSC work involved some coordination with OVP, that coordination was usually a loose one: The NSC charted the path for presidential approval and the clearance process routinely included the appropriate OVP official. In the Reagan administration, then Vice President George H. W. Bush had a particular interest in foreign policy beyond his amused aside "you die, I fly" that took the VP to various funerals.

The National Security Advisor for Bush, Donald Gregg, had been an important partner in my work on South Asia. I had traveled with the VP to India and to Pakistan. Other travels included parts of the Gulf region (i.e., Yemen, Bahrain, Saudi Arabia, and Oman). Given all of the above and my own experience in previous NSC matters, Hadley's admonition "to be particularly mindful of OVP" at our very first meeting in 2003 seemed bizarre. I did not quite understand at that time that Hadley had long been identified as "another of Cheney's 'Defense Dogs.'"[2] Just before we ended the meeting, Condi took me around the corner in the West Wing to meet with the Chief of Staff to the President, Andrew Card. She introduced me to Card and pointed out that I had served at the NSC in other Republican administrations. Just before leaving, Rice told Card that: "Shirin is a Muslim." That was an unusual statement in my experience, as my religion was known and occasionally celebrated, as I recalled from George H. W. Bush's meeting with the Emir of Bahrain on a visit to that country, when I accompanied the VP in 1985.

As we walked back to the NSA's office, she asked how long was I going to be away and urged me to start the process of signing on quickly. I noted it would be six weeks in South Asia and Condi asked that I reduce it to three as she wanted me to start soonest. I left the White House with the feeling that it would be my third round. I was once again struck by the immense activity in the lobby as people moved in and out, those among them whom I knew pausing to say hello.

Upon leaving the White House premises on my way to Dulles airport to start my nearly month-long overseas trip, I pondered the significance of the remark made by Condi noting my religion. That was a first for me in my many years of US government service. The first question that came to mind was the one noted above, why now? But even beyond the obvious connotations of working in the shadow of 9/11, the remark had significance.

As I flew east from Dulles airport after my meeting with Condi in February 2003, I focused on what it had meant to me personally to be a Muslim. Growing up in India, at a young age I was aware that the world familiar to me had many who did not share my religion since they were primarily Hindus, Zoroastrians, or Buddhists rather than Muslim. What were the first memories I had regarding my Muslim heritage? That thought led me to recall my initiation or "Bismillah" ceremony. Always respecting the myriad races and cultures that make up America, I love the mix that allows for a richness that goes beyond mere wealth. I know that for many, including Condi Rice, the sentiment that "In America it does not matter where you come from. It matters where you are going" held true. Yet, I believe that where you come from and what you bring in your identity, education, experience, and outlook surely impinge on your work.

In the George W. Bush NSC, I hoped that my work for the NSC would not clash with the known predilections of so many there who advertised themselves as neocons with suspicion of the world and the belief that US supremacy would only be sustained through denigrating the value of collaborative international work. After all, US leadership is critical. Getting others to join US preferences requires diplomacy and open minds.

But I also knew that neocons did not operate by stealth. They openly articulated their belief, that US supremacy could only be sustained through denigration of collaborative international work. A network of like-minded in the OVP and Defense Department allowed these colleagues incredible coordination and control.

As promised by the NSC Executive Secretary whom I met after my meeting with Rice prior to travel abroad, the paperwork moved fast. I had to send in my updated forms from overseas. I was told that the boss wanted expeditious handling. I was given the commission to become Special Assistant to the President. The title ensured accelerated handling since only a limited number of these are approved by Congress for the President's staff. Without the commissioned position, I knew that access was more limited with the sole title of Senior Director.

I started in my new job on March 24, 2003, the fifth day of the second Iraq war. As I walked into the White House complex that morning I thought: "Is this round very different?" There was a great deal of activity within the White House, a natural response given the seriousness of the war involving American soldiers and material. The George W. Bush Presidency had been staked on the Iraq war and the goal of Saddam's overthrow. The war's raison d'être was the existence of weapons of mass destruction (WMD). The outcome mattered. The President's staff was very focused on events that were unfolding half a world away.

This was the third President I would work for at the NSC. Even as I entered into service in my final foray at the National Security Council, I was struck by how much had changed since my previous assignments commencing in 1984. This was indeed a different White House. It was much more political. Even within that designation, there was a sense of separation based on those who came from Texas, had served as the governor's advisors and/or had worked in the campaign for the 2000 election and those Republicans such as myself who served in the foreign policy world because of their expertise and experience. It seemed as if the painful period prior to the assumption by George W. Bush of the presidency while the election was disputed had left a legacy of suspicion and hostility and an "us versus them" mentality within the staff that I never witnessed in the two previous Republican administrations in which I served.

While to most of its highly placed proponents, the second Iraq war was a continuation of the unfinished effort of the first US–Iraq war, many others, including myself, accepted the official explanation that it was really an aftermath of the attacks of 9/11. Thus, we all agreed with its stated goals: namely the removal of Saddam Hussein, the destruction of Iraq's WMD capability, and the defanging of Iraq as a poisonous threat to the region. The conclusion of the war meant America's full focus would return to the Afghanistan front where there was a real threat: one posed by al Qaeda.

From all published accounts, the Pentagon was surprised by the almost total absence of Saddam's war machine posing a challenge to the onslaught of the coalition forces. General Tommy Franks had reported to the President on March 22 that no Iraqi WMD had been aimed at the advancing forces and that the Iraqi military "are just taking off their uniforms and going home."[3] This seemed to be unexpected and reflected a belief that Saddam Hussein's long reign of terror was now on shaky grounds.

On April 2, 2003, Secretary of Defense, Donald Rumsfeld reported to the NSC that "We've got 116,000 men in Iraq, 310,000 men in the theater."[4] The advance of US forces and the rapid neutralization of Iraqi troops, including the mainstay of Saddam's support, the Republican Guard, were celebrated as the move toward Baghdad proceeded. Yet, the celebration was not worldwide, a disappointing factor for a President and senior administration colleagues who believed that the true beneficiaries of changes being wrought were going to be, first, the Iraqi people and, second, Israel and other regional and international players who were past or potential future targets of Saddam's aggressive policies. I found that contrary to outside simplistic accounts, the President and Rice were aware of the range of options, from disarmament to democracy-building, even as the first bombs fell on Baghdad, but their focus was clearly on WMD.

The model for this Iraq war was deliberately different from the 1990 war evicting Saddam Hussein from Kuwait. In that war, I was witness to the immense diplomatic effort undertaken by the President, the Secretary of State, the US ambassadors to the UN and senior staff at the White House. Multilateral outreach, the hallmark of the 1990 Gulf War, was badly mocked in the White House in the 2003 war. The need for continued pursuit of WMD program was seen in 2003 as a direct consequence of the failure of the UN to force Iraqi compliance with the many existing resolutions of the UN Security Council going back to the 1990–1993 period. Vice President Cheney and his senior staff were convinced that going back to the UN for more resolutions merely extended the period during which Saddam would further deceive international inspectors. For this group, war seemed not just the preferred but the only option. Thus, the UN Secretary General Kofi Annan, the chief UN inspector Hans Blix, several UN Security Council members, and other senior US officials, including Powell and Armitage all were taken by Cheney as those who would prefer to "Wrap the whole thing up in red tape as it's been done for 12 years previously, pass another resolution, call it good, everybody goes home and nothing happens."[5]

As America prepared for the invasion of Iraq, Rice told al Jazeera: "Now, we are in the endgame for UN diplomacy... This cannot go on for very much longer."[6] Rice reminded the Arab news channel that the UN had failed to act in the past when Muslims had been under threat in Kosovo. Nor had the UN done much to prevent genocide in Rwanda costing nearly a million lives. Expressing her views and reflecting those held by both the President and Vice President Cheney, she said: "We really do believe that once the region is rid of this terrible regime in Iraq, if we have to use military force, that will open new opportunities for peace in the Middle East and new opportunities for Arab countries to give greater liberty and greater awareness to their own people."[7]

While this Cheney view, expressing a process of liberation for the Middle East, is widely cited, there is generally less appreciation for the actual anti-multilateral bent within the White House. Most vocal in voicing such misgivings was the VP's confidante and senior staffer, David Addington. On innumerable occasions, Addington offered his condolences to me that I had to deal with "those people" in my UN work. American national interest was seen as being divorced from any UN interaction in the firm belief that few there really wanted change in Iraq as dictated by the USA. In the meantime, the administration was increasingly coming under fire for its unilateralism—a charge that the neocons seemed to wear as a badge of honor.[8]

Philosophic differences in mindset and the preferences for normal tools of American foreign policy were clearly visible in the unfolding events following the attack on Iraq. My previous six years at the National Security Council gave me experience and a prism for viewing interactions within the White House. It was evident that while key players were supportive of the goal of dislodging Saddam, there were critical differences in their respective approaches regarding how best to accomplish the goal. On timing, in the end, the President's belief that time was of the essence and that danger from Iraqi WMD would only mount with time seemed to be the prevailing view.

Given the White House's firmly held belief that the need for the Iraq war was self-evident, the beating that the USA was taking in the propaganda war was puzzling to many in the Cheney circle.

In order to sustain the war effort and any subsequent US occupation, all the senior officials sitting in the Situation Room were cognizant of the need for both domestic support as well as that of the Iraqi population. I had heard similar concerns from Washington leaders in the first Gulf War of 1990, even as I served in New York at the time. In 2003, the case for war was initially made on the existence in Saddam Hussein's hand of WMD. Public opinion was more than divided in offering support. Frustration was evident as President Bush noted to Prime Minister Aznar of Spain, an early member of the "Coalition of the willing," "We are losing one part of the war and this is propaganda."[9]

Iraq obviously occupied a major part of the attention given by the White House to foreign policy in the months after my starting date in the job. There were, of course, additional issues that are of ongoing concern around the world. Among those was the issue of UN actions, past and current, which were addressed. Important among these was the understanding that the UN would continue to play its important role there even absent support for the Iraq war among many of the UN members. National Security Advisor Rice shared my own belief that Kofi Annan, the UN Secretary General (SYG), was important to the postwar effort in Iraq and that keeping lines of communication open to him was key as war seemed in those heady days to be winding down with the early defeat of Saddam Hussein and his once mighty Army. Toward that end, I began to reach out to the SYG and his senior staff, building on personal relationships that harked back to my stint as Ambassador to the UN for Special Political Affairs and that of Annan as an Assistant Secretary General for Peacekeeping Operations in the 1990–1993 period. The President and Rice among many strongly believed that after Saddam's fall, hidden WMD caches would indeed be found. Thus, the primary rationale for the war continued in those early months was non-compliance by Saddam Hussein of many UNSCRs on Iraq's weapons programs and failure to allow UN inspectors unfettered and consistent access.

Vice President Dick Cheney remained particularly focused on the imminent danger of Iraq's possession of a full-fledged nuclear capability as he stated to a variety of people. According to Cheney, Iraq's "ability to miniaturize weapons of mass destruction, particularly nuclear," had been "substantially refined since the first Gulf War."[10] This belief was zealously held by all in OVP and any failure to uncover WMD merely meant that UN inspections system was at fault or that the Iraqi regime had succeeded in hiding its capability more cleverly.

Cheney addressed Veterans of Foreign Wars on August 26, 2002, and said to them: "Simply stated, there is no doubt that Saddam Hussein now has weapons of mass destruction," a charge that is said to have won him a mild admonishment from Condi at the direction of the President.[11] Clearly, the President was less than happy at the constant nudge by his Vice President as he went on to write in his own memoirs. Bush notes that in one of his weekly lunches with his Vice President in the winter of 2003, Cheney asked him directly: "Are you going to take care of this guy or not," but that the President had replied he was not "ready to move yet."[12] Condi Rice echoed some of the same sentiment regarding the Iraqi hidden WMD capability making Saddam Hussein's removal necessary. She said in an interview: "The overwhelming, unmitigated disaster and nightmare is that you have this aggressive tyrant in a couple of years armed with a nuclear weapon...and brandishing it in the most volatile region in the world."[13]

Bush made the pitch against Saddam Hussein's pursuit of WMD in his State of the Union speech in January 2003. The White House was convinced that these weapons existed and that the dictator intended to hide them in order to "dominate, intimidate, or attack." Bush and Cheney were convinced that Iraq's chemical weapons capability existed and that it was only a matter of time when other types of WMD capacity would be fully developed. This is also the address in which the controversial sixteen words "The British government has learned that Saddam Hussein recently sought significant quantities of Uranium from Africa"[14] were noted.

Shadows of Saddam Hussein's war were lengthening. Indeed, the ever darkening antumbra of 9/11 was reaching umbra when the President made the link between the Iraqi dictator and al Qaeda and noted the horror that would ensue should Saddam share "just one vial, one canister, one crate slipped into this country to bring a day of horror like one we have never known."[15]

This round of work at the NSC exposed me to a new format for interaction between senior officials of the US government. From my previous two stints in the Reagan and early Bush 41 NSCs, I was aware that simple issues were resolved below the level of the President. Only key items and tough issues came to the President, and his staff had to manage these. Given that cabinet officials, key ones in particular, maintained their personal access to the President, there were always channels for voicing disagreement. I assumed 2003 was likely to be no different in that respect.

I had seen and expected differences to emerge as the Principals (the term for cabinet-level officials) reflected decision-making in their own style and based on their respective views of what constituted the "best" option for policy on any given issue. But in 2003, the differences went beyond style to substance: The absolute insistence on what was deemed as the best option. Thus, in effect, there was only one possible choice. Critical issues of the day, especially as related to the War on Terror and the Iraq war, were then handled by the neocon mindset that held only to their version of the "right way," as distinct from everybody else which constituted the "wrong way." Still, I was surprised by the reactions of a number of cabinet officials and their deputies who hailed from the Bush '41 time and had been in key positions during the 1990s Gulf War when the cardinal rule was the UN mandate. Clearly some like Cheney, Rumsfeld, Wolfowitz still chafed at what they felt was the untimely conclusion of the 1990 war where the goal, as authorized by UN resolutions, was limited to the eviction of Saddam Hussein from Kuwait rather than his demise. "Now was the chance," their rhetoric implied, "to right the earlier wrong."

In the critical days following the entry of US forces into Iraq, as the overwhelming weight of the problems of Iraq was beginning to be felt at the White House, the Defense Department argued for transfer of ownership of running Iraq to the State Department. Given that the war was continuing and that the US Army was fast becoming an occupation force, State was reluctant to take on a civilian mantle absent any presence in the theater.

Cheney's opinions about the irrelevancy of the UN had the feel of a religious faith and his sermons were those of a profound believer. The atmosphere in meetings was often charged as the Cheney/Rumsfeld/Wolfowitz troika held forth. When Powell stated the President's position that the weapons inspectors go back into Iraq, it was less than well received by the Troika. They proclaimed that it would be a useless maneuver and would result in Saddam Hussein gaining more time for doing mischief. Similarly, any suggestion for greater UN involvement following the start of the war was seen by the Troika as not worth the time. "Make the UN irrelevant" was the oft-repeated mantra. Often these views were forcefully expressed during normal "Principals" meetings which struck me as strange that the Vice President would continue to attend meetings which were slated just for cabinet officials. True that he would be expected to attend the traditional full NSC meetings, which normally the President would chair, but that setting would have been a less suitable location for the VP's proclamations.

Of course, some of these opinions, at least in part, were shared by the President. Yet, at times, Bush admitted that diplomacy counted for something. "I *loved* building the coalition in Afghanistan," he said.[16] But his worry always was what the French, the Russians, and the Germans had in store to prevent American action. He saw the UN as an institution that had long passed its glory. His had not been the experience of his father regarding the UN. Action was what the younger Bush wanted, and he saw the UN as concerned with the "act of talking."[17] He did give it some time because of the wishes of the key allies: Blair (UK); Aznar (Spain); Berlusconi (Italy); and Howard (Australia), all of whom strongly urged it. Still, he believed, there was little chance of success without direct US action. In his earlier speech to the annual meeting of the UNGA leaders on September 12, 2002, on the heels of the first anniversary of 9/11, Bush threw down the gauntlet: "Will the United Nations serve the purpose of its founding, or will it be irrelevant?"

As Special Assistant to the President and Senior Director for International Operations, it fell to me to keep making the case at the White House for the former assumption rather than the latter. There were problems with the UN system which were generally recognized. That also meant the USA insisting at the United Nations that, in order to keep itself relevant for the modern era, it must submit to serious reform. "The UN system had broken down over the years and badly needed fixing" was an often shared opinion. Finally, UN Membership's call for reform provided a much needed opening for the update that was badly needed.

As I listened to hopes and concerns voiced around the table in various Situation Room meetings at the White House in early 2003, my mind flashed back to similar expressions of optimism I recalled from a prior age a world away when I had heard leaders talk of changing history to create a modern, democratic progressive Pakistan. All around me I heard views that the USA would remake Iraq as a peaceful neighbor in a dangerous part of the world. There seemed to be an assumption that fundamental change and political reengineering was a reachable goal.

The rapid demise of the Saddam regime at US hands fed White House hopes that there was a real chance for fundamental change. Hearing one such discussion around the table, I remembered a different country where freedom was seen to be a guarantor for a bright and better future. There was also then the hope that freedom would bring a better life for citizens.[18]

Pakistan had been created out of the Indian subcontinent as a land for Muslims. Freedom meant a chance to fashion a new nation with the hope of equality and prosperity even though all understood that sacrifice would also be required. Given the critical input in education that my father made from the early years of Pakistan, I was privy to discussions around tables where optimism and the can-do attitude was very much the same in 1950 that I heard in the White House deliberations in 2003, freedom was the pathway to a better future. A struggling new nation in the subcontinent and the world's only superpower, respectively, demonstrated the same strong belief that the goal was achievable. In Pakistan's case, it was to create from the ground up a modern, educated, and developed state. In Washington's case, it was to change Iraq through invasion and alter the political map of the Middle East while emasculating all its nuclear ambitions.

On a daily basis in 2003, as turf wars between the Pentagon and the State Department continued, Rice chaired up the group whose job it was to oversee policy aimed at making things better on the ground in Iraq. Each day, with daily charts showing the gains and losses in the electricity grid, Condi would press for better responses on timelines. The NSC Senior Director who was the main liaison with the Pentagon repeatedly expressed his frustration at the difficulty of getting responses. State participants would roll their eyes in a "not our problem" manner. Rice would try and push for better answers and faster progress emphasizing that the President wanted rapid progress and the existing DOD attitude was not acceptable. It was clear that Cheney and Rumsfeld did not care what Rice wanted.

Creating a new ground reality following the overthrow of a dictator in Iraq seemed a mission impossible, even with the world's most powerful country in charge. So it was when a small country newly separated from India was trying to make the lives of its citizens better. Around the dinner table so many years previously, I heard similar arguments: Can political will and commitment to progress be sufficient? Why were there so many impediments and why did people resist progress? How should a government leadership sell the idea of a different future to its people?

Like Iraq, Pakistan is a multi-ethnic Muslim country where regional and tribal loyalties run paramount. I remember the long searching discussions between national leaders and their regional counterparts that the former knew the best way forward. I recall listening to the frustration where the central government representatives could not understand why the local/tribal leaders refused to go along with proposals designed to benefit them. I recall my father conveying some of the hopes and frustration during a tea he hosted for Premier Chou En-lai of China during his first visit to Pakistan in 1956.

Back to the 2003 White House, it was an eye-opener to witness its senior-most foreign policy official, the national security advisor with close links to the President, would herself be involved with the electric grid issues. Here was an invading power who was desperately trying to influence the improvement of life in Iraq so that the Iraqi people would immediately sign on to what they clearly saw as a new and better Iraq.

I could not imagine a parallel in the Indian subcontinent. Perhaps Britain's heavy engagement in the development of newly independent Pakistan in the late 1940s may have come close, had it actually occurred. Nor did the 1971 war and India's role in the formation of Bangladesh after the defeat of the Pakistan Army unleash Indian sentiments for developing Bangladesh on fast track to progress.

Face time with the President is a critical issue within the White House. I had served in a much smaller NSC previously where there was a good deal of time for briefings and decision memos. In the George W. Bush era, my first travel with the President came soon after the fall of Saddam Hussein as Bush journeyed to Dearborn, Michigan on April 28, 2003.

Air Force One is always a great experience when you can ride on it. This one was a 747 much larger than the previous 707s that had been my experience. Much more spacious and much more of a working environment with all of the modern accoutrements, the hustle and bustle of a huge plane with few passengers focused on the mission is dramatic work space.

I went to Andrews Air Force Base in the White House van that carried the staff. In the post 9/11 days, I always rode on the van whereas in previous times driving out to Andrews and parking my car there for the duration of the trip had made sense. As I got into the van, I realized that we were embarking on a domestic policy event. The staff was different from the usual one in my foreign policy experience. Since this was my first travel with the President, the White House photographer duly recorded a photo with the President which he later graciously signed and sent me.

On the plane was Karl Rove who oversaw this domestic trip with all the right props: including the choice of a city where Arab–Americans were certain to offer a warm welcome. The welcome came along with the banner "Renewal in Iraq" emblazoned in the background as the President joyfully made the case to a group of Iraqi-Americans about what he called "new Iraq." Talking about "Operation Iraqi Freedom," Bush gave a rousing account in a speech in Dearborn, Michigan of ways in which the fall of Saddam meant new beginnings for the people of that country, citing the democratic trend that was taking hold each day and the US support for the same. "America pledged to rid Iraq of an oppressive regime, and we kept our word. America now pledges to help Iraqis build a prosperous and peaceful nation, and we will keep our word again," said Bush to thunderous applause.[19] In conversations with audience members, I found a great deal of support for the President. It was a political gathering and Bush was the Commander in Chief. We returned on Air Force One for the flight back to Washington that afternoon.

NOTES

1. Bob Woodward, *Bush at War* (New York: Simon & Schuster, 2002), 336.
2. A reference to a group of former Pentagon officials with links to Cheney, Barton Gellman, *Angler: The Cheney Vice Presidency* (New York: Penguin Press, 2008), 39.
3. Bob Woodward, *Plan of Attack* (New York: Simon & Schuster, 2004), 403.
4. Ibid., 406.
5. Ibid., 235.
6. NSA Rice Interview with *al Jazeera*, Office of the Press Secretary, The White House, Washington, DC, March 14, 2003.
7. Ibid.
8. See, for example, Clyde Prestowitz, *Rogue Nation: American Unilateralism and the Failure of Good Intentions* (New York: Basic Books, 2003).
9. Bush quoted in Prestowitz, *Rogue Nation*, 406.
10. Gellman, *Angler*, 217.
11. *New York Times*, August 27, 2002.

12. George W. Bush, *Decision Points* (New York: Crown Publishers, 2010), 251.
13. Woodward, *Bush at War*, 350.
14. George W. Bush, State of the Union Address, January 28, 2003.
15. Ibid.
16. Robert Draper, *Dead Certain: The Presidency of George W. Bush* (New York: Free Press, 2008), 179.
17. Ibid.
18. Yasmin Khan, *The Great Partition: The Making of India and Pakistan* (New Haven: Yale University Press, 2007).
19. Remarks by the President on Operation Iraqi Freedom, The White House, April 28, 2003.

CHAPTER 28

A Changed Model

The Dearborn visit was symptomatic of the generally upbeat view of expected events in Iraq following Saddam Hussein's fall. This was after the quick entry into Iraq and before the looting and destruction had wrought havoc, signaling the failings of Iraqi and American security efforts. Plans for rebuilding were in progress, and the expectation was that a new Arab democratic showcase was in the making. At this juncture, the White House still fully expected to find significant caches of the WMD. "They were there to be found." And when found, because the USA had no intention of staying in Iraq, they would usher in the new era, disarm the skeptics, and retroactively justify the forceful entry into Iraq. Even before the complete absence of the WMD was fully apparent, the White House was getting poor press. As a result, genuine concern and surprise gripped the leadership. "Clearly it must be because we are not getting our word out correctly. And if so, then getting the message out must become an important part of our overall effort."

The need seemed pressing. The congressionally mandated Advisory Group on Public Diplomacy in the Arab and Muslim World reported its findings on October 1, 2003. Not unexpectedly, the report concluded that: "At a critical time in our nation's history, the apparatus of public diplomacy has proven inadequate."[1] The report noted: (There has been) "unilateral disarmament in the weapons of advocacy that has contributed to widespread hostility toward Americans and left us vulnerable to lethal threats to our interests and our safety."[2] I read the report with care as I thought it would help shape the debate.

To counter the threat posed by extremists to American values and global position, the US arsenal was now to be expanded to focus on "The War of Ideas." The President's senior advisor from Texas, Karen Hughes, led the effort to get the message out regarding America's genuine respect for Islam. To help put distance between the al Qaeda types and the public in constituent Muslim countries, American diplomacy would henceforth offer its own brand of messaging. After all, the 9/11 Commission had pointed out that eliminating al Qaeda requires "prevailing in the longer term over the ideology that gives rise to Islamic terrorism."[3]

Given the new model of diplomacy where no negotiation with new enemies was possible, the war on ideas could then offer an avenue to counter-terrorism through the promotion of democracy and freedom. This was a huge challenge, particularly as poll after poll showed that Muslims worldwide were less than trusting of America's motives and large majorities of Muslims in key countries believed that undermining Islam was a key goal of US foreign policy. Public diplomacy efforts to counter such suspicions were then perceived by Hughes and others to be simply a matter of getting the right message out with greater frequency and intensity. Thus, a number of special programs were launched, including setting up State Department media hubs in London, Brussels, and Dubai seeking to deliver the "right" message with greater intensity and frequency and overcome time differences in the twenty-four-hour news cycle. A Digital Outreach Team began engaging with Arab leaders was expanded to include Persian and Urdu sites in December, 2007.

Another much touted vehicle for winning hearts and minds was personal engagement via educational and cultural exchanges. Calling exchanges "the crown jewels" of public diplomacy, funding for these was doubled from $244 million in 2003 to $501 million in 2008. The highly successful Fulbright program brought nearly 7000 students/scholars to the US. Exposure to America and Americans was hoped to help them understand "our values: generosity, tolerance, compassion."[4]

Much of the above was predicated on the firm belief by those in leadership, including Bush, Rice, and Hughes, that despite various polls, attitudes toward the USA in the Muslim world were more complicated than simple dislike for American policy toward various countries, the war in Iraq (far more unpopular in the Islamic world with a six-to-one ratio than the 50-50 split in the USA at the time).[5] The assumption here was that a better explanation of US goals and policies would build a more tolerant view of America in the Muslim world. After all, as Rice said: The USA is "Still the place where people like to send their kids to school, where people want to start a new life. Sometimes we overstate the degree to which America is not popular, even if sometimes our policies are not."[6] The ongoing decline in US popularity in the Muslim world coincided exactly with the Bush administration effort to get the word out that even after 9/11, the USA understood the conflict with terrorist did not mean a conflict with the World of Islam.

9/11 changed the world of American foreign policy in fundamental ways. Heretofore, the main actors in the international system were nation-states. The USA focused on national governments as the core actors for diplomacy and International Relations. Our national interest required us to convince other governments to coordinate policy in parallel directions to those espoused by us. Under such a scheme, multilateral diplomacy was focused on developing, wherever possible, coalitions that would support US policies.

The post 9/11 world offered a new challenge with the emergence of the non-state actors. Operating with impunity across international boundaries, these players changed the rules of the game. They eschewed negotiation in favor of an inflexible set of demands which were sacrosanct. They sought to discredit the West, while they promoted their own belligerent version of Islam. The USA became their special target. And the threat from these "shock-troops of new radicalism"[7] was keenly felt in the White House.

The USA had to find a new response to a new threat. The nature of the threat had gone from challenges within societies where governments were discredited—as having thoroughly failed to provide justice and governance—to a new menace which was transborder. Because America had become a particular target, ways had to be found to deal with the threat and its "shock-troops." We now lived in an era of asymmetrical warfare, fighting an enemy that has global reach but lives in the shadows of states it tries to co-opt. Any American response to the new threat had to have more than military element in the arsenal. As evident in Iraq and Afghanistan, the theater of operations simultaneously included real and potential use of military force and individuals who assisted in intelligence gathering. In addition, to win hearts and minds, cadres of civilians became involved in reconstruction activities.

The new foreign policy model after 9/11 has had no option but to include the protection of the "homeland" from the new transnational threat that involves terrorists of major consequence. Indeed, as nation-states become ever more vulnerable to these non-state actors, both bilateral relations and multilateral diplomacy are needed to counter them. Because these groups do not subscribe to international norms, negotiation is not acceptable. Their "perfect" vision of the world brooks no disagreement: Issues can only be resolved in death. The USA has, therefore, needed to work with other countries in critical geographical regions to help prevent the menace before it reaches American shores. Under the circumstances, one key response of the USA came from the very top, the President and his key lieutenants. As these officials looked for any possible route to disarm the new enemy, a structure for a new approach began to take shape. Everybody, of course, agreed that whenever and wherever possible, help should be given to those in need. More importantly, knowing that overnight the Muslim world had become locus of a great and henceforth direct threat to the USA, it was decided that special effort had to be made to reduce and possibly counter the profound disenchantment and alienation that existed there. Thus, in the new scheme of things, there would be a push for "inclusion" for the rapidly increasing numbers of young disenfranchised Muslim youth whose only option for inclusion was terror.

Washington assumed that as a target of the 9/11 attack and as the dominant power in the world, it must take the lead in restoring stability in a new world. That stability looked beyond the regimes to the disenchanted group that perpetrated the terrorist attack on the homeland, a group that seemed to draw endless strength from many young adherents across numerous national boundaries. What they had in common, apart from hatred for the USA, was disillusionment with their own respective regimes where even genuine grievances went unmet.

Why was their disillusionment so great that they chose the path of terrorism and self-destruction? The Bush administration concluded that the real problem lay in the alienation of Muslim youth from their respective governments. Lacking any meaningful role in the process of governance, this disgruntled segment of the population sought means to cause grave harm to the USA whom they held responsible for the survival of their dictatorial governments. Demography offered urgency to the administration's task because the rapidly increasing young population needed freedom and democracy in order to gain a role in their respective society.

Thus, democracy promotion took hold as a key foreign policy goal of the Bush administration. The President believed in it and said "the desire for liberty and justice is found in every human heart." Others, especially those around the President, made a persuasive case that "US future depended on making a better world." In the Muslim world that meant a less alienated population who had a stake in their respective country's prosperity. Since many of these countries had non-democratic systems and elite unlikely to promote power sharing with the disenfranchised, the American goal became democracy through developing links and supporting civil society. This again was "Diplomacy without Negotiation" as the regimes in power were obviously unwilling to sign away their privileged position. At best, US interaction with segments of the population was tolerated as an odious accoutrement that had to be worn. The push and pull of America's call for freedom often occurred against a backdrop of power politics and seeking the goodwill of foreign leaders in pursuit of what was named "war on terror," mostly received only a staged response.

The US approach was later articulated in a major speech by Condoleezza Rice as she reflected on the changes wrought by 9/11. Citing her belief and that of Bush that "the root cause of September 11 was the violent expression of a global extremist ideology, an ideology rooted in the oppression and despair of the modern Middle East," she argued that "we must seek to remove the source of this terror by transforming that troubled region."[8] Rice pointed to the mistaken belief of 60 years that stability could be achieved absent liberty and democracy which were the "only guarantees of true stability and lasting security." While pursuit of liberty meant dealing with opponents even as one stood to lose "arbitrary powers and unjust privileges," absence of liberty meant oppression, arbitrary rule, and denial of justice. Rice challenged critics who imply that support of democracy was simply the "export" of democracy, chiding that democracy was not simply "a product that only America manufactured....it is the very height of arrogance to believe that political liberty and democratic aspirations and freedom of speech and rights for women somehow belong only to us...It is not liberty and democracy that must be imposed. It is tyranny and silence that are forced upon people at gunpoint."[9]

As the world worried that the war on terror had changed long-held beliefs in the USA, Rice noted early in her term as Secretary of State that the values that support individual rights and freedom were in place. However, the USA after 9/11 was in a different kind of war "where people who know no boundaries, know no treaties, know no borders or territories are assaulting free peoples, are killing innocents on a wanton scale."[10] Even before the George W. Bush presidency was won, Condoleezza Rice had insisted that peace was most important condition for continued prosperity and freedom. When peace lay shattered in the aftermath of the Iraq invasion and prosperity threatened, Rice as part of the President's inner circle helped shape the response. For promotion of democracy in the Muslim world, diplomacy and engagement would normally be the order of the day. However, the rules of diplomatic engagement became dramatically proscribed after the American invasion of Iraq in 2003. Despite the fact that it was internationally unpopular, the Bush administration worked hard to cobble together a working coalition. To this end, it shunted aside traditional allies who disagreed as simply constituting "old Europe." Often, promotion of democracy meant working with civil society directly outside state interaction. It was a different model, and negotiation was replaced by direct reach into the population.

The second circle for US outreach to the Muslim world involved key components of the global community such as the UN, the World Bank, and UNDP. Here US financial contributions were expected to lead to political clout. But I closely witnessed that the Bush administration was divided on the utility of international organizations, preferring those such as the World Bank, where neocons like Paul Wolfowitz or his successor were seen to be an integral part of the "boy's club." When it came time to work on democracy promotion in Iraq and elsewhere after the demise of the WMD argument for the invasion, Wolfowitz and his friends Shaha Riza and Liz Cheney partnered in attempts aimed at changing the Muslim world. Other multilateral institutions, such as the UN, were suspect because they gave credence to the smaller less important members' grievances against an overbearing disrespectful US. Vice President Cheney, in particular, missed no chance to speak ill of the UN. Indeed, his appointed pals such as John Bolton made mockery of the UN and advised that the top ten floors of the UN secretariat building, where the leadership resides, could be blown off to enhance its work. Clearly, negotiation to promote US goals through diplomacy was not an option.

The outer circle for interaction involved non-state actors, transnational religious, and subnational groups whose aim is to seek a total overhaul of the international system. In this world, there are no referees and the rules of engagement differ according to the actors. There is no meeting ground and no question of negotiation. All communication is reduced to issuing threats and claiming responsibility for heinous acts undertaken to terrorize populations and nations. The work of democracy promotion after 2003 took place within this environment and its circles which set the stage for US foreign policy. The response of the US administration to the challenge provides both the context and the policy of outreach to the Muslim world and the task of democracy promotion there.

NOTES

1. "Changing Minds, Winning Peace: A New Strategic Direction for U.S. Public Diplomacy in the Arab & Muslim World," Report of the Advisory Group on Public Diplomacy for the Arab and Muslim World, October 1, 2003, submitted to the Committee on Appropriations, U.S. House of Representatives, 8.
2. Ibid., 13.
3. *The 9/11 Commission Report: Final Report of the National Commission on Terrorist Attacks Upon the United States* (New York: W. W. Norton & Co., 2004), 363.
4. Glassman, Opening Statement, Senate Foreign Relations Committee Hearing on Nomination as Under Secretary of State for Public Diplomacy and Public Affairs, January 30, 2008.
5. Ibid.
6. Mario Bartiromo, "A Resolute Condoleezza Rice," *Business Week*, July 23, 2007.
7. Fouad Ajami, "The Clash," *New York Times*, January 6, 2008.
8. Condoleezza Rice, Keynote Address, Princeton University, Woodrow Wilson School of Public and International Affairs, September 30, 2005.
9. Ibid.
10. Condoleezza Rice, Remarks at the Department of State Annual Report on Religious Freedom, Washington, DC, November 8, 2005.

CHAPTER 29

Democracy Promotion

There is no country on earth today that is not touched by America, for we have become the motive force for freedom and democracy in the world. And there is no country in the world that does not touch us. We are a country of countries with a citizen in our ranks from every land. We are attached by a thousand cords to the world at large, to its teeming cities, to its remotest regions, to its oldest civilizations, to its newest cries for freedom. This means that we have an interest in every place on this Earth that we need to lead, to guide, to help in every country that has a desire to be free, open, and prosperous. (Secretary of State Colin L. Powell, January 2001)

US fascination with the concept of a Democratic world hails back to the founding of the state. In more recent history, the idea received special notice. President Ronald Reagan spoke eloquently of Freedom's pull. His speech, given on June 12, 1987, to the people of West Berlin contains one of the most celebrated remarks of Reagan's presidency: "Mr. Gorbachev, tear down this wall." Standing before the hundred miles long, twelve-foot concrete wall built in 1961 to keep East Berliners from escaping Communism, the wall symbolized totalitarian control and absolute denial of freedom. Per Reagan: "This wall will fall. For it cannot withstand faith; it cannot withstand truth. The wall cannot withstand freedom."[1]

I served in the Reagan National Security Council at the time that the speech was discussed and penned. I vividly recall the challenge that the President was to throw down during his visit to Berlin. It needed to make an extraordinarily powerful impact as US relations with the then Soviet Union were seen to be in a transformative moment. Peter Rodman and Steve Sestanovich worked the speech and the phrase "tear down this wall" was very deliberately put in as a challenge to the sincerity of the openness that Gorbachev was beginning to espouse.

Among President Reagan's senior staff, there were some who were not sure how the phrase would actually play and what the resulting impact on relations with the Russians would be if the call for the removal of the wall fell on deaf ears. But the phrase stayed in and Reagan delivered it with aplomb. And, when the wall finally fell in November 1989, the Berlin speech was remembered as a watershed moment in the call to freedom. As former Secretary of State, James A. Baker notes recalling watching television as young Germans began to chip away at the wall that fateful day: "I would find it hard to hold back tears of joy as the trickle of people seeking freedom in the West turned into a torrent."[2]

With such a tug of history in mind, George W. Bush made Freedom one of the central themes of his presidency. Even before 9/11, Bush had stressed the theme of "Compassionate Conservatism" as a way of reinforcing self-governance and made the concept a core component of his election platform. Prior to his election, Bush articulated his belief in the importance of a culture that did not turn its back on the poor even as it decried the actions of the welfare state. When asked to explain the origins of the notion, Bush noted that the campaign's mantra "is first and foremost springing from the heart." As early as 1999, there was talk of how candidate Bush would support faith-based social services focused on neighborhoods battling a range of social problems.

Participatory Democracy was important to the President's agenda as the first term started out and survived the terrorist attack of 9/11. Bush called for public service and community efforts for every American. He proposed doubling the size of the Peace Corps and exhorted Americans to commit to at least 4000 hours in community service. According to this view, expansion of the role of the people could also mean a reduction in the role of government, which could be particularly useful in foreign policy, especially in the Muslim world, where governments were unpopular for authoritarianism and large-scale failure to deliver justice and governance to their populations.

The unfolding of the freedom agenda was accompanied by noted bickering within the senior staff of the President. Karl Rove's control over the domestic agenda and his playing to the base ran afoul of moderate Republicans. Even those, like Karen Hughes, who had accompanied Bush to the White House appeared queasy about it. As the 9/11 aftermath brought the need for a focus on ways of dealing with the alienation of youth in the Muslim world, Rove and Cheney put a "political stamp on the War on Terror."[3] Rove argued that Americans "trust the Republican Party to do a better job of protecting and strengthening America's military might and thereby protecting America."[4]

The President continued to bring up the "freedom agenda" as he made his keynote addresses. For example, in his 2003 State of the Union Address, Bush reminded America that: "We exercise power without conquest, and sacrifice for the liberty of strangers. Americans are a free people, who know that freedom is the right of every person and the future of every nation. The liberty we prize is not America's gift to the world. It is God's gift to humanity." Bush's focus on a different future for the people of Iraq and the Middle East was a natural follow-up to the fall of Saddam Hussein. Tyranny led to alienation which in turn led to terrorism was the understanding which provided the context for change. On November 6, 2003, the twentieth anniversary of the National Endowment for Democracy (NED) launched under Reagan provided the occasion for a comprehensive explanation of the Bush agenda for pushing democracy in the Muslim world. It occurred in a large hall near the White House where diplomats, senators, congressman of both parties were assembled.

I went with the President in his motorcade. It was a grand entrance. This was a much anticipated speech, and we were all excited as it began. After the usual words of thanks and accolades regarding important bipartisan support for the NED which "stands for Freedom," Bush zeroed in on the Reagan legacy citing the former President's words that: the "momentum (is) for freedom across the world and for ending the march of Soviet tyranny," etc. Bush lauded Reagan's speech at Westminster in June 1982 as "courageous and optimistic and entirely correct." He noted that in the 1970s there were 40 democracies in the world. As the twentieth century ended, there were 120 democracies in the world and "I can assure you more are on the way" Bush said to enthusiastic applause!

Bush noted that in the space of a generation, the world has witnessed the "swiftest advance of freedom in the 2500 year story of democracy.... It is no accident that the rise of so many democracies took place in a time when the world's most influential nation was itself a democracy." The advance of markets and free enterprise led to the rise of a middle class more insistent on securing other rights. "Freedom honors and unleashes human creativity – and creativity determines the strength and wealth of nations." Building on his theme of "the non-negotiable demands of dignity," Bush noted: "Liberty is both the plan of Heaven for humanity and the best hope for progress here on Earth."

The time was right for freedom's march and for continued support for Democracy as it swept the world. Although the trend was powerful, Bush said that liberty, if not defended, could be lost. He traced ways in which various American presidents supported this call for Democracy in distant lands. And, reminded the audience (which was planned to represent a miniscule version of the world at large) that on nearly every continent, Americans had sacrificed for liberty. It was a noble sacrifice since "Freedom is worth fighting for, dying for, and standing for—and the advance of freedom leads to peace."[5] In a survey of places where freedom was under attack such as Burma, Zimbabwe, Cuba, and China, Bush promised to stand with these oppressed people until they were free. He singled out the Middle East, noting that in that critical region, "democracy has not yet taken root." Challenging the notion that somehow the peoples of the region are not likely to live under liberty, Bush recalled the Reagan term "cultural condescension." He likened it to the then current view that Muslims were destined to live without freedom as being in the same school as past references to the Japanese. Bush further stated that: "I believe that every person has the ability and the right to be free."

Echoing this belief, and the ongoing conversation within his administration, Bush pressed the view that it was incorrect to question whether a given country or a people were "ready" for democracy. Freedom was not a prize to be awarded for meeting Western standards of progress, said Bush: "In fact, the daily work of democracy is itself the path of progress. It teaches cooperation, the free exchange of ideas, and the peaceful resolution of differences...it is the practice of democracy that makes a nation ready for democracy..."

The President then cited the fact that Muslims comprise one-fifth of humanity. They are good citizens in scores of countries, including South Africa, Western Europe, India, Turkey, Senegal, Indonesia, and Niger, "More than half of all Muslims in the world already live in freedom under democratically constituted governments. They succeed in democratic societies, not in spite of their faith, but because of it. *A religion that demands individual moral accountability, and encourages the encounter of the individual with God, is fully compatible with the rights and responsibilities of self-government*" (emphasis added).

Here then was the crux of the issue. Discussions within the White House reflected the President's own belief that it was arrogant to say that Islam was unable to deal with Democracy. The notion of personal search for good life which required accountability meant, according to those promoting democracy for the Muslim World, an appreciation of attributes fundamental to the promotion of democracy. At the time when the speech was under discussion and preparation in October/November 2003, the war in Iraq was in the post-Saddam phase. The fall of a tyrannical regime in Iraq coupled with the banishment of the Taliban from power following a brief Afghanistan war led to a strong sense of optimism for a future of political tolerance in the two countries the USA felt it had liberated. A free people would want a democracy went the logic.

By this time, neocons were fast catching criticism for the WMD rationale for the invasion of Iraq and I found them latch on to the "Freedom" agenda as the positive outcome of a failed argument for war based on Cheney et al. conviction that Saddam Hussein possessed WMD. By the summer of 2003, sentiment against the war in Iraq was mounting. Many Americans felt that the case for WMD was vastly overblown and failure to locate any worked against Bush. Insistence by senior members of the administration that given Saddam Hussein's "intent" to acquire nuclear weapons the war was justified ran counter to the reality of the public view.

At the same time, Bush reached out to other countries to assist in the rebuilding of Iraq. On September 23, 2003, the President went to the opening of the general debate of the UN General Assembly and proclaimed, as many heads of state listened, that the assaults on Afghanistan and Iraq were an integral part of the overall US response to the war on terror. Contrasting with his earlier speech before the same body the previous year—when he had challenged the UN to enforce its own resolutions on WMD in Iraq or step aside—the 2003 speech asked for cooperation from the international body for assistance to a newly free Iraq. Bush reminded his audience that: "Because a coalition of nations acted to defend the peace – and the credibility of the United Nations – Iraq is free" and noted "Iraq as a dictatorship had great power to destabilize the Middle East. Iraq as a democracy will have great power to inspire." His audience was not yet willing to forgive the US refusal to wait for international consensus before it moved into Iraq earlier in March that year. Bush had to hear a sharp rejoinder from the UN Secretary General as Kofi Annan questioned the very idea that the USA would go its own way and invade Iraq.

By September 2003, the WMD stash had still not been found and the USA continued to maintain exclusive control over Iraq's occupation even as it sought the UN's help in governance and re-building of a new free Iraq. In making the case for outside help, Bush stressed: "Every young democracy needs the help of friends. Now the nation of Iraq needs and deserves our aid, and all nations of goodwill should step forward and provide that support."

Inside the White House, particularly in OVP, I saw was no desire to cede any of the authority in Iraq to the "feckless Europeans" who wanted to extract a definite date for US transfer of power to Iraqis before any measurable assistance was delivered. In addition, the French, the Germans, and the Russians (all with veto authority in the UN Security Council where the USA needed their support for a post-invasion resolution) wanted a strong UN partnership in reconstruction. Naturally, it was in expectation of lucrative contracts for the rebuilding of Iraq's oil-based economy. Also, some would say, these countries hoped to influence the choice of the new Iraqi leadership as well as to gain some authority over coalition troops. Thus, while no one seemed to be working for the USA to fail outright in Iraq, at the same time, most were reticent to join forces with the USA.

In Bush's mind and that of some of his senior foreign policy officials (Powell and Rice, for instance), UN help was now needed in the creation of a strong Iraqi constitution, the training of a new civil servant pledged to a democratic Iraq and in the conduct of elections.[6] The latter was a key component as the much touted "new Iraq," and the USA had neither the capacity nor the credibility to conduct elections. The Rumsfeld team was already overburdened and State Department officials were wary of being the foot soldiers of diplomacy while the Pentagon clearly controlled Iraq. The stakes were high as the administration made the request to Congress for $87 billion for Iraq. The US 2004 election was not far off, and the President's popularity at home was dropping. Washington found itself without the requisite tools and resources to bring about democratic change in Iraq all on its own.

As discussions of democracy promotion progressed within senior ranks of the administration in 2004, I noted that the backdrop of 9/11 was ever present along with the urgent need to address the grievances held against many Muslim governments by their respective citizens. To this end, Bush vociferously responded with his pro-democracy chant: "I believe that God has planted in every human heart the desire to live in freedom. And even when that desire is crushed by tyranny for decades, it will rise again." Earlier in his 2001 Inaugural address, Bush had been eloquent in noting that the American story was one of a "slave holding society that became a friend of freedom." He noted that in the last century, America's "faith in freedom and democracy was a rock in a raging sea and now a seed upon the wind taking root in many nations." Bush believed America's destiny was the promotion of freedom—especially in Muslim societies—and absent the USA, the task would be much harder, if not impossible. Under the 1939 Hatch Act, the President's staff with notable senior-level exceptions is precluded from participating in election-related activity. But we were all aware of the political end in play even as we worked to keep the business of the NSC going. As the foreign policy arm of the staff, we dealt with diplomacy, visits, and the issues of building and sustaining support abroad for an unpopular US-led war in Iraq.

As Bush won the 2004 election, there was a sense of seizing the moment to implement a grand strategy to make the liberated Iraq a part of the overall American plan for creating a better tomorrow around the world. Thus, the January 2005 inaugural address was almost wholly focused on "the force of human freedom." Here, the link between President's own deep belief and the pursuit of his foreign policy was forcefully expressed: "We are led, by events and common sense, to one conclusion: The survival of liberty in our land increasingly depends on the success of liberty in other lands. The best hope for peace in the world is the expansion of freedom in the entire world." Calling self-government the "urgent requirement of our nation's security, and the calling of our time," Bush defined freedom as an essential choice but one to be "defended by citizens, sustained by the rule of law, and the protection of minorities...reflecting the soul of a nation....customs and traditions very different from our own. America will not impose our own style of government on the unwilling. Our goal instead is to help others find their own voice, attain their own freedom, and make their own way."

Henceforth, the President's dictum asserted "the moral choice between oppression...and freedom" was to be the role of the U.S. foreign policy. He noted that the U.S. would make it clear to other leaders that "success in our relations will require decent treatment of their own people. America's belief in human dignity will guide our policies." The President went on to define those rights as being "more than the grudging concessions of dictators; they are secured by free dissent and the participation of the governed." Bush reflected that Iraqi freedom was being opposed by terrorists who know "that a free Iraq in the heart of the Middle East would be a decisive blow against their ambitions in the region."

Discussions within the White House focused on the important mission the Endowment had in furthering the democracy promotion agenda for the Muslim world. Indeed, in celebration of Human Rights Week, the President issued a proclamation committing the USA to further the "Nation's support for democracy promotion programs globally."[7] Further, in order "to strengthen support for free elections, free markets, free speech, and human rights advocacy around the world...." he increased the budget dramatically for the NED to $80 million for 2005.

Given the accelerating rhetoric on democracy promotion, visitors to the White House representing civil society from a variety of Muslim countries all took to suggesting that the absence of economic opportunity and justice was the root causes for terrorism. Greater participation and better governance along with opportunity were cited as the requirement of the times. Hope was expressed that the USA would press dictatorial leaders who were now "partners" in the war on terror for satisfying these requirements. Some of the most articulate spokesmen for their respective countries were the many women who visited the USA. In their conversations with the President and senior US officials, they identified the need for assistance in order to change the future of fifty percent of the Muslim population, i.e., the women. The impact of these very articulate groups on US decision makers went far beyond their numbers as visitors. Many came from Iraq and Afghanistan. Recounting hardships over the years, they pointed to the need for change and hoped that America would bring it about. Iraq had once been a place for women as professionals. That had declined over the years as sectarianism and arbitrary rule became the order of the day. The havoc wrought on female students at Baghdad University by Saddam Hussein's sons was painfully recounted. In the new order, women fought for and received American support for greater representation in government and future legislatures.

Many of the special areas of progress that Bush, Rice, and others applauded were of particular note for women. It was held as an article of faith at the White House and among the ranks of senior advisors that around the world, women, comprising half of the world's population, were the natural allies of democracy promotion. After all, they had the most to gain from freedom. The number of women visitors from Iraq, Afghanistan, and other Muslim countries increased dramatically in the years after 2003. Many called upon the President and also Laura Bush. Beyond the White House, these groups saw senior officials in the Pentagon, usually including Paul Wolfowitz and his friend Ms. Shaha Riza—a World Bank official, on leave to work as a contractor for DOD. At the State Department, they visited Liz Cheney who was ensconced in the Bureau of Near Eastern Affairs as a senior deputy assistant secretary. The message resonated.

Given my own portfolio, I often saw these visitors, either alone or as I escorted them to Oval Office meetings with the President. I vividly recall one such meeting which had been hastily arranged for the President by Laura Bush on March 9, 2005. A group of Afghan and Iraqi women were in town speaking on issues relating to their respective experiences in democracy-building. Included among the group were two of particular note: Narmeen Othman,[8] a Kurdish member of the Iraqi governing council and Minister for Women. From Afghanistan came a remarkable woman named Massaouda Jalal. Being a Tajik, it was extraordinary that she garnered fifth place out of twenty-five who ran for President in the November 9, 2004, Afghan election. She was the only woman in Afghanistan's history to rise so high. She was a physician and a political activist who wanted to change her society.

Also well known in Washington political circles was Raja Habib Kuzai, an obstetrician/gynecologist political leader who helped garner support from within the political establishment for a better future for women in Iraq. At a time of particular divisiveness as the Iraqi constitution was being debated, this was a singular achievement for a leader who understood that democracy required sharing power with myriad ethnic/sectarian groups that make up modern Iraq. She stood down many personal threats as she pressed for progress for women and won recognition for her positive role.

At the time that I met Dr. Kuzai at Baghdad's al Rashid hotel in May 2003, she was known as Iraq's top female politician. A Shiite southern tribal leader, she was one of only three women serving on the 25-member Governing Council appointed by the Coalition Provisional Authority. She fought for at least a 25% quota for any future parliamentary seats for women using the simple argument: "If Iraq is to be reborn as a true democracy, women must play an equal part." At a time when other Iraqi leaders—for instance, Ahmed Chalabi—were unfurling their personal gain agendas, Ms. Kuzai rose above it all and acted as an inspiring leader. These many years after the unpopular Iraqi war, it is easy to be cynical. However, the personal bravery of women like Kuzai, Othman, and Jalal made a deep and lasting impression on both their audiences and the US President. Indeed, they engaged the President personally and also unfurled the possibility of potential political gains in the future.

The March 2005 meeting had been hastily arranged. When a few minutes before the scheduled hour I went to the Oval Office to await the guests, the President was outside his office talking to his aide, Blake Gottesman. Looking up from his reading, he asked: "Shirin, are we doing something?" In response, I said: "Mr. President, I am here for your meeting with two fabulous women." "So bring them in," he replied, continuing "I love fabulous women!" The meeting, scheduled for fifteen minutes, ran over time. Both women were very engaged, as was the President.

In meeting Massouda Jalal, the President reminded her that he shared something common with her, namely that both had run for the office of President. Jalal quickly responded: "But with a main difference, you won!" Her host noted that given Jalal's much younger age, she could yet get elected. Beyond the easy repartee, there was a moving discussion on the importance of recent events in Afghanistan and Iraq that made it possible for women to become political leaders. The role of democracy in the future development of both countries was considered. Limits on presidential power as an intrinsic part of the American system was also brought up. Finally, the President gave a tour of the Oval Office and its history and significance and of the various *objets d'art* he had chosen for his term and why. The visitors left ecstatic and spoke to reporters at the White House gaggle and others about what the visit meant to them. They felt that they would continue to see progress for women who had been sidelined for so long in their respective countries.

There were other several wonderful moments involving my human rights work at the White House despite the toughness of the issues involved. One that stands out was a trip to Berlin that I was asked to accompany Secretary Powell on as he headed to the Organization for Security and Cooperation in Europe (OSCE) scheduled for April 28–29, 2004, in Berlin. That particular session was focused on Anti-Semitism and Germans were the hosts. Arriving at Andrews AFB to board the Secretary of State's plane, I was introduced to Elie Wiesel, Holocaust survivor and Nobel Laureate. When we boarded the secretary's plane and moved to our assigned seats in the senior staff section, I found that I was fortunate in having my seat next to Elie Wiesel. Through much of the evening, we talked about many things including his life and the fact that we were headed for a conference on Anti-Semitism in Berlin. He said something that stayed with me: "you won't need conferences when there is really no longer any anti-Semitism." He asked about my experiences as an American Muslim which I recounted. He sent me a signed copy of his book "Night."

Meeting this extraordinary man left a lasting impression on me, and I felt extremely fortunate to have had the adjoining seat on the USAF plane. Because of the few who were on it, there was a silence that allowed me to hear his words. When I returned to Washington, I looked up the citation that accompanied the 1986 Nobel Peace Prize awarded to Mr. Wiesel: "Wiesel is a messenger to mankind. His message is one of peace, atonement and human dignity. His belief that the forces fighting evil in the world can be victorious is a hard-won belief."

The flight to Berlin passed in the blink of an eye. When we got to the OSCE meetings, I was aware that a lot of people wanted time with Wiesel and to hear parts of his life story. Delegates applauded Powell for bringing Wiesel as part of the US delegation.

A subsequent meeting that Powell asked for involved meeting with German Muslim members of the Bundestag. It turned out to be memorable. Powell led the discussion with introductions, pointed to him and me as being "fairly typical" of America. The guests recounted their different experiences as representatives of what they felt was very much at the time in 2004 still considered to be less German end of the political leadership, even though many were born in Germany. Several noted their collective astonishment at the fact that Powell was Secretary of State and I was a special assistant to the President, representing the USA.

Visits to the White House are de rigueur for foreign dignitaries. Those with a global compass are welcomed even if they are not State representatives.

The Dalai Lama was always welcomed with great warmth as the Spiritual Leaders of the Tibetans. On September 10, 2003, I served as note taker for the meeting with His Holiness held unusually at the Residence. Mrs. Bush wanted the President to have his meeting there to show special hospitality and respect. The President had a tight schedule and the movement took time. Secretary Powell was there, and as we entered the elevator to the second floor to await the protocol people who would escort the Dalai Lama, I saw an agitated Laura Bush looking for the tiny clasp to her earring which had fallen on the floor. The President looked impatient.

As the only other woman present, I voiced sympathy for her predicament and set about to cast my eye over the floor. The elevator door opened, the Dalai Lama arrived, and I saw a shiny object which I picked up and passed to Mrs. Bush. Small memories of major themes! The Dalai Lama was not asking for independence for Tibet, but he wanted a measure of autonomy and for the Chinese government not to discriminate against Tibetans. That message resonated with the President who assured His Holiness that he would pass the word to his Chinese counterparts.

An offshoot of the Dalai Lama interactions with the President brought an unexpected visitor to my office. Returning one afternoon from the multiple meetings in the West Wing, I was told by my wonderfully competent and kind assistant, Donna Dejban, that I was to stay in the office as there was another appointment added to my schedule just then. "Oh No!" was my response as the day was already out of control. Just then, the buzzer sounded as doors to NSC offices are kept secured. Donna buzzed the door open and in walked Richard Gere with an aide. "What is going on?" I wanted to ask but even I knew Richard Gere from his movies. So I welcomed him to my office and his aide waited outside in the reception area.

Gere started his conversation with a thank you from His Holiness for the support that President Bush and his administration provided for Tibet. He pointed out right away that he was a Democrat who had actively worked against the election of George W. Bush to the presidency. Nonetheless, he noted: "I am amazed at how much this President and his administration is doing on human rights. His Holiness especially asked me to say my thank you." I knew that Gere was handsome but did not know that he was engaging and knowledgeable. We had a thirty minute plus conversation (a lifetime at the White House and likely also for Hollywood megastars). As we were wrapping up, Gere said: "Aren't you too educated to be a Republican?" "Wow! Are you aware Mr. Gere that there are dozens of educated females on the president's staff especially Condoleezza Rice his national security advisor?" I asked.

Gere looked sheepish and changed conversation to "what else are you working on?" I told him about the Basrah Children's Hospital, a public–private partnership to build a cancer hospital to treat Iraqi children. He appeared genuinely interested and sent me note to that effect along with his book of artfully taken photographs of Tibet. On his way out, I asked if he would stop by the West Wing as the situation room staff really wanted to meet him. "How do they know?" he asked. "We live in a fishbowl" I reminded him.

Support for democracy meant USA would continue to assist countries that were building institutions that embodied the spirit of democracy and were critical to its exercise. Given the plethora of totalitarian regimes in the Muslim world, the assumption in the American leadership's mind remained that political will was absent there. American leaders, including the president, believed that Islam suffered a "freedom deficit" not because of a basic incompatibility between the religion and democracy, but rather because of "failures of political and economic doctrines."[9] Democracy in the Muslim world then meant limitations on the power of the state and of its military, essential to the exercise of the will of the people. Rather than being selective in protecting only the often corrupt rulers and penalizing the rest, the law of the land would be impartial in its application. Seeds of democracy would be firmly sowed if justice prevailed, citizens were provided a modicum of health care and some education, and the rights of women were recognized.

These were the principles that Bush promised to apply to Iraq and Afghanistan. There was a great deal of pride in White House at the changes sought in Afghanistan's political system which had gone through various stages of occupation, external aggression, and internal tribal wars. As the country prepared for the 2004 election, some 500 delegates convened a national assembly in Kabul to approve a new constitution. A great deal of maneuvering ensued, and the constitution established a bicameral parliament, recognized Afghanistan's Muslim identity, gave women the right to participate in the political system, and protected the rights of all citizens. No one expected that all problems would be solved. Yet, there was at the White House a real sense of progress and excitement at the possibilities.

Speaking to a group of extraordinary Muslim women leaders, Condoleezza Rice, by then Secretary of State, noted that it was an exciting time. Women in many countries, Iraq and Afghanistan especially, have gone "through struggle...gone through difficult times....faced down terrorism and terrorists (in order) to vote and to show the way to a better and more democratic future." Rice recounted the sometimes flawed history of America's own search for democracy and the time it took for liberty and freedom to become the law of the land for all of its people. Women were not allowed to vote in America until early in the last century. She recalled her time growing up in Birmingham, Alabama, and the civil rights struggle. She saluted the courage women showed every day, for example, the first Afghan voter who was a nineteen-year-old woman and the Iraqi policeman who threw himself on a bomb so others, including women, could vote. Rice noted that: "these are not the stories of the founding fathers and of people with magnificent degrees and magnificent titles." These are the stories of individual common people, one by one, who say, "Enough, enough of the humiliation of dictatorship, enough of taking away my human dignity to say what I wish, to worship as I please, to educate my children, both boys and girls... these are the actions of those people that lead to freedom for us all." Rice reminded the audience that the journey was always difficult as is the sacrifice to nurture a democracy, be it in America, in Iraq, or in Afghanistan. She added that: "in the United States of America, you have a friend.... So as you go through the struggles, remember that while democracy is a difficult and long journey, it is a journey worth making..."[10]

Rice made the case for increased spending on "our partners in freedom" as she appeared before the Senate Appropriations Committee for the $82 billion supplemental budget request on February 17, 2005, of which $75 billion was slated for the Department of Defense (DOD). Reminding the Senators of the strong bipartisan consensus behind the US diplomatic effort during the Cold War to "win over the hearts and minds of men and women around the world and tip the great scales of power toward the forces of freedom, she stated that the Bush effort was similarly important "to build a safer, better, freer world."[11] Of the proposed additional budget, $265 million was requested for democracy and governance programs in Afghanistan. The focus was to be on assisting in the then upcoming elections, training of parliamentarians, strengthening the rule of law assistance in independent media work, and assistance to civil society, with particular emphasis on women in public life.

Iraq received attention under the supplemental as the USA sought to replace years of Saddam Hussein's authoritarian rule with a reasonable form of democracy where sectarian tensions of the past decades would play out in parliament rather than on the killing fields. The President kept track of these trends and referred to them often as he highlighted the ongoing effort and sacrifice by the coalition forces. In this regard, the NED was used to good effect as it provided support for promotion of women's rights, the training of Iraqi journalists, and with development of requisite skills for political participation. Carl Gershman, the President of the NED, was a frequent visitor to the National Security Council as his views on Afghanistan, Iraq, and the greater Middle East were regularly solicited. The goal was to offer help with the development of the requisite tools of democracy.

Notes

1. Ronald Reagan, "Tear Down This Wall" Speech at the Brandenburg Gate, Berlin, West Germany, June 12, 1987.
2. James A. Baker, III, *The Politics of Diplomacy: Revolution, War & Peace, 1989–1992* (New York: G. P. Putnam's Sons, 1995), 163.
3. Jacob Weisberg, *The Bush Tragedy* (New York: Random House, 2008), 138.
4. Ibid.
5. As National Security Advisor and Secretary of State, Condoleezza Rice often cited this belief and noted that "Democracies do not start wars."
6. "Bush Urges U.N. to Help Efforts to Rebuild Iraq," *Wall Street Journal*, September 24, 2003.
7. "Proclamation by the President," Human Rights Day, Bill of Rights Day, The White House, December 10, 2004.
8. Othman survived an assassination attempt on August 25, 2005.
9. George W. Bush, "Remarks" at the 20th Anniversary of the National Endowment for Democracy, Washington, DC, November 6, 2003.
10. Condoleezza Rice, "Remarks" at the US Agency for International Development, International Women's Day, March 8, 2005.
11. Testimony of Condoleezza Rice before the Senate Appropriations Committee, February 17, 2005.

CHAPTER 30

Ongoing Diplomacy in South Asia

Pakistan continued to present a challenge as I watched the administration try to create a post-9/11 relationship with our periodically important ally. It took months of prodding before the Pakistani Army was deployed to the South Waziristan region. But intelligence cooperation accelerated, and both the USA and Pakistan openly lauded the results in the form of increased arrests of major al Qaeda leaders in Pakistan, including Abu Zubaydah, the head of al Qaeda's overseas operations, and their extradition to the USA. However, by 2003, it seemed that the writ of the state no longer extended into an increasing number of areas within Pakistan, with Pakistani jihadi groups active in the northern areas, including Swat, as well as within the southern part of Punjab, Pakistan's most populous state.

At the same time that emergency funding, debt forgiveness, and US support for the Pakistani Army via Coalition Support Funds (CSF) were adding millions of dollars to the Army's coffers, Pakistani public's views of American policy were moving into a strongly negative direction. During my February 2003 visit to Pakistan just prior to my reappointment to the NSC, I was appalled at the rapid decline in favorable perceptions of the USA. In addition to the usual refrain blaming conditions in Pakistan on the USA, there was now new reasons for doing so. Those who fancied themselves as high-minded proponents of democracy were offended when, during Musharraf's visit to Washington in February 2002, Bush praised him saying: "President Musharraf is a leader with great vision and courage....I am proud to call

© The Author(s) 2018
S. Tahir-Kheli, *Before the Age of Prejudice*,
https://doi.org/10.1007/978-981-10-8551-2_30

253

him my friend."[1] In contrast, Pakistani government officials noted that Pakistan remained "America's most sanctioned ally" while "the man in the street" expressed the view that "America is against Muslims everywhere." No amount of evidence from me showing that the reality was quite the opposite seemed to make any difference! What was also noteworthy is that by 2002, I found few supported US policies in the growing "war on terror" that had become a hallmark of the George W. Bush era.

Others who thought the Bush emphasis on "Democracy Promotion" would yield favorable results for Pakistan were also disappointed. What especially became anathema to the Pakistani liberals, as noted by a well-known Pakistani author, was the fact that "No one (in Washington) raised the issue of democracy with Musharraf," and instead, the Pakistani author noted the US President expressed the view that "Musharraf was indispensable. Conversations with the State Department, National Security Council and the Pentagon reflected little desire in the U.S. for Pakistan to return to civilian government. This attitude was well noted to great (negative) effect in Pakistan."[2]

It was clear from the outset that the war in Afghanistan and the war against extremism made Pakistan an important player for the USA. The Pakistani military had adapted itself to the requirements of American policy and benefited handsomely from the alliance except during times of strict sanctions when all military and economic assistance was banned as a result of Congressional sentiment. Sadly, for most in Pakistan, US assistance, rather than economic support that benefits the people at large, was considered more as military aid primarily focused on benefiting the (secret and undeclared) needs of the USA. Many faulted the disproportionate, even though intermittent, flow of military assistance to give the military a sense of power vis-à-vis the political system. Further, the military continued its adversarial posture toward India in order to strengthen its own position as the guarantor of the nation and turned Pakistan into a "rentier" state, available for hire to do the USA's bidding simply based on its strategic location.[3] Yet, influence proved elusive.[4]

Given the nearly six years of experience that I had serving as the officer for South Asia at the NSC in the previous two Republican administrations, and my familiarity with the complex relationship, I felt it my duty periodically to informally offer my thoughts on the USA–Pakistan relations to my boss, Condoleezza Rice, then National Security Advisor.

To this end, I would occasionally write a short note some weekend, hand the hard copy to Rice, as well as pass it on to Hadley and the NSC Senior Director for Asia. In one such note, dated June 18, 2004, I traced the history of the opening to India under Rajiv Gandhi, which had occurred under the leadership of President Ronald Reagan. This was a time when the young Indian leader was jettisoning the rhetoric of the nonaligned movement days, and his close advisers (which included Manmohan Singh, now Prime Minister) reflected his determination to forge economic and technology links with the USA. I mentioned that that policy had yielded results: The USA negotiated a memorandum of understanding for technology transfer which enabled India to receive its first supercomputer and the GE-404 engine for its defense aircraft venture set in Bangalore. Further, by 1987, the USA became India's largest trading partner, and some 25% of foreign investment in India was coming from the USA.

My note pointed out that the mid-1980s opening to India took place at the same time that US relations with Pakistan were strengthened. In President Reagan's meetings with Rajiv Gandhi at the White House in 1985 and 1987 and each year at the UNGA, which I attended as the NSC officer for South Asia, Reagan did not minimize the important role that Pakistan played as a frontline state against the Soviets in Afghanistan. During the 1984–1988 years, the USA actively encouraged confidence building measures (CBMs), sent presidential missions to both capitals, urging their adoption in the interest of normalization. I had participated in the extensive discussions on various CBMs as I was a part of the presidential missions and noted the seriousness with which US efforts were viewed in New Delhi and Islamabad. I pointed out that most of the CBMs currently in place hail from 1985 to 1988, including the Indo-Pak agreement not to attack each other's nuclear facilities.

The George W. Bush administration made a strategic decision with respect to India–Pakistan relations. There would be a near total focus on India, and, in keeping to Indian wishes, all US interaction with Pakistan would occur only through the prism of the "War on Terror." Thus, while intelligence cooperation between Washington and Islamabad continued and leader-to-leader contact remained in place, there was little focus on nudging forward a constructive Indo-Pak dialogue.

Robert Blackwill, appointed US Ambassador to India, seemed not to have any real work experience with South Asia prior to his appointment to New Delhi. It appeared as though he also did not appreciate the pre- and post-partition history of the two contiguous countries, India and Pakistan. Instead, for Blackwill and his supporters, India stood alone as the prize and that was the starting point to improvement with the USA. To the exclusion of other important points, he pushed through the civilian nuclear agreement between the USA and India. (For this job well done—according to information provided by the Indian Ambassador to the USA at the time—Blackwill was personally rewarded by India, and quite handsomely at that.) As the agreement was heading for passage, I mentioned to Condi that before the agreement is signed there would be a rare opportunity to nudge India to normalize its relationship with Pakistan. India, being the more powerful of the two neighbors, would be extolled for its gallantry, for forgiving any past trespasses, and for its worldliness in securing a trading partner close at hand, one who will be more a buyer than a seller.

But this great opportunity to foster lasting peace in South Asia was carelessly missed by the USA. Further, absent Pakistan's rapprochement with India, Pakistan's military, greatly to the detriment of itself, India and the USA, would never fully commit to taking on the extremists in Afghanistan.

I further mentioned to Condi how Sonia Gandhi had been present during her husband's two official and state visits to the White House. In her party's return to power, she had supported India reaching out to Pakistan. Even when out of power, she had supported Prime Minister Vajpayee's outreach to Pakistan and had even received Musharraf when, after the summit in Agra, he went to Delhi in 2002. There had been crucial back-channel conversations between India and Pakistan involving emissaries of respective leaders on both sides and I myself had been part of some of them.

In sum, it appeared that the leaders and people of both countries were primed for peace. Thus, there was an opportunity, however fragile, for the USA to encourage forward movement. In the absence of such encouragement, India would take it as a signal that a productive peace with Pakistan was neither desired nor expected by the USA. In addition, there would be no full-fledged support for the war on terror from Pakistan vis-à-vis Afghanistan unless its eastern border with India was secure.

Condi noted to me afterward that she found the note very interesting, but she just left it at that.

Fourteen months after I had returned to the NSC, this round with the democracy issue as part of my portfolio, on May 26, 2004, I wrote another weekend note from my home in Pennsylvania, this time on the issue of Pakistan and democracy.

The "Freedom Agenda" was much on the march at the White House. Thus, my note forwarded some thoughts on how Pakistan's President should be nudged forward toward democracy, given that in my view democracy was crucial for Pakistan's security and stability. This was a time when the conventional wisdom in Washington pushed for a close relationship with Musharraf as the sole guarantor of strong support in rooting out America's enemies, particularly al Qaeda. Despite the fact that Cheney and the DOD wanted to focus only on the military dimension, my thought was that the US–Pakistan relationship should not be so one dimensional. Yet, intelligence cooperation was the prize and no one wanted to jeopardize that. Still, it seemed to me that the close collaboration would not suffer in the mid-term and certainly not in the long term. But the USA needed to recognize that despite its generous pouring of holy water, democracy would be slow in evolving and the existence of strong power brokers such as the military, the bureaucracy, and the landed feudal elites would make it difficult and painful.

The challenge therefore would be to assist Pakistan with whatever was crucial to its finding a democratic future while it maintained its friendship with the USA. At this juncture, Pakistan appeared to be at a crossroads where the choices were getting increasingly stark: extremism and loss of political control or the return to civilian government with accountability, transparency, better governance, and the rule of law. I shared my opinion that genuine democracy will serve Pakistan's best interests well and help it in addressing its multifarious problems and in creating hope for a large number of currently disenfranchised Pakistanis.

As I saw it, Pakistan needed to help deliver change without creating chaos. Some specific steps toward that end included: encouraging Musharraf to stand by his previous commitment to step out of uniform by the end of 2004; counseling a reduction in the number of senior Army officers in Pakistan's bureaucracy and semi-autonomous entities; nudging Musharraf to give more power to his appointed Prime Minister; assisting Pakistan to build civilian institutional capacity; requiring that the ISI and other intelligence agencies not be used for domestic political purposes; and encouraging the Pakistan Army to return to its primary mission of protecting the territorial integrity of Pakistan.

US concern that democracy would usher in extremist religious parties in Pakistan was, in my view in 2004, overstated. The majority of the citizens were moderate, and the democratic process would reduce the power of the mullahs and prevent the rise of extremists who preyed on the masses' sense of disenfranchisement, poverty, and lack of economic opportunity, a sure recipe for radicalization. Important contributions by Musharraf to set up a system that strengthens governance at the lowest level and increases the number of elected women at the national, provincial, and local levels seemed to indicate a desire to move in the right direction. After all, as Musharraf proudly noted in his address to the UNGA: "In Pakistan, we are well on our way to transform our country into a modern, progressive, tolerant, democratic, Islamic state, reflecting the vision of our founding father, the Quaid-e-Azam."[5] Musharraf played to Washington even as he personally held to the vision of a moderate Pakistan. In one emotional speech to the country, he noted that it was a false argument some made that it was Islam first and then came Pakistan. No, said Musharraf, Islam was a given, so it was Pakistan first.[6]

As mentioned above, at the NSC, I was told that my paper presented interesting ideas, but the bulk of US focus with Pakistan in 2004 remained the hunt for al Qaeda. American leaders' conversations with the Pakistani President focused mostly on that and related issues. Again, an opportunity was thereby missed: this time to look to a Pakistan that was democratic, inclusive, moderate, and less anti-American.

Compared to what followed, Pakistani public opinion of the USA was still split since criticism was muted by a number of factors. First, the Taliban's Afghanistan had been defeated, and the response to the events of 9/11 were sympathetically viewed by most as constituting a just cause for the American attack on the Afghans. Second, the war in Iraq had not yet discredited American policy. The WMD rationale was operational, and most felt that these caches would be found in time and that success in Kabul and Baghdad reinforced America's image as a powerful country legitimately using its military might to protect itself. Third, the damaging photos of Muslim prisoners' abuse at Abu Ghraib and Bagram had not yet surfaced, causing a massive dent in US reputation. Fourth, drone attacks in Pakistan were few and not an issue.

Pakistan lost its contact at the senior most levels of American leadership, except President Bush himself, when in 2005 Colin Powell left the office of Secretary of State accompanied by his powerful deputy Richard Armitage. Both had extensive experience with Pakistan going back to their tenures in senior policy positions in the Reagan administration. They had deep knowledge of all relevant issues and access to phone numbers of senior Pakistani officials, enjoying close familiarity or friendship with many of them. They also had personal knowledge of the country stemming from earlier service.

Even out of office, they had kept up with their contacts and followed key issues relating to Pakistan. Upon their departure, South Asian matters on the seventh floor of the Department of State slipped down only to ensuring the passage of the civilian nuclear deal with India. Neither Rice nor Nicholas Burns (who was the number three at State) had been to Pakistan or had any experience with Pakistan before its decline into failing institutions and weak leadership. Post-9/11, terrorism was the main filter as the USA worked to bring Pakistan into line. Thus, after 2005, dealing with most other issues relating to Pakistan was downgraded to the Assistant Secretary level.

Of course, this disinterest was upended when crisis struck on October 8, 2005: Pakistan was hit by a destructive earthquake measuring a massive 7.6 on the Richter scale in its northern regions. The damage was extensive with over 100,000 dead, 138,000 injured, and 3.5 million rendered homeless. Entire towns were demolished taking with them schools, hospitals, and means of livelihood. The region, remote under the best of circumstances, was impassable. The USA swiftly reacted to the tragedy by responding to Pakistan's[7] request for assistance. Disaster assistance teams were sent, a 23-member Contingency Support Group from McGuire Air Force Base arrived to provide planning and logistical support.[8]

Within a twenty-four-hour period, the USA dispatched a C-17 military aircraft carrying blankets, winterized tents, and other urgently needed supplies. A flow of assistance began with C-17s delivering goods including shelter, water, medicines and help provided through the Red Cross. Initially, eight US military helicopters (five CH-47 Chinooks and three UH-60 Blackhawks) helped in the grim task of reaching stranded people with supplies and airlift to hospitals, including a US Army field hospital. Despite the war next door in Afghanistan, from where the helicopters were borrowed, the dedication of these aircraft to relief provided a dramatic example of American help to the average Pakistani. The US Senate expressed its sympathy for the plight of the people affected by the earthquake and pledged immediate assistance.[9]

I was in Pakistan on a brief official visit at the time and recall large amounts of assistance arriving daily into Islamabad from the USA and other nations. The only way to get the supplies to the needed area was via the American helicopters. American pilots flew nonstop missions with little rest and earned huge respect and affection of the people they were helping and those watching the mission. Wherever I went, people would talk to me about the goodness of American assistance, and the children would ask for toy models of "Chinooks," a word that seemed to have entered the lexicon in every language spoken in the north! This positive image of the USA, which I had witnessed as a child in Peshawar and which had long faded from Pakistani memories, was resurging. Upon my return to Washington, I briefed Condi, who told the President and other colleagues, of the restoration of very positive feelings among Pakistanis for the USA.

Pakistani leaders acknowledged the great assistance offered by the USA, calling the Chinook helicopters "angels of mercy." They decried the cyclical nature of the USA–Pakistan relationship where periods of intense engagement were followed by phases of distinct estrangement. Citing the fact that both countries had learned from mistakes of the past, Pakistan felt it was now a relationship of mutual benefit and shared interests. Reform, moderation, and self-reliance made the future more secure in fighting extremism and terrorism. US designation of Pakistan as a "major Non-NATO Ally" was celebrated in Islamabad as indicative of the positive trends for the future of the relationship.[10] All this provided breathing room to the leadership and respite from the encroaching forces of extremism that would turn Pakistani cities into killing fields.

When Rice visited Pakistan for a brief stop en route from India in 2005, she noted that the USA had committed to a broad relationship with Pakistan, supporting economic and educational reform. To this end, assistance, totaling approximately $3 billion over a five-year period had been pledged and Rice echoed President Bush in praising Musharraf "for his courage and vision in promoting peace and stability in the region and for his concept of enlightened moderation."[11] Rice told the audience at the same press conference in Islamabad that the USA would "continue to work with Pakistan and we look forward to the evolution of a democratic path toward elections in 2007 for Pakistan." She noted that Pakistan had come a long way since September 11, 2001. She credited that improvement to Musharraf and his advisors along with the people of Pakistan for moving toward democracy and pluralism while shunning extremism.

To some, US policy, as evident in Rice's visit, still reflected the US terrorism agenda and the need to move aggressively against al Qaida. The close link with Musharraf was not popular with some in Pakistan and many complained that beyond the occasional rhetoric, the US administration did little to push Musharraf to allow democratic politics to play a role in the country. When American assistance was cited, Pakistanis felt that much of it was transmitted via American "beltway bandit" contractors who siphoned off the majority amount as overhead. Thus, there was never much to show for and also that there was little in the way of transparency or accountability.

The better part of the cooperation was in intelligence and for the fighting in border areas. As military and intelligence agencies drove that agenda, an opportunity was missed to work with the political leaders and the younger generation. The man in the street's perception once again focused on what he believed was a free hand given to Musharraf and his generals by the USA's financial support for the military. Washington did not dwell on the decades-long association of the Pakistani military with the mullahs in fighting proxy wars in Afghanistan and in Kashmir. By the end of the Bush first term in 2004, there was still a possibility for Musharraf to break with the mullahs and cooperate with Benazir Bhutto and her party, the Pakistan Peoples Party (PPP), at the time a staunchly anti-mullah party with a solid popular base of support. Instead, Musharraf made it look as though he was not one for power sharing, and the steady induction of the military into civilian governance along with expanded perks continued apace. The existence of press freedom, which had occurred much to Musharraf's credit, gave a new voice to the varied opinions prevalent in Pakistan. Yet, there was no outlet for the political give and take that a robust political system would offer and demand.

A "king's party" was launched, and Musharraf went about touting his belief in "enlightened moderation" and in "isolating the extremists": tasks he claimed that only a military ruler could undertake. Pakistan's political opposition shunned the Musharraf exercise and offered no support. The brutal murder of journalist Daniel Pearl earlier in 2002 again reminded one of the darker side of the rapidly changing Pakistan. It was there for all to see, but much of the country, including the political elite, buried its head in the sand.

Even as thousands of extremists were jailed following the January 12 Musharraf speech, none was tried at a time when there was adequate support for a moderate Pakistan. Some said that the Army wanted to keep the focus on winning the parliamentary elections set for October 2002. Others in Pakistan were of the view that the military had begun to distinguish between jihadists who were useful in any enterprise aimed at Afghanistan and India and those who were not because they targeted the homeland. The political map was redrawn with constitutional amendments enhancing the power of the presidency—that is, Musharraf's—and banning previous Prime Ministers from holding future office. The military again imposed the educational requirement for elected office holders with the protestation that it would raise the caliber of the political leadership: an exclusionary clause in a country with barely 54% literacy. Disingenuously, however, madrassa education was given parity with the formal educational structures. Given press freedom, the storm of criticism seemed to catch the military by surprise.

Washington still saw these steps as indicative of Musharraf's desire to move toward democracy. His push for increased participation by women was lauded by an American administration that had begun to talk of women's empowerment regularly and felt that Muslim women were harbingers of better trends in their respective countries. In Pakistan, the US–Pakistan alliance was mockingly referred to as the "Bush-Mush" pact.

Throughout the George W. Bush presidency, Pakistan was an important focus for the war on terror. Even as economic and military assistance was restarted, the problems facing American policy in Afghanistan were the main mover. There was a great deal of frustration on both sides. Washington wanted Pakistan to do a great deal more against the Taliban, in particular denying them sanctuary and support for the war in Afghanistan. It wanted strong military action in the tribal areas, particularly in North and South Waziristan. It pushed for the capture and extradition of al Qaeda leaders, including Osama bin Laden and his lieutenants. Islamabad felt far too much was being asked of Pakistan, especially given the prevailing view that India was the main focus of interest for the USA while Pakistan was simply an ally of convenience and the one "most sanctioned." Many chafed at American demands to flush out al Qaeda operatives in the country's tribal belt saying that the rising Islamic fundamentalist activity in the region was a "blowback" from US actions in Afghanistan. Bush identified Pakistan as the nexus of terrorism and nuclear weapons and therefore "the single largest threat to American national security." In Pakistan, the link between these two elements represented a nightmare scenario for American policy.

These were the years when there was not much interaction with Benazir Bhutto. She was "officially ignored" when she came for her annual visit to Washington. She would always call me and was full of friendship when I met with her, often at her hotel since I did not want her to have to go through the clearance lines to enter State and come into my office. She was always gracious in saying that she would not mind doing that, but it seemed inappropriate to require a person who had twice been Prime Minister of a major country to wait for admission to my office. She complained it was ironic that even as Bush spoke of democracy building in the Muslim world, in Pakistan he seemed focused exclusively on the military dictator. In contrast, the head of the democratic opposition in Pakistan was not able to meet the President or his senior aides, except at the National Prayer Breakfast in Washington. She noted that Cheney was particularly in favor of pushing American policy to stay firmly in the Musharraf camp. To Bhutto, Secretary Rice's comments in the course of an interview in New Delhi in March 2005 that "We have to say that President Musharraf has done a lot to root out extremism in his own country" came across as full support for a military ruler.[12]

By 2005, senior administration officials were firmly touting the strategic opening to India as the key policy change of the Bush years. Engagement with Pakistan remained downgraded to the fight against al Qaeda and other terrorist groups that would destabilize Afghanistan.[13] Further, the prevention of nuclear proliferation—evidenced in the excesses of the A. Q. Khan network—and the containment of the spread of WMD remained a key issue. The multi-year assistance package was to be a downpayment on US interest in Pakistan's security and stability. But, the "major shift in American attention is nowhere more evident than in our newfound strategic engagement with India. This new relationship rests on the solid foundation of shared values, shared interests and our increasingly shared view of how best to promote stability, security and peace worldwide in the 21st century."[14] On the breakthrough in the sale of US nuclear reactors for civilian energy needs, Burns was forced to admit much later that "the problem from my perspective is on the Indian side ... we haven't seen the same degree of commitment to follow [the agreement] through."[15]

In Pakistan, the American recitation of "shared mutual interest" with India meant the end of Islamabad's special relationship and the relegation of Pakistan to client state status or worse. American popularity plummeted further as Pakistanis going through daily bombings and deaths in major cities were confronted by a new enemy that worked against a moderate future and cost some 70,00 lives. The blame for the deterioration in security and economic conditions was often laid at the feet of the American war on terror which was seen to be destabilizing to Pakistan, especially in the face of escalating American demands that more be done. "We should be under no illusion," said the Undersecretary of state charged with dealing with India, noting that the USA was content to remain on the sidelines.[16]

Given that all past sustained success in confidence building between India and Pakistan always involved behind-the-scenes work by the USA, the new attitude whereby Washington appeared publicly to be saying the equivalent of "we are happy not to be involved" and "good luck to you and your future" came across as unrealistic. In the event of Pakistan's collapse at the hands of the extremists, no country would be more directly affected than India and, at some remove, the USA as well.

On the domestic Pakistani front, Musharraf's hand-picked Prime Minister acted more as a buffoon than a leader, interested more in appearing to exert power than in actually wielding it. All the while civil society was making a push for transparency and accountability. The military was in power and while Musharraf talked of "enlightened moderation." some political leaders noted that he had failed to promote a culture of tolerance. The government's worsening record on human rights, including disappearances and arrests without judicial follow-up, suggested that Musharraf used "donor-friendly language to disguise its real anti-democratic tactics on the ground."[17]

Afghanistan forced continued US interest in Pakistan despite a wishful reticence. By the end of 2006, there seemed to be more discussion internally on the need for a democratic Pakistan as a requirement for security in Afghanistan. While Musharraf was being honored as a moderate, military control of civil institutions did not allow for recognition of the political need for ending interference. On the other hand, the Afghans had, with American (i.e., Cheney's) encouragement, begun to play a newer version of the "great game." They approved the building of Indian consulates in Jalalabad and Kandahar, which fed the paranoia in Pakistan's intelligence services that interference by Indian intelligence into Pakistani affairs on the north was now legitimized. No amount of American assurance that the consulates should deal only with the legitimate work of Indian businessmen in the region was either believed by, or mollified, the Pakistani security forces or even the average Pakistani.

When President Bush made a brief stop in Pakistan in March 2006 on his return from a two-day visit to India, he acknowledged again Pakistan's role against terror, noting that there had been some slippage in performance. He endorsed Musharraf who had come under physical attack by terrorists. While the issue of democracy was raised by the American President, it was done so in quiet tones giving the impression that Musharraf was increasingly vulnerable. In any case, the mention of democracy was tied to Musharraf's promise of elections. Never did it imply any expected decline in the powerful role played by the military in all civilian institutions. While Washington said it recognized there was more to Pakistan than Musharraf, reality militated against that assertion.

Domestic events inside Pakistan began to unravel control at the top. As pressure began to mount on the Pakistani President to move toward civilian rule and fulfill his promise to hold elections in 2007, a number of events began to change the political landscape of Pakistan. First, there was the revival of political interest and activity by the two major parties, the PPP and the Nawaz Muslim League. Both Benazir Bhutto and Nawaz Sharif were in exile and both wanted to return home to run for office. Given that each had been dismissed in turn because of corruption and poor governance, Musharraf tried to prevent their return and barred them from running.

Then, on March 9, 2007, Musharraf, apparently following his Prime Minister's exceedingly ill-considered advice, dismissed the Chief Justice of the Supreme Court Iftikhar Muhammad Chaudhry, whom Musharraf himself had appointed in May 2005. The highly unpopular act highlighted the arbitrary nature of the Pakistani system of Justice and brought a large number of influential people, including lawyers, out into the streets of the normally quiescent Islamabad. The little known Chief Justice had unwittingly become a hero. His newly attracted public favor changed him into a newfangled political activist, and he began questioning the various actions of the government while looking into issues of corruption. Many Pakistanis thought that his dismissal reflected the fact that he was getting too close to questioning the integrity of the military elite's economic activities. In all probability, that concern was far-fetched because the apparent progenitor of the idea, Prime Minister Shaukat

Aziz, was not given to having deep political thoughts. As a practiced banker, unless an issue was clearly to his personal benefit, he did not needlessly waste his firepower. I happened to arrive in Karachi a day earlier and had a scheduled meeting with the Prime Minister on that fateful day, March 9th, in Islamabad.

Upon my arrival at the Prime Minister's residence, I was ushered into his expansive office. Shaukat Aziz, whom I had known in his Citibank post in Singapore, received both myself and the senior US foreign service officer who was accompanying me graciously but with a mild reprimand that he had been kept waiting. When I responded that it had taken us over an hour to get through the mob near the residence that was protesting the suspension of the chief justice, Prime Minister Aziz refused to believe any such thing could possibly be going on! He summoned his aide—the word in Pakistan is *Chumcha*—and asked that he check with the civil administration to see if there really was an agitation going on in the streets. When the aide came back (as is habitually the case with *Chumchas* that in order to please their bosses they are prepared to deny a perfectly established fact), he said, "No sir! Nothing is going on!!" I looked at my American colleague in disbelief and had a sad feeling that Pakistan's leaders had chosen to separate themselves from reality. I was later told that eventually even Prime Minister Aziz had to admit the existence of public outrage, especially as it continued for weeks and made a hero of a justice who otherwise was not celebrated for any noteworthy knowledge of jurisprudence.

The events of March 2007 highlighted the first sustained chinks in the armor of the military government. Musharraf was seen to have lost his grip, and street demonstrations, normally not prevalent at the time, began to escalate. At the same time, the "enlightened moderation" that had been made the hallmark of the Pakistani President's program to stem the tide of extremism in Pakistan was coming under increasing challenge right in the heart of the capital, Islamabad. Over an eighteen-month period, the Mullahs of the Red Mosque and its adjacent Jamia Hafsa madrassa were increasingly enforcing their version of Islam. Taking law into their own hands, they were promoting the imposition of Shariah in Pakistan and inciting the public to overthrow the government and President Pervez Musharraf. Violent demonstrations, hate filled speeches, kidnappings, armed clashes with the police, terrorizing of female drivers who were pulled out of cars and shamed publicly were all occurring just a few hundred feet away from some of the most important government sites in Islamabad. Established in the mid-1960s as one of the first mosques in the newly built capital, the Red Mosque was attended by a number of senior government officials. Over time, especially in the Zia period, the mosque grew and encroached upon valuable land belonging to the government-owned capital development authority.

Eventually, the leaders of the mosque baited the government and the military by setting fire to an official building and attacking the Army Rangers who guarded the facility. That was an open challenge to authority, and it appeared that the mullahs felt secure enough in their power to undertake such a dangerous gambit. Given public outrage at the terror being inflicted on Islamabad, the Army took action in July 2007, and military commandos (once the home of President Musharraf) stormed the facilities and captured the (so-called) students and the leadership. Finally, it seemed that Musharraf was doing something concrete to support his call for "enlightened moderation." As women and children were freed from the school, there were casualties on both sides. The mosque was heavily fortified and stocked for a long siege. With the rout of the leaders, the Taliban pressed, rather than surrender, for martyrdom of those opposing the government's actions. In many ways, the battle for the Red Mosque was a watershed that changed the rules of the game. Extremism was now a phenomenon in all parts of Pakistan, and no one was safe. It also meant that the only outcome to such confrontations was fight unto death, which the extremists termed "martyrdom." Negotiation was not possible.

Army action against the militants in the mosque did not mollify the growing opposition to the Musharraf dismissal of the chief justice. Lawyers in thousands came out in support of the chief justice and against the eight-year rule of the President. Public pressure on Musharraf to shed his dual role as President and chief of Army staff escalated, even as the general said he would seek another five-year term in October 2007. When Richard Boucher, the assistant secretary for South Asia, testified before the US Congress, he noted the importance of Pakistan to the fight against terrorism and also that: "Without Pakistani support and cooperation, we would face severe difficulties in supplying, reinforcing, and protecting our troops" in Afghanistan.[18] Once again, the American view of Pakistan, its place in the fight against terror, its hope for a stable moderate state serving as a stellar example for the Muslim world, was noted. The commitment to a long-term multidimensional strategic relationship was voiced. However, the issue of a democratic Pakistan continued to be presented in the context of General Musharraf's pledge to relinquish his military role and hold elections.

Within the administration, some felt that it was not the USA's business to tell Musharraf to "shed his uniform." Leading that view were the Vice President and Rumsfeld. The latter nostalgically noted that it was not "clear to me that we ought to be the ones to judge what a leader in Pakistan ought to wear to the office." According to the former defense secretary, it was foolish for the USA to want the general to have elections and deliver on his promise to move Pakistan to a functioning democracy because "if you're going to fuss at what you have, you better have something better in mind, and we haven't had something better."[19] President George W. Bush notes in his biography the mounting pressure on him to "cut ties with Musharraf." Given the lawyers' revolt over the sacking of the chief justice and the general's reluctance to call an election, preferring the path of emergency declaration, Bush noted to his Pakistani friend, "It looks ugly from here."[20]

2007 was a tough year for Pakistan because of the escalating attacks by extremists in large cities resulting in grievous carnage. The Red Mosque had brought the internal struggle for the soul of Pakistan out into the open. As public calls for the imposition of Shariah by mullahs and devotees became louder, the leadership continued talking of the "silent majority" eschewing imposition of a radical Muslim state and preferring the old Jinnah plan for a secular, modern, prosperous, moderate state. However, many thoughtful Pakistanis grumbled that the USA had not pressed early enough for reversal of military rule in Pakistan with the attendant cost of political paralysis ensuring a worse future. As noted in the Boucher testimony, even when the vision of a progressive moderate Pakistan was spelled out, it was done in the name of the military leader, General Musharraf: "This is the vision that President Musharraf has articulated and demonstrated by reiterating his resolve to stop the Talibanization in the frontier areas as well as in the urban areas…. It is strongly in the U.S. national interest that Pakistan succeeds in realizing this vision."[21] There was no mention that the vision of most Pakistanis was for another try at democracy. There was a national stake in a moderate Pakistan, and people realized it. A free press debated the issues endlessly and noted the steady growth of extremists. But the USA pinned its hopes on the will of its most reliable friend who wanted clearly to do the right thing but his writ now was more limited.

Eventually, the USA did get involved and helped broker a deal for the return of Benazir Bhutto to run for office. By that time, it was clear that internal support for the President was fast eroding. The normally staid lawyers took to the streets ostensibly to protest the ousting of the country's top judge. There was discontent over Musharraf's declaration of emergency on November 4, 2007, where he suspended the constitution and rounded up political opposition and jailed human rights activists. That move made it impossible for the USA to continue business as usual and precipitated the final showdown with the general.

Pakistanis believed that Washington had been consulted by Musharraf prior to the emergency declaration in the belief than any elections held in the future would yield him another five-year term and such would be the case even if the general gave up the top Army post to the Deputy Chief of Army Staff General Kayani. This view was further strengthened when the State Department spokesman, Sean McCormack, commented that parliamentary elections should precede the presidential ballot. Most believed that this procedure would give an advantage to Musharraf's party since he was in a position of authority and could influence the outcome. He argued that the Pakistani people should be responsible for choosing their next President through the parliamentary elections, which implied that if the general took off his uniform, Musharraf's earlier pledge would be fulfilled. In Pakistan, Bush, Cheney, and Rice were noted as being "Musharraf's enablers"[22] for hedging their bets in continuing to work with him despite his proclamation of an emergency and subverting of the constitution.

When Prime Minister Shaukat Aziz ordered the arrest of lawyers, judges, and human rights workers, America's Freedom agenda suffered another blow and Pakistan's leading human rights activist, Asma Jahangir, appealed for the Bush administration "to stop all support of the unstable dictator as his lust for power is bringing the country close to the worst form of civil strife."[23] When questioned in the course of an overseas trip whether the US administration would continue American assistance to the tune of $150 million a month despite Musharraf's declaration of an emergency, Secretary of State Rice responded: "I would be very surprised if anybody wants the President to ignore or set aside our concerns about terrorism ...But obviously the situation has changed and we have to review where we are."[24] After being briefed by the White House on the evolving situation, Senate Foreign Relations Committee Chairman, Joseph Biden, said on CBS' "Face the Nation," "I am not sure how much good the military aid we give [Musharraf] is doing us.... I don't know that they [White House] have any notion of what they're going to do right now." The administration finally backed away from Musharraf, but only after all options had been exhausted.

Public opinion polls conducted by the International Republican Institute showed that by November 2007, Washington's alliance with the general was costing the USA. Not only did the respondents note that Musharraf's grip on the system and his performance had affected a more negative view of the Army, 82% said that Pakistan should not cooperate with the USA on its war on terror. By January 2008, that figure not supporting Pakistan's cooperation with the USA had gone up to 89%. Indeed, after the September bombing of the Marriott hotel in Islamabad, the most blatant act of terrorism in full view of the central government's base, when asked whom the respondents held responsible for the suicide bombing, 20% said America while only 2% said India.[25] All of the public diplomacy unleashed by the Bush administration was having little effect on winning hearts and minds in Pakistan. While two-thirds agreed that religious extremism is a problem in Pakistan, only 10% listed the suicide bombings and other manifestations of extremism in their daily lives as the most serious issue facing the country. Rather, it was inflation, said nearly 58%. Also, 73% said they would not support American military incursion in the tribal areas.

The sense of frustration in the USA–Pakistan relationship continued as Pakistan neared the promised general election. Nawaz Sharif and Benazir Bhutto became more engaged. Washington's continued frustration at the perceived double role in the fight against the Taliban reflected a genuine worry about the future of the war effort in Afghanistan. Despite the American role in pushing Karzai and Musharraf at least to enter the same tent, it was clear that the two loathed each other. In watching the leaders of all three countries dine together hosted by Bush at the White House in 2006 and 2007[26] and meet at the margins of UNGA, I was reminded of President Reagan's meetings when he brought together Indian Prime Minister Rajiv Gandhi and Pakistan's President Zia-ul-Haq in the mid-1980s. Karzai and Musharraf refused to look at each other or to shake hands at a Rose Garden meeting or at the dinner table, whereas Gandhi and Zia had not been personally discourteous.[27] Still, neither Bush nor his senior advisors focused on the need to help normalization in the subcontinent as the necessary ingredient for greater cooperation from Pakistan on the Afghan front. Unlike the Reagan years, when the USA had taken a great deal of care to bring India and Pakistan closer together on a broad front, Bush simply noted that: "Part of the problem was Pakistan's obsession with India.... the fight against the extremists came second."[28]

Finally, when Pakistanis took to the streets and demanded a change, the Bush administration had little choice but to spend serious energy on democracy building in Pakistan. The vehicle for the effort was Musharraf's pledge to hold free and fair elections but the onerous task of holding him to the pledge was still that of the USA. In terms of the two party leaders who likely were to lead the effort, Benazir Bhutto was Washington's preferred choice. She was a known quantity and had spent her time out of power, maintaining some links with the USA. But with Musharraf's hold on American decision makers, her circle had shrunk. As Rice, and intermittently Bush himself, engaged in conversations to coax the Pakistani President to shed his uniform and set a date certain for the election, Bhutto seemed to emerge as the only viable and acceptable candidate. Her rival, Nawaz Sharif, had been exiled after Musharraf carried out his coup. Sharif had other strikes against him. He was less palatable to Musharraf because of Sharif's pledge that he would try Musharraf for subverting the constitution, a crime carrying the death penalty. In addition, Sharif was a more conservative leader whose stay in Saudi Arabia during his exile had only further reinforced his sympathies for Islamist Wahhabist tendencies. These sympathies were also encouraged by his wife, who, by her own declaration, is herself a (female) mullah.

Talk of power sharing between Musharraf and Bhutto, begun while she was visiting New York in 2006, accelerated. Encouraging his friend to leave power was not a conversation Bush relished, so it fell to his Secretary of State to convey the unwelcome though simple message: "Hold a fair election and abide by its results." To this end, Musharraf agreed that when Bhutto, who had previously been banned from holding office ever again, returns to Pakistan, she would not be prosecuted for the still pending official charge of corruption in office.

Bhutto, remembering that both of her prior tenures had been curtailed by an unhappy military, seemed happy enough with the new, USA-sponsored, arrangement. Before her return to Pakistan, we met, and I asked her if she felt safe returning and also whether she had faith that the new agreements would be honored when she returned home. Bhutto poignantly noted that she had few choices. She was a "people's leader" with a serious following in Pakistan. She eschewed extremism and felt that Pakistan's future hung in balance. She had a responsibility to her country to try and arrest the decline and move back toward moderation. Bhutto had an amazing degree of fatalism regarding her own safety in Pakistan. I pressed upon her the need to be careful, and she said with a smile that her friends, me included, were all urging the same.

Just prior to her fateful return to Pakistan on October 18, 2007, Benazir Bhutto wrote that she was returning to her country in order to prove that the fundamental battle for the hearts and minds of Pakistanis can be accomplished only through democracy. Capturing the growing frustration in Washington with the weak record of the military in the fight against terrorism, Bhutto chastised past American actions in dealing with military regimes in Pakistan throughout its tortured 60-year history even though religious fundamentalism was never a part of that history. Citing Pakistan as a moderate, centrist state, Bhutto stated that it failed "political dictatorships and social helplessness that create the desperation that fuels religious extremism."[29] Bhutto pledged that she would lead the battle to stand up to fanaticism by mobilizing the moderate middle.

Bhutto had been targeted by various extremists groups, including Baitullah Mehsud, the Taliban leader who publicly threatened to kill her. In October, upon her return during a meeting with an American expert on the region, Bhutto expressed that some of those conspiring against her included "another structure that is giving ... encouragement."[30] Washington continued to support Musharraf with the President noting he had no reason to doubt the Pakistani leader's pledge to hold elections: "I take a person for his word until otherwise ... And he made a clear decision to be with us and he's acted on that advice."[31]

A free and fair election in Pakistan meant that Nawaz Sharif too had to return from his exile. While Musharraf was not willing to permit the man he overthrew coming home from exile, the country's Supreme Court ruled that Sharif must be allowed into compete. He came home with special Saudi blessing and quite possibly all the needed funds for his security and the election campaign. The polarization of Pakistani politics began even before the election. Critics of Bhutto's engagement with Musharraf, before her return home, needed to be answered. She said it was to ensure free and fair elections and to make the military a partner in the battle against extremism, which neither the military nor the political leadership could undertake on its own. She repeated George W. Bush's words that the most powerful antidote to extremism is not bullets or bombs but the universal appeal of freedom because "Freedom is the design of our maker, and the longing of every soul."

Presciently, Bhutto acknowledged that she could not be sure what would happen to her upon her return to Pakistan, except that the people would welcome her as head of the largest political party. She ended by writing "I pray for the best and prepare for the worst...I am going home to fight for the restoration of Pakistan's place in the community of democratic nations."[32] She wanted an end to extremism in Pakistan and was willing to fight for that. While campaigning for the election at a public gathering, she was assassinated on December 27, 2007. Her final words to the nation implored her countrymen: "Wake up, my brothers! This country faces great dangers. This is your country! My country! We have to save it."

Condoleezza Rice issued a statement expressing deep sympathy for her passing saying she had known Bhutto as a "woman of great courage and had been impressed by her dedication and commitment to democracy and to the future of Pakistan."[33] Yet, while the freedom agenda was much celebrated after Bush's second inaugural speech, Washington's South Asia focus at the highest levels of the administration singularly remained focused on the prized nuclear agreement with India, rather than bringing democracy to Pakistan.

The nuclear deal was touted in both New Delhi and Washington as the singular achievement of the Bush–Singh collaboration. Launched at the meeting of the two leaders in July 2005, for more than three years, the agreement required active hand-holding by Bush, Rice, and her Undersecretary. Bush signed the new agreement as law on December 18, 2008. Its congressional approval empowered the US government to expand civil nuclear cooperation with India and lift long-standing legal restrictions. With singular deliberateness, Rice pushed the deal to give India a different status under the US law, international nuclear regulatory regimes, and international safeguards, including the 45-member Nuclear Suppliers Group (NSG) and the IAEA offering a "foundation for a new strategic partnership."[34]

Benazir Bhutto's death forced a scramble for Bush and Rice to find an early acceptable alternative. A shocked Pakistan, understanding that her demise ended any hope for mounting a political challenge to the extremists whom she had vowed to defeat, needed help. US interaction with Pakistan thus meant an essentially on-time election. Musharraf obliged in February 2008 while noting that a successful effort to defeat terrorism and extremism in Pakistan required a military as well as political and economic effort. Noting that thousands had died fighting al Qaeda and the Taliban, that 112,000 Pakistani troops were deployed along the border with Afghanistan, he reminded the USA of the sacrifices of the Pakistani military. With this in mind, he felt it appropriate that he remain a player to help shape the future.[35]

But the outcome was sealed when Zardari, Bhutto's husband—who, upon her death, had taken over the stewardship of the PPP—and Nawaz Sharif, the opposition leader, joined hands to talk of impeachment for the general for subverting constitutional rule through his 1999 coup. Upon failing to secure a reconciliation between Bhutto, Sharif, and Musharraf, who left Pakistan after resigning on August 18, 2008, Washington backed off. It was the end of an era and the USA had to once again start its engagement with a different set of players. In a clear shift, anticipating tougher times in Pakistan, President Bush approved orders in July 2008 that for the first time allowed American Special Operations forces to carry out ground assaults in Pakistan without the prior approval of that government. This became necessary because the situation in the tribal areas was deemed intolerable.[36]

Notes

1. "Bush Promises to Facilitate Pakistan India Talks," *The Nation*, February 14, 2002.
2. Ahmed Rashid, *Descent into Chaos: The U.S. and the Disaster in Pakistan, Afghanistan and Central Asia* (New York: Penguin, 2009), 149.
3. Husain Haqqani, *Pakistan: Between Mosque and Military* (Washington, DC: Carnegie Endowment for International Peace, 2005), 323.
4. See Tahir-Kheli, *The United States and Pakistan: The Evolution of an Influence Relationship* (New York: Praeger, 1982).
5. Address by Pervez Musharraf, United Nations General Assembly, New York, September 22, 2004.
6. Speech by Pervez Musharraf, National Students Convention, Islamabad, May 24, 2004.

7. The White House Press Office statement noted that "the U.S. is robustly responding to the request of *President Musharraf* and the Government of Pakistan..." (emphasis added), October 9, 2005.
8. The White House, Office of the Press Secretary, "Statement on U.S. Assistance for Earthquake in Pakistan," Washington, DC, October 9, 2005.
9. Senate Resolution 274, October 17, 2005.
10. Shaukat Aziz, Speech to the Council of Foreign Relations, New York, November 18, 2006.
11. Remarks by Pakistan's Foreign Minister Kasuri at the Joint Press Conference with Secretary Rice, Office of the Spokesman, U.S. Department of State, Washington, DC, March 17, 2005.
12. Interview with Shivraj Prasad, New Delhi Television, March 16, 2005.
13. Remarks by Condoleezza Rice en route to India, U.S. Department of State, March 15, 2005. Rice noted that in her conversations with Musharraf in Islamabad, she would expect a commitment to a democratic path for Pakistan. She lauded the Pakistani President for his effort to rid Pakistan of extremism and make Pakistan a model for other Muslim countries.
14. R. Nicholas Burns, "The U.S. and India: The New strategic Relationship," *Asia Society*, October 18, 2005.
15. Simon Denyer and Rama Lakshmi, "U.S.-India Nuclear Deal Drifts Dangerously," *Washington Post*, July 15, 2011.
16. Ibid.
17. Sherry Rehman, President, Central Planning, Pakistan People's Party, letter to author, November 25, 2005.
18. Boucher, Statement before the House Committee on Oversight and Government Reform Subcommittee on National Security and Foreign Affairs, July 12, 2007.
19. Peter Baker, "Unrepentance Day: Questions for Donald H. Rumsfeld," *New York Times Magazine*, February 13, 2011.
20. George W. Bush, *Decision Points* (New York: Crown Publishers, 2010), 216.
21. Boucher, Testimony before the House Committee on Oversight.
22. Ahmed Rashid, "America's Bad Deal with Musharraf goes Down in Flames," *Washington Post*, June 17, 2007.
23. Ahmed Rashid, "A Second Coup in Pakistan," *Washington Post*, November 5, 2007.
24. Karen DeYoung, "Rice Says U.S. Will Review Aid to Pakistan: Portion Funds Effort against Terrorism," *Washington Post*, November 5, 2007.

25. The International Republican Institute (IRI), Pakistan: Public Opinion Survey, 2007, 2008, 2009.
26. These meetings led to the establishment of a trilateral effort at coordination against terrorism. The meetings continued at the presidential, foreign minister, and military experts' levels until Pakistan refused to attend the March 2011 meeting slated for Brussels because of the civilian deaths caused by American missile strikes in the tribal areas of Pakistan leading to a rare condemnation from the country's powerful Army Chief who called the American attack "unjustifiable and intolerable." The Pakistani foreign office statement stated: "It was evident that the fundamentals of our relations need to be revisited. Pakistan should not be taken for granted nor treated as a client state." By 2007, Pakistan had become the highest recipient of American weapons calculated at $5.1 billion in value of agreements. India stood second at $3.5 billion and Saudi Arabia at third with $3.2 billion. See Tom Shanker, "U.S. Is Top Arms Seller to the Developing World," *New York Times*, December 1, 2007.
27. George W. Bush, *Decision Points* (New York: Crown Publishers, 2010), 215.
28. Ibid., 213.
29. Benazir Bhutto, "When I Return To Pakistan," *Washington Post*, September 20, 2007.
30. Steve Coll, "Time Bomb: The Death of Benazir Bhutto and the Unraveling of Pakistan," *New Yorker*, January 28, 2008.
31. Bush quoted in Rashid, *Descent Into Chaos*, 388.
32. Bhutto, quoted in ibid.
33. Statement by Rice, "Assassination of Benazir Bhutto," Department of State, Washington, DC, December 27, 2007.
34. Upon retirement from the Secretary of State office, Rice and Steve Hadley set up a consulting company, taking with them Anja Manuel, the junior officer responsible for the USA–India deal, for advice in emerging markets such as India, ensuring some of the spin-off from the expected $40 billion in potential sales to India. Ironically, the post-earthquake and tsunami events and the Fukushima Dai-ichi nuclear power crisis in Japan in March 2011 may restrict Indian enthusiasm for nuclear power, especially with the memory of the accident at Bhopal chemical power plant in central India in December 1984 which resulted in massive number of dead and injured. The litigation for compensation from Dow continues with the Supreme Court of India issuing notice to Union Carbide of India and Dow in February 2011.

35. Pervez Musharraf, "A Milestone on the Road to Democracy," *Washington Post*, February 22, 2008.
36. Eric Schmitt and Mark Mazzetti, "Bush to Give Orders Allowing Raids in Pakistan," *New York Times*, September 11, 2008.

CHAPTER 31

Return to Democracy

Even with the return to democracy, security and stability remained elusive. Yet, there were some new good firsts in Pakistan: the election of more women, the establishment of a bipartisan women's caucus in parliament, and the election of Fehmida Mirza by the legislator as Pakistan's first female speaker of parliament.[1] Despite this, in answering an opinion poll, Pakistanis stated that in many ways they felt less secure each successive year that the International Republican Institute (IRI) survey was conducted after 2004. In the March 2009 poll, when asked to choose between a stable and prosperous Pakistan run by the military dictatorship or a democratic government that led to instability and insecurity, 75% selected the democratic option while 23% opted for the military.[2] This was obviously based on promise and not performance. Indeed, as in 2009, whenever the memory of military rule is still fresh, the eternal hope for a more responsive democracy always shines bright. This has happened every time the military has had to vacate the throne. Yet, the inevitable outcome always has been an inept civilian government focused on lining its own pockets and the beating of drums for freeing Kashmir from the repressive dictatorial rule of the world's largest democracy across the border.

Despite their repeated assurances of Pakistan's commitment to the war against terrorism, Pakistani leaders sounded less than convincing to American ears. To many observers, it is the mirror reflection of America swearing to a lasting strategic relationship with Pakistan and avowing that this time around, the USA would not walk away. It appeared to be a dialogue of the deaf in which neither heard the other but firmly delivered its well-practiced speech.

Pakistan's Ambassador noted that in singling out Pakistan for criticism for not doing more against the extremists while ignoring the problems caused by the government in Afghanistan, the critics were "keeping one eye shut and one open."[3] Various mechanisms to correct the perceptions of each other included the high-level Strategic Dialogue, set up in March 2006, to review policies, dispel irritants, and provide impetus for progress.

While US criticism continued, Pakistani perceptions, governmental and public, persisted that in the global (read, USA) fight against al Qaeda, Pakistan was bearing a disproportionate burden and losing its soldiers to the effort. Also, that most of the al Qaeda fighters were arrested in Pakistan. The American view, however, was somewhat more nuanced. The fact that the Taliban and al Qaeda were "sworn enemies of a progressive Pakistan and its current leadership" should by itself make it Pakistan's business to undertake action against them. Indeed, Pakistan's truce with the tribal leaders had clearly been a negative because it in effect handed a free pass to the foreign fighters in their midst.

According to Islamabad, the problems lay in Afghanistan where warlords, drugs, corruption, and lack of governance made success impossible. Reluctantly, however, Pakistan was willing to acknowledge that despite mutual distrust, fighting the extremist in both Afghanistan and within Pakistan was an unusual shared objective possibly the first in the history of USA–Pakistan relations.[4] Yet, despite increased consultations via the Strategic Dialogue, military-to-military discussions, and intelligence agencies communication, the lack of trust persisted. Pakistanis resented the pressure "to do more" when they felt they were fully committed. They pointed to a number of unfulfilled pledges, namely to enhance counterterrorism capacity, the 2006 promise to develop Reconstruction Opportunity Zones (ROZs), that remained unfulfilled. Hoping to win "hearts and minds," the USA had talked of spending $750 million over a five-year period in the tribal areas of Pakistan. The legislation to move the assistance forward and the development plans for massive spending in an infrastructure starved region with a population of 3.2 million remained the challenge. Unveiling the plan for the FATA region, Boucher noted during a June 2007 visit to Pakistan that the main aim was counterterrorism. Reflecting a point made by Musharraf to Washington, it was said that the objective of the proposed plan was to offer an alternative future to the people of the FATA, provide basic human services and infrastructure, and bring them on par with the rest of Pakistan so that they would not welcome the Taliban and al Qaeda.[5]

Then came November 27, 2008, when 10 gunmen laid siege to Mumbai, India's most populous city with 14 million people, murdered 164 innocent people and wounded 308 in three days of carnage. Planned and fingerprinted in Pakistan, this engineered a crisis that might well have led to an Indo-Pak conflagration. For Rice, who rushed to Delhi to show support and to prevent precipitous response from the Indian military, the bloodbath had once again shown that things in Pakistan were out of control. And that the progenitors of these actions came from Pakistan constituted another headache for which she had little time. Rice issued a stern warning to Pakistan en route home from India. There, she pointed out that the attack had been masterminded by the leader of the Pakistani militant group Lashkar-e-Taiba, a group that, in response to previous attacks against India's parliament, had ostensibly been banned (by Pakistan) in 2002.[6] Rice acknowledged that she had told the Pakistanis that "the argument that these were non-state actors is not acceptable" because they had traveled from Pakistani territory (where they in fact lived) and thus they were the responsibility of the Pakistani government.

Zardari needed to crack down on militant groups, irrespective of whether they operated against Pakistan, Afghanistan, or India. "This is a qualitatively different set of circumstances than we have seen in the past and it requires a qualitatively different response" said the American Secretary of State.[7] Pakistan vowed action to curb the militant groups and claimed that it had put their leaders under house arrest. What went unacknowledged, however, was the fact that the terrorists had achieved one of their prime objectives: to derail plans for normalization between India and Pakistan. Talks between the two leaders in New York had launched serious effort to normalize trade relations and open up each market to goods from the other. With the Mumbai attack, efforts by Pakistan's Foreign Minister Shah Mehmood Qureshi, who had been in Delhi talking about diplomatic steps toward rapprochement, all came to naught.

As the Bush administration's tenure came to an end, Rice noted that Pakistan was the most difficult problem the administration was leaving for incoming President Barak Obama. It did not have to be so. From Rice's perspective, Pakistan was an unattractive headache where Osama bin Laden had found sanctuary. It was a rapidly crumbling perhaps even a failing country, while its neighbor next door was a rising star—a mega nation, with an established democracy. Thus, India was the real prize for US diplomacy. Answering a question after leaving office, Rice noted that Indian interest in destabilizing Pakistan was simply a myth. "Pakistan has nothing India wants," she noted, suggesting that the Pakistani obsession with India was unwarranted.[8] While restating only the obvious, she failed to mention the well-known truism: a four-alarm fire is a mortal danger also to the contiguous neighboring house. In the view of some, Musharraf deliberately raised the profile of jihadi groups in order to make himself invaluable to the USA. Unfortunately, in the process, he provided an opening for the local Taliban to take root in Pakistan's cities. Richard Boucher, the assistant Secretary for South Asia, stated categorically that Ahmed Rashid was "totally wrong" in saying that the USA relied exclusively on Musharraf.[9]

While Washington demoted Pakistan as a positive concern in the newly realigned Indo-US equation, the USA continued to press Pakistan to solve the Afghan imbroglio, which was passed on to the Obama administration and remains unresolved in the Donald Trump era.

NOTES

1. Mirza, a supporter of Benazir Bhutto, is a businesswoman and a physician, elected three times to parliament and garnering 249 out of 324 votes cast in the National Assembly. Her rival male, a Musharraf's man, received 70 votes.
2. The IRI, Pakistan: Public Opinion Survey, 2009.
3. Mahmud Durrani, *Daily Times*, Lahore, May 3, 2007.
4. Mahmud Durrani, "Pakistan–U.S. Relations," USIP, July 8, 2010.
5. Jane Perlez, "Aid to Pakistan for Tribal Areas Raises Concerns," *New York Times*, July 16, 2007.
6. In 2005, the UN Security Council committee also sanctioned groups that target individuals and organizations believed to be assisting al Qaeda and the Taliban.
7. James Blitz, "Rice Urges Islamabad to Root Out Extremists," *Financial Times*, December 2, 2008; Rice interview with George Stephanopoulos, ABC News, Washington, DC, December 7, 2008.
8. Remarks at the World Affairs Council of Philadelphia, May 4, 2009.
9. Richard Boucher, "Pakistan at the Crossroads," Hearings of the House National Security and Foreign Affairs Subcommittee of the House

Oversight and Government Reform Committee, July 12, 2007. Boucher was grilled extensively on the reason for exclusive administration support for Musharraf. As late as February 2008, Boucher continued to answer a question from a member of Congress that he, Boucher, found Musharraf "indispensable." This was also the time when State Department colleagues kept muttering about the difficulty of getting President Bush to give up on his friend, the general.

CHAPTER 32

The Freedom Agenda: What Went Wrong?

> America's vital interests and our deepest beliefs are now one. From the day of our Founding, we have proclaimed that every man and woman on this earth has rights, and dignity, and matchless value, because they bear the image of the Maker of Heaven and earth. Across the generations we have proclaimed the imperative of self-government, because no one is fit to be master, and no one deserves to be a slave. Advancing these ideals is the mission that created our Nation. It is the honorable achievement of our fathers. Now it is the urgent requirement of our nation's security, and the calling of our time.
> So it is the policy of the United States to seek and support the growth of democratic movements and institutions in every nation and culture, with the ultimate goal of ending tyranny in our world.
> —President George W. Bush, Inaugural Address, January 20, 2005

By 2004's end, it was abundantly clear that Iraq was in serious stress. Continued breakdown in delivery of services and security were spiraling out of control. Given that Saddam Hussein posed a mortal danger to the region with his WMD, the President and his senior advisors believed the war was an honorable option. Still, the lack of success on finding WMD after the war shifted the focus to the alternate goal of the war: namely, democracy promotion. As the case for war was originally articulated, the rationale did not include efforts to promote democracy in the Middle East. But by 2004, democracy promotion had become *the defining noble goal*. It included the rise of Iraqi democracy which, it was said, would bring hope to reformers in the Middle East, bring dismay to Damascus and Tehran, and signal a decisive defeat for extremists and terrorists in hopes of undercutting the appeal of radicals' extremism and nurturing the appeal of a free and tolerant country.

Several immediate benefits to the change in emphasis and strategy were assumed: First, democracy promotion was a positive goal in itself. Its importance derived from the very essence of America's strength as the world's most powerful democracy. Here was an instance where the USA wanted for others what it itself had benefited from. The rhetoric was altruistic and the President couched it as a US strategic goal. Within the White House, senior advisors and presidential speechwriters put in a great deal of effort to create the right message. For Bush, this was a commitment he believed in, and he saw it as a reflection of the American destiny.

Second, the failure to unearth any WMD was telling. Despite public denials, the White House was despondent. As detailed later, discomfort also began to build regarding CIA's assessments of Iraq's nuclear capability and intentions. In other words, the central rationale for the invasion and the resultant costly US engagement in Iraq was unraveling. A certain amount of defensiveness appeared as official spokesmen and advisors sought to frame the right message on why the war had to be fought and the supplemental requests for funding were a critical element of the response to the fight against terrorism.

Third, the neocons, including Cheney, had actively promoted the war with their espousal of the WMD rationale. Absent WMD findings, the credibility of the presidency was at risk. Thus, for neocons, an alternate explanation was badly needed. They climbed on to the Democracy promotion agenda and the "creation of a democratic nation in the heart of the Middle East" then became the noble pursuit that provided an altruistic *rationale* for the invasion.

In the lead up to the invasion, the USA argued that Iraq's WMD represented an immediate and a growing threat. Condi Rice's remark that the evidence of Iraq's culpability does not have to be a "mushroom cloud" spoke to Bush's firm view that Iraq possessed the capacity to do great harm. Bush himself noted that the "Intelligence gathered by this and other governments leaves no doubt that the Iraq regime continues to possess and conceal some of the most lethal weapons ever devised."[1]

As the non-existence of any WMD became undeniable, serious individuals with requisite expertise began to unveil what they saw as a deliberate misreading of Iraq's capability in order to make the case for war. Cheney, Rumsfeld, Wolfowitz, Hadley (who later took responsibility for the 18 word misrepresentation of Iraq's acquisition of nuclear material in the President's State of the Union speech involving Iraq's purchase of uranium from Niger), Addington, and Rove—all had declared themselves totally convinced that US national security was directly under threat from Saddam Hussein's nuclear, chemical, and biological programs.[2]

Woven into this declaration of distrust was the obvious dislike of the UN by these neocons. They felt all UN institutions were under suspicion because of the generally anti-US-anti Israel sentiments at the UN and the particularly anti-George W. Bush feelings that were rampant in the run-up to the invasion of Iraq in March 2003. They were unwilling to accept that Iraq's nuclear program had been dismantled by UNSCOM and "there was no convincing evidence of its reconstitution. Regarding chemical weapons, UNSCOM discovered that Iraqi nerve agents had lost most of their lethality *as early as 1991*. Operation Desert Storm and Desert Fox and UN sanctions had effectively destroyed Iraq's large-scale chemical weapons production capabilities."[3] There were greater uncertainties with regard to biological weapons. White House officials were concerned on all three scores, with near obsession by Cheney and his staff. As the siege mentality set in, the neocons continued rationalizing their pursuit of war against Iraq on their firmly held belief that Saddam was a man who had the desire and the capacity to inflict serious harm on the USA and Israel. They did not believe public assertions by UNSCOM and its leader, Rolf Ekeus, that Saddam's WMD capability had been fully neutralized. Indeed, even if they were to believe this assertion, they wanted proof that Saddam's intentions had also been "decapitated."

That meant a robust program post-invasion must remain focused on eliminating his capability in addition to unearthing any hidden WMD. Thus, the White House sought, and Congress approved on November 3, 2003, the Bush request for a supplemental which included $600 million to the ISG that was to work under David Kay and subsequently Charles Duelfer.[4] The ISG acted as an independent entity and did not follow the normal chain of command since it reported directly to Donald Rumsfeld. The set-up made it easier for the ISG teams to live and work in various parts of Iraq where WMD was believed to have been located. After six months of work, the ISG issued an interim report on October 3, 2003, noting that while it had found evidence of "WMD-related program activities," it had found no actual chemical, biological, or nuclear weapons. It did, however, find evidence of some non-WMD programs banned by UNMOVIC.

Inside the White House and the Pentagon, the existence of the banned programs but no actual WMD caches was more evidence of the lack of credibility of the UN inspection teams. There was much gloating about the uselessness of relying on the UN for anything bearing directly on US national security. Cheney and his senior staff led this unfavorable assessment. Cheney had already stated that a return of UN inspectors would provide no assurance of Saddam's compliance with previous UNSC resolutions.[5] Whenever the UN inspectors discounted reports of the Iraqi WMD, especially in the run-up to the invasion, Cheney or Rumsfeld termed the return of the UN inspectors "a sham."[6]

Colin Powell's speech to the UN Security Council on February 5, 2003, provided detail on how the administration firmly believed that the Iraqis were fooling the inspectors.[7] On March 16, 2003, Cheney gave a scathing view of the IAEA view that components such as the aluminum tubes were not meant for the Iraqi nuclear program, noting: "If you look at the track record of the International Atomic Energy Agency and this kind of issue, especially where Iraq is concerned, they have consistently underestimated or missed what it was that Saddam Hussein was doing. I don't have any reason to believe they're any more valid this time than they've been in the past."[8]

There also existed intense dislike of the Egyptian head of IAEA and when his contract came up for renewal in 2005, neocons, led by John Bolton, wanted to dump him. However, failure to put together an alternative viable candidate in a timely manner and to garner sufficient international backing for a US pick was impossible given the lack of international support for the USA at the time. This made the re-appointment of El Baradei to a third term a *fait accompli*.

Though initially reluctant, the Cheney group went along largely because Gregory Schulte, an OVP insider and who as executive Secretary of the National Security Council had directed the NSC staff to share all emails with the Vice President's staff (a previously unheard of procedure), was being sent to Vienna as the US Ambassador to the IAEA to keep pressure on El Baradei, particularly vis-à-vis sanctions on Iran.

El Baradei subsequently lamented: "We were spied on by the same intelligence agencies we relied upon to inform us when they detected anomalies; we were given selective intelligence information, which was difficult to authenticate. We were dependent on Member States, some of whom had their own agendas, to supply state-of-the-art technology we could not afford. We were pressured by those who believed that funding the Agency came with the right to influence its work for political ends."[9] El Baradei specifically refers to a conversation that he had with the number three State Department official, Nicholas Burns, where Burns handed a list of US demands and pointedly noted that the USA pays 25% of the IAEA budget.

As the complicated search for WMD continued, the ISG leadership came under a great deal of pressure to find something. It was an article of faith in the White House, and among Cheney staff in particular, that the stockpile existed. Thus, to put pressure on the ISG was not seen as an unreasonable request but rather simply as encouragement to do a better job! But the pressure was telling. On January 23, 2004, David Kay resigned his position as head of the ISG, stating that he believed that WMD stockpiles would not be found in Iraq. "I don't think they existed," said Kay.

The Kay resignation was greeted with some trepidation but also a measure of relief due to the neocon insiders' belief that the WMD really existed. And all that was needed were competent diggers! Therefore, a new head, more attuned to the administration's sensitivities, was needed.

One day, as I traversed the lobby of the West Wing, I ran into Charles Duelfer, whom I had met in 1990 when we were both in a small intensive French language class at the Foreign Service Institute. Back then, I was heading out as one of the US ambassadors to the UN, and Duelfer was training for an assignment. Meeting now in the White House, we had a brief chat and he told me he was waiting to see a number of West Wing principals. I did not ask but assumed he had been brought in to discuss his becoming the new chief of the ISG: our own man to do more competent digging! However, the final Duelfer Report, released on September 30, 2004, found nothing new as it reiterated that Saddam Hussein had ended his nuclear weapons program in 1991 with no evidence of any concerted effort to reconstitute a nuclear weapons program; Iraq's chemical weapons stockpile was destroyed in 1991 with only a small number of old, abandoned chemical munitions discovered by the ISG; and that Saddam Hussein's regime had abandoned its biological weapons program and its ambition to obtain advanced biological weapons in 1995.

9/11 provided the critical overlay to the fear of a nexus between rogue states and terrorists bent on doing harm to the USA. Prior to 9/11,

Condi Rice had written that Iraq was effectively deterred because "if they do acquire WMD, their weapons will be unusable because any attempt to use them will bring national obliteration."[10] After the terrorist attacks of September 11th, the focus shifted to prevention rather than reaction and the phrase "taking the war to the enemy" made its rounds in the White House. Some, such as Rumsfeld, pointed to the changed interpretation of evidence caused by 9/11 when he said apropos the invasion: "We did not act in Iraq because we discovered dramatic new evidence of Iraq's pursuit of weapons of mass murder. We acted because we saw the existing evidence in a new light, through the prism of our experience on September 11th."[11] The worst case scenario as painted by neocons was the marriage between Saddam Hussein and the al Qaeda leadership.

The above lengthy recounting of the WMD issues is relevant to this analysis of what went wrong with the democracy promotion effort. I found neocons agitated as failure to find weapons stockpiles inside Iraq made the rationale for the invasion less credible. They lashed out against the UN. And Cheney often led the attack. Thus, it became distressingly evident to all that the "slam dunk" WMD statement in the run-up to the war in Iraq had been false. However, despite the evidence to the contrary, Cheney et al. continued asserting that Saddam must have very cleverly hidden or transferred out of the country most of his existing WMD stockpiles. Besides, the same argument stated that failure to find existing stockpiles or even destroy them meant leaving intact Saddam's will to resurrect a viable, deliverable WMD program.

As Senior Director for the Directorate with responsibility for international operations, I had to deal with the OVP staff in getting buy-in for the work we had to continue, including the various UN Security Council resolutions that dealt with Iraq. It was never an easy task, but Bush himself was willing to engage as I made the case to Rice that we needed presidential input in order to bring the UN Secretary General, Kofi Annan, on board. We worked to be responsive whenever Annan reached out to the President or to Rice. Rice met with Annan on June 11, 2003, when some of the early shared disillusionment was dormant. Whenever they met, Cheney was present, sitting silently throughout the meeting. As the White House reputation for unilateralism in diplomacy became firmly set, both because of the invasion and the many statements that administration neocons had made, we sifted through the American foreign policy record to challenge the prevalent popular belief that the UN had been ignored by the administration.

32 THE FREEDOM AGENDA: WHAT WENT WRONG?   291

Despite the general dismissiveness by his critics of the overall Bush record on UN engagement, the record of the administration's engagement with the UN since 2001 was actually quite respectable in some areas. Several issues are worth noting. While there had been some 72 UNSCRs since 1990, there had been 17 resolutions in the 2001–2003 period all of which required serious engagement by the USA, which wields veto powers. The President had raised the issue of non-compliance with 16 UNSCRs by Saddam Hussein speaking to the UN General Assembly in September 2002. UNSCR 1441, which was adopted unanimously determined that Iraq was in material breach of its obligations under relevant UNSC resolutions; the statement made by Bush (along with Blair and Aznar) at the Azores summit in March 2003 prior to the invasion of Iraq, that if military action were required, the coalition would work in close partnership with international institutions, including the UN: "We plan to seek the adoption, on an urgent basis, of new United Nations Security Council resolutions that would affirm Iraq's territorial integrity, ensure rapid delivery of humanitarian relief, and endorse an appropriate post-conflict administration for Iraq." Following the invasion, in my NSC tenure, the USA pursued and won unanimous adoption of three comprehensive resolutions (UNSCRs 1483, 1511, 1546) that laid out a vital and leading role for the UN in Iraq; the UN assisted the Iraqi people in a political process leading to free and fair elections under a new constitution drafted by representatives of the Iraqi people.

The above-noted engagement with the UN took place despite the disdain of the Cheney staff and the VP's key advisors. There was collective mocking of the UN's impotence in the face of defiance by Saddam Hussein. Any other alternate course was deemed preferable for enforcement on the WMD front given that the USA would lead such action. Therefore, physical entry into Iraq was necessary. However, there were other strands of policy within the White House.

Rice, in bringing me on as Senior Advisor, knew that I would push for multilateral engagement. Further, despite her voiced skepticism of the UN record on Iraqi compliance on WMD, she understood that the USA could not have a sustained effort on Iraq without involving the UN and its leadership. She convinced Bush along the same lines, and the President was very engaged in his conversations with Kofi Annan on post-invasion issues. He joined with Blair in welcoming UNSCR 1472, which allowed for shipments of humanitarian items to Iraq under the Oil for Food program. He welcomed the April 2003 appointment by the UN

Secretary General of a Special Advisor for Iraq to work with the people of Iraq and coalition representatives. Bush and Rice lobbied Annan to send Sergio de Mello to head up the UN's Iraq effort given his record of dynamism and outreach. When de Mello was killed in the massive bombing of UN headquarters in Baghdad in August 2003, the President and Rice shared the sense of loss, especially as it led to the departure of all UN personnel from Iraq within weeks of the terrorist bombing.

Thus, when it finally became clear that no WMD caches were found even by armies of inspectors, the neocon focus and the rationale for the invasion of Iraq shifted to "Democracy Promotion." Once Cheney made the rhetorical switch, others piled on. Liz Cheney, for obvious reasons, was appointed to head the State Department's Middle East partnership effort and helped put in place a cadre of people, including Paul Wolfowitz's friend Shaha Riza, who became a consultant on leave from the World Bank. Essentially all the funding allocated to the Department of State for these purposes was allocated to Liz Cheney for distribution. The funds for the BMENA initiative and the Forum for the Future were also used. Many participants, who were tied into the Liz Cheney effort, were invited. A sense of entitlement was apparent, for as questions were raised, the typical response was: "Vice President Cheney was nationally elected: you were not." No one seemed to acknowledge that it was Dick Cheney, not Liz! However, the symbiotic relationship between Cheney et al. and Democracy Promotion cast a negative shadow on democracy promotion as an important undertaking by George W. Bush. American policy had a tough time recovering from this awkward attachment since the main proponents for the war were now dressed as public spokesmen for democracy.

Beyond the negatives of the war occasioning much loss of blood, there were specific ways in which the neocon legacy in the Bush administration had negative impact on the effort to promote democracy. First, Iraq became a laboratory for political change. The callous attitude embodied in the now infamous Rumsfeld remark "stuff happens" was a consequence of the firm belief that this was to be a short war. As the USA became the sole arbiter of change and no government-in-waiting emerged after the fall of Saddam Hussein, it was obvious that the USA "owned" Iraq. There, only the DOD had the presence on the ground and State was loathe to acquiescing to the authority of the Pentagon where Rumsfeld, Wolfowitz, Feith, etc. called the shots. Also, it was clear that Powell had been "used" when he spoke to the UN in February

2003 about WMD in Iraq, a fact not easily overlooked by the State Department when asked to step in.

As early pages have noted, the muddle of Iraq made it easier to focus on issues relating to democracy, which seemed to be the obvious alternative to multi-ethnic Iraq shaking off the tight Sunni Baathist control that had lasted decades. As the Coalition Provisional Authority (CPA: the name carefully selected by the proponents of the invasion to imply broad-based support, the temporary nature of the undertaking) got set up to oversee Iraq, the need to develop a civil society structure surfaced quickly. This was the phase when large numbers of Iraqi leaders came to Washington and made the rounds in favor of their personal or the neocon agendas in which the need for a more representative Iraq was made.

Once the WMD issue faded, those inside the White House with a distaste for multilateral diplomacy including Cheney and his staff were now expressing interest in greater UN involvement to help with the "sign-off" from the US occupation of Iraq. This sudden interest in multilateral diplomacy among those who long derided it emerged as it became clear that the USA did not have the capacity to effect any real change inside Iraq's atrophied political system without outside help. The UN was the one institution that had undertaken civilian remakes after conflict in a variety of places. Thus, even as the US viceroys—first Jay Garner and then Jerry Bremer—worked to get Iraqi representatives on board for a postwar government in Iraq, the need for outside help, from those with experience in such matters and not simply from the "coalition of the willing," was obvious. But the UN had withdrawn from Iraq after the bombing of its headquarters that resulted in the death of the Special Representative and 22 other UN staff.

We had a lot of work cut out for us as we made the case to Kofi Annan to re-engage the UN in Iraq. In my many conversations, I found that the ongoing reputation of neocons as dismissive of UN intentions and capacity had escalated and further soured feelings toward the George W. Bush administration. Many countries (e.g., Germany and France) who possessed the capacity to help rebuild Iraq saw the invasion as a unilateral Bush action, absolving them from responsibility for follow-on actions. Therefore, they were loath to help, in keeping with the Kissinger sentiment: "Why are you asking me to participate in the crash landing when I was not in on the take-off?"

I left on July 10, 2003 on a week-long trip to Iraq to see postwar democracy building efforts and to work with a team from the White

House looking at children's health facilities. Flying in from Kuwait in a C-130, we flew to Mosul first. The planes corkscrew landing made clear the danger of ground fire but July was still quiet and the insurgency was not yet in full swing. When we got to Baghdad, the cavernous hangar where American visitors (limited in number) and incoming soldiers (a growing number) were processed was blisteringly hot. My first image was that of a large dumpster inside the hangar, filled with thousands of bottles of cold water. It was a welcome ever present sight wherever one went in Iraq where American troops were present. Given the high temperatures, sometimes nearing 125 degrees in the shade, cold water was a lifeline.

Transferring from the airport to the Green Zone by a secure vehicle with body armor and helmet, I was warned of snipers and the need to heed the security protocol. Checking in at the al-Rashid hotel (where a week later Paul Wolfowitz's room was the target of a rocket attack), my colleagues and I were warned about movement, even within the Green Zone. As White House staff, we were told of our special vulnerabilities. We were also given a history of some of the bizarre goings on at the hotel, which used to operate a disco where Saddam Hussein's sons, Udai and Kusai, terrorized guests, especially attractive females. It was pointed out to us that all of the hotel rooms were equipped with cameras (turned off by the US military) from which hotel guests were once monitored by Saddam's goons and used for blackmail or worse.

It was an extraordinary time in Iraq. I found in my meetings with Iraqi members of the Governing Council, a great deal of hope for their country's future and a firm belief that the fall of Saddam Hussein would finally loosen the grip of arbitrary rule. The women were impressive in their determination to make a difference, sometimes even as they faced physical threats. They lamented the mass graves that were just then in 2003 being unearthed and vowed that the Iraq of the future had to be inclusive and tolerant. They voiced sadness with the plight of young girls who were often kidnapped at the behest of Saddam's sons and their goons from the streets or the University. Many never came back. The bodies of some were sent back in plastic bags with signs of physical torture evident. We saw a "palace" where it was said the sons kept torture instruments and used them frequently. The commitment of US soldiers and officers serving in Iraq was total and humbling. From the lowest in rank to the serving general, there was fearlessness about the mission in 2003 as it was unfolding.

What struck me inside the palace where the CPA was headquartered was the hum of activity and the large-scale presence of self-selected, young, inexperienced American civilians who had attached themselves to the Pentagon-led leadership. These individuals had seldom been outside the USA, some had not even traveled beyond state borders. They had no experience or knowledge of the world, let alone one as complex as Iraq. They had a messianic mission to "bring democracy to the barbarians" and clearly they were an inappropriate face of America to the Iraqis. Many did not venture outside the Green Zone, so were not in direct contact with Arabs. But they sat in places where they could control paper and policy as it wound its way to Washington. The rush to get the American administration of Iraq up and running by the Pentagon in the shortest possible time had offered an avenue for the inexperienced political adventurers a job in Iraq. The result was often not best for projecting the American image in an occupied Muslim country. I briefed Dr. Rice on my impressions of personnel on the civilian side of CPA when I got back to the White House.

Upon returning from the Iraq trip, at Rice's request, I worked with the UN leadership. It was an important task. In October 2003, seeking broader support for Coalition efforts, the USA again approached the UN Security Council. Work on UNSCR 1511, which brought in the UN in an enhanced role inside Iraq, was complicated. The resolution was scripted in Washington but Negroponte, who remained close to Powell, was the one who had to sell it at the UN.

Toward the end, Rice sent John Bellinger, the legal advisor, and me to New York. We were to be there for the final moments before the vote. At the last moment, various members of the Security Council asked for a twenty-four-hour postponement of the vote in order to receive instructions from capitals. Much to the annoyance of the White House, Negroponte agreed as he wanted a unanimous vote and did not want to lose the chance because of deadlines imposed by Washington. Hadley, undoubtedly listening to Cheney and Rumsfeld, wanted Negroponte to proceed. Bellinger and I called Rice to explain the postponement, and Rice asked if the delay would hurt the chances of securing the resolution. We responded that we thought not. Condi ended the call by saying: "make sure it works or don't come back." We hoped she was jesting.

In the end, the next day, the Security Council unanimously adopted Resolution 1511, which endorsed the Iraqi Governing Council, set out a timeline for Iraq's transition to sovereignty, outlined a vital role for the UN in Iraqi reconstruction, and authorized a Multinational Force (MNF) to provide security in Iraq.

Annan was under pressure from the UN employees union and his security team to restrict the UN's presence in Iraq. But, at the same time given the expanding UN mandate, that presence was essential, even critical. Many lamented Sergio de Mello's loss, noting that he was going to be irreplaceable. Annan, whom it was said treated de Mello as a son, was reported to be suffering from depression. In my dealings at the time, I found him engaged but sad. His meetings with Bush, at the UN and at the White House, were comprehensive. On one of the visits, the President invited Annan to a working lunch, an unusual event under normal times. In the several hours spent together, the leaders discussed the Iraq operation and focused on the transfer of sovereignty to the Iraqi people, which Bush promised would take place by June 2004.

The transfer made it easier to deal with issues relating to UN engagement. Annan appointed Lakhdar Brahimi as Special Advisor to the Secretary General and Under Secretary for Conflict Prevention. Brahimi had been the UN's point person in Afghanistan and was known to Annan and to US officials. While there was a collective sigh of relief at the White House that finally UN leaders were focusing on assisting Iraq return to civilian rule, the anti-UN segments within the Bush administration wanted to make sure that Brahimi at best played a secondary role. Iraqis wanted the UN and understood the wide unpopularity of the war among the very Western countries that could be helpful in re-building their country and also assisting in keeping the American agenda in check. Yet, all recognized that the USA had the upper hand. With Brahimi's involvement alongside the USA, in May 2004, the Iraqi Governing Council and the CPA announced the formation of the Iraqi Interim Government.

Speaking to a meeting of the UN Security Council, Iraqi Foreign Minister Hoshyar Zebari said in his statement (written by the USA) that the interim government was the result of extensive consultations undertaken by Brahimi in Iraq, who traveled to all the regions despite the poor security situation. Further, the CPA (i.e., USA) led an exercise over months to reach out in broad national consultations that included outreach to tribal, religious and community leaders, political parties, and women's groups. Iraq wanted the passage of the pending resolution in order to ensure smooth transfer of sovereignty over its own assets.

Zebari noted that the Transitional Authority Law (TAL), which covered the transitional period until the election resulted in an elected government that reflected the will of the people to form a free, unified and democratic Iraq. The principles in TAL reflected, said the foreign minister, Iraq's preferred path of reform and democratization. The assembled representatives of Security Council member countries understood that while the rhetoric was fashioned by Washington, the sentiment was shared by Iraqis. Everyone wanted the USA to end the occupation, and resolution 1546 would make that possible. Yet, the minister asked for the continued presence of MNF on Iraqi soil in order to stabilize the situation and prevent regional interference in Iraqi affairs and to protect Iraqi borders.

On June 8, 2004, the UN Security Council unanimously passed Resolution 1546, which noted that the occupation would end by June 30, 2004, endorsed the Iraqi Interim Government as the sovereign Government of Iraq, laid out a role for the United Nations in the political process that would lead to democratic elections held under a new Iraqi constitution, and reaffirmed the presence in Iraq of the MNF. The UN was thus asked to assist the people and the government of Iraq in a variety of ways: to aid in the convening of a national conference to select a Consultative Council; to advise on and provide support for the holding of elections; and to help promote a national dialogue leading to a consensus for the drafting of a constitution. In addition, the UN advised the Government of Iraq in the development of effective civil and social services, coordinated on the reconstruction effort, assisted in the work of human rights protection, national reconciliation, judicial and legal reform and the planning for a national census.

Upon the resolution's passage, US Ambassador to the UN Anne Patterson noted that despite war and Saddam Hussein's legacy of oppression, the Iraqi people were determined to create a new reality. Washington hoped that finally the international community would help Iraq and "match advice with assistance!" She recalled that Bush had said that "Free Iraq deserves the full support of the international community." Finally, said the US Ambassador, a unanimous vote for the resolution "should be a reflection of international resolve to help improve the situation on the ground for the lasting and permanent benefit of the people of Iraq."

The White House put out a statement on behalf of the President upon adoption of UNSCR 1546 celebrating the unanimous support for a "stable, prosperous and democratic nation." The statement noted that by calling for elections by January 31, 2005, the UN resolution sent a clear message: "The international community stands united with the Iraqi people in opposition to all who attempt to halt that nation's march toward freedom."[12]

By mid-2004, violence inside Iraq had escalated, with the insurgency taking hold in most places. Along with it came the ethnic/sectarian strife that pitted Arab against Kurd and Sunni against Shia. Regional countries had varying degrees of influence but Iran had the most in the south. Militias became the order of the day, making assassinations commonplace. Even as Iraqi political leaders geared up for the January 2005 elections, they faced many challenges beyond the issue of waging a successful campaign.

Despite authorization from the Security Council and with increased awareness in the international community that postwar Iraq badly needed assistance, Annan and his senior advisors were nervous about the huge task the UN had been handed. Security was a growing impediment to political development and Annan found US control over the unfolding political process restrictive. From the very start, Cheney, Rumsfeld, and Wolfowitz had played favorites in terms of particular Iraqis that they wanted to promote, such as Ahmed Chalabi.

Annan wrote to Bush on October 31, 2004, stating that elections were due to be held in three months' time and pledging that the UN was committed to doing everything possible to supporting credible elections and assisting with Iraq's political transition as mandated by UNSCR 1546. In meetings and conversations, Annan noted that he believed elections were key to restoring stability and legitimacy in Iraq. However, in order to be credible, the elections needed to field a more inclusive, broader spectrum of Iraqis. The process could not succeed if certain elements who felt alienated from the transition process were not brought in. Only inclusiveness, thought Annan, might help ameliorate the tough security environment. The Secretary General repeated to many his concern that the security environment would not be helped if the MNF undertook action against the insurgents in Fallujah and other places where large civilian casualties would result.

Annan remained unconvinced that military action would bring security. Rather, he cautioned that only dialogue and an inclusive political process would restore security to Iraq. He felt that the threat of military action would only deepen the sense of alienation among sizeable numbers of Iraqis, keeping them from achieving consensus required for elections and peaceful transition. In particular, the election that was to replace military occupation with political transition would be made all the more difficult once the MNF went into Fallujah. Offering the services of his Special Representative, Ashraf Qazi, Annan counseled dialogue in order to forge a conducive political and security environment for successful elections. All the while, Annan pledged his commitment to work closely with the USA, Tony Blair, and the Iraqi leadership (Ayad Allawi was Prime Minister at the time).

Cheney, Rumsfeld and other neocons on their respective staff were extremely unhappy at Annan's suggestions. They felt his warnings simply reflected a proclivity against the USA and would make MNF action all the more difficult. Within the White House, the President, Rice, and others chafed at Annan's statement to BBC in the course of an interview on September 14, 2004, that the war in Iraq was "illegal as it was not in conformity with the UN Charter." In the same interview, Annan had said that credible elections could not take place if the security situation stayed as it was at the time. Countering the statement, the White House press Secretary put out the word that with all due respect for Annan, the USA did not agree that the war failed to conform with the UN Charter.

The White House response to Annan was that the USA had previously made clear its position on the legality of the Iraq war and felt "confident that coalition forces had authority under international law to use force against Iraq." This authority was deemed to be based on UN Security Council Resolutions 678 (dated 1990) and 687 (1991), which provided clear legal authority against Iraq based on the latter's repeated material breach of the 1991 cease-fire conditions over more than a decade. Of course, no one wanted to mention that the pre-Gulf war resolutions envisaged a very different plan of response, i.e., a fully multilateral approved effort led by the USA but carrying the UN's imprint. Within the White House, the OVP emphasized that, in 2002, UNSC passed Resolution 1441, concluding that "Iraq has been and remains in material breach of its obligations under relevant resolutions, including 687," all of which justified the use of force.[13]

The USA pretty much drafted the Iraqi Prime Minister's response to Annan via the work of senior US officers seconded to various Iraqi officials in Baghdad who were involved with external correspondence. Allawi wrote to Annan that he was committed to the election timetable set under UNSCR 1546 and felt that any delay would be a victory for those bent on violence and intimidation. He said that it was true that violence would be very disruptive to Iraq's political transition. Therefore, in order to stop it from escalating, "we" are arranging for a robust response. Allawi used a phrase popular with neocons when he recounted that parts of Iraq had been "hijacked by the terrorists and insurgents" resulting in high level of atrocities committed against civilians. Allawi worried that despite his reaching out for a broad consensus; the insurgents had shown no interest in joining the political process, eschewing the rule of law so necessary for democracy to gain a foothold in Iraq. The Fallujah process, per Allawi, would spare civilians, offer humanitarian aid and be led by Iraqi security forces with his direct approval.

NOTES

1. Joseph Cinncione et al., *WMD in Iraq: Evidence and Implications* (Washington, DC: The Carnegie Endowment for International Peace, 2004), 22.
2. One of Cheney's neocon experts told me on July 22, 2004 that WMD definitely existed in Iraq and it was merely a matter of time before huge caches would be uncovered "if the UN inspectors did their job." Author's meeting with John Bolton.
3. Cinncione et al., *WMD in Iraq*, 6.
4. The ISG was a fact finding mission setup following the invasion in 2003 to find expected caches of Iraqi WMD which provided the main reason for the invasion. Consisting of some 1400 members of an international team put together by the Pentagon and the CIA to hunt for WMD stockpiles and any supporting research programs and infrastructure that could be used to develop WMD. The ISG replaced the UNMOVIC led by Hans Blix and Mohammed ElBaradei of IAEA which was mandated by the UN Security Council to search for illegal weapons before the conflict. Neocons refused to accept the UNMOVIC verdict that no WMD were found as they mounted the case for the invasion in March 2003.
5. Richard Cheney, "Remarks to Veterans of Foreign Wars 103rd National Convention," Nashville, Tennessee, August 26, 2002.
6. Donald Rumsfeld, "Interview with the National Journalist Roundtable," August 7, 2002, available at www.defenselink.mil/transcripts/2002/t08072002_t0805sd.html.
7. Cinncione et al., *WMD in Iraq*, 46.
8. Ibid.

9. Mohamed EL Baradei, *The Age of Deception: Nuclear Diplomacy in Treacherous Times* (New York: Henry Holt and Co., 2011), 239–240.
10. Condoleezza Rice, "Promoting the National Interest," *Foreign Affairs* 79.1 (January/February 2000) 61.
11. Donald Rumsfeld, "Testimony on Iraq," Testimony before Senate Armed services Committee, Washington, DC, July 9, 2003.
12. The White House, Office of the Press Secretary, June 8, 2004.
13. The White House, Office of the Press Secretary, September 16, 2004.

CHAPTER 33

GTMO

The Iraq war took a toll on the reputation of the USA and the President. The argument offered by senior officials that the USA had gone into Afghanistan and Iraq to bring democracy and better governance failed to resonate outside the USA, particularly in the Muslim world. Even within the USA, critics, including conservative Republicans, were taking the administration to task for invading a country that was not a threat to the USA, had not attacked American forces, and did not want war—only to disarm it of weapons that did not exist. The criticism included ridicule of the idea that Iraqis would welcome US soldiers as liberators who would go on to establish democracy throughout the Middle East. The idea that criticism of the war was unpatriotic also stung conservative opponents. Arriving days after the invasion of Iraq, I witnessed in the George W. Bush White House that Cheney's staff operated completely differently from the VP staff in the Reagan or George H. W. Bush administrations that I served. In the W. Bush White House, the Vice President dominated the national security apparatus and often sought to speak in the name of the President.

The interagency process, which I had closely witnessed and participated in during two other Republican White House periods, was certainly different in the George W. Bush period. The Vice President was more intrusive, his staff more belligerent, and DOD more demanding. The NSC staff often had to broker personalities and issues way beyond the norm. Outsiders commented that "Rumsfeld simply ignored decisions made by the President in front of the war cabinet, according to several senior administration officials. Condi Rice, who was supposed to be managing the interagency policy process, seemed either unwilling or unable to rein in Rumsfeld, so the defense Secretary simply got away with pursuing his own foreign policy."[1]

I recall that early in my stint at the NSC in 2003, Scooter Libby, Cheney's Chief of Staff and National Security Advisor whom I had known since we both served in the Reagan administration under Paul Wolfowitz at the State Department's Policy Planning Staff, told me that Wolfowitz came by the OVP to see Scooter nearly every morning before going to the Pentagon. It seemed highly unusual for the Deputy Secretary of Defense.

Beyond the usurpation of the democracy agenda as justification for the 2003 war, other problems cropped up. Among the most damaging were the repugnant photographs of extensive prisoner abuse at the Abu Ghraib prison in Iraq. Several issues then surfaced requiring immediate response as I sat in the directorate that dealt with Human Rights for the NSC.

The international human rights community, already critical of the US treatment of prisoners, including those who were confirmed dangerous terrorists threatening America, was up in arms at the visual record of abuse by US military officers in charge of the prison. The fact that these photographs were taken by some of the officers themselves stripped the moral high ground from US action and its declared intention to build a better future for Iraq.

There was no explaining how this could have happened to my many interlocutors. I assured them that the President as well as National Security Advisor Rice was shocked by the reality reflected in the photos and condemned what had transpired and ordered an inquiry.[2] In his May 8, 2004, radio address, the President noted that: "What took place in that Iraqi prison was the wrongdoing of a few, and does not reflect the character of our military or our country. America is a compassionate country that believes in justice and freedom. Americans believe in the worth and dignity of every person." Bush was emphatic that the individuals given the responsibility of overseeing Iraqis in American custody were expected to do so "in a decent, humane manner consistent with our military code of conduct." Any practice to the contrary the President iterated would not be tolerated. However, he carefully absolved the military at large of the excesses of the few, saying: "Our people in uniform are the best of America. And the shame of a few cannot diminish the greatness of their achievement in Iraq or the respect they have earned by fighting and sacrificing for this country." This was the time when insurgent attacks inside Iraq were intense, and areas such as Najaf and Fallujah were in violent turmoil.

As the photographs circulated rapidly in the Muslim world, immense damage was done to America's image as a liberator in Iraq and a protector of human rights. That these prisoners were Muslims seemed to engender particular resonance in the Muslim world and the criticism was fierce. Specifically, charges of abuse at Guantanamo (GTMO) and the treatment of those interned at the American base in Cuba were voiced by many inside and outside the USA noting that extreme interrogation techniques were put in place by Rumsfeld using the argument that GTMO housed "enemy combatants" not regular prisoners of war. On the other hand, Iraq was occupied territory and there the USA was obliged to follow the Geneva Conventions covering treatment of prisoners of war. Under these rules, the Army interrogations were to follow rules prescribed in the Army Field Manual and Uniform Code of Justice, which prohibits US forces from engaging in "cruelty," "mal treatment," or "oppression" of prisoners.[3]

As the storm began to erupt internationally, I realized that we were caught in a strange situation at the NSC. Given the debunking of the original rationale for the Iraq war, the unearthing of Saddam's torture chambers and mass graves provided a small measure of respectability to the American intervention. Cognizant of this fact, the President and Dr. Rice seemed to strongly support human rights protections in Iraq. Yet, Cheney, Rumsfeld, and others seemed "hell bent" on moving in an opposite direction.

In discussions on the status of the detainees in GTMO, it became clear that the OVP role, particularly that of David Addington who was legal advisor to Cheney, was key. On October 21, 2001, the *Washington Post* reported that the President had signed an intelligence "finding" on September 17, 2001, removing CIA restraints on covert action against al Qaeda and bin Laden. As per the report, one senior official noted that "The gloves are off. The President has given the agency the green light to do whatever is necessary. Lethal operations that were unthinkablepre-September 11 are now underway."[4] Views of Addington, Yoo, and Haynes (representing OVP, Justice and Defense Departments, respectively) remained central to the effort on detainee matters. That pattern continued until late in the administration as scandals leaked and the role of the Vice President—particularly in the aftermath of the Scooter Libby affair—surfaced.

While the administration asserted that those declared "enemy combatants" did not have Geneva Convention rights, the International Committee of the Red Cross (ICRC), charged with oversight of prisoners of war, fought to have access also to those incarcerated at GTMO and (few) elsewhere. The struggles to allow due process, and the limits of interrogation techniques are detailed at length via interviews with key players.[5] The story makes sorry reading. Even as early as 2003, when I arrived at the NSC, the tension between those who argued for due process and those who did not believe that GTMO and Abu Ghraib violated either international law or American ideals was palpable. My colleague at the NSC who served as Counsel to the President and Legal Advisor to the NSC, John Bellinger, worked with me as we dealt with ICRC issues. We made the case internally that the administration needed to be responsive to ICRC concerns and accommodate them as best as possible because American soldiers serving abroad would need protection against arbitrary behavior by other governments. Alienation of the ICRC did not seem a good idea. Rice gave us a sympathetic hearing but she had left detainee issues to the lawyers, and here, Bellinger was outnumbered.

On June 6, 2003, Bellinger and I accompanied the Counsel to the President, Alberto Gonzales, on a day-long visit to GTMO.[6] Bellinger headed the Detainee Policy Coordinating Committee (PCC) at the NSC. I was the Senior Director for human rights and international operations, with responsibility for some of the issues pertaining to detainee policies. As I climbed into the White House van that took me to Andrews Air Force Base to get on the Gonzales plane, I assumed it was to be an NSC contingent going with Gonzales since we had voiced concerns. Upon arrival at the base, I was startled to see OVP and DOD representatives David Addington and William J. Haynes climb on board. I felt that they were there to keep an eye on the NSC and get a sense of what questions we would have of the officials in charge there including Major General Geoffrey Miller, the base commander. In addition, public sources noted that on December 2, 2002, based on recommendations from his legal counsel, Jim W. Haynes, Rumsfeld had approved additional categories of harsher treatment against GTMO prisoners "including the use of 'hooding,' 'exploitation of phobias' and 'stress positions,'" ordinarily forbidden by the *Army Field Manual*.[7] Addington and Haynes undoubtedly had their own items on the day's agenda since they were aware of the reported authorization cited above.

It was a strange experience, flying over the blue waters off Cuba, landing in a place which was US territory, taking a boat to the base and going on the tour that followed. Given all of the human rights issues that I heard from various organizations such as the ICRC, Amnesty International, the International Crisis Group, and Human Rights Watch, I wanted to see first-hand how the incarceration was handled. We were all, including Gonzales, taken to some of the sites, including the future military commissions facility where we were briefed on pre-trial and post-trial detention, the Mental Health Facility at Camp Iguana. It was obvious there were others sites where access was especially controlled, and I was excluded. However, the commander was keen that Bellinger and I see the special facility where a single underage Afghan was held. It was a small house with pleasant rooms, including a teaching room where the boy was taught English by a specially appointed teacher. He was reported to be doing well and had expressed a desire to go on to make his life in America once he was educated and set free.

The majority of those held at GTMO whom I saw were in a common area. The ICRC had voiced some concerns that I shared with the officers of the base. They offered to take us around to see how they had tried to handle the relevant issues and stated with a good deal of assurance that the commander had been responsive to the ICRC on all issues that he was authorized to handle, including the provision of reading materials, exercise, and a place for prayers. (I noted that the direction of K'aaba toward which all Muslims face in prayer was carefully marked with an arrow in each cell.) But the total absence of communication between two alien cultures was clearly evident, and it was stark. The inmates did not appear to respect the officers, and officers saw them as evil people who wanted above all to do harm to America. As we walked through the individual open metal cages that held those deemed less dangerous, I understood some of the languages being spoken. There was a strange ongoing commentary by the group who might as well have been on the moon as far as they were concerned. In one comment, I heard one inmate say to another in Urdu: "Hey, Bush has sent people to take you out of here!" Responded the other: "Not so. Because that would be an important visit. And if so, it would not have included a woman." He said this as he pointed at me.

We were shown the medical facility and the brand new sparkling dental clinic recently completed. All of us saw the elaborate facilities that had been built as a venue for the expected military commissions for trying the enemy combatants which the DOD felt were imminent. The lawyers in the group discussed procedures for these commissions and issues relating to its timing. As we took off for the return to the White House, I thought of the day's travels, the sights seen, and the two groups of fellow travelers who represented starkly different views about human rights.

The NSC group briefed Condi on GTMO on June 11, 2003.

More compelling for me was a better understanding of the vast divide between the President's desire for outreach to the Muslim world and the cold reality of the obvious hits America's image would take from its interrogation of prisoners incarcerated at GTMO. Yet, I felt that a majority of the detainees could not be held indefinitely. After all, this was America where court challenges were already beginning to surface, and the US image was taking a beating abroad at the very time that we needed to build international support. As GTMO detainees returned home, they would likely spout hatred of the USA. Theirs was not the dislike of a distant people but the hate generated by exposure to an extremely rare but painful and distressing interaction with American officials which they would conveniently use to depict angst toward the USA at large. They would get credibility for their message of violence and support for recruitment of more terrorists. With the discovery of abuse at Abu Ghraib, the problem became even more severe. Could the USA ever recover? This was a key issue faced by those of us at the NSC who felt a wing of the administration had created a nightmare and the President's pledge to champion the growth of freedom and the end of tyranny was being hampered by the pictures of the US government's official sanction of excesses in the name of interrogation. How is the challenge within and abroad to be countered? That was the question.

One obvious way to counter it was to deal head on with the issue of torture. Everyone around me at the White House kept assuring me that the USA did not and does not engage in torture and from the President on down all stated that that continues to be the policy of the government. Of course, I was unaware at the time that the nature of what constituted torture had now been carefully redefined and that Addington was holding in his office safe CIA's relevant program documents. This was reported publicly by the Obama administration.[8]

Not having any knowledge of the existence of the closely guarded memo that had supposedly "legalized" harsh interrogations and not knowing that CIA was also carrying out "renditions," and believing the President's statement that the USA does not torture, also repeated by Rice, my directorate consulted with colleagues at State and the NSC. Matt Waxman, a bright young colleague in our directorate who went on to become Rumsfeld's deputy assistant Secretary of defense for detainee issues after the Abu Ghraib scandal, and I went to see the legal advisor and asked for his help in drafting a presidential statement against torture that would have to be approved by the President and issued in his name on the upcoming occasion of the day celebrating US accession to the international Convention Against Torture. That Convention, which the US Senate ratified in 1994, declares that it is the policy of the USA "not to expel, extradite, or otherwise effect the involuntary removal of any person to a country where there are substantial grounds for believing that the person would be in danger of being subjected to torture." This was to apply to anyone held in US custody anywhere, not just within the borders of the USA.

Given international worries about US actions, a presidential statement to be issued on June 26, 2003, on the United Nations International Day in Support of Victims of Torture made sense. Working with colleagues at State and the NSC, we drafted a statement for presidential approval and circulated it to the appropriate officials within the NSC, OVP, and State. Comments came back, and the draft was also referred to DOD since it involved military matters. OVP clearance was not forthcoming, and there was never an explanation for why that was the case. Subsequent public reports have shed light on why Addington, Cheney's lawyer, who carried Cheney's proxy, would not give OVP clearance.[9] The failure to secure OVP clearance ensured that the document would go nowhere. Believing the assurances that I kept receiving—namely, that torture was not US policy—I continued pressing for action as the anniversary of the "U.S. accession to the international Convention Against Torture" was fast approaching.

As it happens, the "torture memo," as it was referred to internally, was one of my first major undertakings after my arrival in George W.'s NSC. The need for it was self-evident, the hurdles puzzling, and enormous. Bellinger and I met a number of times with Steve Hadley, NSC deputy, who seemed less than pleased that we wanted the statement approved and released. "Why is this necessary?" was Hadley's query. I offered up that the administration was under full attack by all of the human rights NGOs and other governments whose help was needed for reconstruction and democracy building in the postwar phase of Iraq. I also kept noting that given that the President and other senior officials had reiterated that the USA does not torture, where was the harm? Again and again Hadley pressed Bellinger and me to make sure that all of the concerns expressed by OVP and DOD were taken into account as their role was critical to getting any approval. Unhelpful though this response seemed at the time, I later determined that it was fully in keeping with the usual Hadley support for all OVP and DOD positions. Clearly, I thought, an appropriate version of the draft memo needed to be drafted so that OVP and DOD would come on board given that at least Hadley was eventually willing to go along with the idea of some presidential statement to be issued on the UN International Day in Support of Victims of Torture.

The NSC offices responsible for human rights and legal affairs, respectively, finally obtained all requisite clearances for an appropriate draft that included only a brief statement to be issued in the name of the President. It said: "**…the United States declares its strong solidarity with torture victims across the world. Torture anywhere is an affront to human dignity everywhere. We are committed to a world where human rights are respected and protected by the rule of law….the United states is committed to the world-wide elimination of torture and we are leading this fight by example. I call on all governments to join the United States and the community of law-abiding nations in prohibiting, investigating, and prosecuting all acts of torture and in undertaking to prevent other cruel and unusual punishment. I call on all nations to speak out against torture in all its forms and to make ending torture an essential part of their diplomacy**" (emphasis added). The statement ended with the President's urging that: "**No people, no matter where they reside, should have to live in fear of their own government. Nowhere should the midnight knock foreshadow a nightmare of state-commissioned crime. The suffering of torture victims must end, and the United States calls on all governments to assume this great mission**" (emphasis added).

The following year, the relevant statement was more detailed and we incurred less pushback, though there was a measure of inexplicable squeamishness about mention of the phrase "elimination of torture." Because precedence had been established the previous year and since the USA needed to bring in the international community for work inside

Iraq and Afghanistan, the statement was approved by the President and issued in his name on June 23, 2004. I hasten to add that OVP and DOD once again managed to insert some language at the end of the statement reflecting their strong interest in and involvement with GTMO and other relevant places. However, this time they agreed to sign on to some of the critical points we at the NSC had pushed. For example, the USA reaffirmed its support for the worldwide elimination of torture and noted that freedom from torture was an inalienable human right. The USA committed itself to "building a world where human rights are respected and protected by the rule of law."

The presidential statement aimed to reflect officially the President's shock at the excesses committed at Abu Ghraib and add his critical voice to the call from all quarters that cared about human rights. The blame for the excesses at Abu Ghraib fell squarely at the door of the of Defense and the December 2002 Rumsfeld approval of a series of harsh questioning methods at GTMO, which the *Washington Post* and *The Wall Street Journal* noted, included removal of clothes, use of "stress positions," and use of dogs to elicit fear. Finally, when exposed to the world press, Rumsfeld decided to deem these techniques as "grievous and brutal abuse and cruelty." His new view was that Geneva Conventions do not apply in GTMO but they did in Iraq.

Further, the statement celebrated the fact that the USA joined 139 other nations in ratifying the Convention Against Torture and Other Cruel, Inhuman or Degrading Treatment or Punishment. Then came the line that I felt justified months of internal wrangling: **"America stands against and will not tolerate torture. We will investigate and prosecute all acts of torture and undertake to prevent other cruel and unusual punishment in all territory under our jurisdiction. American personnel are required to comply with all laws, including the United States Constitution, Federal statutes, including prohibiting torture, and our treaty obligations with respect to the treatment of all detainees"** (emphasis added). The NSC lawyers felt that the last line stating it is "U.S. policy" not to tolerate torture and stating that American personnel are required "to comply with all U.S. laws," covered all necessary ground. When I asked that a reference to the commitment to eliminate torture be included, even NSC legal felt that while it was true that we supported the elimination of torture, a specific reference would create a new firestorm among the human rights community. Unaware, as I was at the time, that Rumsfeld had approved "rigorous methods of interrogation," the hedging against a strong commitment did not make any sense to me.

In order to make the case internally in the White House, I continued to press that the statement was in our national interest because we would want others to treat our military with decency. Internal NSC deliberations for the annual memo against torture were helped by the direct call for an amendment to the defense authorization bill by Congress requiring Rumsfeld to provide guidelines reaffirming the commitment that the USA does not engage in torture. It was said that "the administration's policy decisions have cast doubt on whether this country accepts the fundamental principles of human rights."[10] It now seemed imperative to get out the presidential statement against torture on the anniversary of the Convention against Torture on June 23, 2004. With Rumsfeld under direct attack and the Iraq record of American behavior in serious jeopardy, even the recalcitrant White House players—Hadley, Addington, among them—signed on.

With their un-enthusiastic approval, the final statement noted: "The United States remains steadfastly committed to upholding the Geneva Conventions, which have been the bedrock of protection in armed conflict for more than 50 years. These Conventions provide important protections designed to reduce human suffering in armed conflict." And, of course, with their enthusiastic approval, the words: **"We expect other nations to treat our service members and civilians in accordance with the Geneva Conventions"** (emphasis added). The statement further noted that: "Our Armed Forces are committed to complying with them and to holding accountable those in our military who do not."

The statement to be issued in the President's name was an excellent document. It addressed both international and US public concerns. As the statement made its internal rounds for clearance before moving to the President, a direct response was approved. Thus, it was noted, under the presidential insignia, that: "The American people were horrified by the abuse of detainees at Abu Ghraib prison in Iraq. **These acts were wrong. They were inconsistent with our policies and our values as a Nation**" (emphasis added). The statement went on to announce: "I have directed a full accounting for the abuse of the Abu Ghraib detainees, and investigations are underway to review detention operations in Iraq."[11]

Abu Ghraib had a lasting impact on the Muslim world's views of America, and the scandal also destroyed some of the urgency that went with the US efforts for democracy and political change in the Muslim world. It weakened the belief that the USA would either really want or could manage the rapid democratization of the Muslim world. Following public reports of the President's approval of the intelligence "finding,"[12] in hindsight, I understand why the Addington crowd fought hard to include the following paragraph in the final statement and why they were willing to agree to language that I felt was crucial to specifying the US strictures against torture. "**These times of increasing terror challenge the world. Terror organizations challenge our comfort and our principles. The United States will continue to take seriously the need to question terrorists who have information that can save lives**" (emphasis added). Indeed, Addington and the rest of the OVP appeared to justify—to those who supported them—their agreement to the memo by citing the last paragraph as the needed loophole reflecting the reported CIA "finding." It would have been better that the statement end with the following words: "**But we will not compromise the rule of law or the values and principles that make us strong.**"[13] But that was not to be.

Around May 11, 2004, I learned that in some measure the human rights groups felt betrayed by the predicted presidential statement because the statement was to be issued at the same time that tougher physical and psychological techniques were approved. The release of the President's statement was, however, greeted with relief by the human rights community. Yet, according to conversations with the White House press colleagues, while there was praise for the presidential clarification, the application of tough measures on detainees by Rumsfeld was very unwelcome. In hindsight, it would seem that the neocons had worked to neutralize the presidential statement by approving contradictory measures, thereby using the statement as a cover for their intentions toward continued use of harsh methods.

In the aftermath of the presidential statements and speeches, as we continued to deal with the press and the humanitarian NGOs regarding the torture issue, we made the following points: "U.S. policy is to comply with all U.S. laws, including the Constitution, federal statutes, and U.S. treaty obligations with respect to the treatment of all detainees; We are obligated to comply, and our policy is to comply, with the Geneva Conventions with respect to the treatment of all detainees in Iraq, which is a party to the Geneva Conventions. The president remains committed to building a world where human rights are respected and protected by the rule of law." The last point was one that our office felt was needed in order to show ongoing commitment to the President's statement against torture. These were the points that we suggested the White House press office use in its May 12, 2004, response to media queries. Cleverly, Cheney's office and his supporters did not challenge this suggestion. Rather, they dealt with it by ignoring it altogether and continued with the imposition of the Rumsfeld sanctioned stronger interrogation techniques.[14]

In an attempt to deal with the aftermath of Abu Ghraib, my office helped organize a comprehensive roundtable that brought together human rights leaders to meet with Dr. Rice. And she received many accolades for the president's statement pledging abhorrence of torture. Rice seemed pleased. The respite the June 23 declaration won the USA in terms of public diplomacy, both domestically and overseas, was not long-lived. Shortly afterward, another issue surfaced that once again brought controversy.

The emerging story of I. Lewis (Scooter) Libby, senior most advisor to Cheney, came out into open. Scooter had served in the Reagan administration, first on the Policy Planning Staff (S/P) of the of State with Paul Wolfowitz as Director and then at DOD when Wolfowitz became the number three official there. I have known Scooter since October 1982 when we worked together under Wolfowitz in S/P at the State Department. He wrote speeches for Wolfowitz, and it was clear that he was close to the boss. When I showed up years later in 2003 at the White House and quickly found the OVP impossible to get requisite clearances from for essentially all issues relating to multilateral diplomacy, I found that one course of action to get an override to the OVP staff objection was to explain the rationale for the issue and then appeal to Scooter as a former colleague as the Cheney senior aide. He held two very senior titles: namely, Assistant to the President and Chief of Staff to V.P. Cheney and Assistant to the Vice President for National Security Affairs. This placed him high in the hierarchy and having his agreement counted.

In the summer of 2003, rumors began to circulate that someone had deliberately leaked the name of a CIA undercover agent to various reporters. As the matter was heating up, one afternoon I invited Ruth Whiteside, my very first foreign service friend from 1982 and by 2003 a senior official at the State Department, to lunch at the White House Mess. In the course of our conversation about matters at hand, the issue of the unauthorized leak came up. Ruth suddenly asked me: "Who do you think did it?" My instantaneous guess was: "Scooter Libby or possibly someone in his entourage." Later, when news of the *New York Times* reporter Judith Miller broke, Robert Novak named Valerie Plame in his comment on July 14, 2003, and the Grand Jury started its deliberation, Ruth wondered how I had come up with Scooter's name. Ruth and I had served alongside Scooter in the Wolfowitz S/P. Because of my experience with the OVP world (which Scooter headed as Cheney's chief of staff) where anyone who disagreed with them on human rights issues or detainee policy—this included most Democrats and the *New York Times*—was villified, Scooter's name was self-suggestive. There was complete non-acceptance of dissent on issues relating to what was called "the war on terror." Thus, it was natural to think that the perpetrator was possibly in the OVP.

On October 28, 2005, Libby was indicted for obstruction of justice, false statements, and perjury charges regarding the matter that he disclosed to reporters the then-classified information concerning the employment of the Central Intelligence Agency agent Ms. Valerie Wilson.[15] Libby was found guilty of trying to deceive investigators and the grand jury. Libby resigned his White House post. He was convicted and sentenced on June 5, 2007, to prison and a $250,000 fine. President Bush commuted the 30-month prison term calling it "excessive," but left the rest of the conviction in place.[16]

A government official indicated that the Justice Department had not been consulted by the president prior to the commutation. I thought that Cheney must have directly weighed in. The neocons immediately set up a defense fund to help defray the legal costs that Libby had incurred. Whatever the overtones of the legal decision, Scooter is a gentleman, civilized to the core, and has respect for international rule of law. David Addington, Cheney's lawyer, on the other hand, has an amazing disdain for diplomacy and international norms. Therefore, it was not a good moment for American foreign policy when Scooter was replaced by Addington.

For us, at my directorate, statements regarding what was postulated as America's fall from grace on human rights issues were tough to take. We were pummeled both from the outside and from the inside: on the one hand, with expressions of sympathy regarding the extraordinary circumstances that 9/11 had created and on the other hand that America was failing to remain the beacon in promoting human rights and the rule of law. It was pointed out that the 1949 Geneva Conventions were established to deal with the horrors of WW II and to provide for humane treatment in armed conflict. In 1977, following the liberation movements of the 1960s, the concept was modified to also include intrastate conflicts rather than only the interstate ones that are the traditional boundaries for the Geneva Conventions. Additional Protocols 1 and 2 of the 1949 Geneva Conventions (signed by the USA but not ratified), respectively, bring wars of national liberation and guerrilla conflicts within the scope of the Geneva Conventions and call for application of the Geneva Conventions for treatment of fighters who fall under the jurisdiction of a single state.

My colleague, Sandy Hodgkinson, a trained military lawyer, briefed Colin Powell and his team on human rights—when we visited northern Iraq in 2003 and spent the day with the Kurdish leaders. (I was impressed and asked Sandy to join our directorate at the NSC.) Subsequent to my request, she laid out the DOD approach. DOD saw terrorism as a law enforcement measure to be dealt with as any other international crime. In the shifting paradigm of International Relations after 9/11, non-state actors are increasingly attacking states with the intent to do harm. Often these terrorists possess sufficient force to inflict damage and they show no interest in negotiations. Mostly, the global war on terror is directed against them.

Sandy explained that: "Because no particular government can be held accountable for the actions of these non-state actors, traditional law enforcement measures fail to apply. Also, the Geneva Conventions do not provide sufficient guidance on how to deal with such enemy combatants since they do not meet the following criteria: follow a chain of command, wear distinctive insignia, carry weapons openly, and follow the laws of armed conflict. Absent these criteria, they do not qualify for the traditional Prisoner of War (POW) status with the attendant obligations. Neither are these individuals and groups engaged in the traditional 'non-international armed conflict' that would carry some responsibility under the Common Article 3 provisions."[17]

However, no matter how much the administration made the case that those picked up in the global war on terror constituted a threat to the USA and were enemy combatants in a new kind of war, most other nations did not agree, and thus, the USA was denied international legitimacy which has traditionally been ours around the world. Due legal processes that are held to be the mainstay of the American system of Justice are also denied those captured or extradited to the USA in the war on terror. Further complicating the case was that some of the individuals held at GTMO and elsewhere are there because of their armed attack on the USA or its allies. Others are captured in the course of committing criminal acts which would afford them due process.

Within the White House and in the administration, through months of turmoil on detainee issues, the call for liberty continued. The president used the occasion of July Fourth celebrations in 2004 to renew the call, even as he was under pressure on interrogations. Recalling that on the 4th, Americans are proud of their founders, Bush stated that the "founders would be proud of America today. They would take a look at this great country and see a place where opportunity is common, where all stand equal before the law, where all can hope for a better life.... They would see a nation that is the world's foremost champion of liberty."[18] The president went on the recall the sacrifices that the American military made in order to "keep this country safe and to bring freedom to others."

Bush acknowledged that the war on terror had placed new demands on the military. He said that the September 11, 2001, attacks necessitated America's war on terrorism, and America's actions had freed Afghanistan from the Taliban turning that country into a rising democracy. But he did not mention any abuses and scandals. Referring to Iraq, he pointed out that the dictator who "tormented and tortured the people of Iraq ...was sitting in a prison cell, and will receive the justice he denied so many for so long." America was dealing with a new kind of enemy **"You can't talk sense to them. You can't negotiate with them. You cannot hope for the best with these people.... We have got a job to do, and that is to protect our country...Our immediate task is in battlefronts like Iraq and Afghanistan is to capture and kill the terrorists...We will engage these enemies in these countries and around the world so we do not have to face them here at home"** (emphasis added).[19]

Bush believed that the USA had brought peace for the future by supporting the rise of democracy as he asserted that the path to democracy brings hope as an alternative to hatred and terror, and this was particularly true in the broader Middle East. All this was held as an article of faith: "In democratic and successful societies, men and women do not swear allegiance to malcontents and murderers.... When justice and democracy advance, so does the hope of lasting peace."[20] Bush and Rice pointed to recent gains where "from Cairo and Ramallah, to Beirut and Baghdad, men and women are finding new spaces of freedom to assemble and debate and build a better world.... it is possible to envision a future Middle East where democracy is thriving, where human rights are secure, and where hope and opportunity are within the reach of these people."[21]

Notes

1. James Risen, *State of War: The Secret History of the CIA and the Bush Administration* (New York: Free Press, 2006), 161.
2. However, the 368-page report released in April 2005, headed by Vice Admiral Albert T. Church concluded that "there was no link between approved interrogation techniques and prisoner abuse." The breakdown in discipline and the use of unusual cruelty and humiliation depicted in the photographs was judged by the report to be rare and a case of combat stress, insufficient training, and a "breakdown of good order and discipline."
3. Joseph Margulies, *Guantanamo and the Abuse of Presidential Power* (New York: Simon & Schuster, 2006), 55.
4. Bob Woodward, "CIA told to Do 'Whatever Necessary' to Kill Bin Laden" *Washington Post*, October 21, 2001; and Woodward interview with CNN, November 4, 2002
5. Jane Mayer, *The Dark Side: The Inside Story of How the War on Terror Turned into a War on American Ideals* (New York: Doubleday, 2008).
6. Also in the entourage were: William J. Haynes, General counsel of the Department of Defense; David Addington, Counsel to Cheney; Anna Perez. NSC Advisor for Communications.
7. Mayer, *The Dark Side*, 220.
8. Mayer, *The Dark Side*, 316–326.
9. For analysis of David Addington's relationship with Cheney, see Barton Gellman, *Angler: The Cheney Vice Presidency* (New York: The Penguin Press, 2008), 136–137, and 173; and Mayer, *The Dark Side*.
10. *Washington Post*, "Torture Policy." June 16, 2004.
11. "President's Statement on the U.N. International Day in Support of Victims of Torture," The White House, Washington, DC, Office of the Press Secretary, June 23, 2004
12. Bob Woodward, *The Washington Post*, October 21, 2001.
13. Ibid.
14. May–June 2004 time frame. Work done after the White House press office alerted us on May 11, 2004, that the *Washington Post* was writing a story scheduled for publication on June 23, 2004, covering the expected

UN Convention Against Torture day statement from the President. The Human Rights groups sense of betrayal at the near simultaneous timing of the statement with the issuance of the harsher interrogation techniques authority had led to press interest in the internal process that led to the issuance of the presidential statement. Prior to the NSC's involvement in formulating the response to the inquiry from the *Post*, I heard (but never saw the note) that the president's counsel, Alberto Gonzales, had passed some press guidance to Scott McClellan, the press, which my office did not see, even though we were integrally involved in generating the statement against torture.

15. Office of Special Counsel, Patrick J. Fitzgerald, Washington, DC, October 28, 2005.
16. Cheney pushed Bush hard at the end of the administration in 2009 for a full pardon of Libby, but did not succeed.
17. These provisions included minimum standards of humane treatment.
18. Remarks by the President at the 4th of July Celebration, Charleston, West Virginia, July 4, 2006.
19. Ibid.
20. Remarks by the President, Oak Ridge National Laboratory, Oak Ridge, Tennessee, The White House, Washington, DC, Office of the Press Secretary, July 13, 2004.
21. Secretary of State Condoleezza Rice, "Keynote Address," Woodrow Wilson School of Public and International Affairs, Princeton University, US Department of State, Office of the Press Spokesman, September 30, 2005.

CHAPTER 34

Forum for the Future

Central to the US effort to promote freedom was the Forum for the Future. American hopes for the kind of multifaceted push as detailed in the previous chapter ran almost immediately into trouble. The economic dialogue became more cantankerous and the political effort, meant to promote democracy and freedom, lagged as reality ran up against presidential wishes. For example, the Democracy Assistance Dialogue was envisioned as core to the political reform agenda, but quickly ran into difficulty because its three co-sponsors (Italy, Turkey, and Yemen) were struggling to organize a robust dialogue. The American suggestion was for them to lead an effort with a serious plan for civil society representation and to bring key Muslim countries together.

Unfortunately, the co-sponsors had no experience in dealing with this novel idea. Consequently, there was growing in-fighting among various civil society groups, each asserting its legitimacy as "the" true representative. While the Forum provided new and exciting venues for civil society to meet with governmental leaders and to engage in discussion, the access thus provided started an unhelpful competition rather than the hoped for coming-together of civil society elements.

Resources were limited and soon after its launch the US effort ran into funding problems. Also, European partners became unwilling to underwrite what they perceived as an American venture. Further, key Muslim countries, such as Egypt and Saudi Arabia, sensing a possibility of greater accountability in the Forum and potential embarrassment

© The Author(s) 2018
S. Tahir-Kheli, *Before the Age of Prejudice*,
https://doi.org/10.1007/978-981-10-8551-2_34

at the hands of civil society deliberators, never came through with the anticipated funding for future activities. Instead, these governments attempted to wrest control over the reform agenda itself. In addition, they put pressure on multilateral institutions such as UNDP and the World Bank to discourage them from funding unrestricted activities recommended by civil society. Incomprehensibly, these activities also included education. Looking to the G-8 never became a serious option as even the UK, while claiming to be interested in the American-led initiative, made it clear that the Forum was not a top priority. The Foreign Secretary, Jack Straw, absented himself from the Forum, suggesting a lack of commitment by the foreign office even though his American counterpart Colin Powell chaired the meeting.

When writing her January 2000 *Foreign Affairs* article "Promoting the National Interest," prior to the 2000 election, Rice noted the following items as constituting a refocus in a Republican administration's foreign policy priorities: ensuring military strength; promoting economic growth through free trade and a stable monetary system worldwide; renewing "strong and intimate" relationships with allies where the burden of promoting peace, prosperity, and freedom can be shared; building comprehensive relationships with the big powers, especially Russia and China; dealing decisively with rogue regimes that threaten international order through terrorism and development of WMD. These were, of course, the usual aspirations of a government-in-hopeful-waiting.

Obviously, the 9/11 attacks turned these assumptions on their head. A new enemy with potentially huge reach made the course of engagement different. The nationalities of the attackers served as a strong reminder of the common thread that bound them: repressive dictatorial regimes that denied hopeful futures to an ever-expanding population of illiterate, unemployed youth. Absent even a marginal state engagement of citizenry emerged as the gaping void that cried for urgent US attention. Rice ended her view of foreign policy with the sentiment that "America can exercise power without arrogance and pursue its interests without hectoring and bluster."[1] Once in office, the search for a more hopeful future for millions in the Muslim world was put on the front page of the administration's agenda even as it collided head-on with reality. The case of Egyptian reformer Ayman Nour served as a poignant reminder of the limits of US policy.

As noted earlier, the January 2004 inaugural speech highlighted Bush's deeply held belief that "the call of freedom comes to every mind and every soul." The president went on to speak to the peoples of the world to say, "All who live in tyranny and hopelessness can know: the United States will not ignore your oppression, or excuse your oppressors. When you stand for your liberty, we will stand with you. Democratic reformers facing repression, prison, or exile can know: America sees you for who you are: the future leaders of your free country." The clarion call for regimes "with long habits of control" to start on the journey to justice was voiced by Bush as a warning that unless this journey is started they would incur US wrath. He also called for all free nations to undertake a concerted push to promote democracy as "a prelude to our enemies defeat."

With all of the presidential rhetoric promoting democracy and the dedication of resources for the freedom agenda via the NED, etc., in many countries, the push for reform took an optimistic turn. Given American patronage, regimes in the Muslim world took note even as they (publicly though not internally) decried interference. The call for democracy from the USA made it possible for opposition movements in the Muslim world to act more boldly. By mid-2004, the effort to promote democracy was firmly in play in Iraq: a country that was repeatedly referred to by the administration as situated "in the heart of the Middle East."

Because of its central place in the Arab world and as a partner of the USA in Middle East peace, Egypt came into sharp focus. In Egypt, the press showed signs of becoming free and calls for Mubarak to relinquish power emerged with the formation of a new movement, the Al-Ghad party—tomorrow party—with Dr. Ayman Nour as its leader. The party began challenging Mubarak's long-held position as president. Feeling some pressure, Mubarak announced elections for September 2005 and in February 2005 asked his parliament to amend the constitution to allow for multicandidate election for the presidency.

Secretary of State Rice made a trip to Egypt in June 2005. In an open speech, at the American University of Cairo, on June 21, she called on Mubarak to ensure that the upcoming election was free and fair. She praised Mubarak for opening up the presidential election to more than—what was hitherto the case—one candidate, and Rice urged for international monitors to ensure the election's sanctity. She assured her audience that as reflected in the 2004 inaugural address, the US aim was to help people find their free voice and not to impose a US-style government on them. "The people of Egypt should be at the forefront of this great journey, just as you have led this region through the great journeys of the past." In a clever reference to his longevity in office, Rice noted that Mubarak as president had been an important leader meeting with American presidents going back to Ronald Reagan![2] At the end of the speech, noting the upcoming Egyptian election, Rice warned: "Throughout the Middle East, the fear of free choices can no longer justify the denial of liberty. It is time to abandon the excuses that are made to avoid the hard work of democracy."[3] Following the speech, Rice met with civil society activists including opposition leader Ayman Nour.

Rice's speech had White House clearance including from NSC Middle East deputy, Elliott Abrams, who earlier beat multiple felony counts and indictment in the Iran–Contra Affair through a plea agreement in October 1991 and secured a pardon from departing president George H. W. Bush in December 1992 for his role in Iran–Contra. The speech was a calculated risk, and it was expected to pay off dividends given that Mubarak had already changed election rules for the better. Yet, Arab dictators chafed at what they perceived to be American interference in their affairs. The call for recognizing "human dignity that comes from democratic values" meant that rulers whose fiefdoms allocated benefits to the populace as "noblesse oblige" now needed to grant participation as a matter of right. Women were to be included, said Rice as she voiced a powerful message that she had been handed by a Kuwaiti woman saying "Half a Democracy is not a Democracy." Rice also referred to the Saudi denial of access to women and the jailing of three peace activists who had petitioned for change. Following this historic speech, Rice moved on to Saudi Arabia for an official visit to that country.

Egypt's September 7, 2005, election was quickly followed by charges of widespread fraud, manipulation, and buying of votes. On September 8, 2005, Ayman Nour contested the election results and called for a repeat election. The government responded by charging that it was Nour who was really the guilty party! It accused Nour of forgery in the petitions that were signed to launch his party in the fall of 2004 and on December 24, 2005, and sentenced him to five years of hard labor.

In an unusual move, the White House Press Secretary released a statement on behalf of the President reflecting the anguish the Nour case had engendered. The statement noted: "The United States is deeply troubled by the conviction today of Egyptian politician Ayman Nour by an Egyptian court. The conviction of Dr. Nour, the runner-up in Egypt's 2005 presidential elections, calls into question Egypt's commitment to democracy, freedom and the rule of law. We are also disturbed by reports that Mr. Nour's health has seriously declined due to the hunger strike on which he has embarked in protest of the conditions of his trial and detention. The United States calls upon the Egyptian government to act under the laws of Egypt, in the spirit of its professed desire for increased political openness and dialogue within Egyptian society, and out of humanitarian concern, to release Mr. Nour from detention."[4] Rice spoke to her Egyptian counterpart and noted that she hoped the Nour issue "is resolved soon." Egyptians responded with disdain by stating that the USA should appreciate the fact that it was solely a legal matter, to be handled only by the judicial system, and not a political issue that the minister for foreign affairs should deal with.

Despite the Nour setback, US push for democracy promotion continued. The BMENA effort was recognized as a way of engaging authoritarian regimes and their civil society toward a common effort for the "freedom agenda." In these meetings, Egypt had participated and had even offered to host a meeting of the Arab League and the G-8 to discuss reform. That offer seemed to be a breakthrough, although civil society representatives complained that the Egyptians merely wanted to co-opt the exercise without making any real changes.

After weeks of "giving the Egyptians time," there was no movement and Nour still remained in prison; Rice took the unprecedented step of canceling an official visit to Egypt. In addition to being singled out by the President in his second inaugural and the Rice Cairo speech, this was too much for Mubarak, and he, according to a senior official from the region, "got his back up." The same source noted that Mubarak knew well that sooner or later the USA would need him for help with the Arab/Palestinian/Israeli issues. Given the clash of the democracy promotion effort against the cold reality of Middle East priorities, Mubarak knew the USA would "cave." He had simply to bide his time and point out that he was preoccupied in dealing with the internal Egyptian threat that stemmed from the Muslim Brotherhood and that Mubarak was America's best bet for stability in the region. Putting some clout into his policy, Mubarak canceled the hosting offer for civil society dialogue by the G-8 and Arab League in Cairo. After Nour's jailing on trumped up charges, the meeting was unlikely to have been productive in any case.

As normal business of the government overtook the Nour case, it seemed that this brutal handling of a democratic challenge to Mubarak's rule was yet another reminder of Mubarak's ability to muzzle all potential rivals. The Nour case starkly demonstrated the inability of the USA to affect Egypt's behavior regarding human rights. In fact, focusing on the maltreatment of a single individual as representing the entire democracy promotion thrust of the Bush administration exposed American policy to the charge that Washington made it easy for dictators to ignore the freedom agenda. All they had to do was detain one activist. And an example was set for others to completely back off the whole agenda. Despite the NSC talk of how the USA must eschew contacts with Mubarak's chosen successor, namely his son Gamal, in the end, Gamal was invited to the White House for meetings with the very people who had earlier condemned his muzzling of the opposition. The victory of Hamas over Fatah in Gaza (Palestine) gave pause to ambitions for democracy promotion. The many tiered web of Middle East politics had now got further entangled, and a democratic Middle East at peace with Israel had become even more improbable. One clairvoyant observer of policy noted: "Bush's demand that freedom and democracy become the beacon toward which all nations in the region should advance is neither inherently flawed nor clueless, as critics maintain. The post-colonial Arab political order of militaristic or hereditary authoritarianism is tottering toward collapse in any event. American efforts to help channel were, and are, appropriate."[5]

There was a call for better understanding of political Islam in the West beyond the conduct of elections where radicals might draw temporary advantage. That America should pursue promotion of moderate forms of political Islam had been the insignia of the Bush effort. In her Cairo speech, Dr. Rice implied that ignoring democratic reforms in the past had got the USA nowhere. Henceforth, therefore, the administration would focus on assisting democratic aspirations and work for the emergence of moderates. But when the trend seemed to go in the opposite direction, because the extremists were better organized and played effectively to the prevailing anti-American popular sentiment, the policy of focusing on democratic aspirations lost its patina. Down went with it years of presidential and rhetoric and the appealing alternate justification for the invasion of Iraq.

After 2005, with Rice already Secretary of State, the same cast of characters who had proclaimed to be democracy czars started to serve as key overseers of the Israeli–Palestinian peace efforts. That brought rapid modifications in focus and policy at the presidential level. Mike Gerson, the senior Bush advisor who had penned many of the freedom agenda's ringing words,[6] became weary of the ensuing internal battles with the

Cheney entourage. He was audibly critical of the Bush administration's unwillingness to stand up to Egypt and Saudi Arabia to further the freedom agenda. According to Gerson, the cost of invading Iraq was even heavier for the distraction it had caused the President. Moreover, there was the impact of political reality influencing diplomacy.

For instance, Bush's previous wistful talk of the promise of real democracy in the Muslim world was diluted by the reality of America's need for Mubarak to continue honoring the Egypt–Israel peace treaty. The process of writing presidential statements was often wrenching, unless it involved known unfriendly regimes such as those in Cuba, Syria, Iran, or Burma. Toward the end of the administration, the lines for reform had softened and the president became susceptible to pressure from Arab leaders to tone down his rhetoric. Still, Bush felt particular concern about lack of freedom in Egypt and early in 2008 gathered his speechwriters noting that unless Mubarak leaves, democratic reform was impossible in Egypt. The 2008 World Economic Forum meeting scheduled for Sharm el-Sheikh in Egypt offered a unique opportunity for Bush to make a dramatic presidential proclamation. Bush, who considered himself to be the "dissidents' president,"[7] could thereby build on the call already relayed in his second inaugural to end "tyranny in our world." Some of the writers felt such action would be close to Reagan's historic words, "Mr. Gorbachev, tear down this wall," cried right in front of the wall that divided East and West Germany.

For some of us who had worked with the presidential speechwriters on democracy issues, there was a sense of excitement that something big was in the making. I was surprised that even the normally cautious State Department colleagues were hoping for a forceful statement. I remembered well how Rice had been a committed supporter of democracy promotion in Egypt and had pressed for the release of Ayman Nour and even canceled a scheduled visit to Cairo when Nour was imprisoned by Mubarak. She expressed her frustration with Mubarak to the speechwriters by noting: "They've screwed it up," and hoped for a speech that had some "edge."

As initially drafted, the speech would have noted: "The change that the people in the Middle East have been looking for is before us. The only question left to be asked by the leaders and intellectuals of this region, and in this room, is this: Will you be left behind by this change – or will you choose to lead it?" At this point, right there on Egyptian soil at Sharm el-Sheikh, sitting prominently next to him, Bush would ask Mubarak to send a message of "goodwill" by ordering his guards to open prison doors and release Ayman Nour. Recall that an earlier mention of Nour had irked Mubarak.

It was a massive disappointment when Bush missed the Reagan moment.

Perhaps, he decided to listen to the Saudi King whom he visited just before he went to Egypt. The Saudi King clearly would have wanted him to tread lightly on Mubarak. As told by the speechwriter, Rice too changed her mind noting that she had not been sufficiently thanked by Nour for her earlier support to release him from prison where he had been beaten and tortured! She needed Mubarak's help in the search for peace, and she was done with "the Ayman Nour business." In the end, there was no challenge to Arab leaders present at the speech but only vague, unexpressed hope for reform at a future date. Instead, Bush lauded Egypt as "a model for the development of professional women." Ayman Nour was never mentioned.[8]

In the end, the four-year election cycle of American diplomacy came into play. Just as Iran had done years earlier, soon after the installation of the new commander in chief, Ayman Nour was released. This happened on February 18, 2009, in advance of Obama visit to Cairo on June 4.[9] The new administration in Washington announced that it would not promote the freedom agenda the way its predecessor had done. Obama would not push American foreign policy to support democracy-building as a means of dealing with an age of terrorism. In the meantime, Mubarak called for presidential elections for 2011. One of the emerging contenders was Gamal Mubarak, whom I had met over dinner at a mutual friend's house in London. He was very conscious of the stark security picture that faced Egypt. The other contender was Mohamed ElBaradei, a Nobel Laureate and former head of the International Atomic Energy Agency, who said that he was being pressed by Egyptians to run and who noted: "I'm not seeking the Presidency – I'm seeking to nudge Egypt toward democracy. To put it bluntly, democracy here is a farce."[10]

Even in Iraq, as the post-election government had yet to be formed, Ayad Allawi, the challenger to Prime Minister Nouri al-Maliki in 2007, voiced an opinion which could be just as applicable today: "Building democracy in Iraq will be a long-term process, established through the rule of law, a stable security environment, functioning state institutions and an emerging civil society."[11] While recognizing the difficulties inherent in the process, Bush saw Iraq slightly differently. "They're striving to build a modern democracy on the rubble of three decades of tyranny, in a region of the world that has been hostile to freedom. And they are doing it while under assault from one of history's most brutal terrorist networks."[12]

The administration worried about public opinion around the world which was hostile to the USA. Even in Europe, it was a difficult issue. Three quarters or more of Muslims in Britain (94%), France (75%), and Germany (73%) have an unfavorable view of the USA. European Muslims tend to be critical of the war in Iraq and American policies toward the Israeli–Palestinian issue. Only about half of French and German Muslims express support for the war against terrorism, while nearly all British Muslims oppose it. According to surveys, support is limited because of suspicions of US motives rather than because of any backing for bin Laden's cause.[13] With these numbers in view, a serious attempt was made to change world opinion.

Karen Hughes, a close confidant of the president and of Mrs. Bush, was brought into the State Department as the Undersecretary of state for public diplomacy. She arrived with great enthusiasm for the job and for making a difference. Hughes had also been a key voice in George W. Bush's visit to the Washington Islamic Center soon after 9/11 to articulate that America's fight was not with Islam but with those who used religion for terror. I had always been grateful to Karen for her judgment.

Rice noted in her long tribute to Hughes that: "I asked her to come and help make public diplomacy strong and central to the mission of transformational diplomacy and she has done that."[14] Some of the programs she put in place are detailed in the previous chapter.[15] Despite all of Karen's efforts, the basic issues dividing the USA from the Muslim world, namely the wars in Afghanistan and Iraq, the continued Palestinian–Israeli stalemate, etc., there was no respite from negative opinion. As Hughes finally planned to return to Texas "to spend more time with her family," she responded to the intractability of her task with: it would take decades for the USA to overcome the intense hostility it faces around the world. She acknowledged that opinion polls showed a sharp decline in the image of the USA in Pakistan, Turkey, and Indonesia, exacerbated by the US decision to invade Iraq. In Hughes words: "We are in the early stages of a long struggle. We didn't get here quickly. Reactions have been exacerbated by images of war and disagreements about our decision to go into Iraq." Given that "the cauldron of hate" has been brewing for many years before 2001, Hughes felt it would take a long time to simmer down.

Hughes characterized her stint at the State Department as a time when "seeds" were planted for a significant improvement in America's image at a later time. Her tenure was difficult because, as she noted: "It is legitimate to say this is what the polls show but to expect they would change in a time of war without other dramatic change is not reasonable." The obvious need to help bolster the American image plus Karen's celebrated access to the president ensured all desired funding. Yet, after all that, upon her departure when asked for advice for the incoming president on how public diplomacy makes a difference, she noted somewhat sadly: "It is hard to say what impact it will have."[16]

NOTES

1. Condoleezza Rice, "Campaign 2000—Promoting The National Interest," *Foreign Affairs* 79.1 (January–February 2000).
2. Hosni Mubarak was appointed Vice President in 1975. He assumed the presidency upon the assassination of Anwar Sadat on October 14, 1981. He was the longest serving ruler of Egypt since Muhammad Ali Pasha.
3. Condoleezza Rice, "Speech at the American University in Cairo, Egypt," Department of State, Office of the Spokesman, Washington, DC, June 21, 2005.
4. The White House, Office of the Press Secretary, Washington, DC, December 24, 2005.
5. Jim Hoagland, "Squaring Islam with Democracy," *Washington Post*, February 2, 2006.
6. Although one of his speechwriting colleagues at the White House, Matthew Scully, accused Gerson of having assumed exclusive authorship of presidential speeches when it was not warranted. *Washington Post*, October 31, 2007. See also, Michael Gerson, "Arab' Urge for Self-Government Shouldn't Be a Surprise," *Washington Post*, February 1, 2011.
7. See "Freedom Agenda" in George W. Bush, *Decision Points* (New York: Crown, 2010), 395–438.
8. Matt Latimer, "When Bush Caved to Egypt," *Daily Beast*, January 30, 2011.
9. As an appropriate footnote to the Egyptian saga, Mubarak noted in January 2010 that he would hold presidential elections in 2011 and that

the presidential election would be open to all, even as he was said to be carefully grooming his son to succeed him.
10. Joshua Hammer, "The Contenders: Is Egypt's Presidential Race Becoming a Real Contest?" *New Yorker*, April 5, 2010, 28.
11. Ayad Alawi, "How Iraq's Elections Set Back Democracy," *New York Times*, November 2, 2007.
12. "Remarks at Wright-Patterson Air Force Base, Dayton Ohio," The White House, Office of the Press Secretary, Washington, DC, March 27, 2008.
13. "Muslims in Europe Generally Hold Negative Views of U.S." Office of Research, Department of State, Washington, DC, July 7, 2003.
14. Rice, "Remarks, Departure of Undersecretary of State for Public Diplomacy and Public Affairs Karen P. Hughes," Office of the Press Spokesman, Washington, DC, October 31, 2007.
15. Included in the Hughes effort were: New Media Hubs in key countries for timely rebuttal of anti-American rhetoric, engagement by US ambassadors in the field using commonly supplied themes; involving the private sector "you are all American ambassadors" theme; expanded English language programs; setting up of a Counter-Terrorism Communications Center to develop culturally sensitive message to undermine terrorists; doubling of the education exchange program; outreach to women.
16. James Blitz, "U.S. Faces 'Long Struggle' to Overcome Worldwide Hostility," *Financial Times*, November 7, 2007.

CHAPTER 35

Vice President Cheney

No recounting of what went wrong with the Bush policy for democracy-building and the freedom agenda is complete without an assessment of the role of Vice President Cheney. In addition to all the speculation and writing on the subject, my own exposure to that office as an NSC senior staffer, and my previous NSC tenure during two Republican presidents, Reagan and Bush 41, provides me with a comparative frame of reference. And my experience at the NSC during two previous Vice Presidents, namely George Bush (senior) and Dan Quayle, had taught me that Vice Presidents are "merely seen and not heard." Thus, Cheney's dominating role as V.P. was a new experience for me. Under Cheney, the neocons flourished. His tutelage offered them access, legitimacy, and power.

As the Bush W. administration got underway, the familiar faces were often those who had been part of the so-called Vulcan advisory group that had been set up to tutor a young president. "This was not to be a repeat of the father's administration" was the operative word on the Republican street. In this round, the right wing was to have special authority in promoting the White House agenda. The DOD, with Rumsfeld as Secretary and Wolfowitz as his deputy, would have daily planning meetings and coordinate closely the work that went on. Cheney's self-selection as the vice presidential candidate was a harbinger of the ascendency of the controlling neocon agenda. Placed in the White House as policy experts were personal political aides who had been part of the president's entourage from his Texas days. Rice was the exception. The selection of Hadley to be her deputy ensured the Cheney/DOD supremacy and the induction of unusual new procedure to share all internal e-mails with the Cheney staff even when the Vice President's office was not required to reciprocate.

The level of OVP involvement in foreign policy oversight and the interagency process was, in my experience, unprecedented. OVP staff attended all Situation Room meetings and offered views on everything. While the NSC norm is that VP attends only those NSC meetings that are chaired by the President, Cheney himself was present in meetings that were not chaired by the president. Often, it seemed that he had shown up to buttress Rumsfeld and DOD positions, especially when their differences with State and Colin Powell became more pronounced. Cheney's cover offered Rumsfeld a level of arrogance against the National Security Advisor that was unprecedented in my experience. Rice herself mentions one such incident where Rumsfeld got up and left a principal meeting on Iraq she was chairing as it started to address the issue of detainees. When she queried: "Don, where are you going?" Rumsfeld responded: "I don't do detainees."[1] Even when he was absent from Washington, Cheney's image appeared over the screen as he held forth on what (he claimed) constituted "the president's position." The NSA, who saw the president innumerable times in the course of any day, was somehow not accepted as representing his "true position" by the Cheney crowd. Cheney's manner often displayed arrogance and disdain for the non-Defense department participants.

From the outset, it seemed clear that the invasion of Iraq was promoted by the neocons led by Cheney. For months preceding the invasion in March 2003, these advisors had voiced growing impatience with Saddam Hussein, as noted in an earlier chapter. When war came, their confidence that the invasion would unearth a King's ransom in WMDs knew no bounds. As mentioned before, when that hope came to naught while the US forces were still mired in Iraq, democracy-building in Iraq "as an instrument to advance U.S. strategic interests"[2] became the oft-stated rationale. Removal of the "bloodthirsty dictatorship" and the introduction of democracy in Iraq were promoted as the key to getting at the root causes of terrorism and freeing the entire region from its scourge. The Cheney group became owner and operator of the democracy promotion agenda and started both to allocate and control (essentially all the allocated) resources for the enterprise. The very group that was seen in the Muslim world as less than sympathetic became the progenitor of the idea that they needed democracy for their salvation. Thus,

American engagement was thrust on the unwilling and by those with little historical perspective and overseas exposure, this greatly reduced the appeal of the message and diminished its power.[3]

Because of the wide unpopularity of the Iraq war, the Bush White House became even more insular as the "us versus them" mentality took hold. During the 1990 Gulf War, I had experienced a vastly different mind-set. Post-2003, the daily tussle between Rumsfeld and Powell, and the lack of interagency agreement was disconcerting and had a negative impact on the selection of the frontline cadre in Baghdad. Iraq became a war zone after the war. It left DOD with prime authority. But DOD lacked diplomatic and linguistic expertise and as it happened they stationed hardly any of it in the field. The choice model thus became hiring contractors through a maze of DOD neocon connections.

It was reported that those chosen were rewarded for "100 percent loyalty to Bush, even if they were 100 percent ignorant of Iraq."[4] The result was a near total absence of foreign policy experience. Even White House staff members who had graduated from the Texas campaign tailgated on the act. One, Kristen Silverberg, serving as a deputy to domestic policy czar Karl Rove, signed on to serve in the office of the Iraq viceroy. The president was clearly aware of the lack of foreign policy experience of some of those signing up. On a plane flight to Detroit on Air Force 1, I overheard him tease Kristen saying that "I know why you are going to Iraq. It is to keep an eye on your boyfriend who is also going." Her friend had signed on to do duty in the Bremer press office.

As a result of the absence of expertise, American occupation's early interaction with Iraqis (when it may have mattered the most in setting the tone of the occupation) was limited to those Iraqis who either dared to enter, or were invited to, the Green Zone. Interviews were arranged inside the palace. I recall one such incident in May 2003 when I was in Baghdad when Dan Senor, the press man for Bremer, had arranged for NBC's Tom Brokaw to come into the palace for an interview with Bremer as part of the Brokaw's five night coverage from Baghdad. Brokaw who normally would report from the streets of the city had driven into the fortified Green Zone, surrendered his car to Senor, and went in. Upon his exit, no one could find what happened to Brokaw's car. My White House colleagues and I were waiting to see Bremer and witnessed much consternation as Brokaw needed to proceed to his base in the city for his next assignment. In the end, a very nice, but young inexperienced, girl from the staff personally drove Brokaw back to his hotel in her own car outside the Green Zone. I asked someone if that was right given that Dan Senor had the responsibility and here was a young staff member, named Olivia, driving herself into harm's way! The answer was: "This is Iraq and her boss is looking for his next job!" Upon my return to Washington, I heard that Senor wanted to become the president's press Secretary when Ari Fleischer left. Fortunately, that did not happen.

Cheney and company were dismissive of multilateralism and international law because they saw them as an attempt to tie down America by reducing its freedom of action. Thus, they held forth against international engagement **at the very time** the USA was looking for allies prior to the invasion of Iraq. They were said to be financial conservatives and yet launched the 2003 Iraq war with astounding miscalculation of its cost and its longevity: The war is ongoing and has cost upward of $750 billion.[5] They answered only to God and the Vice President: "a secretive man by nature whose unmatched power is largely veiled but whose secretive governmental operations have changed the world – and not for the better."[6] America's image took a beating as Iraq became a costly foreign policy experiment.

The fact that at the end of Bush's term V.P. Cheney would not run for the presidency greatly helped neocons. As election time nears, there is always tension between the office of the president and that of the V.P. I witnessed this first hand during two presidential elections (1984 and 1988). However, 2004 was different. Here, Cheney and his staff were fully integrated into the workings of the White House.[7] For Bush, the partnership with Cheney was desirable because Cheney would not be guided by his own political ambitions. Thus, at least theoretically, loyalty to the sitting president would be paramount. In practice, however, Cheney used this apoliticality issue to promote his own agenda by overlaying it with the president's imprint and became the public face of the administration.

It was clear that the president liked having familiar faces around him, and his senior staff and aides reflected that bent. Most of these had come from Texas. He was always gracious to me. He knew that I had served on his father's staff. Often, he would engage in a certain amount of presidential banter in the few free moments prior to formal meetings. However, in contrast, Bush's personal level of comfort with Cheney's staff appeared different.

With others present, in the Oval Office or in the Situation Room, in meetings when Bush presided, Cheney kept his opinions to himself. However, whenever he himself was the senior-most person present, he made his thoughts known in no-uncertain terms and emphatically demanded total deference. Only once, when it was abundantly clear that Cheney's interpretation of the presidential mind was completely at odds with Rice's own recollection, did I hear her say in total frustration: "Mr. Vice President, we will just have to take this to the President!" Cheney's coming into office without the attendant neocons might have left a very different imprint on the Bush presidency.

The contested nature of the 2000 election and the weeks that followed before the outcome gave perfect opportunity to Cheney to become "by any measure the dominant force in creating the Bush administration to be."[8] It is said that Cheney shared the Reagan suspicion of permanent government and those who manned it. Hence, the adage "personnel is policy" was played to the extreme at the start of the administration and in its most telling foreign policy decisions, such as the invasion of Iraq. Just as Bush wanted his Texas crowd nearby, Cheney wanted the old DOD group in his immediate vicinity and as well to populate critical parts of the US government.

Indeed, the primary role that Cheney's staff such as David Addington played in selecting others in the administration ensured a particular bent of mind. For example, Steve Hadley who became the deputy NSA was known as one of Cheney's "Defense Dogs," an informal group of former Pentagon advisors, having served as an assistant Secretary of Defense in the 1990s. Hadley noted in an interview that Cheney intimidated him.[9] The White House interaction that I witnessed reflected Hadley as being particularly deferential to the Vice President. Rich Armitage, former Deputy Secretary of State who had many dealings with Hadley in the deputy's committee, noted privately that Hadley was "Cheney's mole."[10]

The atmosphere at the White House following the 9/11 attacks created an opening for Cheney with his motto "this is no time for debate and diplomacy. This is the time for action." As Rice later told a group of entrepreneurs at Google in 2008, "We were in an environment in which saving America from the next attack was paramount."[11] For the OVP staff, the likelihood of an attack was a near certainty as they talked about a biological, chemical, or even a nuclear attack on American cities. There was also a sense that in these extreme times whatever measures they suggested and the president authorized were permissible. According to the president's lawyer, Alberto Gonzales, if Bush were to approve a procedure, it would "not constitute torture."[12] Even before the issue relating to torture became known beyond the extremely narrow confines within the OVP and some on the White House staff, neocons were running with the argument that diplomacy was passé given its irrelevance to the new and real threat posed by al Qaeda and its cohorts.

Therefore, the OVP deemed this was the time for no diplomacy and no negotiation. Opposition to the war abroad was dismissed simply as reflecting "anti-Americanism." When the media was challenging policy, the reaction was also severe. In particular, al Jazeera was treated with a great deal of contempt and their reporting and commentary against the USA in Iraq often ignited the ire of the Vice President who was often heard to say he would call the Emir of Qatar to complain about al Jazeera coverage and ask it be shut down. I found it odd that Cheney would want to do that especially in view of the commitment to democracy promotion which included development of a free press in the Muslim world.[13]

Cheney, his daughter, and his policy supporters believed that the Vice President had provided foreign policy cover for the inexperienced Bush during the campaign. Moreover, because of his experience as Chief of Staff to President Gerald Ford and Secretary of Defense to President George H. W. Bush, the proverbial query "who takes the call at 3 a.m. in an international crisis" was answered by this group with the retort: "Cheney, of course!" It was, therefore, expected that Cheney would reign supreme on domestic, defense, and foreign policies. This, of course, would leave pretty well nothing for President Bush to direct. Indeed, the OVP fully believed that Bush sanctioned such a course of action.

Given the selection of Condoleezza Rice as the NSA, the above scenario seemed all but assured to unfold. Arrayed against Rice were Cheney and Rumsfeld. This duo hailed back from President Ford's White House, where Rumsfeld had in some ways been Cheney's mentor. To this "fabulous duo," it seemed natural that when Bush was not present, Cheney would chair NSC meetings. Adding to this feeling was their feeling that Rice's previous White House experience was only as a mid-level NSC official (under Bush, senior). Somehow these feelings failed to acknowledge the history of her tenure because given the momentous events of the early 1900s when the former Soviet Union was falling apart, Condi had indeed played a central role in policy formulation.

It seemed unfathomable to Cheney and Rumsfeld that Rice would have the stature, even if she had the president's ear, to challenge any of their preferences. This is also the reason, I felt, Cheney showed up regularly in principals meetings where traditionally only cabinet heads had participated. In my early weeks at the George Bush NSC,[14] I was struck by the ubiquitous Cheney presence in the Situation Room. Perhaps, I thought, this was an anomaly caused by the early days of the Iraq invasion because there was much anxiety and Rumsfeld as manager of the war needed Cheney to be nearby. However, that pattern continued in times when less seemed to be immediately at stake. And it helped the duo score points in turf wars and show disdain toward Rice. During my service to five NSAs prior to Rice,[15] I had seen many egos clash, but eventually come to an agreed course of action. I had never witnessed a Vice President and a Secretary of Defense hold forth on critical issues with no sense of responsibility to find common ground with the rest of the participants. It seemed ironic that Hadley would press on me the view that "this is a collegial NSC process."

It must not have been easy for Rice to acknowledge that she had to go to the president and ask Bush to inform his first NSC meeting, on January 30, 2001, that: "Condi Rice is my National Security Advisor. She will run the meetings in my absence."[16] As Rice told later, she had "to get it fixed" since past Vice Presidents had not played that role and thus it "wasn't appropriate."[17] This rationale is a less painful explanation than another which implied total lack of respect for Rice.[18]

So, much of the desire to see a change in the Middle East and by extension in the rest of the Muslim world came from the invasion of Iraq. With no WMDs found, the full focus turned on democracy. Bush was as idealistic about it as was Rice.[19] As she noted in an interview: "I have believed from day one that Iraq was going to change the face of the Middle East. I have never stopped believing that....There's nothing that I'm prouder of than the liberation of Iraq.... Did we screw up parts of it? Sure. It was a big historical episode and a lot of it wasn't handled very well... It wasn't my responsibility to manage Iraq....The fact of the matter is, as National Security Advisor you have a lot of responsibility and no authority."[20]

A fitting epitaph to the entire period is the assessment of Lady Manningham-Buller, who led Britain's domestic security service, the MI5, during the 2002–2007 years. Testifying to the panel investigating events leading to the Invasion of Iraq and mistakes made, she noted:

"Our involvement in Iraq, for want of a better word, radicalized a whole generation of young people...Who saw our involvement in Iraq, on top of our involvement in Afghanistan, as being an attack on Islam." She was particularly critical of the decisions that led to the attack noting that "Saddam Hussein had nothing to do with 9/11[21] and I have never seen anything to change my mind ...It was not a judgment that found favor with some parts of the American machine ... That is why Donald Rumsfeld started an alternative judgment." Citing that Britain had been provided only "fragmentary" intelligence on WMDs before the invasion, Lady Manningham-Buller stressed that MI5 had not believed that Saddam Hussein was amassing WMDs. She closed her testimony with the scathing assessment that: "By focusing on Iraq, we ceased to focus on alQaeda....that was a long-term, major and strategic problem" leading to an overwhelming increase in homegrown terrorism.[22] That is a far cry from the president's firm belief on the march of history following the overthrow of Saddam Hussein: "Liberty is transformative."[23]

The highly anticipated British report on the UK's role by John Chilcot heading up the independent Iraq Inquiry Committee published in the summer of 2016 blamed Prime Minister Tony Blair for blind support for Iraq war with his "I will be with you whatever" comment to President George W. Bush. The exhaustive report implicated Blair, political, military, and intelligence establishments for misjudgments and "occasional ineptitude." That Blair committed Britain to the war before diplomatic options were exhausted was as condemnatory as the judgment that Saddam Hussein posed "no imminent threat" in March 2003 as the war began.[24]

Conventional wisdom has the Palestinian election results of January 2006 as meaning the end of "transformational diplomacy," at least as far as democracy promotion was concerned.[25] The excitement that there was to be an election in the Palestinian areas was indeed palpable inside the administration, particularly as so many neocons felt that the Arafat years had been riddled with personal corruption and opportunities missed. Here was to be proof of a new era where personal responsibility was to be reflected in people exercising the most sacred of democracy's attributes: the direct selection of their leaders. American support for the two-state solution had meant involvement in new ways, including economic assistance to help the moderate secular Mahmoud Abbas. This was a time of great interaction with his leadership in finding new innovative ways to seek international help in making the lives of Palestinians better. I participated in a number of meetings where we examined concrete programs and sought financing to get those off the ground. It was an exciting moment with firm belief that if the elections would allow Abbas to consolidate power, ground reality in favor of a moderate Middle East could be assured.

Thus, the fact that immoderate Hamas won a landslide victory in the Palestinian legislative elections trouncing the moderate, secular Abbas's Fatah party came as a shock. Particularly, as it meant that Hamas, considered a terrorist organization by the USA, had earned the right via the election to form the new government. Some thought Hamas' victory meant that "transformational diplomacy" assumptions held by Rice were "at least for the moment, in ruins."[26] The President and Rice's response to this momentous event was to put it in context and offer up the explanation that the election reminded the President of "the power of democracy…when you give people the vote, you give people the chance to express themselves at the polls, and if they're unhappy with the status quo, they'll let you know."[27]

However, in terms of the central Bush commitment to promoting democracy, in the end, some said, "promoting democracy is too difficult to be a truly viable doctrine."[28]

Notes

1. Condoleezza Rice, *No Higher Honor: A Memoir of My Years in Washington* (New York: Crown, 2011), 275.
2. Francis Fukuyama, "The Neoconservative Moment," *National Interest* (Summer 2004), 60.
3. "More than half according to one estimate, had gotten their first passport in order to travel to Iraq" and most of the self-selecting Americans who went to Iraq after the invasion had never traveled or worked outside the USA. Rajiv Chandrasekharan, *Imperial Life in the Emerald City: Inside Iraq's Green Zone* (New York: Vintage Books, 2006), 17.
4. Thomas Friedman, "Can We Talk?" *New York Times*, July 18, 2010.
5. Candy Crowley, "State of the Union," *CNN*, July 4, 2010.
6. John W. Dean, *Worse Than Watergate: The Secret Presidency of George W. Bush* (New York: Little Brown, 2004), xv.
7. Mary Matalin, a senior Cheney staffer, noted that Cheney chose a structure that was "not separate and contributing, but integrated with the West Wing in ways that I know were a radical departure from previous white Houses." Barton Gellman, *Angler: The Cheney Vice Presidency* (New York: Penguin Press, 2008), 49.
8. Ibid., 35.

9. Ibid., 39.
10. Ibid., 189.
11. Ibid., 180.
12. Ibid., 193.
13. I recall a small lunch given by the first lady, Laura Bush at the residence for the Qatari first lady, Sheikha Mozah in 2007 in honor of the joint interest both had as UNESCO education ambassadors. The Sheikha took her host to task for failed American policies, especially the war in Iraq. Laura Bush was less than happy with the conversation but reacted only afterward.
14. I joined the NSC on March 24, 2003.
15. McFarlane, Pointdexter, Carlucci, Powell, Scowcroft.
16. Elisabeth Bumiller, *Condoleezza Rice: An American Life A Biography* (New York: Random House, 2007), 137.
17. Ibid.
18. Comments I heard at an early stage where I was seen as part of the club having worked in Policy Planning at State under Wolfowitz along-side Scooter Libby.
19. I do not agree with the assessment that Rice discovered democracy-promotion in the adoption of the "transformational diplomacy" agenda as Secretary of State. She shared the president's idealism and strong support for the American push for Democracy in the Muslim world from the very outset. See Bumuller, *Condoleezza Rice*, 254.
20. Bob Woodward, *The War Within: A Secret White House History 2006–2008* (New York: Simon & Schuster, 2008), 421.
21. As Cheney and the neocons insisted.
22. Sarah Lyall, "Ex-Official Says Afghan and Iraq Wars Increased Threats to Britain," *New York Times*, July 20, 2010.
23. Woodward, *The War Within*, 424.
24. Henry Mance, "UK Report into Iraq War Delivers Damning Judgment on Blair," *Financial Times*, July 7, 2016; "Iraq War Lies: 13 Years Later," *New York Times*, July 7, 2016.
25. See, for example, Bumiller, *Condoleezza Rice*, where she writes, "Transformational diplomacy brought new definition and passion to her work, although the phrase and the ideal behind it would not survive reality two years into her tenure as Secretary of State," 254.
26. Ibid., 279.
27. "Press Conference of the President," Office of the Press Secretary, The White House, January 26, 2006.
28. Richard N. Haas, "Is There a Doctrine in the House?" *New York Times*, November 8, 2005.

CHAPTER 36

The American Legacy of the Basrah Children's Hospital

> Everyone involved in the building of the Basrah Children's Hospital can be proud. Iraqi parents and children are hopeful for a bright future. Every country's success depends upon the health and well-being of its children. And by working together, we can help future generations of Iraqi children grow up strong and healthy. (First Lady Laura Bush, Remarks at the Project Hope Gala, October 18, 2005)

> As President Bush has said, we will continue to stand with the men and women of Iraq every step of the way as they build brighter tomorrows for their children....the Basra[h] Children's Hospital will make tomorrows possible for many suffering children. (Secretary of State Condoleezza Rice, Remarks at the Project Hope Gala, October 18, 2005)

> In small wars, tolerance, sympathy and kindness should be the keynote of our relationship with the mass of the population. (The 1930s U.S. Marines "Small Wars Manual")

The building of the first pediatric hospital in Iraq dedicated to cancer treatment for Southern Iraq is a tale worth telling. Coming out of the unpopular US invasion of Iraq in March 2003, the Basrah Children's Hospital (BCH) was forged as a public–private partnership between the US government and Project HOPE. It offered a bold approach to making a difference for Iraqis and won support from the President, the First Lady, the then-National Security Advisor who subsequently became Secretary of State, and a host of others within the USA and beyond. Sadly, however, the project received no approbation from Paul Wolfowitz and other neocons who strongly believed in fighting the war, but apparently not helping, the Iraqis.

In April 2003, it became clear that while the invasion had resulted in a quick rout of the Iraqi Army and the fall of Saddam Hussein, the American presence was likely to be prolonged, and real "victory" remained elusive. When Condi Rice took over stewardship of the Iraq Coordination Group (ICG, set up to deal with the myriad issues cropping up in the field and given existing tensions between DOD and State), the daily work of the group for the National Security Advisor was to hear about the state of affairs, possible scenarios for meeting the multiple challenges, and to provide direction. With DOD and State at war with each other, Rice was the only one who could pull together the interagency group with some coherence.

On March 27, 2003, only three days after joining the NSC, I participated in the ICG meeting. As I walked into the Situation Room, a familiar place from my previous stints at the White House, I was struck by the somber mood of the group even as the battlefront news indicated success and a melting enemy field. It also appeared odd that a coordinating field group would be headed up personally by the NSA given the presence of a number of senior NSC staff who might traditionally have done the chairing. Despite the heavy fog engulfing wartime decision-making, at least two problems seemed apparent. First, DOD and State were not collaborating. It was wartime, and the time for diplomacy in Iraq was not yet there. State felt that "DOD owned the problem." Having eschewed international diplomacy in the run-up to the war, the administration was in a weakened position regarding diplomacy. This fact clearly disadvantaged the State department. Second, information was not being shared by the Pentagon. The DOD leadership had poor relations with other agencies and at times even with the NSC.

At the second meeting of the ICG on March 31, it was clear that the President and his National Security Advisor wanted fast action in helping alleviate the suffering of the Iraqi people and to do all possible to make their lives better. There was genuine interest in ensuring that years of political and economic deprivation be replaced quickly with an open political system, more economic activity, better health, and greater opportunity for the average Iraqi. More than fourteen years later today, it is easy to be cynical about the motivations of Bush and Rice as they tried to change the ground realities of an internationally despised invasion. Given that the USA became an occupier in Iraq, the responsibility for governing Iraq fell squarely on Washington. Into this milieu entered the focus on remedies for fixing old and new problems such as health, education, food, water, and electricity.

In keeping with my normal routine whereby generally on weekends I left Washington to return home to my family in Pennsylvania, I used my journey time to think of what the USA could do on the civilian side that would reflect the traditional American generosity toward the vanquished. There had to be a reason why a majority of people everywhere made the distinction between Americans, who they liked, and American policy, which they often disliked. As I drove home, this point kept going through my mind. Nearing Philadelphia, I ran into a traffic jam on the expressway near the University of Pennsylvania campus. Sitting there in sight of the Children's Hospital of Philadelphia, it came to me! What if we were to build something for the children of Iraq? A modern medical facility dedicated to pediatric needs and in a location where the need was really acute.

Excited at the possibility I called a distinguished medical expert, a great humanitarian, and a friend Doctor Donald Silberberg, Chair of Neurology at the Hospital of the University of Pennsylvania (HUP). I mentioned my interest in probing the possibility for the USA building a Children's Hospital for Iraq and asked whether he had time the following morning to discuss the feasibility of such a project and also what it would entail. I knew that Don with his vast experience of the medical world would understand the complexities of creating such a Hospital, especially in a war zone. Over the next several days, Dr. Silberberg consulted with other specialists and put together a paper with some of the key elements for moving forward.

In a few days, I received a thoughtful paper that highlighted what a children's hospital typically encompasses in the USA. It noted the lack of material and human pediatric care resources in Iraq. Regime neglect over the years had left Iraq indicators paralleling the rates of some of the world's poorest countries. These low rates applied to maternal mortality, neonatal mortality, and under-the-age-of-five mortality. He also mentioned widespread malnutrition. On the other hand, the paper noted Iraq's available well-educated workforce and its fiscal ability to sustain a children's hospital and a children's learning center and to make it available to the region. The bold concept envisioned a set of medical school affiliations with hospitals throughout Iraq. There was also the possibility of clinics in select locations. The paper proposed development of regional integration of children's hospitals in Cairo, Jerusalem, and outreach programs to serve the entire Middle East.

US models which could be helpful included the Children's Hospital of Philadelphia, which had helped develop the Children's Hospital of Shanghai. Dr. Silberberg noted that the latter had been assisted by the private nonprofit, Project HOPE which could become a private part of the effort on an Iraqi children's hospital. It was the first time that I heard of Project HOPE and noted it along with the other ideas for my mention in my draft for briefing Rice.[1]

Returning to Washington, I worked further on the hospital project. I wanted the stated hope of the president and others that the invasion of Iraq would result in a better future for its people to come true. Forty-nine percent of the population of Iraq is under the age of fourteen, compared to twenty-two percent of the US population. A Children's Hospital would bring the long-isolated medical community in Iraq into contact with the latest in training as well as a modern hospital. The Pentagon with its responsibility for Iraq was looking at immediate ways to fix existing health problems. There would be money in the Iraq supplemental budget specifically earmarked for health. USAID was also focused on clinics for dealing with infections and water purification.

I met with Rice on April 9 with details of my initial discussions with Dr. Donald Silberberg and with others in the medical arena and in the bureaucracy. She seemed excited at the idea and asked if I would be willing to go to Iraq with a small team to survey existing pediatric facilities before focusing on a particular specialty and location. We talked about the possibility of making this a public–private effort given the humanitarian nature of the project. Sensing this interest, I proposed the idea of building a children's hospital with emphasis on treating cancer. Basrah, ravaged during the Iran–Iraq war, had received heavy dumping of fatal carcinogens and pollutants. As a result, the incidence of cancer, particularly among children, was very high. Based on great need, Rice supported my idea to build BCH.

Day after day and week following week, our directorate, which was charged both with humanitarian assistance and issues relating to international operations, prepared charts of services needed and the Pentagon supplied elaborate figures on what they thought was the state of play. Given the highly centralized Iraqi system under Saddam where information was power and sharing information was suspect, getting reliable information about Iraq's medical facilities required Herculean effort. Optimism shared by the president and Rice that Iraqi lives could be made better was reflected in many of the earliest discussions, including those in the ICG. Rice graciously helped task people to "make it (meaning, the BCH) happen" and regularly asked me for a "to-do list" for her to follow up on.

I had served sufficiently long at the White House over previous administrations to understand the need to bring the Office of Management and Budget (OMB) on board. All initiatives required money, and OMB was the keeper of the purse. Consequently, I met with Robin Cleveland who was the OMB liaison for the NSC. While I had previously seen Robin in meetings, this was my first direct interaction with her, and I was completely unprepared for the hostility and foul language she used to convey her disapproval of my involvement with any project dealing with Iraq. When I reminded her that I was doing so at the direct request of Rice and appropriately since my portfolio included humanitarian issues for the NSC, Cleveland remained unmoved.

Upon checking around, I found out that Robin was a close confidante of Paul Wolfowitz and often felt an obligation to do as he would want her to do and also to protect what she deemed to be his "turf" whether or not the National Security Advisor wanted something done.[2] She would obviously go along with an issue if Condi was directly present given that Rice had her own link with the President and the OMB boss. Robin's job seemed to be to use foul language to try and intimidate the rest of us. I was struck by this anomalous behavior given that the White House always tended to be a civilized place where even tough talk was delivered politely. A core member of the neocon club, Robin clearly sang to their shared tune, so each conversation with her was a huge struggle. While I was able to carry the first round in the meeting discussing Children's issues for Iraq, Cleveland was to make life impossible during much of the 2003–2005 period I spent at the Bush White House: screaming all the while that Hadley agreed with her views and even her besmirched tactics. When I finally pointed this out to Hadley, he demurred.

In matters dealing with Iraq, it quickly became obvious that the task of replacing the then existing leaderless system with focused activity was going to be difficult. The DOD had sounded as if it expected a short-lived occupation, but that was clearly not a correct assumption. There was talk of quick remedies for water quality and health. USAID and the Pentagon discussed ways of setting up health clinics for remedial action against water-borne diseases.

Condi kept asking for imaginative ways in which we could spearhead private–public action for linking American and Iraqi people and for showcasing the spirit of American generosity. I kept meeting with others in the White House and at State who dealt with humanitarian issues. We cast a wide net for ideas and I relayed Condi's exhortation to "think big!" While many in various offices focused on how we might link up Iraqi rehabilitation efforts with American communities, most of the ideas that came out in response to Condi's suggestion to "think big" were not suitable for US governmental involvement. For instance, it was suggested that we should get school children in the USA involved and encourage them to pass UNICEF-type contribution boxes and hats at church services.

We had serious work to do. The months after the American invasion of Iraq did not go according to plan. But the desire to do good did not diminish despite the failure to locate WMDs. Rice continued her supervision of the ICG, while we continued to remain under pressure to help turn around the deteriorating situation inside Iraq. Daily reports of problems left most participants sitting around the table with a sense of frustration. Quick fixes beyond water purification efforts and generators were few.

Decades of Iraqi negligence in infrastructure maintenance had left a void that could not be fixed with band-aids. The problems were compounded by the limited DOD non-combat presence on the ground. Governance was the key issue and the dispatch of Jay Garner as overseer of Iraq brought its own problems. Thousands of jobs needed to be filled in a hurry. As neocons filled positions, it appeared that the criteria for employment related to political leaning rather than substantive expertise.

The running of Iraq's health system went to James Haveman, Director of a faith-based organization, recommended by John Engler, former Republican governor of Michigan. Apparently, that recommendation from Engler to Wolfowitz was based on the simple fact that Haveman had run a large Christian adoption agency in the state. Wolfowitz then summarily fired Fred Burkle who had the health charge for the USA during the invasion and had extensive disaster-response and public health issues experience in post-conflict Somalia, Kosovo, and 1991 Gulf War. Despite his obvious experience, it was commonly known that the White House (namely the Domestic Policy side headed by Karl Rove and his deputy Kristin Silverberg, who worked to enforce the neocon agenda) wanted "loyalists" rather than experts.

Back at work, a great number of interagency meetings were held at the White House where health issues related to Iraqi reconstruction were discussed. Rice chaired some of them, and I chaired several that included key players from USAID, DOD, OMB, Health and Human Services, Dr. Silberberg, Dr. Howe, and others. We were clarifying the preliminary concept for a children's hospital. Given DOD reticence about allowing ideas from outside its own sphere to take hold and its general hostility toward other agencies, Rice, who was excited at the possibility of doing something major and unique for Iraqi children decided to send me to Iraq to survey the state of pediatric medicine. In a meeting with her on May 7 and 12, 2003, I gave Condi an update of the Iraq hospital issues, and all the bureaucratic hurdles that stood in the way.

The National Security Advisor also felt that we should brief the First Lady, Laura Bush, and see if she would be willing to be a patron saying, "Mrs. Bush is great and highly under-utilized!" She asked that we get a meeting put together, and I made the request of Condi's scheduler and executive assistant, Liz Lineberry. I followed up by reaching out to Mrs. Bush's staff scheduler to set up a briefing. It also occurred to me that I should brief Scooter Libby, Cheney's chief of staff, who saw Wolfowitz daily, and I hoped might be helpful in getting Paul on board. Subsequently, I met with Scooter on May 16 and shared Rice's view that something major on pediatric health for Iraq would be worth pursuing. I also mentioned my puzzlement at DOD's negative attitude and asked if he could speak to Wolfowitz.

On the same day as my meeting with Scooter, I met with the First Lady's Director for special projects, Anne Heiligenstein. Anne was enthusiastic about the concept for the hospital and said she would share it with the appropriate First Lady's staff and then with Mrs. Bush. I explained that Rice wanted to brief the First Lady and ask if she would be amenable to involvement with the project. Given the interest that Laura Bush had regarding children, and recognizing that the USA was now firmly in Iraq, a hospital ensuring better health would, I hoped, resonate with the First Lady. I also mentioned to Anne that prior to going too much further, we would travel to Iraq to survey existing pediatric facilities there before formulating any final recommendations.

Although I had met Laura Bush for the first time in 1987 in Washington at a small dinner in honor of her husband and herself (I met Barbara Bush in 1984), I had never had a chance to meet her in a small White House setting until May 27, 2003, when I went with Condi to the East Wing for the briefing. That was my first foray into the first lady's offices and I was uncertain of the entrance door in the East Wing of the residence to go to the second floor. I realized too late that it was a mistake for me not to have tried to find the best path in advance of the meeting. Somehow, I had imagined that there would be Secret Service agents posted en route who would insist on passes being checked and would point us in the right direction. That anticipated scenario was misplaced in two ways: one, no one ever questioned Condoleezza Rice's progress within the White House given that she was one of the most recognized faces in the administration; two, once inside the inner sanctum of the White House, passes were not checked, although they were worn visibly by the staff (but not by principals).

Condi was familiar with the residence portion of the White House. We made our way up the stairs and to the meeting with Mrs. Bush. It was clear that Condi and Laura Bush were good friends. Condi told her about the poor state of pediatric health in Iraq. That meant that the proposed children's hospital would offer care to future generations of Iraqi children, become a center of excellence for the country, draw in accomplished physicians from the region and become a center for the training of young interns and nurses resulting in an elevation of the quality of care. Under Saddam, there had been utter degradation in the Shia South. He had severely punished Shias in all sorts of ways including denying them modern health care available to the elite in Baghdad.

There followed a discussion of the type of facilities under consideration for a children's hospital, a 100-bed hospital for specialized care. Given the importance of bringing in partners into this humanitarian enterprise, it was suggested by the First Lady that perhaps Project HOPE, an institution founded in 1958 that had built similar hospitals in China and Poland, could become a part of this exciting public–private partnership. Laura Bush knew John Howe, the head of Project HOPE, from Texas, and he was a respected medical leader, having served as President of the University of Texas Health Science Center at San Antonio for some fifteen years. (As mentioned before, I had already heard of HOPE from Dr. Silberberg and briefed Condi on that possibility.) Rice noted her desire that USAID would be the US government lead for the public part of the partnership. Rice mentioned that she would send a team to Iraq for an on-site review of existing facilities and needs.

I left the meeting with the clear go ahead to contact Dr. Howe and coordinate a potential visit to Iraq. It was getting close to Memorial Day and Howe was on vacation in Martha's Vineyard. We finally located him, and I requested him to come to a meeting to discuss a project in Iraq. On June 4, 2003, Anne Heiligenstein, her deputy Sonia Medina, and I met with John Howe on the second floor of the White House East Wing to discuss a potential public–private partnership for a children's hospital in Iraq. John recounted Project HOPE's (of which he had been president since 2001) experience in creating a pediatric heart hospital in Shanghai and another in Krakow in Poland and how both these institutions had become leaders in medical excellence in their respective countries. We spoke of the problems that any new major venture would have in Iraq because it was an active war zone. We all appreciated the fact that the USA was now committed in a major way in Iraq. We felt that if Iraq was sufficiently important to shed American blood and expend its treasure it was worth saving the lives of Iraqi children. That argument did not resonate with the neocons, Robin Cleveland, and Paul Wolfowitz, in particular, who undoubtedly complained to their friend, Steve the deputy National Security Advisor. Hadley summoned me to a meeting on June 5, 2003, to receive a full briefing on how matters were progressing. He listened with "enthusiasm" of someone who wished he had never heard of the issue. It was not his to stop but never was he very supportive either. As a follow-up to the earlier Condi Rice–Laura Bush meeting, I met with Andrew Natsios, USAID Administrator, on July 2, 2003 to brief him on the proposed project.

Rice told me to proceed to Iraq along with Howe and Heiligenstein for a survey of existing pediatric facilities in the country prior to selecting a site and focusing on the final project reflecting a lasting legacy of American goodwill. The sniping from the neocons did not cease, so we went to Iraq with the permission of the CPA which had authority to admit or refuse any Washington travelers. Our usual travel orders had to be amended for travel by military aircraft since that was the only way in and out of Iraq.

As I went to say good-bye to Condi before setting out for Iraq with the White House team, she greeted me and said: "travel safe."

Some Images of the Completed Children's Hospital in Basrah

36 THE AMERICAN LEGACY OF THE BASRAH CHILDREN'S HOSPITAL

36 THE AMERICAN LEGACY OF THE BASRAH CHILDREN'S HOSPITAL 355

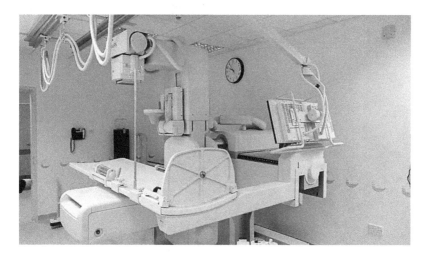

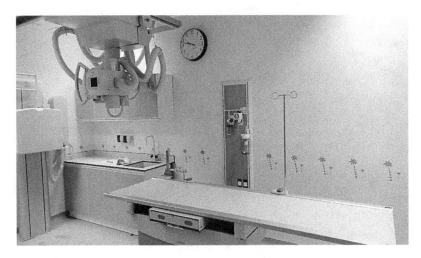

36 THE AMERICAN LEGACY OF THE BASRAH CHILDREN'S HOSPITAL   357

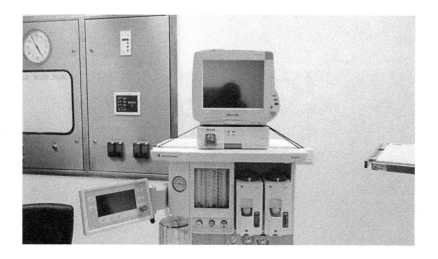

Notes

1. Dr. Donald Silberberg, "Children's Hospital in Baghdad: Concept Background," April 20, 2003. It is worth noting that the draft recorded that a state-of-the-art hospital of the kind envisioned would cost nearly $500 million if built in the USA. Silberberg also noted that the source of funding could come from Iraqi sequestered funds, the Gates Foundation, and the Rockefeller Foundation, among others and partner for institutional expertise with US academic institutions.
2. Wolfowitz appointed Cleveland as his chief of staff when he went as president of the World Bank. Her modus operandi and use of choice language with one and all was one of the first indications of Wolfowitz's troubles at the Bank, from which he ultimately had to resign. The Government Accountability Project noted that Cleveland received $250,000 tax-free salary at the Bank, which it deemed "grossly inflated with respect to previous experience."

CHAPTER 37

Trip to Iraq

There were several hurdles for travel to a war zone, including the absence of commercial flights. The DOD controlled Iraq, and a certain amount of training was required, including in the quick application of masks in case of chemical attacks, which were deemed a real possibility at that time. None of the three on the White House mission were military and thus needed some very basic training. We also signed on for basic training at Fort Belvoir the day of our departure on July 10, 2003, and came back armed with our duffel carrying equipment including the face mask and battle boots! Even as we were preparing to leave that same night for Frankfurt en route to Kuwait and there to board a C-130 into Baghdad, we met with more DOD reluctance and its Assistant Secretary for Health William Winkenwerder came by to discourage anything other than whatever the DOD proposed in Iraq.

It was a nine-day trip of which four days were spent in travel to Iraq and back. Anne, John, and I left for Frankfurt on a commercial flight from Dulles and connected with a Kuwait flight into Kuwait City, where we were met by the American embassy's political/military officer and taken to our hotel. Early the next morning, we were picked up at the hotel in official transport and taken to the Kuwait military airport, where we met the Combined Forces Land Component Command (CFLCC) Surgeon Team. We departed for Baghdad on July 12, 2003, by C-130. Sitting in the wartime configured aircraft was a new experience, and we were told by the pilot that we were first headed for Mosul and that our arrival into Baghdad would be delayed.

It was a blistering time of the day when we finally did get into Baghdad's airport. The terminal was a huge hangar where thousands of people seemed to be moving around. Arriving military flights carried US soldiers (male and female) who were being processed for deployment at the facility. While we waited for our security detail (since we arrived late, the arrangements were delayed.) We wondered at the hardship borne by the young soldiers in heavy fatigues in these unaccustomed high temperatures rising above 120 degrees.

Finally, the security detail was in place, and we were told we had to be guarded since we were a senior White House mission. All were asked to wear bulletproof vests and helmets since the road from the airport into the Green Zone was an active combatant zone for attacks on coalition vehicles (mostly American). We departed for the al Rasheed Hotel in the Green Zone, were checked in, and given a special identity card to carry at all times.

As mentioned earlier, the hotel was close to the various palaces that Saddam Hussein and his sons had inhabited. It was a multi-story structure with all of the trappings of a flashy Middle East hotel. It even sported a discotheque, where it was said that Saddam's son's Uday and Qusay took as they pleased any good looking girl they saw. On the tour of the hotel, we were told by an escorting military officer that the rooms in the upper floors of the hotel had cameras which recorded everything that went on and upon occupying the hotel after the invasion, American soldiers had found a room in the basement of the hotel where video and sound recording equipment stored massive collection of tapes. We were assured that these had now been de-activated! We heard from almost every Iraqi mother we met, horrific tales of rapes at will by the Hussein progeny and their goons. Early in the occupation, I sensed a huge collective sigh of relief at the end of oppression and the beginning of a better comfortable future for Iraq.

In this atmosphere, I was ready to help plan something good for the future welfare of 58% of the population, the children. As a member of the trio from the White House, I fully expected to get access to those inside the CPA and in the Iraqi medical system as warranted. We had come a long way and looked forward to the briefings. Our first set of these was with the medical czar, Haveman, who was openly hostile to the whole notion of our wanting to learn the state of the healthcare system in order to determine, with Iraqi help, what if anything might be done as a public–private partnership. The neocon rep that he was,

Haveman thought Iraqi's needed no consultation as they had got used to too much public support for health and all aspects of medical assistance, including access to medicines. "We are here to change Iraq" was his mantra, but it was changed in his and the DOD bosses' image. It was indeed startling for me to note the issues of turf which took precedence over the issues of substance. After all, this was not Washington infighting. This was US occupation of Iraq with the entire attendant issues. Haveman wanted me to know that I would need to go through him to see "the bosses," in particular, Jerry Bremer, America's proconsul in Iraq. Haveman even had the domestic side of the White House checking how our group had arrived in Iraq for the medical survey in the first place and whether we all had the requisite clearances! Had it not been for the seeming fact that he was interested only in delaying our schedule, this would have been a bizarre worry given that Iraq was a war zone and there were no commercial flights into that country.

Indeed, in order to fly to Iraq, all proper procedures needed to be followed including permissions and assistance for military air travel. Much of the time Anne, John, and I laughed off his clumsy approach, but it was a sad chapter in US policy when a man with little on the ground experience in Iraq or in foreign or national health policy makes the categorical statement that "this children's hospital that you are proposing will NOT happen." We were all stunned, but put his words aside as we proceeded with our schedule.

Given our charter and our past experience in the field along with the fact that our trio came with the specific blessings of the National Security Advisor and the First Lady, we received extensive support from Bremer, Pat Kennedy, Bremer's chief of staff overseeing thousands of civilian staff in the CPA[1] and Reuben Jeffery, economic advisor to Bremer. We met with individuals from the military side attended briefings with Lt. Gen. Ricardo Sanchez, the commander of US forces in Iraq at the time. Later, Lt. Gen. Sanchez wrote about the total inability of NSC to synchronize all of the government agencies in a milieu where the State Department would not deal with the CPA, and the CPA would not deal with the Defense Department or the State Department. Sanchez deemed the NSC "either incapable, incompetent, or unauthorized to perform the task" [of coordinating the inter-agency process] thereby leading to the failed first year in Iraq.[2]

Most of our conversations in the Green Zone and elsewhere in Iraq started with an explanation of why we were there and why we hoped to visit available pediatric facilities in different parts of the country. It was in one of my meetings with Bremer while we were talking about the hope for a new facility for Iraq's children, he mentioned that perhaps it made most sense for us to see if the facility could be built in the south in Basrah, which was quiet at the time and where the Saddam regime had spent virtually no funds in updating any medical facilities for decades. Bremer urged our trio to travel to Basrah to see the state of pediatric medicine there. His office arranged with the military to give us a lift into and out of Basrah for a daylong visit. Bremer said it was important for the USA to build support in the south, an area that lay close to so many American interests and where the people had been victimized following their 1993 revolt against Saddam Hussein.

The CPA helped make it possible for John, Anne, and myself to fly to Basrah on July 13, 2003. The airport was brand new and unused, except by the occupation. There were no commercial services in the recently completed facility as war had come on the heels of its opening with the expectation of making Basrah the hub for business travelers in the region. The area was under the control of the British, and we were met upon arrival by a British officer who had familiarity with health issues in the city. Basrah was indeed quiet at the time, and we moved around the city in one vehicle with no armor and no security detail. We were taken to all existing facilities and hospitals, including the Maternity and Children's Hospital built by a Kuwaiti family that had become the best of the existing medical treatment centers. Most of the facilities we saw were in dire need of updating. What also made a deep impression was the dedication of the doctors who worked under difficult conditions and the patients whose families had no place to sit/sleep with their loved ones in a culture where someone close to the patient was always by their bedside.

One glaring need was for treatment for children who faced high rates of cancer in a country with no full-time surgical oncologists, no nurse oncologists, and no pediatric chemotherapists. As a result, children under five accounted for more than half of registered cancer cases in Iraq, and 150 out of every 1000 Iraqi boys and girls were likely to die before they reached the age of five. The situation was even worse in the South where cancer was more prevalent. Thus, it made sense to locate a potential hospital, geared to the treatment of cancer, in Basrah.

Pediatric medicine was even more affected. As we traveled around to facilities, doctors pleaded with us for medicines and supplies. It was a wrenching scene as pediatricians appealed for simple items, such as syringes, saying that they were now forced to use adult size needles on premature babies, and we reached out to colleagues in Baghdad to see if any could be spared and forwarded south (we did succeed). There was an acute shortage of incubators in hospitals, and even those became inoperable once power failed. We met physicians and administrators of the hospitals and asked to see potential sites where the new hospital could be built. One site, next to the existing women's hospital, seemed to be a possibility, until we were told that the land had been a medical waste dumping ground for years and thus was toxic.

As we moved around Basrah with freedom (compared to elsewhere in Iraq), we saw several burnt out buildings and palaces which we were told were remnants of Hussein's retribution against the Shias of the South in the mid-1990s. At lunch in a hotel restaurant, there was prolonged discussion of the political differences between the mostly Sunni North and the Shia South and what it meant to the British command in the governance of the Basrah region. We were told that the political and religious groups were important and that their consultation would be crucial in the creation of anything in Basrah, a lesson never pressed with the same eloquence by the neocons in Baghdad whose mantra was "Wolfowitz does not want a hospital." It struck me that the British seemed much more experienced and their long history of engagement with the Muslim world had left them with better perspectives on the region.

As with all aspects of the visit to Iraq for our group, the day in Basrah was heart-wrenching. The problems seemed immense. Yet, the dedication of the medical community and its sense of service despite huge handicaps was inspiring. We returned to Baghdad later that evening via military transport, and as we were landing, the pilot told us that there was enemy fire in the area and that we needed to be braced for a corkscrew landing descending rapidly onto the airfield.

As the C-130 lumbered to a stop, we saw vast numbers of military aircraft and other vehicles. We saw scenes very different from those in our normal international travel, especially as we climbed into the armored vehicle with security for the travel to al Rasheed hotel where we were staying. Our security detail warned us that there had been enemy activity on the airport road into town, so we needed to hit the floor should an attack seem to occur. We were braced!

However, this was still a time when Americans were greeted with friendship. As we traveled in different neighborhoods on our way to medical meetings, children in the area would come out and wave. When we waved back, they smiled at us with the typical friendliness of a child. I noticed that when we got out of the vehicles, we were often surrounded by people and they were curious, but not unfriendly. This was a period when the invasion was over, Saddam Hussein was overthrown, and there were great expectations that American occupation would lead to a renaissance.

The DOD had sent Winkenwerder to Iraq from his Washington base at the same time that the White House group was there. He came to some of our meetings in Baghdad. We were invited to a fancy dinner he threw at the Ishtar Sheraton outside the Green Zone. The invitation said that the dress code would be "coat and tie for the Iraqis and best civilian or military dress available" for Americans. It was a large affair and after the speeches came the entertainment, belly dancing! It was a bizarre performance by an aged, less than talented dancer, and the Iraqi medical guests present seemed to feel embarrassed by the strange selection of what they felt Americans thought represented Iraqi culture.

July 17, 2003, was spent attending a medical conference organized by the DOD. The large guest list included physicians and bureaucrats. Discussion ranged over several issues regarding the remaking of the health sector. After all, the White House had requested $8 billion in supplemental funds for Iraqi reconstruction from Congress for 2004. Haveman got a chance to talk about the fact that in a free Iraq, people paid for medical services commensurate with their need. The broken health sector would have to be privatized in order to bear the costs. While Iraqis recognized that the previous enormously corrupt pharmaceutical distribution system had left gaping holes, they were dissatisfied with the envisioned new privatized system, where the required payments would not be commensurate with ability to pay. Since this was our final day, I tried to squeeze in meetings with CPA officials following my larger NSC portfolio, particularly democracy and human rights. I got a sense of the major work underway and the contact between some of the professional State Department civilian and Foreign Service members with fieldwork. It was an ambitious agenda, and money was beginning to flow from Washington to hire contractors to train Iraqis. Work with women's groups seemed to be particularly promising.

I attended a meeting of the Governing Council as an observer and was struck by the articulate women representatives who appeared familiar with their constituencies and were so full of hope for their nation. I had a separate meeting with Dr. Raja Kuzai, a medical doctor from the North, and mentioned the concept of a specialized children's hospital in the South. Her response was wonderful and reflected the esprit de corps we had found throughout our meetings. Kuzai noted that although she was herself from the North and knew there were tremendous needs in the South as well, she was happy that America would do something special for the children in the South, where Saddam had visited so much suffering on the population. I came away encouraged that Bremer's recommendation for the children's hospital to be located in Basrah was indeed the right way to go. The hospital could become a beacon of hope for families in Southern Iraq who in 2003 had few options for care when their children became gravely ill.

One of the memorable hours spent within medical facilities was our visit to the US Army field hospital in the desert. Travel by a Blackhawk helicopter was the only option. On an extremely hot day when outdoor temperatures were above 140 degrees, we were dropped onto the site as the helicopter could not land in the sand dunes. The last several feet we had to jump because of the heat and desert sand. Clothed in protective bulletproof gear with a helmet on our heads, we leapt into the hot sand and were grateful for helping hands that lifted us out. That was a memorable experience that I knew my son would be impressed I had managed.

The hospital cared for wounded American and coalition soldiers, but they were also treating burn victims, Iraqi children who were playing close to fuel lines that were often tapped illegally to provide gas for the families. Looking at the worry on the faces of the mothers and the care with which American doctors and nurses were tending to the Iraqi civilian patients was moving and demonstrative of the spirit of gratitude that I recalled in my early years in Peshawar in northwestern Pakistan, where my first contact with America's gracious generosity had occurred in the mid-1950s.

We departed Baghdad on July 17 after a visit to Camp Victory, located en route to the airport in another of Saddam's huge palaces with sweeping marble staircases, rooms with gold thrones, vast grounds and a real sense of opulent unreality that is consistent with many of the oil-rich sheikhdoms of the Arab world. We exited again through Kuwait and continued the twenty-four hour plus journey via Dubai and London back to Washington. Anne, John, and I were firm in our belief that the visit to Iraq had been critical to our understanding the state of health facilities in that country and what the USA might do to ameliorate some of the suffering we saw.

We had many experiences to share as we returned to brief the First Lady and Dr. Rice. Upon our return, we put together a comprehensive briefing paper in which we outlined the needs of Iraq, a concept of a flagship children's hospital.[3] The hospital project made even greater sense as a public–private enterprise, since we had seen the level of expertise needed would be better met if it came from organizations with experience in equipping and training which seemed to be completely absent in the DOD appointed health officials in Iraq.[4] We also came away understanding the problems of operating Iraq from the Green Zone.

If the children's hospital was to be built with public funds, it needed to gather support inside Iraq from the very outset. That meant political leaders of Basrah would have to offer the land with a clear title, so that once the hospital is completed, no one comes forward with a claim to the land or that it was not land that Saddam Hussein had seized illegally from rightful owners. I was also well aware that in the Muslim world, land ownership, and a stake in the upkeep of whatever was and is built on it is heavily prized. We needed another Iraqi stake right from the start. Apart from the land, those who stood to benefit from the hospital needed to become the spokesmen for the project. The families, particularly the mothers, would be the likely supporters of a project as they understood its meaning for the care of their suffering children. That involvement would actively be sought by the people in charge of building the hospital.

Building of the Basrah hospital would project the image of America's compassion and a marked difference with the cruelties of the former regime whose actions had been reflected in the 2003 discovery of mass graves of some 300,000 individuals. I recalled the powerful words of Dr. Muayad Al Hussaini: "There are many projects where the United States could build stronger and more trusting relationships with the Iraqi people. However, projects which address the health care of children are dearest to everyone's heart."

I reported back to Condi on our main findings, and she asked when we were briefing Laura Bush. I told her that John Howe, Anne Heiligenstein, and I were meeting with Mrs. Bush on July 22, 2003. The First Lady was extremely interested in our reporting on what we saw in Iraq in all of its manifestations. Anne asked me to talk about the overall context of what we saw and what we had worked on. John Howe, as the medical person in the group, reported on the specifics of the state of health and what the proposed hospital would mean.

Jerry Bremer came to the White House for a meeting with the President, followed by a statement in the Rose Garden. I managed to catch a moment with Bremer and reiterated the Rice and Laura Bush interest in following up on his suggestion for the children's hospital as a modern cancer treatment facility to be located in Basrah. I mentioned internal discussions on the subject were ongoing, and there were many hurdles yet to be cleared, including financing. Bremer remained supportive and graciously volunteered to keep an eye out at CPA.

I also worked on a briefing with the head of USAID (the initial public partner), Andrew Natsios, before his meeting with Rice. The full team that included Dr. Donald Silberberg met with Rice on July 24, 2003, where we put forward details of the proposed hospital and also shared the word that the Iraqis wanted it to be called the Basrah Children's Hospital (BCH). I had earlier noted the intense bureaucratic hurdles for the project that existed in the Green Zone given that health officials from the DOD, both in Iraq and Washington, had not been forthcoming. We had, however, met some terrific military members such as US Army Colonel (R) Fred Gerber, who had knowledge and interest beyond the Green Zone.

I felt it important to let the National Security Advisor know that we faced internal USG hurdles and those created by the OMB's Cleveland were likely to be the hardest to overcome. There would be no cooperation from the neocons without directives from the Boss that the building of the 100-bed hospital is to be a priority especially since it would need a $100 million from the $971 million being allocated to Iraq's health sector in 2004 supplemental. Although that would still leave $871 million for projects dear to the neocon heart, the DOD continued to demur, and I received yet another call warning me of the personal and project pitfalls of continued pursuit of BCH by Winkenwerder who called on August 12, 2003, to re-register reservations on behalf of Wolfowitz.

I reiterated that for BCH we would follow a more efficient model different from all the other DOD projects which had already garnered a lion's share of the USA allocated health budget. We would ask for Iraqi support and solidify it through their provision of suitable land, both in size and in having a clean, clear title. They would "own" the hospital and become stakeholders early in the project. We would also build community support to help protect the hospital as needed if/when the war spreads to Basrah. The people of the area (motivated by the mothers) already seemed passionately to want to guard any such facility. Further, that John Howe and I would travel to the region and elicit community and country support. We noted that the public–private nature of the enterprise made it possible for Project HOPE and its CEO Howe to reach out to partners in the training and equipping part because he brought professional experience in successful hospital projects overseas.

Once it became known within the administration that Rice and Laura Bush were firmly supportive of BCH, internal USG struggles for face time with these White House luminaries began. Health and Human Services (HHS) Secretary, Tommy Thompson, wanted to be in charge for the public side of the effort. His staff was very keen that their secretary meet with Rice to press the case for why HHS rather than USAID needed to be in charge. Thompson's junior staff, Bill Steiger, came into remind me that theirs was a "conservative" connection with the White House domestic policy shop, which meant that they had a privileged link to all White House initiatives. This was an unprecedented and amazing line of reasoning in my experience, but I heard it often when I joined George W.'s NSC in 2003. I heard everyone out and promised that we would stay in touch. They received invitations to the meetings I chaired on BCH. However, once it became clear that the lead would not go to HHS (given its known poor record in overseeing smaller projects elsewhere), its personnel stopped attending the working meetings, preferring like so many others, to snipe from the sidelines.

But neocons were not yet done with their opposition. Once they heard that the project was on track, the big guns came out! Now, Liz Cheney wanted to hear about our Iraq trip. I met with her on July 31, 2003, to discuss what we saw. I mentioned to her that I kept hearing that Wolfowitz did not want BCH to be built and that I was at a loss to understand why. Given the deep American involvement in Iraq following the invasion and the commitment to rebuild Iraq, opposition to BCH puzzled me immensely, and I said that I had continued to ask the question: "If Iraq is worth sacrificing our young soldiers, why is it not worth saving Iraqi children for a different tomorrow?" Liz replied that building democracy would bring a different future (and I pointed out that that goal was not incompatible with a healthy Iraq), and she asked my impressions of life and leaders in and outside the Green Zone. She was amazed that our trio had traveled so extensively in a war zone. I responded that Rice felt that we needed a full review of all Iraqi pediatric facilities before making a final decision on any American hospital building effort.

As we continued refining the model for BCH and dealing with the CPA along with the relevant Iraqi medical professional, we continued to deal with the issues of preference that perpetually came up in conversations with the key neocons in the DOD, HHS, and OMB. At times, it appeared that the president's request for supplemental, when approved, would not leave sufficient time for an orderly implementation of the plans earmarked for funding through the supplemental. The internal bickering within the various agencies continued.

Also, escalating problems in Iraq began to spread across the country. Finding money for and the implementing important projects inside Iraq rapidly became extremely difficult. BCH got caught in funding issues and the constantly changing array of health ministers and senior officials.[5] Reflecting his frustration, General Sanchez wrote of this period: "The absurdity of the U.S. government's bureaucracy really came to the forefront in February 2004 when the congressional supplement, which had been passed back in November, finally became available. At this point, after the long wait to receive the funding for critical projects, the CPA was put in the position of having to spend $18 billion in a little over four months."[6]

With all this dithering, the hospital, initially envisaged as a 250-bed facility, was earmarked to receive only half the requested amount. Even this amount, namely $50 million, was allocated after a great deal of effort by Condoleezza Rice. Indeed, she had to call congressional leaders arguing that despite the DOD qualms US legacy in Iraq would be burnished by the gift of a modern much needed pediatric facility and that the building of the cancer treatment hospital was the right thing to do. However, even the Republican leadership within appropriation did not want to go forward against neocon naysayers exemplified by Robin Cleveland, who had once served on Kentucky Senator Mitch McConnell's staff and where she was dubbed by some colleagues as being "wild eyed" nasty.

The conservative staff of the House leadership summoned John Howe and me to a briefing on the Hill. At my request, the White House waived the usual reluctance to have presidential staff appear before Congress. I went to the briefing, armed with materials showing the need, the different model for BCH which ensured Iraqi support after US departure from their country. I was stunned at the open hostility masked as concern from staff who did not want to hear about the need and the prospect of what the hospital would mean for the children. We kept hearing that "this will never be built," which we had heard so often from Haveman and others in the DOD. In the end, we received fifty percent of the request after a series of phone calls from Rice to McConnell.[7] While the allocation of funds was greatly welcome, delay in funding and internal US government wrangling cost precious time in construction. The region, which had been a low security issue as BCH planning took place, began to escalate in violence. The Shia revolt was in full swing soon after the construction began. Therefore, further delays were all but assured.

Reduced US funding meant greater need to look elsewhere for additional funds. That, in turn, required making a powerful case to donors in the USA and abroad why support for a pediatric hospital to serve the children of Iraq was important and worthy of contributions. Given the public–private nature of the BCH effort, Project HOPE and US officials cast the net wide. Laura Bush had offered to host an event for BCH at the White House. Immediately, Karl Rove's shop went into swing. They reminded all that the hospital was controversial and the involvement of the First Lady made it nearly impossible to host any event unless each and every potential invitee was first vetted by the White House lawyers. Given the lawyers' rather full plate, including issues related to terrorism, and Guantanamo and Abu Ghraib issues, sparing anyone to do the vetting in a timely fashion was declared impossible.

Amazingly, there came an offer from Nanette Iverson in Gonzales' White House Counsel's office who graciously volunteered to do the vetting on her own time and compiled several large binders with the cleared list from the initial names submitted for an invitation to the First Lady's lunch. Nanette told me how the concept of the hospital had moved her deeply, and she was willing to undertake the immense effort and contribute toward the realization of the dream. This was a huge achievement given that none of us would want to compromise the clearance process and wished for an orderly procedure for getting the right people for the event. Anne Heiligenstein and her deputy Sonia Medina were extremely helpful in trying to get all of the issues ironed out so that the event would be successful in showcasing an important US gift to future generations of Iraqi children.

As usually happens with events at the White House, when time for the lunch drew closer, even people who did not want to help in the building of BCH wanted to be invited. Our interest was in accommodating an appropriate audience to help build and sustain the public–private effort.

Anna Perez, the Senior Director for Communications at the NSC, was supportive of also inviting the press as indeed were others when I mentioned it to colleagues during preparations for the President's annual UNGA speech.[8] As Senior Director for the UN at the NSC, I traveled with the President and Rice to New York for the UNGA opening and the President's speech and his reception for heads of state. I discussed the hospital concept with several interlocutors from other countries: All said it was exactly the sort of project that would elicit international support. Yet, neocon opposition was making the domestic dealings ever harder. Some briefed the media that the First Lady was involved in a "dubious project in the health sector."

The annual UNGA reception for the Heads of State/Government was hosted by the President at the Museum of Natural History in New York. By the time the schedule was set for September 23, 2004, the usual Waldorf ballroom was already taken. Protocol did a great job of finding an alternate site even as it complicated arrangements for the reception and the speech by President Bush to the assembled dignitaries. Navigating the labyrinth in high heels flying across a concrete floor en route to the assigned duties, I knew better than to miss the White House motorcade waiting near the entrance for the return to the Waldorf where the US delegation was ensconced. Yet, I lingered too long so that I could hear the president and see which edits from the earlier draft had survived in his remarks. To my utter horror, I soon realized that I had tarried too long and in those elegant heels, no way could I run fast enough the long distance to the assigned car in the motorcade. Knowing all roads around the museum were closed for the reception traffic, and there was no hope for a taxi, I was panicked! As I surfaced at the exit door, there stood the president by his limousine awaiting Laura Bush's arrival within seconds. One look at my face, he said with a twinkle, "You aren't going to make it are you Shirin?" I replied, "No Mr. President, I am not" to which he replied, "So get in this one, we'll give you a ride back." I hesitated, and Andy Card, the chief of staff, said: "get in, he is serious." So I quickly took one of the jump seats and off we went. Certainly was the fastest ride through New York I ever had, even via Times Square. Back at the Waldorf, I thanked the President as he took his elevator up to the suite.

On November 13, 2003, I updated Condi on the hospital state of play. I mentioned that we were refining the BCH model, that the Iraqis wanted the hospital to be named the Basrah Children's Hospital, and that Project HOPE was already getting deeply involved and USAID was working toward the start of the work leading up to construction, once obligated funds were available.

The signing ceremony for the Iraq/Afghanistan Supplemental Appropriation Bill occurred in the East Room of the White House on November 6. Rice was instrumental in getting the funding, and I took this as a sign of her constant support for the BCH effort. As always, Condi said on the issue: "give me a 'to do' list," and I always happily obliged. She was very pleased that Mrs. Bush's office was being kept fully in the picture.

The BCH team briefed the First Lady and worked closely with her staff. In addition, I chaired the NSC effort in getting everything on board for the US reentry into UNESCO. We were greatly cheered when the announcement finally came that the President had decided to reenter UNESCO in September 2003, after an absence of eighteen years, and also to appoint Mrs. Bush (who became UNESCO Ambassador for the Decade of Literacy) as head of the American delegation. But much work still needed to be done including the finding of the requisite funds that the USA was required to pay to cover its share of the annual costs.[9]

Rice met for over half an hour on December 1, 2003, with Dr. Charles Sanders, Chairman of the Project HOPE Board and John Howe, its CEO. This is a long time in the West Wing world! The discussion centered on the collaboration for BCH and settling any concerns Sanders may have on the commitment of the White House to the children's hospital. The meeting was a cordial one, and both Rice and Sanders seemed satisfied, and each understood that the effort would be a difficult one given that Iraq was a war zone where delays and difficulties would occur. I was struck once more by the firm commitment to the hospital and the sense that we would work around the multiple problems that would undoubtedly crop up before completion of BCH. Our pessimism was well placed.

Rice spoke to Laura Bush on the telephone on December 8, 2003, to update her on the state of play. Condi noted that she would be meeting on the 17th with the Iraqi minister of health along with someone from Bremer's shop, the CPA. At no time did either Laura Bush or Rice hint that BCH should not be completed because of the expected problems of launching a project in wartime Iraq or the political attacks from some inside or outside the US government, once Laura Bush's name got closely associated with the hospital.

Notes

1. Bremer says of Pat Kennedy with whom he had worked for decades at the State Department, that Kennedy "was recognized as the best administrator the modern Foreign Service had produced." L. Paul Bremer, *My Year in Iraq: The Struggle to Build a Future of Hope* (New York: Simon & Schuster, 2006), 9.
2. Ricardo S. Sanchez, *Wiser in Battle: A Soldier's Story* (New York: Harper, 2008), 314. Among the anecdotes, Sanchez recounts in his book as he recounts Iraq and what Sanchez terms "a strategic blunder of historic proportions," was a sample of presidential "pep talk" to his generals where the killing of four contractors in Fallujah in 2004 led Bush to tell his military to "Kick ass! If somebody tries to stop the march to democracy, we will seek them out and kill them."
3. Shirin Tahir-Kheli, John Howe, and Anne Heiligenstein, "Children's Tertiary Care in Iraq: Assessment Team Report," July 21, 2003.
4. For example, the DOD health senior official, Jim Haveman, extolled the virtues of a redesigned privatized system for Iraq's procurement and distribution of drugs with a harshly curtailed generic list of USA produced drugs under a new "formulary." By the time Haveman leaves Iraq, the Health Ministry estimated that of the 900 drugs it deems essential, 40 percent are unavailable.
5. By the time of BCH's opening in October 2010, there have been 8 Iraqi ministers of health. However, each one of them has been a strong supporter of a state-of-the-art children's cancer treatment hospital.
6. Ricardo S. Sanchez, *Wiser in Battle: A Soldier's Story* (New York: Harper, 2008), 314.
7. White House rumor had it that Robin Cleveland had made her own calls to the appropriators saying that her "job was on the line" if there was no funding for BCH, a statement that seems unlikely given her flaunting authority to one and all!
8. The 2003 UNGA speech raised, for the first time, the issue of Human Trafficking as "a modern day form of slavery." September 2003 also saw a great deal of work focused on promotion of democracy in Iraq.
9. Laura Bush, *Spoken from the Heart* (New York: Scribner, 2010), 293. I was indeed surprised that the former First Lady chose not to mention the children's hospital in her book given that it is likely to be her main lasting goodwill legacy on a daily basis for the future in a country of note to her husband's administration. A colleague who said he had asked her that question, told me that she told him that she did not say a word in her book because she did not want to draw any attention to the hospital, uncompleted at the time the book went to press, for fear it would become another source of criticism for the Bush administration.

CHAPTER 38

Rallying Support

The "us versus them" mentality inside the White House, particularly acute in the George W. Bush White House where political operatives like Karl Rove had special status, complicated dealing with the media. Also, the world of 2003 was certainly different from that of 1984 when I first entered the NSC when the great communicator himself was president, and there was only gentle sparring with the press and undoubtedly mocking jokes on the outside, but the media "spin game" was of a different variety all together. The invasion of Iraq in March 2003 did nothing to abate the disdain with which the media covered the Bush presidency, especially given the drawn out manner in which the 2000 election was finally resolved. Therefore, stories about BCH were covered with a great deal of skepticism. Adding to the prospect for mischief making with the press was the presence of two major personalities, Laura Bush and Condoleezza Rice, as patrons of the project. Those inside the administration who opposed BCH for their own reasons found willing listeners in the media as they griped about approval of any non-neocon idea. Besides, as the Iraq war took a beating in the press, another health project in Iraq such as BCH was viewed as unlikely to get completed.

Again and again, when the issue of Iraqi reconstruction came up, we were pounded by charges of waste: first, in terms of the lack of progress under Bechtel, which was given the construction contract because it was in 2005 the only company with reach inside the administration. There was also a great deal of public angst because, according to some reports from CIA sources to the *Washington Post* in early 2005, at least 50% of

© The Author(s) 2018
S. Tahir-Kheli, *Before the Age of Prejudice*,
https://doi.org/10.1007/978-981-10-8551-2_38

the $40 billion intelligence budget for the year would go to private contractors. Additionally, there were also many critics of the close links that contractors such as Halliburton and Bechtel had with Cheney and other senior officials.

BCH had become a recurring critical story in the press on September 20, 2004, as I left for the President's annual visit to the UNGA. At a dinner that night with NSC communications Senior Director, Anna Perez, I learned that the *Wall Street Journal* was all set to do a negative piece on BCH. I asked to speak on the record to the reporter and respond to whatever he may have heard from others regarding the reasons that Laura Bush and Condi Rice were supporters of an American-built pediatric cancer hospital in Basrah. In the midst of the hectic New York schedule of meetings that is the stuff of a presidential visit to the UN, I had a long telephone interview with the reporter. The thrust of what he had heard as genesis of the hospital idea implied that it had come out of non-serious efforts to create work! I detailed the statistics for children's cancer in the south and the very limited options that children there had for recovery. I also noted the fact that Mrs. Bush's Projects Director, me, and John Howe the CEO of Project HOPE had seen all this first hand when we visited pediatric facilities in all parts of Iraq. After a detailed account of the serious effort that we were making to help future generations improve their chances of survival from cancer, the reporter seemed mollified. I then asked why it seemed that there was little appetite for the good that might be done and why only the inaccurate headlines proclaiming: "the hospital would be nothing but a hole in the ground"? In a startlingly honest rejoinder, the reporter admitted: "The negative makes for a much better copy!"

That interview was a seminal moment for me. I realized that there was an important task ahead. We owed it to America's goodness and Iraqi children's future that BCH get built. We needed to insulate the negative talk and do the job at hand. Completing the hospital would be the only way to silence the skeptics. So the meetings that needed to coordinate the work of the hospital went on. We were extremely fortunate for the resolute support offered by the National Security Advisor who became Secretary of State. From time to time, Condi asked for an updated "to do" list for her on BCH matters, which was provided and she was gracious and judicious in meeting the requests for her input.

In the spirit of moving ahead, we met with the requisite agencies involved in various ways, including: NSC, First Lady's Office, White

House Counsel, USAID, OMB, and HHS. The meeting was a way to decide on how to respond to congressional staff inquiries regarding the nature of the hospital, the construction timelines, the staffing and training issues, design costs, etc. We believed these were legitimate issues that needed to be addressed and answered because of the responsibility of public funding and the need for private funding for the Project HOPE's equipment and training contribution effort. We also knew that certain neocons were prompting friendly congressional staff to ask these questions. We talked about seeking reduced overhead costs for the contractors and an off-the-shelf hospital design with some Iraqi cultural motifs built into blend the design into the local setting.

USAID estimated that a 250 bed hospital, as initially envisioned, would cost $145 million for design, engineering, and construction. The cost worked out to $2360 per square meter, an estimate that American and Iraqi experts agreed on. Given the $50 million approved by Congress, other ways to supplement were discussed. Among them was the possibility of moving money from other parts of the Iraq supplemental to make up the shortfall. While that procedure was legal, it would simply further complicate matters with Congress. In any case, shifting of the funds required a 15-day notification which is long enough for all manner of objection to rise and trouble to brew up.

What were the other options that would allow the hospital project to move ahead quickly and get past the endless Washington insider games that had already cost dearly in funds, in time, and indeed even in lives? The first alternative option was to refurbish an existing hospital. While that option would garner a positive reaction from those in opposition to the project, experts in the group deemed updating an existing Iraqi facility more costly in the end because of years of neglect and the crumbling infrastructure needed for a modern hospital. Project HOPE also thought it would be far harder to garner private donations for an old facility since few if any of the western major medical equipment companies such as Phillips, GE, or Siemens would want to offer anything for a facility where electricity was often off and even safe water was not always available.

A second alternative option we considered was to use the $50 million toward the addition of a pediatric wing to a hospital that the CPA was refurbishing. This option required convincing CPA to shift plans back to Basrah which had been taken off its list once BCH had secured funding.

Experts in the group cautioned against a process where new and old facilities would have to be integrated and share the same systems.

The third option was to give up the concept of a critical care hospital (which was the rationale for the $50 million from Congress) and instead build a pediatric clinic to provide only primary health training for doctors and nurses. This option was unlikely to attract much private funding as envisaged in the original public–private partnership for BCH.

The final option was to opt for building a smaller hospital, using the $50 million allocated and reach out to potential partners to augment the funding toward a 100-bed facility. A 30–50-bed facility was said by the experts to be difficult to call a hospital. Nor could such a small hospital provide the range of modern care that was so badly needed. Funders from outside, including those that Project HOPE wanted to appeal for contributions of state-of-the-art equipment, were less likely to be generous in support of a small facility. We discussed whether it made sense to start small with private donors adding build-out modular units as money became available. However, that option was put aside because of the medical opinion that a proper facility needed to be built as an integral unit and that a 100-bed hospital was the best way to go.

It became clear that the hospital was among US projects in Iraq complicated enough to require a great deal of coordination. Even after the $50 million came through in funding, the public–private nature of the enterprise meant that the interagency process required continued conversations with supporters and detractors. We were keen to share all information and did it happily and often. In return, we looked for support from all helpful quarters. During the nearly two-year delay, events on the ground had changed for the worse, and Basrah had become less secure. Therefore, the need to proceed with alacrity became paramount. In addition, hospital construction was one way to provide jobs to unemployed Iraqis. Thus, once initial funding became available, USAID made Iraqi employment a requirement in the BCH contracts with Bechtel (Bechtel and others).

No doubt that BCH was an entirely different sort of project for the USA in war-torn Iraq. Delays had both raised the costs and worsened security. Questions often asked were: what is the probability of the USA managing a complex project such as the BCH when USAID and their contractors were neither able to stay on schedule nor get any Iraqi buy-in for the much smaller clinics and the simpler jobs of improving water treatment plants. Democrats in Congress questioned whether it was politics that had led to the selection of the hospital as "an unusual alliance between the White House and the National Security Council to fund a state-of-the-art children's hospital in Iraq."[1] Even the usually very sensible Senator from Vermont, Patrick J. Leahy, the ranking Democrat on the Senate Foreign Operations Subcommittee, was said to have expressed that he was "concerned about spending large sums on a state-of-the-art hospital that may be more the result of political pressure than the best use of taxpayer dollars."[2]

A *Los Angeles Times* story included an interview with Laura Bush who acknowledged her support of the hospital project, stressing the importance of improved health care for Iraqi children with one of the highest cancer mortality rates in the Middle East. Addressing questions regarding the genesis of the project, Mrs. Bush noted that the idea had been brought up in her conversations with NSA Rice and me. Although the genesis of the idea had preceded the linkage with Project HOPE, yet there was criticism that somehow it must be because Laura Bush knew project HOPE's CEO, John Howe. The article noted that Laura Bush's "determination to build the hospital comes as the first lady seeks a higher profile in government and politics during a presidential campaign year." However, the fact that the occupation had already committed the USA to oversight of Iraq and funds for reconstruction had also been approved by Congress was not even mentioned.

Another criticism that came up had to do with those who said, "Why build a hospital in Iraq and not spend the money in America where the needs are also great?" I treated that as a very legitimate question, but made the point that clearly it would have been far better not to have invaded Iraq at all and spend the trillion plus dollars doing it. But now that the deed is done, Saddam has been dispatched, and the majority of the costs have been incurred, it is no longer a case of one against the other. At the NSC, we deal with issues relating to America's relations with other countries. Iraq is deemed to be a critical issue for the USA. Now, it is important to build a legacy of good will and positive relations for the future. And saving lives of the children of Iraq offers a good place for creating such legacy.

BCH was a product of Iraqi preferences to a greater extent than most American reconstruction efforts in Iraq. At least nine different ministers of health supported the idea of a specialized cancer treatment facility. The Iraqi MOH established a priority of reducing child mortality by 50% and agreed that BCH will lead the southern governorates in meeting that objective over five years and by serving more than one million children living in the region. The situation is made more poignant by the fact that childhood cancers are 8–10 times more common in Iraq than in developed countries. The most common cancers are leukemia, lymphomas, and brain and nervous system tumors.

The new American built 100-bed BCH, which is set on 13 acres of land given to the project by Iraq, is placed to address the abovementioned childhood diseases with the goal of prevention, early diagnosis, and cures using therapies that are standard elsewhere, but not available in Iraq. BCH offers Iraq the first functioning linear accelerator and the southern region its only radiotherapy facility (two other such facilities exist in northern Iraq but they are outdated and mostly deteriorated). In addition, BCH offered a chance to get modern medical oncology training for Iraqi physicians, nurses, and pediatric chemotherapists on an ongoing basis. Also, it offered the possibility of additional needed equipment and support through private partnership and help from regional countries. According to Project HOPE, BCH's annual pediatric admissions would cover 360 cancer patients, 468 intensive care patients, 354 neonatal intensive care, and 2230 acute care patients.

Training is to be a critical part of the BCH effort. As we noted in our 2003 trip report, Iraqi doctors, almost to a person, begged for better training for all medical professionals, including nurses, few if any of whom were certified. Nurses were ill-educated, ill-trained, and greatly underpaid. At best, they could barely read and according to what we observed were not even able properly to take patients' vital signs, much less perform more complex tasks. We found families straining to look after patients themselves in the hospital including procuring appropriate medicines and blood supplies as needed.

Project HOPE, with similar efforts in China and in Poland, was the perfect match to provide crucial training for BCH hospital staff ensuring appropriate expertise for the immediate, medium, and long term. They coordinated and implemented multi-tiered training for the pediatric staff using international board certified experts in specific specialties along with a consultative group of physicians, nurses, administrators, and technicians to set up the curriculum and training programs as the hospital readies for the opening. Iraqis were extremely interested in proper training through Fellowships, Certificates, Short Courses, Workshops, and Visiting Scholars programs. Training included classroom, laboratory, and clinical observation in recognized training centers with a focus on

"Train the Trainer." One special aspect of the program is the provision of training in state-of-the-science health programs in secure regional facilities or in the USA.

Iraq's MOH asked that the emphasis should be to train some 250 nurses at a multi-level effort. During our tour of Iraqi health facilities, we observed that doctors routinely performed duties which would be the purview of nurses in the USA. Thus, training was to focus on pediatric nursing care, operating room nursing, intensive care nursing; neonatal intensive care, emergency room nursing; oncology, endoscopy, infection control, education, quality assurance, and medical/surgical ward nursing. As a pediatric referral hospital, BCH needed pediatric oncologists and surgeons who were trained at centers outside Iraq, including the King Hussein Cancer Center in Amman, Jordan in a Project HOPE partnership set up in coordination with the MOH. BCH is a modern day model requiring management training for its successful operation. Training of healthcare managers at senior executive and staff level was to occur in collaboration with a Transition Team gearing for the phased hospital opening.[3]

Creation of jobs and provision of essential services were an important American goal from the outset. While USAID contracted with Bechtel for constructing BCH, the US Army Corps of Engineers became involved in the plans for building a health sciences academy and with numerous other facilities' renovation. By December 2004, US efforts were focused on renovations of health facilities including 19 small hospitals and 59 primary health centers. In addition, USAID gave a $36.7 million grant to UNICEF for medical supplies and other humanitarian assistance to areas with ongoing hostilities.

We continued to fight internal US government battles over BCH even as Iraqis donated suitable land, approved the hospital concept, formed a joint steering committee, celebrated the start of construction, and proceeded for medical training. For the US government, the personnel in charge included Jim Kunder, a senior deputy to Natsios at USAID as overseer, Leslie Perry as the point person in Baghdad, plus support from US Ambassador John Negroponte. Leading the private effort was Dr. John Howe.

Project HOPE hired retired Colonel Fred Gerber for the implementation/training phase. Fred knew the landscape well both from the Iraqi point of view and that from that of the US bureaucracies. The HOPE senior leadership, including Jim Peake and Dr. Fox, worked with the

Iraqi MOH in identifying needs and personnel for BCH. By the end of 2005, the public–private partnership seemed to have gelled. However, the deteriorating security situation caused steady delays, and Bechtel seemed unable to find the requisite number of Iraqi contractors and workers to move ahead steadily.

In mid-October 2005, USAID reported on its efforts on behalf of BCH. These updates were structured for presentation to Rice and also for keeping the bureaucracy on board. Given my move to the Department of State with Rice, I had no further dealings with Robin Cleveland who went with her mentor, Paul Wolfowitz, on her disastrous and short tenure at the World Bank. At State, BCH-related problems were addressed in a spirit of getting things done. Although, at times, the frustrations ran high when deadlines were constantly missed and security inside Iraq continued to plummet.

We were keeping the First Lady's staff fully integrated into the BCH plan. With the departure for Texas of Anne Heliegenstin, who as Projects Director for Laura Bush had been part of the trio Rice sent to Iraq in 2003, the BCH initial team began to break up. Sonia Medina, Anne's deputy, stayed on for a while, so that continuity was possible. However, once Anita McBride, a card carrying neocon—who told me proudly that she was a John Bolton protégé—became Laura Bush's chief-of-staff, I found an unpleasantness that was reminiscent of an earlier time with Robin Cleveland. McBride's tenure in the first lady's office ended the camaraderie and problem-solving approach we had developed for BCH implementation. She constantly assaulted me with complaints and man-handling regarding delays and how the "project is not going to get anywhere" a refrain from earlier years from other neocons. I briefly complained to Condi about it. This was perhaps the second time I ever complained to Condi about anyone. The first prize had clearly gone to Robin Cleveland!

Project HOPE began to reach out to regional countries for assistance in training as it asked for help from different companies for equipment. Cairo and Amman began to respond. In one of our regular meetings, I asked Dr. Howe how he foresaw achieving his training goals given that it was difficult to find needed numbers in Basrah and the fact that the tense security picture made it difficult to fly in trainers. Howe offered the view that Cairo and Amman, Jordan were already on his list for potential help. He mentioned that neighboring Oman had one of the best health systems in the region. I volunteered that I was planning to visit Oman in connection with some other matters and while there I could bring up this issue with the National Security Advisor to the Sultan of Oman, Dr. Omar Zawawi, who is a personal friend.

On December 5, 2005, I went to Oman. In meetings, I mentioned to Dr. Zawawi the concept of a children's hospital for cancer treatment. I reiterated the needs-based location in the South in Basrah, not far from Oman. Dr. Zawawi said that this seemed to be exactly the sort of project that regional countries could get behind in support of helping suffering Iraqis. He prefaced his remarks with the statement that Oman had not found the US invasion of Iraq to have been a good option. But, the USA was now there. As a medical doctor, he was acutely aware of the deficiencies in pediatric care and noted that Oman had an excellent team of Iraqi doctors who had moved there during the Saddam years. Dr. Zawawi noted that with Laura Bush and Condoleezza Rice as patrons, the BCH project clearly had high-level support, which gave it the necessary credibility for outside assistance and he would convey these thoughts to His Majesty the Sultan along with some thoughts where Oman might be of help.

Upon my return to DC, I briefed the Secretary and Dr. Howe who immediately said he would follow up with specific proposal for nurses training in Oman for Dr. Zawawi. In addition, Howe asked he might meet with Dr. Zawawi when the latter came to Washington in May. The Omanis kept their word and came back with a commitment to train in Muscat any Iraqi nurses slated for BCH. They also allocated $500,000 toward the effort along with the promise to continue the process even after the hospital opens, so that the quality of nursing keeps improving.

The actual construction by Bechtel commenced in April 2005 with extensive excavation and site preparation. Bechtel said it was going to move forward on a fast track to completion scheduled for March 2006, then adjusted to September 2006. When I mentioned the date to hospital experts in the USA, they were amazed at the notion that a new full-fledged pediatric oncology facility in a war zone could be stood up that fast. Three to five years was given as the more reasonable time frame for a new 100-bed hospital to be built and fully equipped before doors could open to patients.

Basrah, which had been quiescent after the US invasion and even after the insurgency spread to many areas of the North, began to spiral into violence in the summer of 2005. Competing militia violence and political assassinations became a regular and increasing challenge for the UK forces in control of the region. The deteriorating security environment led to more delay as Bechtel seemed unprepared to carry out its commitment citing the difficulty of construction in a war zone. USAID's deputy Jim Kunder reported that by October 2005 meetings on BCH had begun to include military security in addition to Bechtel and Project HOPE. As the primary US contractor, Bechtel seemed unable to find appropriate foreign sub-contractors who would then employ the local work force. By this point, labor and materials cost surged by approximately 40%. And this meant more funds needed to be found. Bechtel's senior management noted that as security threats increased, their capacity to provide on-site protection for the contractor staff declined. By spring 2006, Iraqi Army units began to replace the British contingent in Iraq, and Bechtel felt increasingly more exposed.

The Directorate of Health in Basrah had begun to identify several possible candidates for the BCH Senior Executive Leadership Group for consideration by the MOH in Baghdad. The selection of candidates in Iraq remained highly centralized, and the Saddam model for governance was not yet dismantled. USAID also began looking for potential funds remaining from Iraqi reconstruction accounts to fill the gap caused by security and construction delays. Further, integration of all of the complex project details required the assistance of trained medical specialists who had to be paid to create a plan for smooth delivery of a new state-of-the-art functioning hospital. Construction was ongoing, and progress was being made in laying the foundation slabs. However, high water levels in Basrah made foundation work costly as 1300 concrete pilings needed to be installed, causing another six month delay and costing an additional $1.4 million.

The work to build support continued. Laura Bush and Secretary Rice were keynote speakers at an extremely well organized and attended Gala hosted by Project HOPE on October 18, 2005, in Washington. Condi was introduced by John Howe, and she referred back to the genesis of the project, noting that: "After decades of neglect under Saddam's brutal dictatorship, the challenges that confront Iraq's health system are great and so are the medical needs of Iraq's children." She went on to note that BCH had come together as a combined effort involving the White House, Project HOPE, Iraq's MOH, USAID, and the medical community. Rice termed BCH as, "this important humanitarian effort that truly reflects the generosity of America."

In her remarks, Laura Bush noted that Rice "came to see me when she was serving as the National Security Advisor in the White House and ... asked me to join her in this effort to bring a children's hospital to Iraq. I immediately wanted to be a part of that." She went on to thank Rice for her involvement with BCH as Secretary of State, "even in the midst of the many responsibilities you have." The Gala took place shortly after the Iraqi election, and Rice and Bush noted their excitement that Iraqi parents had hope for their future in a democratic Iraq, where "a new generation would see democracy." Mrs. Bush summarized the need for a cancer-specialized pediatric facility given the great need and continued suffering by asking: "Imagine your child being desperately ill and the best care available is halfway around the world." She stressed that BCH would help Iraqi healthcare needs "through generations of children by training future doctors and nurses in critical care pediatrics."[4] She ended on a note of thanks to BCH supporters conveying her deep gratitude as well as that of the president for making BCH possible.

NOTES

1. T. Christian Miller and Johanna Neuman, "Politics Questioned in Hospital Plan: Proposed Children's Facility in Iraq is Backed by First Lady and Linked to a Bush Family Friend," *Los Angeles Times*, February 24, 2004.
2. Ibid.
3. James Peake, Project HOPE paper, delivered, June 15, 2006.
4. Remarks at the Project HOPE Gala, Andrew W. Mellon auditorium, Washington, DC, October 18, 2005.

CHAPTER 39

The Big Picture

By May 2006, USAID estimated that the hospital was 33 percent complete and some $16 million had been accrued in expense. USAID, the oversight provider for BCH, found the situation difficult both because of the prevailing security environment and because of Bechtel International's demobilization. Bechtel now seemed interested in ending its relationship with USAID. In May 2006, USAID halted construction, and HOPE put donor contributions on hold. As official US government efforts came to a halt, the Basrah community surrounding the hospital site swung into action. Large numbers holding signs stood at the site calling for a resumption of construction. From the outset, the BCH model had invited the community to become a part of the effort. Clearly, that had worked, and Iraqi mothers who would stand guard under declining security were a testament to the enormous need for pediatric oncology and their sense of being stakeholders in BCH. Such local zeal and enthusiasm was a first for American engagement in Iraq.

With the support of the Iraqi MOH and local political, religious, and health leaders, the USA switched construction responsibility to the US Army Corps of Engineers (USACE) in July 2006. That was the one institution that had the capacity and the willingness to construct the hospital and was able to handle the security issues both to protect the site and its workers. For a two-month period, USAID shared the mutual lead with USACE. However, in October 2006, USACE assumed program lead for BCH and signed an MOU with HOPE. At that time, the residence building was nearly complete. The sewer lines had been laid. Some

400 construction workers were on site along with 30 supervisors. Some 100 security workers were on site, and construction was 30 percent complete. By November 2006, the concrete structure for the hospital was to be completed. As usual, these updates were shared with the secretary and the First Lady's office.

Public funding was a key to the construction of BCH. As such, accountability and oversight for all US efforts in Iraq's reconstruction were legislated. Congress appointed a Special Inspector General for Iraq (SIGIR) to provide an assessment of how the money allocated to Iraq reconstruction ($18.7 billion in 2004) had fared. The $50 million for BCH also came under scrutiny, especially given the visibility of Laura Bush and Condoleezza Rice, who lent their respective names to the effort.

At the same time, the American agenda in the Middle East was under pressure. The battle for Lebanon raged, and the two-state solution articulated by Bush seemed to recede ever further. While Rice attempted to be a peacemaker in the Middle East, her job to broker one within the inner circle of the NSC seemed even more demanding.[1] During August 2006 Israeli bombing of Lebanon, the Bush administration was being accused in the Muslim world of refusing to reign in the Olmert government. With all this activity in train, we continued to strain to work out the myriad issues accompanying BCH.

The Stuart Bowen report on Iraqi reconstruction effort by the USA and its failings came out in July 2006. Bowen, as SIGIR,[2] aimed special criticism at USAID. As we worked to tighten oversight, an assessment team went to Iraq and sought an alternative partner to replace USAID on the public side of the effort. Project HOPE remained as the private partner for equipping the hospital and training its administrative and medical staff.

Constant internal squabbling had, if anything, made us more able and determined to deal with criticisms. All of the BCH team was aware that the project was worthy of American support and that it carried two very important patrons: Laura Bush and Condi Rice. USAID incurred a great deal of criticism in failing to provide adequate oversight for the full $1.4 billion under its purview, of which only a small fraction, namely $50 million, was for BCH. Unusual though it was for USAID to respond positively to criticism, it did try to change the model for contracting by asking its partners to utilize fewer layers of subcontractors, employ larger number of Iraqis, and generally speed up construction. Also, USAID officers in Iraq were pushed to coordinate better in the field, and a direct link with the Army Corps of Engineers was established for security issues in Basrah.

The neocon chief of staff to the first lady, McBride, made life difficult, leaving endless nasty messages pointing to the media coverage of the criticisms levied in the SIGIR report[3] and getting petty about the number of her phone calls to various State Department offices that went unreturned. I had, once again, to pass on all the relevant phone numbers for any future queries, along with a reminder that, as the State Department Spokesman, Sean McCormack had said in his briefing to the press, that BCH issues involved security, and that working in what had become a war zone meant additional effort was needed for the site. Nonetheless "we believe there is a need for it, The Iraqi government continues to believe that there's a need for it... it will save the lives of many children."[4] However, it was clear that we needed to sort out the priorities and see how the funding gap could be met. Approaching international sources would add to the partnership for BCH. The reality was that the American invasion of Iraq, with the exception of the active coalition, remained highly unpopular abroad.

As I talked to various colleagues at the State Department, including Dan Fried and Narissa Cook of the European bureau, I got a sense of which European countries might be amenable to providing help. Normally, one of these would have been Spain because it had hosted the October 2003 Madrid Donor Conference, where the USA and others had pledged to help rebuild Iraq after the war. But Spain rapidly opted out of helping once the conservative Prime Minister, Jose Maria Aznar, was defeated at the polls in 2004. This was specially the case because Aznar's defeat had been occasioned, in large measure, due to his support for the American invasion of Iraq and his close dealings with Bush. With some 92% of Spain voicing opposition to the war, the newly elected socialist party Prime Minister, Rodriguez Zapatero, quickly made it known that Spain would henceforth not be a member of "the coalition of the willing" and withdrew all of Spain's contributions to the American venture in Iraq. The Bush White House was less than pleased, and Zapatero found himself frozen out. There were no invitations to the White House, and Rice, along with senior members of the US government, were loathe to go to Madrid. However, in June 2005, Eduardo Aguirre was appointed US Ambassador to Spain. A Spanish–speaking native of Houston, Texas, Aguirre wanted to re-connect the two countries and was a dynamic US Ambassador in Madrid. In the course of my official travel, I went to Spain in March 2006 to discuss UN Reform and had a number of meetings with leaders. Ambassador Aguirre was a gracious host. He expressed sensitivity to the fact that Spain had political issues, and a new reality obtained. Yet, despite the departure of Aznar, who had been close to President Bush, he felt that deep down even the new Prime Minister, Zapatero, wanted to move forward. I promised to convey this hopeful message to Rice and did so upon my return.

USACE resumed construction of BCH on October 6, 2006, and the pace of construction picked up. Neighboring countries, Kuwait, Oman, UAE, Jordan, and Egypt, came forward to help in what everyone said was an important American legacy effort in Iraq. There were still no takers in Europe where money for assisting Iraq after the invasion had been pledged but not delivered. Thinking back to my Madrid meetings, I felt perhaps we should request Ambassador Aguirre's assistance. The Ambassador's response was quick and positive. He asked that we send details on the project and what would be helpful as coming from Spain. He hoped that Zapatero's Spain would come through for BCH as "this is exactly the sort of project they are looking for."

European bureau colleagues as well as Wendi Dick, then-Iraq desk officer, were excited and helpful in transmitting the requisite details including the criticism that had become public regarding the delays and cost increases and how we were working to meet them. In early August 2006, the USA responded to the requirement for a possible Spanish role in BCH by forwarding all the information needed, including the fact that BCH was still a high priority for both the USA and the people of southern Iraq and that Laura Bush and Secretary Rice hoped for an early completion.[5] The project required an additional $67.4 million, and Congress was being notified of plans to reprogram $45.5 million from the unspent funds available; that the USA appreciated Spain's consideration of the remaining $22 million gap, and its possible provision before the September 30, 2006 Iraq Relief and Reconstruction (IRRF) deadline. The USA promised to work with Spain to identify the best use of the money even if the allocation came through after September 30 since additional needs would surely remain.

The good news finally came in the course of a visit to Madrid on October 18, 2006, by the Deputy Secretary of the Treasury, Robert Kimmitt. Spain's Foreign Minister Miguel Angel Moratinos told Kimmitt that Spain strongly supported Iraq's compact[6] and would disburse some $22 million for BCH. Subsequent to this announcement, the foreign minister received a letter of thanks from Laura Bush. The money was pledged to come for the hospital through the UNDP (WHO was an alternate if the money was to be used for equipment) as Spanish rules precluded a handover for the construction directly to the US government. Spain stipulated that the funds for BCH would come via the UNDP—Iraq Trust Fund. This was not a simple "pass-through" of funds, but rather a complex system requiring multiple approvals, accounting, and audits.

Even as we celebrated Madrid's contribution, we worked to see how the money could be utilized effectively in a timely fashion avoiding UN bureaucratic hurdles. BCH was a new sort of engagement for UNDP, but they were willing to see how they could accommodate mechanisms aimed at moving the effort rapidly. Then, there was the issue of the normal 6.25 percent fee that UNDP typically charged for its management services, and $2 million was deducted by UNDP for its services for BCH. We provided details of the construction needs for BCH. UNDP, Iraqi Strategic Resources board (ISRB), GRD, Midcon (contractor), USACE, Project HOPE, and Iraq's MOH began to work out the details for receiving Spanish funds and disbursement of the same through a mechanism set up in Amman, Jordan. Over a two-week period, UNDP Amman worked with Iraqi and US offices to create a Project Document creating positive interactions between the UNDP Iraq and BCH partners. Community involvement in Basrah led to support from local sheikhs, which was significant as the competing militias were ever-present in the daily life of Basrah, once a quiet city.

State Department experts on Iraq reconstruction management along with colleagues at the American embassy in Madrid worked diligently to get questions answered and helped obtain the Spanish contribution. Ambassador Aguirre kept his promise to push for an opening for Spain in terms of funding for BCH in Iraq. The discussions over Madrid's $22 million contribution to BCH had positive reverberation beyond the money. First, it allowed us to make the case that even previously reluctant countries were forthcoming for a project worthy of support, such as BCH, in Iraq, and leverage that for engagement by other countries. Second, given that Secretary Rice was a strong supporter of the Basrah hospital, the fact that the Zapatero government committed itself to funding at a time when it was critical, meant that a thaw in the previously chilly relationship was beginning. The State Department announced on May 21, 2007 that Rice would visit Madrid for meetings with the foreign minister, her first to that capital as America's top diplomat. When the press asked why it had taken so long, the press spokesman, Sean McCormack noted: "Every relationship has some bumps in the road, but you work through those in a respectful way and try to build up mutual understanding so you don't talk past one another."[7]

Help also came from one of Iraq's neighbors: Kuwait. The gift was all the more poignant given that Saddam had invaded Kuwait in 1990. In early 2007, Rima Al-Sabah, the wife of the Kuwaiti Ambassador, known for the patronage of causes considered important, offered to host an exclusive gala titled "Healing for Peace" to raise funds for BCH. She worked with John Howe to find the best ways funds could be added to those pledged for equipment and training by Project HOPE. The first issue was to find a date when Laura Bush and Condoleezza Rice were available to attend. We found March 7, 2007 worked for both. The invitation noted that the gala was in support of the Basrah Children's Hospital termed an "extremely important humanitarian initiative desperately needed to address childhood cancer." The host then put together a spectacular event where major corporate donors[8] gave generously to attend. It was designed as a small event and thus became much in demand since it offered up Laura Bush, Secretary Rice, Ambassador of Iraq Samir Al-Samadaie,[9] Chief of Staff Josh Bolten, several congressional and cabinet members, and so many senior White House officials that the emcee for the evening, television's Charlie Rose, quipped: "I could do my show from here for the next two years. ... I just wonder who is having dinner with the President tonight!"

I updated Secretary Rice on BCH progress and problems on May 30, 2007, just prior to her Madrid stop. Given continued instability in Iraq Laura Bush's office was always partnered in all updates to Condi. In order to prevent nasty surprises for the bosses, we felt it important that the top was always kept informed of both problems and progress. I recall that mid-2007 brought us to the 50% completion point for construction, and that 700–900 workers were on site daily and there had been as many as eight Iraqi ministers of health thus far. In addition, USACE was working hard, both to coordinate with UNDP and to retain the support of the community in order to enhance security at the site and the surrounding area.

Project HOPE continued its training of the medical staff including nurses and administrators. Brigadier General (retired) William Fox, a veteran of American operations in Iraq, Kuwait, and Afghanistan, was hired by HOPE upon his retirement from the command of the Great Plains Regional Medical Command and Brooke Army Medical Center in San Antonio, Texas. Fox was familiar with the complexities of the region and was an ideal addition to the Project HOPE team when he came on as Executive Vice President and CEO. He worked with the US team on BCH as we continued to sift through complicated issues in Washington, Baghdad, and Basrah. He traveled to the site which even in 2008 required security escorts. On one of his visits in early 2008, General Fox was badly injured when his vehicle hit an Improvised Explosive Device (IED). He was evacuated to Frankfurt and then back to the USA with multiple serious injuries requiring prolonged recovery and rehabilitation. It was a testament to John Howe and Project HOPE in general that despite this immense setback, the effort continued unabated.

The US administration changed in January 2009 as the Bush baton was passed to the Obama administration. Gratefully, the BCH construction stayed on course. The opening date slipped some largely because of the inevitable delays associated with coordination, execution, and connections for water and electricity from Basrah authorities. Throughout the tenure of nine health ministers, each reiterated the need for the hospital and Iraq's commitment to getting it completed and maintained for the future at a cost of some $15–20 million in annual operations. Project HOPE continued its training and equipping role. The promise of the Sultan of Oman to help with nurses training into the future buoyed the prospects of the advanced nature of the pediatric hospital as envisioned.

Construction was completed in June 2010. Connection to the main electricity grid, water, and sewage was finalized. By August 2010, even the press began to mention the unique success that BCH represented. Noting that as the USA draws down in Iraq, "it is leaving behind hundreds of abandoned or incomplete projects. More than $5 billion in American taxpayer funds has been wasted, more than 10 percent of the $50 billion the U.S. spent on reconstruction in Iraq." The report went on to note that: "By contrast, the Basra[h] children's hospital, one of the largest projects undertaken in Iraq,[10] looks like a shining success story."[11] On September 26, 2010, BCH initiated a phased "soft opening" with general radiology services, pharmacy, laboratory, and dental clinic opening up for outpatient service. The following week, October 5, 2010, oncology patients from the local Basrah Maternity and Children's Hospital began to transfer to the BCH oncology ward.

October 21, 2010 saw the opening ceremony of the Basrah Children's Hospital. The regional and local authorities came together with strong support of the governor, the religious authorities, and the community to celebrate the completion. Dr. Ahmed Al Shawny, Director of BCH, represented the hospital; US Ambassador Peter Bode represented the State Department; USACE, Iraq's Minister of Health and Basrah Governor, represented the government of Iraq; and Colonel Frederick Gerber Project HOPE's Country Director for Iraq represented the private partner. Some of the other donors were also present. In his remarks, Bode noted the high collaboration between the public and private partners of the project along with other countries and Iraqi health and political leaders that brought BCH to fruition. More work needed to be done, and Iraq must go on to fulfill its pledges to make this a center of excellence.

Dr. Janan Hasan of BCH noted that Iraq's first specialist cancer hospital for children was built in its neediest location because in the years since 1993, Basrah province has seen a sharp rise in childhood cancer. "Leukemia among children under 15 has increased about four times."[12] Thus, this "hospital is a very important achievement, and I thank everyone who helped build it." Brigadier General Randal Dragon, Deputy Commander for Support of the US Army base in Basrah, noted: "This project will have a capability to serve the people of Iraq and its children for many years to come. From that perspective, all of us should be proud and hope that this project will pay big dividends."[13]

Laura Bush and Condoleezza Rice each sent a letter addressed to all supporters of the hospital. They were read out at the opening ceremony celebrating the "lifesaving work of this hospital"[14] noting the "sacrifice of the American men and women in uniform–as well as their partners at the State Department and Project HOPE–to see this project come to fruition." Of special mention was "extraordinary commitment of Iraqi nurses, doctors and medical professionals who will soon fill its halls." Finally, the "leadership of the Government of Iraq in this effort and its burgeoning institutions, particularly the Iraqi Ministry of Health, should be celebrated as its officials deliver much-needed medical services to the country's children."[15]

Here then is an example of a much needed reconstruction effort in Iraq which succeeded. This was largely due to the fact that Iraqis were made partners as committed stakeholders from the beginning. And all of us who played a role and dealt with a mountain of problems for over six years in a war zone take a great deal of comfort in what was achieved as we hope that the progress continues into the future. The commitment of the Government of Iraq is a key to BCH remaining a beacon for cancer treatment for Iraqi children and as a much needed pediatric center of excellence into the future.

Toward the end of 2014, the Governor of Basrah, the Chairman of the Provincial Council, and the city's planning committee confirmed their funding to construct, staff, and equip a Pediatric Hematology wing adjacent to the existing BCH at a cost of $25–30 million. The center is expected to provide treatment for the majority of pediatric blood disorders and cancers, except for bone marrow transplant.

The current commitment by the Government of Iraq and the regional authorities in Basrah to maintain a high standard for the USA-built hospital and to commit its own $18 million a year for operating costs of the hospital is a testament that the USA built a worthy institution of lasting value even in an unpopular war. The fact that the Iraqis are now expanding the facility to add a pediatric Hematology wing to BCH is a tribute to what the USA built in the 2004–2010 period. As Condoleezza Rice, who gave unstintingly of her support notes: "It is really heartening to see what the hospital has become."

For all who lent their name and support to the building of BCH, it is indeed heartening that discussions between Project HOPE, the Governor's office, and the Basrah Medical University indicate ongoing strong support for BCH, renamed Basrah Children's Specialty Hospital (BCSH). They note that as the only dedicated pediatric cancer hospital in Iraq, BCSH is highly sought after by interns, residents, and fellows as a training location.

My own dream of American assistance worthy of USA which I focused on during a traffic jam outside Philadelphia thus became a reality in 2010. So many wonderful colleagues from so many countries turned the idea into the reality of healing. And Iraqi children began to receive treatment to battle cancer. It was gracious of Condi to note my proposal to her for building the Basrah Children's Hospital in her memoir of her Washington Years.[16] As I left the US government and my last assignment on January 17, 2009, and headed for a quiet period in New Mexico, I was indeed grateful to have thought of and helped build the Basrah Children's Hospital.

Notes

1. Helene Cooper, "Rice's Hurdles on Middle East Begin at Home," *New York Times*, August 10, 2006.
2. Appointed by Congress to provide oversight of the appropriated funds for Iraq. The SIGIR report also meant summons on August 17, 2006, for USAID to speak to Senate and House staff on priorities, problems with BCH and whether given deteriorating security in Basrah it made sense to "mothball" the project. The old debate on health clinics versus a hospital surfaced again, but no one asked how well the clinics had fared. USG briefers noted that BCH had the strong support of the Governor of Basrah as well as that of the community who agitated to continue work on BCH to completion.
3. James Glanz, "Audit Finds U.S. Hid Actual Cost of Iraq Projects," *New York Times*, July 30, 2006; and Lisa Myers, *NBC Nightly News*, August 2, 2006.
4. Daily Press Briefing, Department of State, Washington, DC, July 30, 2006.
5. I recall one on February 15, 2005, where Andrew Natsios reported that Bechtel (the design-build contractor) noted increased security costs along with price escalation for the project.
6. Spain pledged $300 million for Iraq's needs at the Madrid conference of 2003. Of that amount, Spain noted that it disbursed $160 million in 2003–2004; $62 million in 2005; allocated $77.5 million for Iraq in 2007, but no Spanish business wanted to go to Iraq, and the money remained undisbursed, except for the $22 million pledged and delivered by Spain to BCH.
7. Reuters, "Rice set to Make Fence-Mending Trip to Spain," May 21, 2007.
8. Chevron, The Dow Chemical Company, ExxonMobil, Shell Oil Company, CONOCO, Kuwait Petroleum Corporation, Valero, and others contributed through the Kuwait–America Foundation some $2 million for Project Hope's use for BCH.
9. The Iraqi Ambassador noted that the evening proceeds will be donated to "Project HOPE to assist in the development the Basrah children's Hospital, which will administer care to Iraq's ailing children, and especially those with cancer...Iraq's future lies in the hands of its children; they are Iraq's most valuable resource. It is my hope that in helping to heal Iraq's children, Project HOPE will help Iraq's children to heal Iraq."
10. Yet, costing $100 million of US funds out of a total of $50 billion committed to reconstruction projects by the USA in Iraq.

11. Kim Gamel, Associated Press, August 30, 2010; and *The Daily Beast*, August 29, 2010.
12. Some of the reasons for the high incidence of cancer remain as they were when Basrah was chosen as the site in 2003: industrial pollution including high chemical pollution from nearby oil wells and Basrah's frontline location in three wars including the 1980–1988 conflict with Iran and the use of chemical weapons by Saddam Hussein in 1991 to put down the Shiite uprising in the south.
13. Anwar Faruqi, "Iraq City with Soaring Child Cancer Rates Gets New Hospital," AFP, October 22, 2010.
14. Letter from Laura Bush, October 19, 2010.
15. Letter from Condoleezza Rice, October 19, 2010.
16. Condoleezza Rice, *No Higher Honor: A Memoir of My Years in Washington* (New York: Crown Publishers, 2011).

CHAPTER 40

Women's Empowerment

As Secretary of State, Condoleezza Rice established the first ever office for Women's Empowerment with an Ambassador in charge as an integral part of her own office of Secretary of State. She did not scream from rooftops about her work for that part of her portfolio, but it was substantial. Given that Rice came from a national security background and embodied women's empowerment, her showing the flag as a Secretary of State drew plaudits around the world. For example, the Women Leaders Working Group was set up with nineteen ministers, and heads of government, including notable ones like Ellen Johnson Sirleaf, president of Liberia. Within two years, the group grew to sixty-four. Its work included coordination and leadership, especially meetings with newly appointed Secretary General of the UN Ban Ki-moon for including women in UN senior ranks and as special representatives of the Secretary General.

The group's ministerial, including in New York, Vienna, and Athens, respectively, brought together for the first time to discuss education, political empowerment, justice, and economic opportunity for women ministers from the Arab states and the foreign minister of Israel, Tzipi Livni. Without any rancor, they worked alongside.

The State Department under Secretary Rice and with her present in the chair along with Justice Sandra Day O'Connor launched the Women and Justice Program that brought together senior justices from Africa to discuss best practices and create a network. Access to justice for women was a key component of the effort and ways in which we could partner to promote the same.

© The Author(s) 2018
S. Tahir-Kheli, *Before the Age of Prejudice*,
https://doi.org/10.1007/978-981-10-8551-2_40

I went to India as part of my work and met with the senior officials in charge of the police training programs, including Kiran Bedi. With them helping, we launched a contingent of all women peacekeepers deployed in Liberia. Within six months of their deployment, as told to me by the foreign minister of Liberia, attacks on women declined by a third, reporting of violence against women doubled, and Liberian women started to apply for police work.

On June 19, 2008, Secretary Rice chaired a UN Security Council meeting (which made this a ministerial from all member countries and the attorney general of the UK), which adopted UNSC Resolution 1820. That resolution, passed unanimously, made rape and other forms of sexual violence a "potential act against humanity or a constitutive act with respect to genocide." Strict training of peacekeepers was imposed to bring down horrendous acts against the most vulnerable in zones of conflict. The resolution called for prosecution of violators who went to conflict zones as peacekeepers but sanctioned or perpetrated sexual violence.

As we flew with the Secretary on her plane on June 19, 2008, final negotiations with some of the member states of the UN for the passage of the resolution were still ongoing. Over a period of months, in Washington, New York and in world capitals, we had negotiated the resolution. We wanted something robust that laid benchmarks for behavior and for follow-up by the UN. The need all acknowledged was great. Several conflicts in Africa and elsewhere led to major reports of sexual violence against women in these areas. While UNSCR passage was no guarantor of cessation of sexual violence, the absence of internationally sanctioned penalties made subsequent accountability for violators impossible. All states needed to sign on to prevention of sexual violence. It was time to act. Condoleezza Rice showing the flag for the effort was important to its success. Secretary Rice presided over the Security Council in the month of June 2008 (in accordance with with the procedures for a rotating presidency). High-level attendance for the passage of the resolution meant high-level attention to a critical issue for women.

As we boarded the plane at Andrews AFB for the short flight up to New York on June 19, 2008, I received a call from my colleague Alex Wolf who was the Ambassador in charge at the US Mission to the UN. Alex had worked alongside all of us pushing for a robust resolution and we had made considerable headway. We wanted to have unanimous passage as a signal that Women's Empowerment was a uniting, not a divisive, issue. Alex told me that the Russians wanted more changes even as the session was due to start very soon. "Let me talk to the Secretary here on the plane" I told him. I went up the plane to Condi's private office and brought her up to date. "What do you recommend?" she asked knowing that the Russian negative vote constituted a veto which meant all the work was for naught. "I think we should call the Russians on it," I advised, fully aware of the consequence of my advice. "You should give the U.S. statement and call for a vote. Let the Russians veto a resolution calling for prevention of sexual violence against women in conflict zones."

"Let's do that" was Condi's affirmation. I called Alex back and asked that we close the negotiation with no more time for changes that weaken the resolution.

As the Secretary's motorcade sped through Manhattan (a side benefit of these hurried trips), I was excited that we were going to make such an important commitment from the international community on a grave matter. As we entered the Security Council chamber, I noted that never had I seen it more packed. Senior women leaders from around the world were present and the energy in the room was amazing. The US delegation took its assigned seat with Rice at the podium. I sat right behind her. I noticed a minor commotion in the area where the Russians sat. They were looking for signals from Ambassador Alex Wolf that they had some diplomatic wiggle room on the resolution before us. We sat poker faced behind the American Secretary of State. UN Secretary General Moon was nearby.

Condi gave the US statement on why we were all gathered and why the resolution before us mattered. Always a good speaker, Rice held everyone's attention. She then called for a vote with a show of hands and proudly raised hers to cast the US vote in favor.

I held my breath as I looked to other delegation's show of hands. The Russian Ambassador's hand was also up! We got unanimous passage of UNSCR 1820.

On the plane journey back to Washington that afternoon, Condi and all of us were more relaxed. She seemed particularly pleased. Her chief of staff who had to block off her time for the day despite other items vying for her attention also was happy. Personally, I knew of Condi's commitment to Women's Empowerment. Using that support for her legacy on full international display was worthwhile and enjoyable.

In the last days of my work at State in December 2008, I helped Hillary Clinton's staff Melanne Verveer understand the work at State where she was inexperienced. I also mentioned that Rice in her outgoing meeting with Hillary had said that we had built on the latter's work as first lady. We hoped she would do the same to support our efforts on Women's Empowerment. I conveyed that I was told that Clinton was touched and agreed with the sentiment. I guided Melanne through the thicket of foreign policy, not her forte as former chief of staff to the first lady. I also gave her bureaucratic tips and handed over my physical office space.

Hillary's transition head, Wendy Sherman, who went on to become the number three at the department, noted to me when I ran into her at State in the C Street Lobby that Melanne had told her about all the help she got from me. "Of course, it's my duty and I am happy to help" was my reply. Melanne did write me a note of thanks. However, to my utter disappointment and contrary to my urgings that women's empowerment remain a bipartisan issue in the Clinton State Department, Verveer's response essentially was: "We Democrats own women," an unfortunate mindset for the women of America and women of the world.

CHAPTER 41

Reflections

I have been fortunate to have lived an extraordinary life. There are several contributing factors.

The most important, perhaps, was watching my parents make the massive transition from India to Pakistan and live out what could have been trauma with grace, joy, and purpose. That early lesson gave me a sense of adventure, even fearlessness. Moving to the USA or moving to Albuquerque in New Mexico without friends or family and making a life was thus possible and enjoyable. In the final months of Mama's life, as I spent the time talking to her and sitting endless hours with her and Baba as we read the Arabic version of the Quran with Baba's translations, we finally had a chance to look back at the decades past, our family history and the changes planned and unplanned that altered our destiny. "Why did you leave Hyderabad, India, and the settled life," I asked him. The answer from my father was a simple one: he was asked to serve a new nation and help bring it education and science.

"Did you know what you would be giving up in terms of your position in India, your place in Hyderabad society, your house, bank accounts etc.?" Without a moment of hesitation, Baba responded: "Saying no to helping Pakistan was not an option. No one thought of what they were leaving, only of what they could contribute to a new nation."

I have often wondered if my parents realized that the divide between India and Pakistan would go so deep and last so long. All their lives, they lived above the fray of hostility and continued to build bridges between India and Pakistan. That was an early lesson.

Underlying the desire to study a world away in the mid-western USA and the total belief that it would work out were typical of the fearlessness of youth. The option of getting to do that was my parents' trust that that their daughter, even at fifteen, was sufficiently grounded that they could let her go far away and know she would do the right thing.

Looking back, I see my willingness to be open and take chances as setting the trajectory of my life. I consider the milestones as the choice of the USA for university, my marriage, my return to the USA, joining the US Army War College faculty on a year–long fellowship and the opening to work on defense issues there. What followed—years of service at the White House in dream jobs that I never applied for—was humbling as well as profoundly satisfying.

Academia gave me a base. I was picky about jobs and bosses. It is important to have a specialization which grounds one. A Ph.D. is critical to establishing one's credentials even though it is not a guarantor of satisfying employment.

The freedom to speak one's mind, when based on knowledge of issues and people, made my time in government productive. I give the same advice to young students who seek a public service career. It is important to know what you stand for and what you propose as options to policy makers when your time is there. To understand the "why" of your recommendation is important. Particularly as there are other viewpoints vying for attention at the same time. In the end, I feel my willingness to walk away from any job rather than settle for the minimum acceptable decision allowed me freedom to work and to live with dignity. I always took my father's advice: "If you are educated and hard-working, remember you can work anywhere."

After having been a part of the American fabric for more than fifty-eight years, assimilation is internalized. Yet, in this age of controversy and conflict about what it means to be an American and what it means to be a Muslim in America, it is important to discuss how we as Muslims lived our lives here as citizens and parents.

Starting with my university years in 1959, I witnessed the decency and welcome of America. When I came back for the 1962–1964 years, I was part of an academic grounding with exceptional and warm people who became lifelong friends. When Raza and I returned to the USA in 1966, we were already parents of a baby daughter. We were later blessed with the birth of our son, who was born in Philadelphia. We knew that we were not going back to live in Pakistan. Our future was America. But we were and wanted our daughter and son to be proud of their heritage even as we embraced our new country of choice. An academic calendar meant that our summers were free to work and live in different places. Raza's place in Physics took us all over the world for summers where we lived in mostly university surroundings be they Oxford, Paris, Ljubljana, Trieste, Recife/Rio de Janeiro, and Stuttgart. Then, there was time spent with our parents in Pakistan for part of each summer as both children were growing up.

Pakistan offered not only the care and love of grandparents for my children but also exposure to a completely different milieu. Child care included spoiling in households where staff was present which meant needed relief for this multitasking mother. The trips to Raza's ancestral villages along the river Indus set in verdant valleys, and fruit orchards were stunning. Family members and younger cousins thought our kids exotic even as ours were intrigued by differences in experiences. Bonds were renewed each successive year. But year after year during the formative phase of our children's growth, as we landed at John F. Kennedy airport in New York close to the end of summer and the start of the school/university year, all of us in the family shared a sense of homecoming.

By the time our daughter entered high school, we felt we had somehow managed to make our children citizens of the world in that they could be comfortable anywhere. However, they were absolutely American. And, they and we were proud of it. Why else would we choose to live here if not to participate fully on an equal footing with everyone else? We were educated and came from backgrounds rich in culture so we could make a go of it anywhere. By coming to the USA, becoming citizens and joining in the American dream, we found fulfillment. Even though ours was not a rags-to-riches version of the American story, it is nonetheless a truly American story.

Religion had always been a private issue in our own upbringing. Neither Raza nor I felt any need to change the focus with our own daughter and son even as each was given a "Bismillah" experience. Raza, a Pathan, came from the Northwest frontier area of Pakistan which before partition had Hindu and Sikh neighbors. I grew up in Hyderabad, India, before coming to Peshawar. My parent's circle of friends, and mine, was not confined to any one religion. My years as an undergraduate at Ohio Wesleyan University cemented ties across religions. In any case, even if we had felt the need, which we did not, there were no community centers in Philadelphia of the early 1960s where we would haul our children on the weekend. Religion and values were taught at home and practiced in a quiet personal manner.

Public service offered me a perfect way of connecting with people and making America home. There were obviously more lucrative professions in this land of opportunity. From childhood I witnessed grandfathers and father enjoy respect and satisfaction in giving back. That was the compass, and it served me well.

I remain convinced of the power of friendship in shaping my world. Family and friends have been the anchors of my life. They multiplied the joys and shared the sorrows.

Our choice of friends and lifestyle was shaped by our place as academics. Raza was a professor of Physics, and I was a graduate student at the University of Pennsylvania, where our 1962–1964 stint had already given us friendships with extraordinary people that continue to this day. When I received my Ph.D., I was the mother of two. It was an active life, and there was a great deal of work, travel, and socializing. Our friends invited us into their homes, and we reciprocated. Cuisine and culture were our entry points, and there was appreciation on both counts. We had a sense of belonging from the very start. As I look back, a lot of that had to do with the ease of friendships based on professional links with Physics but developed through a great deal of give and take over meals shared and children growing up together in the same school system.

Of particular note in our early married life in Philadelphia are several who all were initially based at the University of Pennsylvania. Central among them were Anna and Bob Schrieffer; Ruth and Alan Heeger; and Pat and Don Langenberg. Over the years, we pledged to meet up at New Years in different cities across the USA. Only later did I focus on how illustrious the group was: two Nobel Laureates Bob Schrieffer in Physics; Alan Heeger in Chemistry; and one University Chancellor, Don Langenberg. Through good times and tough times, we remain a tight group suffering loss such as the death of Anna Schrieffer, a most glamorously beautiful Danish woman. We were having a dinner party where these friends were present in a multicourse French meal that evening in 1972 when we found out that Bob Schrieffer was awarded his Nobel.

Raza opened up celebratory bottles of champagne, and I still have a cork that Bob signed for me that night from one of the bottles!

Ruth and Robert Gales were New Yorkers transplanted in Philadelphia whom we met through Dilys and Saul Winegrad in 1963. Robert hailed from Detroit and was a publisher with deep knowledge of politics, jazz, and sports. I could share the first two and learn from him, especially as he personally knew so many legends of jazz. Sports left me out, so he taught me a bit about baseball but gave up on football. Ruth taught me so much of how to get along, from finding pediatricians to best locations for the multiple items that make up a household. For more than fifty-three years, she celebrated the joys of my life with me and shared the sorrows. Her generosity knew no bounds, and even in the last years of her declining health, she was important in the life of our family. Ruth vouched for me when I became a US citizen in 1971. She drove me to the hospital for the birth of my son as in the pre-cell phone days I could not reach Raza who had just left for the university. She insisted that I not give up on my Ph.D. Time and again she sat with various members of the federal investigative services when I was going through security clearances for White House and State Department jobs. My family was lucky in being part of the wonderful Thanksgiving tradition with the Gales. Besides the traditional fixings of turkey, etc., we added some flavor of the subcontinent with the addition of "pakoras" to the appetizer portion of the meal. In all, we had forty-nine Thanksgivings with Robert and Ruth.[1]

While preparing for my graduate degree, I decided that I wanted to master French sufficiently so that I could manage the sabbatical time in Paris that Raza was planning. I already was carrying the full course complement so could not add another course. However, I could "audit" a course which meant the work but not the credit. Undaunted, I looked around and found a young teaching assistant with a lovely English accent (as she was English) in the Department of French. Dilys and I connected up right away, especially since it turned out that she had been an undergraduate at Oxford at the same time as Raza although they did not know each other at the time. She too was a recent bride having married Saul Winegrad, a professor of Physiology at the University of Pennsylvania. The Winegrads visited us in Pakistan just before my daughter Shehra was born. They introduced us to Marilyn and Don Silberberg who have been a very important part of our circle of friends.

Beyond faculty friendships, others became important to our lives, including Saundra and John DiIllio (she later became a lawyer though we shared a class in the Political Science department at Penn and met in our student period and he was an outstanding architect). They too remain an important part of the family and friends circle that gave us both a sense of belonging in a country and a family.

When our family residence, my parent's house, in Islamabad, was disbanded after their deaths, I decided to find an alternative closer to Philadelphia.

In 1963, when the Morris Minor had taken us west, I was enchanted by the American Southwest. The vast empty spaces, the red rocks, and the Cowboys and Indians landscape reminded me of my childhood in Banjara Hills in Hyderabad, India, and the vastness of the rugged terrain around Peshawar in Pakistan.

In mid-1997, I received an invitation from Arian Pregenzer of the Cooperative Monitoring Center (CMC) of Sandia National Laboratories in Albuquerque New Mexico. She asked if I would speak on the Track II BALUSA effort as it was of growing interest to CMC. I accepted saying it would be great if I could combine it with the opening of the presidential library and fly into Albuquerque from Houston on that Friday for the Monday talk.

Consequently, on November 6, 1997, the George Bush Presidential Library was dedicated by the 41st President in College Station Texas on the campus of Texas A & M University. I went to the opening and the attendant festivities, which became a reunion of the White House staff and others from that time.

Just before leaving for Houston, I heard from Patricia Dickens, the most efficient and nicest administrator at CMC. She wanted flight details and offered to meet me at the airport and take me to the hotel. Patricia asked if I wanted to do anything over the weekend. I asked if she knew of a real estate agent that I could contact. Patricia told me that a colleague knew of a great realtor she would put me in touch with. Patricia and Lee Dickens continue to help make Albuquerque a home for us. Thus, I met Revonna Barber, a tall stylish woman full of mirth and knowing everything about the area. We had a few conversations about my interest in the area and the limited time I had to get a sense of potential places to buy in Albuquerque. That Saturday morning after arrival, Revonna picked me up at the hotel and talked about what I wanted to look at and why was I interested.

"This is such spectacular scenery and something about it is very evocative," I replied.

"Well, it is the 'Land of Enchantment' and we can visit a number of different options in space and price" Revonna noted. And so we set out. I mentioned that facing west toward sunsets was an absolute requirement. The setting was important, not the size, as our home would remain in Philadelphia.

Since we only had Saturday but because Revonna had done her homework following her earlier phone conversations with me, we set out to look at a number of places with views in the traditional adobe style of New Mexico. Many were spectacular.

The rationale behind the search and possible purchase was simply that I felt a sanctuary was important. While parents were alive, their house served the purpose. After them, a small place with a large view of spectacular scenery made for a desirable place for the last part of my life. This had to be an almost spiritual place close to the heart as a place for periodic habitation.[2] I found the more popular Santa Fe too self-consciously cute. Besides, given Raza's medical history, we needed a major hospital system and an airport. Toward the end of that blustery November day as suddenly snowflakes descended, Revonna asked if I was ready at that time of sunset to view something in the planning stage but not yet built. "Sure," I happily replied.

We drove into a unbuilt area in the shadow of the Sandia mountains. There was a finished road where we stopped with a twenty feet high ridge above. Casting a glance at my sandals, Revonna asked if given the light falling snow, I could walk up to the ridge. "I'm from South Asia and my feet are always hot" was my reply. We did and walked along the several city blocks length of the ridge as the sun turned everything crimson and I selected the perfect spot with the best view of the city below and Arizona in the distance. Seven small houses were to be built by a reputable builder and because Revonna was so plugged into the scene she knew of it. All sites were available so the selection was easy.

When I got back to my hotel that evening, I called Raza. "We need to buy this and have to put down a small amount as a commitment in the morning," I said. "Why do we need a house in New Mexico?" was his very understandable response. "Because it speaks to my soul," I noted. "Well then, we must get it," said Raza without missing a beat.

We drove across the east coast to the plains and then onto Albuquerque in July 1998. Crossing into New Mexico from Colorado along Interstate 25 Raza, and I loved the spectacular scenery on both sides of the road. As we got closer, I had a few moments of panic. What if the house, which we had not seen finished but simply in blueprints, was a disaster? What if Raza hated it? What if we never met anyone and lived totally isolated? We stopped for gas. I got out to stretch and ran into a very impressive tall gentleman who clearly was a Native American. He looked like a Chief of tales I read as a child. His handlers were with him, showing him great respect—he was undoubtedly a man of consequence. The chief noticed me and strode over to say "Good afternoon!" "Where were you born?" he asked me. Interesting question I thought as most simply asked "where are you from?" "I was born in India," I responded. "Oh, so you are Indian, me too!!" was the Chief's comment and he had a twinkle in his eye as he said that I should be in touch with him if I had any problems in New Mexico. I was too tongue-tied at this happenstance to come up with a clever comment or to ask for his contact information.

The chance conversation was a perfect welcome to our life in the Southwest.

Coming into town, we drove directly to Revonna's office to pick up the keys. Arrived at the house, unlocked the door with some trepidation and were thunderstruck with how perfect it was for us. Although I expected the details of the house to be as they were, what really surprised us was how expansive the view to the west and the limitless horizon. "My Sanctuary," I noted. Baba and Mama were no more, but this place reminded me of years passed in their company. They would have loved being here, enthusiasm undimmed by age.

So the pattern of fall through spring in Philadelphia, with summers in Albuquerque became the norm. The two abodes could not be more different, and we enjoyed each. Our summers in Europe or in Pakistan declined after my parent's death. We even managed a winter trip in 1998 soon after the move-in when our New Years group, named the "Pennguins" for the fact that we all began at the University of Pennsylvania. New Year's Eve in 1998–1999 was spent in Santa Fe with local cuisine and music to mark the year and celebrate the friendship. The set of friends who came understood our desire to be southwest-based during the summer months.

Revonna had shown me a local art gallery which she described as owned "by an artist of great talent who gave the gallery her name as Weems Gallery." Be sure to check it out, she said. So began my forays on each visit to Albuquerque for the distinctive art by noted artists of the region. On one such visit, I came across a painting done in oil of what looked like a sunset. The view reminded me of our view out west. "Must have it," I thought. Of course, limited budgets for public servants can put a crimp into art purchases. The person working at the gallery told me that Mary Ann Weems was the artist herself. She asked if I would like to meet the artist who was painting in her studio at the back of the gallery. "Could I?" Off went Pat, and I remembered that my hope in earlier life was to be a textile designer and paint on the side. After a lengthy interval, Pat emerged with the artist. She was impressive, and as Mary Ann herself recounts it, Pat had to work hard to get her to come out to meet me. We connected the moment we met. I realized this woman of talent was also great fun and as a native-born New Mexican (from Carlsbad in the south), my first local friend.

Along with friendship, Mary Ann gave us family in New Mexico. She offered the generosity of time, a circle of her lifelong friends and a place to call home. She introduced me to art of the Southwest which I love. She shared her group of exceptional women, especially Thelma Dominici, Judy Zanotti, and Marty Wilson. Many of these dear friends were born in New Mexico and shared either childhood or adult life friendships with Mary Ann. Patricia and Lee Dickens, Dave Davis, Rod Wilson are extremely important to our life now.

Revonna's close friend Jane Bickelman became mine as we both grieved Revonna's loss after she died of cancer just two years after we met. In subsequent years, Jane and I have traveled the Southwest in great camaraderie and friendship. She is a very special lady. These friends are all generous, fun-loving and empathetic, and extremely hospitable. They make our annual summers in New Mexico exceptional in so many arenas, especially intellectual and travel.

Throughout my life, I have had wonderful opportunities for travel. Some of it was in the course of my work in the US government. There, it was the senior colleagues in overseas governments, and what is known as "representational" meals. I saw places I might not otherwise have. Our family travels and my work as an academic scholar gave me a chance to go to places I really wanted to and meet leaders in countries I researched. Baba used to say that, as a family, we had travel in our genetic makeup. Raza and I saw much of Europe by car. We drove through great cities and beautiful countryside, stopping where we pleased. When our children were young, they were part of this road journey. Our world was not limited by our immediate surroundings, and I am always grateful for that.

Some travel was particularly unusual. My journey with colleagues and students from Johns Hopkins SAIS during March 21–24, 2000, a Staff Ride to Jerusalem, was just that. Before going, I needed a visa. My friend Harvey Sicherman introduced me to the Israeli Consul General in Philadelphia. The diplomat was curious about my service in government, and I had a feeling that he was aware of it even before raising it with me. "These are tense times" he noted, and I wondered when exactly they are ever not! I got my visa, and the Consul General said he would alert his colleagues in Tel Aviv so I would get through airport formalities smoothly as a US Ambassador. I was grateful for his help, especially as the rest of the twenty in the group were also expedited through Ben Gurion airport.

As we settled into the hotel in Jerusalem, I decided to take a short siesta given the overnight travel from Baltimore to London to Tel Aviv. Then, it would be dusk and time to walk in Jerusalem. Sapphire evening skies are unique to Jerusalem. That hue reflects in surrounding hills of biblical landscapes. With its combined history of significance to Christians, Jews and Muslims, Jerusalem is a very special place. Turning right on exiting the King David Hotel, I was immediately caught up in the landmark buildings on hills with the soft glow of illumination. The temperature was perfect, and I was totally at peace walking in these very new yet strangely familiar surroundings. It was the path of Prophets and Saints. Walking in their footsteps was a humbling experience. I appreciated the quiet of being on my own on this first ever trip to the city.

I walked to the famous gates into the Arab and the Jewish quarters. Walking past the Wailing Wall, I noted the notes stuck in crevices. I looked up to the Temple Mount, Judaism's holiest site known to Muslims as Haram al-Sharif, Islam's third holiest site after Mecca and Medina. The Dome of the Rock and the Al-Majjid Al Aqsa as signposts I had previously seen only in photographs. Even jaded travelers know that this is an extraordinary place and I was no different. After three-plus hours of walking, I returned to the hotel for a simple dinner and bed.

The international staff rides that the strategic studies program organizes with Eliot Cohen as head is vigorous in physical and historical exertion. We went to battlefields and participated in simulation exercises. We fought like soldiers and thought like generals. We met with Israeli and Palestinian senior officials. But some free time was built in, and I mentioned that I wanted to wander into Old Jerusalem. "Where, and by yourself?" came the universal query. "Yes, I responded but if anyone wanted to go with me that would be great."

There was a Palestinian student at SAIS who was on the ride, and she offered to accompany me after understanding that my knowledge of Arabic was restricted to the Quran. I assured the group that I felt no discomfort wandering around on my own but would be careful.

My colleagues and I walked through East Jerusalem with its multistoried stone buildings that had cheerful gardens and reminded me of some of the Mediterranean towns I had been to. The cafes and shops were full, and we sat and had some coffee with the sound of chatter and laughter around us. In 2000, I did not feel any discomfort being part of the scene where many Israeli women of all ages were present.

I then wanted to go to the old Arab Jerusalem. Several of my colleagues voiced discomfort and again talked of the tension there and the need to stay away. "But how can I stay away and not see the Arab part and pray at the al Aqsa Mosque?"

So I set off, and my Palestinian colleague followed with a worried look on her face. We wandered through the much narrower streets where, it was said, demonstrations could start any moment making escape difficult. I went into shops and chatted as best I could with the owners, who seemed friendly. I bought souvenirs for my family. Some of the streets reminded me of similar venues in South Asia, so I felt at home. Then, I wandered toward the al Aqsa Mosque and asked my colleague where to find the entrance. "There are several" she responded. "You have to find the one where there is an Israeli checkpoint and entry into the Mosque is allowed," she replied.

We then came to the entry gate for that day. I noticed a crowd of Arab men inside the mosque compound near the entry. In front of the entry, controlling access was a long table with about six very young armed Israeli soldiers checking identification for those going into the Mosque. As I came forward alone, the soldier who took my passport looked at it and then me with great puzzlement. "Why are you here?" he asked. "I want to go pray in the Mosque, which is a sacred one for me as a Muslim," I replied. "You don't look like a Muslim" was the response. "But I am," said I. In the meantime, a crowd was gathering inside the Mosque compound, and there was growing unease at the table. My US passport was re-examined, and I was once again asked why I was there.

I gave the background of the visit to Jerusalem and noted that I tried to pray in the great Mosques wherever I traveled. "There are recitations I could recite to prove my religion but I won't," I told the young soldier. "How long will you be there?" he asked reasonably. "Just long enough to pray, up to an hour," I said. "Come back through this same check point"! I promised I would and then the soldier let me pass. I walked through the crowd to the Mosque, said my prayers in its beautiful interior. Then, I walked around alone turning down offers of guides. This was a spiritual place, and it meant something beyond its history. When I finally exited at the same checkpoint as promised in an hour, I noticed my colleague was waiting anxiously across the street. I greeted the soldier who smiled back, and we left.

Within six months, the same site was aflame as the Palestinians launched the Second Intifada protesting the presence of Israeli minister Ariel Sharon on Temple Mount. Thousands were killed in the violence that followed. I understood the nervousness behind the "things can happen fast" warnings I kept getting in Jerusalem.

After memorable historic visits, it was time to leave Jerusalem on March 25, 2000. Eliot Cohen had offered me the name and phone contact of a trusted driver he used when visiting and said I could book him for my travel to the Allenby Bridge as I was not returning to the USA but going on to Amman, Jordan to attend a meeting hosted by Crown Prince Hassan.

Prior to my travel, I had arranged with the chief of Jordanian Protocol for their car to pick me up at the Allenby Bridge crossing for the short drive to Amman. The Protocol office referred to the crossing as the King Hussein Bridge. This mode of travel between neighboring countries seemed better than flying back to London to fly back to Jordan. Comfortable with my newly acquired expertise in the region, I met the taxi driver at the hotel, loaded my suitcase, and clearly told the taxi driver who spoke only a little English: "Take me to the King Hussein Bridge and then I will cross over into Jordan, where a car is waiting for me." He said fine, and we set off.

I saw the city of Jerusalem receding, and I kept watching this beautiful sight as long as I could. Then, we passed fertile fields of fruits and vegetables, and the scenery changed. We still kept driving. There appeared a lot of signs in Hebrew. Then, an occasional word in English told me that we were nearing a military base and that the Golan Heights frontier with Syria was not far. How could that be, I thought as the bridge to Jordan was not far, Eliot had told me. I asked the taxi driver if we were headed to the King Hussein Bridge. He replied that we were. Soon thereafter, we came to a gate where we stopped. The driver rolled down the window on his side as a soldier came up. What they said I did not understand. The soldier asked us to wait and called someone.

Soon, two other soldiers appeared, and conversation between them and the first soldier ensued. Still, we were asked to wait as they again talked via phone to someone. After five more minutes, with the taxi driver getting impatient that he had not charged enough for the day-long journey (in lieu of the short ride I should have had), we were finally allowed inside the base. I was asked to alight, my bag was unloaded. The driver wanted payment and would not wait, so I paid him and he took off.

My colleagues were still in Jerusalem, so I thought if all else failed; I would take a taxi back and fly out with them the next morning to London. Not nervous and not realizing there could be problems, I was escorted into the office of the officer in charge. I believe he was a colonel in the Israeli Army.

"What brings you here?"

"Well I'm at the end of my SAIS visit to Jerusalem and need to get across the King Hussein Bridge as the car from the protocol office of Crown Prince Hassan is waiting for me there to take me to Amman."

Then why are you here at this base?

I do not know, as I thought it was a short ride to the bridge.

The colonel got on the phone and spoke in Hebrew for a couple of minutes. By this time, he was on a first name basis with me. From my passport, he knew my name and citizenship. He hung up the phone and with a broad smile said: "Shirin, you are at the wrong bridge. I just checked. There is a Jordanian protocol car waiting for you at the Allenby Bridge and they are worried where you are." How could this have happened, I thought but realized from the conversation that the Jordanian protocol had used a different name for the bridge. But there was an actual King Hussein Bridge north, and the Army base at that bridge had not been used since the 1967 war!

"Could I get a taxi to go to the right bridge?" The colonel replied: "You could but it is a long way. Why don't we ask the Jordanians to bring the car to their side of the bridge here? It will take a while as the road is not too good. You can stay here and once we know the car is across, we will get you across also to meet up. In the meantime have some coffee and relax." And that is what I did. We spent some time talking about the region and my own experiences. I never felt worried, which in retrospect is amazing!

There were many telephone exchanges, and the Jordanians were asked to meet me at the new location. The Jordanian side finally signaled that the car had arrived and could I make my way across the bridge. But how?

There was barbed wire on the bridge that needed to be temporarily removed. A non-military vehicle had to be found to take me to the Jordanian side. Finally, an old bus was located, and its driver pressed into service. The colonel came to see me off, likely relieved I was leaving. Just as he turned to go, I called him to ask if he could lend me or exchange for US dollars the equivalent of five Israeli Shekels as the driver insisted the fare be paid in Israeli currency only, and I had given all of mine for the taxi ride along with the remaining as a tip. So I crossed the King Hussein Bridge not used by civilians since 1967. When I got to the Jordanian side, I noticed a fancy limousine with the elegant protocol chief waiting as I alone alighted from the old bus. "And I was worried earlier how I would recognize you!" noted the Jordanian official who had a sense of humor. We drove on to Amman, and when I told the story, the Crown Prince and others were genuinely surprised at what they termed my "sangfroid!"

Travel came easily and brought all kinds of experiences. Another one of note was my very first visit to Saudi Arabia in 1983. I was already on the Policy Planning Staff at the Department of State and was headed to Jeddah where the foreign ministry was located at the time. My colleagues had mentioned that the US embassy, then under veteran diplomat Richard Murphy as Ambassador, was wondering if as a Muslim woman I was coming alone (frowned upon in the Kingdom) or with my husband? I said that I would check with Raza.

Raza immediately informed me that although he was very supportive of my career in Washington, he was not about to head to Saudi Arabia simply in order to help get me entry into the country. "Just come back if they refuse you entry because you are a Muslim woman arriving without a husband, brother or father!" Well, that settled it. I got the requisite visa in my diplomatic passport as the State Department handled that request and set out. I changed planes in Amman Jordan and immediately noticed that there were only two women travelling alone: myself and the wife of the ambassador of Spain to Saudi Arabia.

We decided to disembark together and approached the immigration officer in Jeddah. "You women wait!" he yelled.

We moved to the side as all other passengers were cleared through. Then, noticing a long line of new arrivals disembarking from a Boeing 747, we decided to press our luck. I gave the officer my US diplomatic passport. He checked the name carefully. "You are Muslim?"
"Yes" I replied.
"Where is your man?"
"At home in America, teaching Physics."
"Where is his permission for you to come here unescorted?"
"I am here for my job at the Department of State for talks with the foreign ministry officials of the Saudi government." That really threw the officer off and he and I both noticed that an officer from the US embassy who was clearly there to receive me was hovering nearby watching all this.

Finally, after asking if I was carrying any "objectionable" materials (later explained to me as pornography) and my saying "of course not," I passed through.

Given that I was in Saudi Arabia, the chance to perform "Umrah" (similar to Haj in non-prescribed time as Haj occurs each year on a specific date based on the Muslim lunar calendar). I had a nephew on Baba's side from Hyderabad, India, who worked in Jeddah. He and his wife offered to take me to Mecca to pray. Umrah is a formalized ritual with very specific prayer and dress. I asked the US embassy to schedule my official work so that I could go to Mecca.

My American embassy colleagues told me that they were thrilled at my being a Muslim American official. Thus, I would be allowed into Mecca. "Tell us what it is like" was the often repeated comment. Just before we entered the city of Mecca, my nephew drove up to a checkpoint that noted that only Muslims were allowed to proceed into the city. A soldier looked into the car and moved us on.

Despite my anticipation, I was unprepared for the impact of actually seeing Mecca, entering the Mosque, and viewing the Kaaba, toward which Muslims face "qibla" wherever they are in the world for prayers. As we entered the al-Masjid al-Haram, Islam's most sacred mosque, tears welled up in my eyes that I was actually there. In 1983, it was a much smaller mosque, and the Kaaba was clearly within reach for the Tawaf, the circumambulation seven times around the Kaaba in a counterclockwise direction that is part of performing Haj or Umrah.

We got in line to pray in the mosque at the call to prayer. There were thousands, but in 1983, the mosque was smaller, people fewer and the environment around the mosque simple. Men and women of all nationalities were there, side by side. No religious police were hounding women into a different direction from the men. There was calm and everyone present intent on prayer. It was an immensely spiritual experience. As I performed Tawaf around the Kaaba, I could not believe that I was close enough to touch it.

This was exactly as Baba had taught me about my religion so long ago. In Islam, there are no priests between you and God. Each soul connects individually. I felt that connection that evening and night in Mecca. The second time I arrived in Saudi Arabia was as part of a five-member team to support the visit to the Saudi Kingdom of George H. W. Bush, Vice President of the USA. I was the NSC representative on the visit of the Vice President and Barbara Bush in April 1985 that took us to Yemen, Bahrain, and Oman, besides Saudi Arabia.

In preparation for the travel, White House protocol shared many of the "do's and don'ts" of the upcoming visit. There were special instructions for women. But Barbara Bush and I were the only two women. She was the wife of the Vice President. I was NSC staff and promised to follow requests.

In Washington, I had come to know Prince Bandar bin Sultan, who for decades, was the Saudi Ambassador to the USA. Thus, as we disembarked in Riyadh from Air Force Two, I noted that Bandar was there and he came forward to say something to me: "Shirin, you are the first Muslim to arrive with an American Vice President or President. Thus we are overlooking the normal exclusion of women from meetings between your Vice President and our king and allowing you to attend. Also, you are invited to the king's state dinner for the Vice President."

"Thank you Excellency. What are my other options for the dinner?"

"You could attend the dinner given by the Princess for Mrs. Barbara Bush."

"I'll do just that," I replied recalling photographs of dinners where all sat and watched the King.

As we were watching the Vice President and Mrs. Bush get into their limousine, I mentioned to the latter that I would accompany her to the dinner in her honor. Then, I climbed into the limousine dedicated to me as part of the motorcade that took each of us in separate cars to stay at different palaces in the royal compound; I thought this was amazing. The driver was from Pakistan as was the household staff at the palace. They were thrilled to see one of their own, and a woman to boot, arrive with the US Vice President as an official rather than as a servant of the royal household. They went out of their way to look after me during that short stay in Riyadh.

That night, all dressed up, I went with Barbara Bush in her limousine to the dinner in her honor. It was another palace with high walls. A hundred or so extremely elegantly dressed in couture fashions princesses of varying ages but mostly young were assembled. Crystal shone and opulence was in full display. Never having met any Saudi women since I worked in a man's world and in the mid-1980s, there were few Arab women in the diplomatic service of their respective countries, I had a number of interesting conversations with these educated women on a variety of issues.

After a resplendent dinner, the music started, and after a while, various women got up to dance. I gave Barbara Bush a mischievous look. "Don't even think about it," she replied instantly. I shall always recall her words to me as we parted from her car upon return to the palace: "Shirin, you have made the Vice President and me proud." My American journey allowed me so much.

Family is where the journey began and where it must end.

I have shared some of my memories of my parents. My life has also been blessed by having siblings. My brother Toufiq has been an incredible source of comfort, friendship, generosity throughout my life, and that of my own family. Raza and he were fellow students in Peshawar in the early 1950s, so they became friends and family.

Toufiq would take me, his little sister, with him when he went to the movies in Peshawar with his friends. In the Peshawar of that time, western films came regularly on release in Hollywood. He picked up my Little Lulu Comics from the city bookstore when he went for his own selection. We listened to hit songs on the Binaca Hit Parade during the summer vacations in Nathia Gali when the family moved up with the rest of the government to the hills to escape brutal heat. When he left for Cambridge University in 1955, there was a huge gap in our household. I missed him terribly. He went to Frankfurt for his doctorate in Nuclear Physics where he added German to his repertoire of languages.

My brother was the head of his class, captain of the university cricket team, a tennis buff and handsome to boot. I remain his proud sister. When he and his wife Ulrike decided to move to Honolulu in 1976 after his tenure at Indiana University in Bloomington, they introduced us to the magic and beauty of the Hawaiian Islands. They always welcome us, our children and grandchildren to their homes in the Hawaiian Islands, in Neustadt, Germany, on the Costa del Sol in Spain. Toufiq and Ulrike helped us eliminate distance as we maintain family ties across continents and oceans.

Raza has been my rock. He insisted I get graduate education, paid for it cheerfully and lived with the consequences of a working wife away in Washington for prolonged periods of time. I married him by choice, and it is a journey still. He sometimes says to friends who marvel that we have been married nearly fifty-five years: "Well the first fifty two were the hardest!"

Shehra, my daughter is smart, beautiful, caring, and generous. A mother needs a daughter, and I am lucky to have an exceptional one. She chose a wonderful mate, Ethan, whom she calls the "love of her life" and he has been a son to us. Their two children, Gladia and Cyrus, now sixteen and twelve, respectively, make this part of life's journey enchanting. We have been fortunate to live five minutes away from each other, so they have grown up with us. I admire the way they have been raised to be wonderfully warm, responsible, and good people. As a parent, one worries about one's child, regardless of age. As a good friend of mine would note in my White House years, "parenting never ends." But I know, these grandchildren will be great citizens and have a wonderful future, hopefully in a more secure world than the one I inhabit.

When I left for my out of town employment, first Carlisle in Pennsylvania, then Washington, New York and back to Washington, Shehra was initially in High School, then away at Oxford University as a student. She was busy with her music (she went to Magdalen College as a scholar in music), viola and piano. She "read" Jurisprudence at Oxford and received her American law degree from Georgetown. She was always a poised young lady who had traveled the world. With us, she had been to Brazil, the Caribbean, South Asia, Europe, and England. With her Philadelphia Youth Orchestra travel, Shehra had been to Australia, Scotland and other places. Wise beyond her years and gifted with a phenomenal memory, Shehra became our family's network keeper.

A mother's bond with her son is special. And my son, Kazim, grew up in the wake of my career. He turned into a smart, caring, and handsome man with a career spanning many continents from Africa to Asia, Europe, and Latin America. He graduated early from Lower Merion High School and went off to Harvard during the period I went to Carlisle, Pennsylvania, and then Washington. Women feel guilt no matter how well things are going when they leave family for even the work week because of the requirements of a job. On those occasions that I would fret that long absence was not good for Kazim, Raza would happily say "Maybe he is so good because you're away?"

Maybe.

During his vacations, Kazim would come visit me in Carlisle Barracks and in Washington. I talked at length with him recently in preparation for my memoirs. He made some very interesting points about my being away but also that being where I was, initially in Carlisle at the Army War College, was really "cool" for a boy of nine. He said that Carlisle Barracks was unique and a great place to visit on weekends or during school breaks as he could wander about in a safe environment in the gym, library, or the playing fields.

I heard that by the time the 1980s rolled around, my son knew that half of his friends had mothers who worked. Also, kids adapt easily to a parent's work life (good to know). Kazim pointed out that back then there was "not so much connectivity," whereas today there would be texts and face time. Carlisle was easier than Washington as it was a campus. And, it was closer.

As a young kid, Kazim did not know most of my colleagues during my years of service for the Presidents, except for Oliver North, who was involved in the Iran–Contra scandal, which Kazim recalled only because he had met Ollie.

With some relief, I heard my son recount that by coming home each weekend to Pennsylvania, I had made life less traumatic for him. However, I experienced my own day of agony when Kazim took Amtrak Train 94 back to Philadelphia the winter morning of January 4, 1987. To his chagrin, I had walked him to the train (you could in those days), and he got in the second car. For whatever reason, I got him out of that car and into the third car. As a frequent commuter, I recalled the conductor who was nearby. I reminded Kazim that he was going to be met by friends at the Philadelphia 30th Street station. He was staying with friends for the week as Raza was in Germany for work. Kazim had school the next day, Monday.

Mid-afternoon, shortly after 1:30 I saw a news flash of a massive Train collision involving Amtrak regional train number 94, which travelling at 108 miles per hour at the time of the accident. Signal problems seem to be the issue, and the collision occurred just short of the bridge over the Chesapeake in Maryland. Turning on the news, I witnessed the horror of the details and overhead photographs of wreckage on my son's Amtrak train. The third car in which he sat was buckled and off the track.

There was nowhere to call. No cell phones in those days. So I just sat. A friend from the White House who heard about the accident called, and I told him Kazim was on the same train. I asked if I should get in the car and drive. He replied that it was better I stay put in case Kazim tried to reach me on my home phone. "Are you OK?" "Should we come and stay with you?" offered my friend and his wife.

I was not OK but wanted to sit and stare at the phone alone.

In the meantime, the photographs became more detailed. People had died in first two compartments! I saw off Kazim in the third car but how could I be sure he did not move forward to the second after the train left the station?

The news announcer said that there were several bodies and the train engineer and conductor, whom I had just seen, were among the dead. The tally was sixteen dead. There were badly mangled cars, but rescue workers were going through.

Another hour went by. My phone rang!

My son had walked several miles after helping people more injured than he get off the car. He had found a house where kind owners allowed him and several others to make quick calls to let loved ones know they were safe. "I'm fine, just a few bruises. Yes, I was thrown from the back of the car to the front when the seats collapsed. Can't talk long as there is a line of people who need the phone." he said. "I'll call you once they get us to Baltimore," ending with "please stay home and don't come here as you can't get through."

To say I was relieved does not adequately express how I felt.

It was so long ago but the horror stays with me. My son is now a senior executive with global experience. He is married to beautiful and loving Victoria. They have twin children, Taisiya and Alexander, born in November 2016. Our life as parents seems complete.

So much of my life's work focused on bringing India and Pakistan into a better relationship. While at the NSC I had the honor to work on that effort as part of my portfolio. I started BALUSA to bring key leaders together in order to lessen the animosity and create new friendships. My hope that these crucial links would influence policy was in some ways successful. It did not, however, result in peace breaking out.

Connectivity in public and private sectors meant a change of mindset. However, India and Pakistan lurched from crisis to crisis, and the willingness of one to reach out to the other was seemingly always out of phase. It was as was once said of the Arab-Israeli relationship: "They never miss an opportunity to miss an opportunity."

I had to leave BALUSA Track II work when I reentered the White House NSC in 2003. Toufiq carried on work to finalize the South Asia water study that Carnegie Corporation of New York funded at Johns Hopkins SAIS to the tune of nearly $500,000. This was Carnegie's first ever grant for Track II in South Asia, and I was very proud of this seminal study in looking at water disputes between countries of the subcontinent and within its countries. We started a network of experts who stay in touch on this issue of growing importance.

BALUSA members in India and Pakistan took on the work of building bridges together and individually through other subsequent Track II efforts. The media in each country, which was hostile to the other in 1990s, had created its own links. Liberalized visa regimes in the last decade meant a greater exchange of views. Sports, cricket in particular, led to much more exposure. All that came to a halt in 2008.

Pakistanis lament that while Indians are welcomed and feted in Pakistan, India does not reciprocate. Poor treatment of Pakistani cricket teams when touring India has muted the desire for travel.

What does the future of the bilateral relation between India and Pakistan look like? Under Prime Minister Narendra Modi, India talks of moving on into a different era and a powerful destiny. The model is China, and Pakistan is viewed as being left in the dust. The issue of Indo-Pak relations takes second place.

What, then, should we expect in the future?

In my view, India has indeed moved on into a sense of self-awareness and a desire for modernity for its billion-plus population. It relies on the technologies of tomorrow to move the bullock carts of yesterday into a future of progress. The growing list of Indian billionaires is testament to the ingenuity of its people and the desire to catch up with the modern world.

But there is also the other side of India, where nearly "450 million subsist on less than $1.25 per day and nearly half of India's children are malnourished."[3] Even as one of the fastest growing economies in the world, India has a great deal to catch up on, with its broken infrastructure, a crumbling power grid, and a massive need for energy.

The great strength of India is its Democracy. Democracy implies inclusion and responsibility.

India has a 150 million strong Muslim community that is totally Indian. Yet, it remains suspect. I seldom saw Muslim names in the ranks of senior officials in the ministries of defense or external affairs. Muslim graduates of India's famed Indian Institutes of technology are few. Those in the armed forces are even fewer. Their aspirations to study, work, and live where other successful people do is stymied by a sense of denial of access. It seems as if there is an unspoken assumption that given the formation of Pakistan as a homeland for Muslims of the subcontinent, Indian officials feel that even those living as fully fledged Indians are simply waiting to go across the border. I have over the years raised the issue of the dearth of senior-level Muslims in India's premier services and positions, especially where the government is the employer. After one such conversation with former Foreign Minister Jaswant Singh, I was asked to go to the Indian Planning Commission, where I had a very good meeting with a Muslim woman who was a deputy of the commission.

I often joked with my Indian friends that it is good to have Muslims as Bollywood megastars. Muslims are musicians and singers. But where are the Muslim generals, university presidents, and Prime Ministers?

By 2050, India will have 311 million Muslims, the world's largest Muslim population.[4] The gap between India's constitutional guarantees of political, economic, and social equality and the reality will be increasingly reflected in the sense that Muslims are being left behind in ways that are unhelpful to Indian democracy.[5]

A real thaw in India's relationship with Pakistan where neither feels threatened could, in my view, lift the burden of Muslims in India being sidelined. When even the world's leading female doubles tennis star, Sania Mirza, an Indian Muslim from Hyderabad, who lives in India, is referred to as "Pakistan's daughter in law" in major Indian commentaries for the simple reason that she is a Muslim, it is a crying shame.

Add to the alienation, the situation in Kashmir which both India and Pakistan claim. Wars have been fought over this area, and no change has occurred. The BALUSA effort deliberately side-stepped Kashmir as we understood the issue carried just too much baggage for early reconciliation. Instead, we focused on the lower hanging fruit in improving relations between India and Pakistan. A major uprising in Indian Kashmir in 1989 tempted Pakistan to interfere by proxies to the detriment of all.

A massive Indian Army and paramilitary presence resulted in alienation of many Kashmiris. The Pakistani governments exploited the issue and reached out to the UN and China for support. Today, both are wary of jihad as a means of securing Kashmir's future.

As a noted Pakistani scholar said, "Everything has been tried: war, repression, elections and inducements."[6] Pakistani leaders claim Kashmir and hope that they can keep the issue active even as Pakistan itself is in a state of political disrepair and under siege from extremists.

India has a major military presence in Kashmir with nearly 600,000 soldiers and paramilitary personnel. Their treatment of Kashmiris is instantly shared via social media these days, as we saw following the killing of a Kashmiri youth Burhan Wani in 2016, which went viral and led to massive Indian security force reprisals with lethal force.

Pakistanis have harbored extremists, as Mujahidin who have sought to wreak havoc inside India. They murdered 164 in killing Hindus and Jews in Mumbai in November 2008 in a killing spree that lasted four days. In Kashmir, Hindu Pandits have been killed along with political leaders, and there has been a continuous attempt to bring greater control over the women along with pushing sectarian violence.

Recent past history details backchannel efforts going back to 2002 to help India and Pakistan to keep the peace and build a stable relationship. Though the political changes on each side, the trusted counselors made an effort for creative thinking whereby some middle ground could be found in Kashmir between "no change in the border" and "line of control existing is unacceptable" that represents the existing position of India and Pakistan, respectively. One attempt at reconciliation in Kashmir occurred following Prime Minister Atal Bihari Vajpayee's visit to Islamabad in January 2004 for the SAARC regional summit. Shortly thereafter, cricket teams of each side reconnected for tours, visas were liberalized for people to people contacts, and trade between both sides in Kashmir was opened as was a celebrated bus service connecting up divided families.[7]

Scholars of the region believe that the future requires a spiraling down of violence in these dangerous times. That means no more proxy wars regardless of how tempting or low cost the Pakistani security establishment believes them to be. Subsequently, as per one knowledgeable Indian economist and scholar, Prem Shankar Jha, three steps are required by India: First, that Indian security forces declare "a unilateral cease-fire with an accompanying deletion of police records on citizens;

second, work with the current Kashmiri Chief Minister Mehbooba Mufti to heal the wounded Kashmiri psyche; third, police to be equipped with lower end technology for crowd control against stone throwers instead of current use of pellet guns that maim permanently. The 1989 uprising which lasted into the early 2000s killed nearly 90,000 civilians, militants, police, and soldiers." We do not want to see things go down that path in the future.

I still believe that India and Pakistan can normalize relations. But I also know that such a move will not occur without active US encouragement. A collapsed Pakistan with an arsenal of nuclear weapons and animosity with India will make India's dream for modernity and grandeur just that. We all understand that the trajectory of US relations with India and Pakistan, respectively, will be different as the USA pursues its interests. But one of the key interests, especially for the development of a vibrant developed India, is stability. Indo-Pak normalization is critical to that goal.

Reflecting on my own life has to end with thoughts about what it means to be a Muslim in today's America. These are harsh times for America's Muslims. The attack by Osama bin Laden on the homeland on September 11, 2001, occasioned the shift. "So, it is the Muslims' fault," say some.

While it is true that all of the perpetrators of the heinous act were Muslims from Saudi Arabia and Egypt, it is vastly unjust to lay the blame for that grievous act at the feet of America's Muslims. We have come here to this great country by choice and consider it home and give it our undivided loyalty. We are the mothers, fathers, sons, daughters, wives, and husbands who believe that American values of freedom, liberty, justice, and fair play make all things possible in this land. We understand the concept of giving back as exemplified in the three tours that my nephew did as a Marine serving in Iraq even though as an only child of a widowed mother he could have got a deferment after his first tour. "I will not leave my Buddies" was his cry when his mother talked to him and to me about his sense of duty beyond requirement.

Muslims have sacrificed for America and would again if needed.

The 2016 presidential election has made matters much worse as Americans are asked to equate those who perpetrated terror in the name of Islam with the commitment or decency of American Muslims living and serving as citizens. We have nothing in common with those people who want to take the world back to the fourteenth century. The equivalent would be to accuse every white American of being a member of the Ku Klux Klan.

Our commitment to this country is permanent. Our children have been born here and have grown up here. When the standard-bearer of the Republican Party (which I carefully studied and then joined in 1971), first the 2016 nominee and now the President, talks of "banning Muslims" from these shores or his surrogates propose questioning of American Muslims about their belief in Shariah Law as a test of their continued residence, words fail me. If Muslims wanted to live under Shariah, they would not be living here in this country. It is a bogus issue used to divide and debase a people and a religion.

During these forty-six years of my US citizenship, I have traveled extensively for work and on vacation. Many of the countries of Europe, where I lived for periods of times, are so vastly different for Muslims compared with our American experience. From UK to France to Germany, I sat with parliamentarians, teachers, disgruntled youth, mothers, administrators, and politicians in a variety of settings from the House of Lords in London to the banlieues of Paris to the mayor of Karlsruhe in Germany.

For hours on end, we discussed the different models of immigration and assimilation between the USA and Europe. Why was it that American Muslims, the majority from outside arriving in the last thirty years, feel integrated as Americans while in Europe immigrants did not have a sense of belonging to their respective countries? In the UK, there are large swaths of areas in the midlands and the north or even in London where immigrants mimic the culture and customs of what they left behind. Their young, born in the UK, often still feel as outsiders.

In contrast, Muslim Americans are spread out throughout the land and live in all sorts of communities: military bases, inner cities, suburbs of major cities, and farmland. They are factory workers, farmers, truck drivers, nurses, teachers, doctors, scientists, soldiers, marines, taxi drivers, office workers, government bureaucrats and policy wonks, ambassadors, mayors of small towns, political leaders, and participants in the political system. We live where we can afford to live, pay taxes as required and partake of the school system, which gives our children a base for the future. Family ties are strong even as the new age of social media challenges the traditional family's ability to supervise its young.

Being a "Muslim" should never become an epithet. False charges that President Barack Obama was a Muslim was touted as a disqualification from his holding the highest office in the land. I recall being in Helsinki, Finland for official business in 2004 where my friend Barbara Barrett was the American Ambassador, when I watched former Chairman of the Joint Chiefs of Staff and former Secretary of State Colin Powell, my admired former boss, answer a questioner on Obama's religion. While stressing that the Democratic candidate of 2004 was a Christian, Powell asked: "What is so wrong with being a Muslim in America? There are innumerable Muslim soldiers buried in Arlington National Cemetery who fought for and died for this country."

When Tom Kline, a Senate staffer made fun of my looks (and by association, my religion) as a nominee before the Senate for an ambassadorship in 1990, I laughed it off as sheer ignorance and stupidity. It was the same when growing up in Pakistan in the 1950s and visiting there in the 1960s, 1970s, and 1980s, I joined in with my acquaintances and friends in laughing off the Mullahs who spewed hatred toward women, foreigners and tolerance of differences and moderation of political views. By 1990s, I saw Pakistani power shift toward intolerance of differences as preached for decades by ignorant Mullahs as the country verged from crisis to crisis. Terror, death and mayhem struck, and Mullahs became an important arbiter of governance.

Thus, I feel it extremely important as a proud American and a proud Republican to repudiate this "lynching by association" of Muslims that is becoming part of the rhetoric of political discourse. Tolerance and acceptance, the hallmarks of my experience in America, are being cast aside for short-term political gain. Assimilation, understanding, and appreciation for the freedom of religion that is unique to the American experience means that Muslims cannot give up by clustering into separated places out of a sense of fear. We are and must remain a part of the fabric of the country to which we came by choice. This is the future of our children and grandchildren as we nurture in them the same sense of belonging to this great country we call home.

Notes

1. We lost Robert in December 2015 and Ruth in June 2016 bringing an era to an end.
2. I thank our wonderful friend Thelma Domenici for the discussion of what constitutes a sanctuary.

3. For a discussion about the challenge of exclusionary benefits, see Atul Kohli, *Poverty Amid Plenty in the New India* (New York: Cambridge University Press, 2012).
4. Pew Forums, "The Future of World Religions, 2010–2050," Washington, DC, 2015.
5. Riaz Hasan, *Indian Muslims: Struggling for Equality of Citizenship* (Melbourne: Melbourne University Press, 2016).
6. Pervez Hoodbhoy, "Cooling Down Kashmir," *Dawn*, July 30, 2016.
7. Zahid Hussain, "Kashmir Issue: The Story of a Lost Opportunity," *Dawn*, August 26, 2015.

Appendix

DE-CLASSIFIED REAGAN WHITE HOUSE UNITED STATES
GOVERNMENT DOCUMENTS IDENTIFICATION
(IN ORDER OF INCLUSION)

1. The White House, October 11, 1984. **National Security Decision Directive 147. NSSD 147**
A critical document, prepared through the interagency process overseen by Shirin Tahir-Kheli as Director, South Asia, National Security Council. Signed by President Ronald Reagan, NSSD 147 serves as the road map for US relations with India and Pakistan, respectively, following the Soviet invasion of Afghanistan in 1979. The document outlines US policy for the 1984–1989 period in some detail as the planning approved for implementation by President Reagan.

2. The White House, October 2, 1986. **Memorandum: "A Legacy of Peace in South Asia."**
From the National Security Advisor, John Poindexter, to the Secretary of Defense, Caspar Weinberger, prior to the latter's official visit to India and to Pakistan.
Attached alongside minutes of the meeting of the **National Security Council chaired by the President, on October 3, 1986.** Drafted by Shirin Tahir-Kheli, the documents stress the continuing effort by the President to help foster peace between India and Pakistan. As noted, the NSC met to review ways in

which the USA could build a legacy of peace between India and Pakistan. The White House directed US government-wide effort promoting Indo-Pakistani normalization is detailed in the paper for the President's review prior to his chairing the NSC meeting.

3. December 17, 1985. **Cable from American Embassy, New Delhi recording the India–Pakistan Agreement Not to Attack Each other's Nuclear Sites.**
Successful conclusion of a key confidence building measure first proposed to India and Pakistan by the USA in 1985 and pushed by Tahir-Kheli to White House and State Department senior officials in 1983–1984.

4. September 17, 1985. **Schedule for the Visit to Pakistan by Deputy National Security Advisor Donald Fortier and Undersecretary of State Michael Armacost.**
One of several such missions between 1984 and 1989 to the subcontinent to discuss confidence-building measures between India and Pakistan understood as critical to winning the war against the Soviet Union in Afghanistan.

5. January 1985. **Memorandum for the President for the Second Term, from National Security Advisor Robert McFarlane.**
Drafted by Shirin Tahir-Kheli, the memorandum details India–Pakistan normalization efforts as part of the select number of themes for the Reagan second-term foreign policy agenda. Normalization of India–Pakistan relations remains a goal for the success of US policy in South Asia.

6. April 4, 1986. **Note from Shirin Tahir-Kheli to Grant Green.**
Executive Secretary of the National Security Council on USA–India Relations.

7. June 29, 1984. **Decision Memorandum from Deputy National Security Advisor Donald Fortier to National Security Advisor Robert Mc Farlane.**
The memorandum proposes nineteen key areas for study aimed at establishing foreign policy priorities in the second term. Specific experts in each field are selected to undertake the work. Shirin Tahir-Kheli is the author for item number 8 on Indo-Pakistan Normalization.
The list is approved and the work undertaken prior to a briefing of the President on each issue.

APPENDIX 433

8. **March 1988. Memorandum to the Chief of Staff, Howard Baker, from National Security Advisor Frank Carlucci.**
   The Reagan White House presses hard for Pakistan to limit its nuclear weapons ambition and to agree to a non-attack on nuclear facilities with India. Simultaneously, India is urged to pursue confidence-building measures with Pakistan.
9. **January 1985. Internal National Security Council Document.**
   A planning document authored quarterly by Shirin Tahir-Kheli highlighting administration wide milestones for US government priorities in the subcontinent.
10. **July 3, 1987. Cable from Ambassador Arnold Raphel, American Embassy Islamabad on Nuclear Issues.**
    The cable reflects the seriousness of the discussions aimed at limiting Pakistan's nuclear weapons program as a requirement for continued US economic and military assistance. The effort demonstrates continued importance of Pakistan for the expulsion of Soviet troops from Afghanistan. Also reflected in the discussion is critical confidence-building measure on nuclear non-attack agreed to by New Delhi and Islamabad.
11. **October 20, 1987. List of Attendees, US and Indian Delegations, Working Visit of Prime Minister Rajiv Gandhi, The White House.**
    This, the second Rajiv Gandhi visit to the White House, builds on progress made after his first official 1985 state visit. A working lunch scheduled in the private dining room demonstrates the growing ties. The agenda is ambitious and the camaraderie exceptional.
12. **March 5, 1986. Draft Response for the President's Signature for Letter to Senator John Glenn on Pakistan.**
    Senator Glenn expresses his concern regarding US certification of Pakistan's non-nuclear status as required under law for continued assistance to Pakistan. The Senator highlights Pakistan's march toward nuclear weapons capability and cautions against continued US aid.
13. **March 29, 1984. Department of State Cable to American Embassy, Islamabad on Schedule and Agenda of upcoming Meeting of the USA–Pakistan Military Planning Group (MPG).**
    The MPG aimed at building institutional links between the US and Pakistani military establishments on a range of issues.

14. **September 15, 1985. Cable from American embassy, New Delhi with Schedules for visit to India by Deputy National Security Advisor Donald Fortier and Undersecretary of State, Michael Armacost.**
Details of program in New Delhi for this Presidential mission.
15. **December 18, 1985. Cable from American Embassy New Delhi on meeting between Prime Minister Rajiv Gandhi of India and President Zia-ul-Haq of Pakistan.**
The cable details key agreement by Prime Minister Gandhi and President Zia on a key nuclear agreement long promoted by the USA
16. **May 25, 1985. White House Memorandum on Safeguarding the USA–Pakistan Relationship.**
Drafted by Tahir-Kheli, the memorandum lays out US policy objectives in Pakistan at the height of Soviet occupation of Afghanistan.
17. **April 5–12, 1985. Schedule of Vice President George H. W. Bush Visit to Bahrain, Saudi Arabia, Oman and Yemen.**
Shirin Tahir-Kheli accompanies the Vice President as NSC Director for Political-Military Affairs.
18. **February 1985. Department of State Strategy Paper for Securing Support of the FY 88–93 Security Assistance Package for Pakistan.**
19. **January 15, 1987. White House memorandum for the President's Signature of Letters to President Zia of Pakistan and Afghan Resistance Spokesman respectively.**
Letters from the US President to key leaders reflect presidential priorities. These letters were hand delivered by Ambassador Robert Oakley and Undersecretary Michael Armacost on a Presidential mission to Pakistan.
20. **March 20, 1987. Cable from American Embassy, Islamabad Reporting American Ambassador's Meeting with Prime Minister Junejo on Nuclear issues.**
As Pakistan moved toward nuclear weapons, the USA continues to press for restraint. Washington reminds Islamabad of the consequences of its nuclear program for the proposed 1988–1993 US assistance package.

APPENDIX 435

21. May 17, 1988. **National Security Council Memorandum for National Security Advisor Colin Powell providing an Update on USA–India Relations.**
Prepared by Tahir-Kheli, the memorandum updates on issues discussed during the visit of Prime Minister Rajiv Gandhi to the White House on October 20, 1987. Attached is the official list of the New Initiatives announced at the conclusion of the Reagan–Gandhi meeting.
22. May 23, 1988. **Memorandum of Conversation between P. K. Singh Senior Ministry of External Affairs Official with Robert Oakley and Shirin Tahir-Kheli at the White House.**
The conversation on Afghanistan covers clarifications of respective US and Indian positions. Indian worries about Intellectual Property Rights for US pharmaceuticals produced in India and other related items covered. US Science Advisor to the President's visit to India confirmed.
23. June 2, 1988. **President Ronald Reagan's Letter to Prime Minister Rajiv Gandhi.**
Gandhi notes his interest in disarmament issues. The US President provides an updated vision of US arms control efforts with the Soviet Union. The letter once again notes the importance of Indo-Pak efforts for mutual nuclear restraint.
24. September 3, 1988. **Prime Minister Rajiv Gandhi Letter to President Ronald Reagan.**
The letter highlights the "critical significant changes in the substance and atmosphere of our relationship." Noting White House's imprint on improved relations, Gandhi notes the positive trajectory in USA–India relations. He refers to the upcoming visit of the US Science Advisor to Delhi.
As officer in charge of South Asia for the NSC, Tahir-Kheli accompanies the Science Advisor.

These materials can be accessed via this link: http://extras.springer.com.

Index

A
Abbottabad, 71, 72
Abrams, Elliott, 324
Abu Ghraib, 258, 304, 306, 308, 309, 311, 312, 314, 370. *See also* Torture
Addington, David, 220, 305, 306, 315, 318, 337
Afghanistan, 14, 101
 al Qaeda and, 207–210, 219, 262, 263, 274, 281
 Bush, George W. and, 262, 303
 democracy in, 122, 127, 241, 244–246, 250, 251, 303, 317
 India and, 83, 84, 86, 88, 97–100, 102, 109, 111, 123, 124, 127, 161, 209, 211, 254–256, 262, 263, 271, 281
 Iraq and, 218, 219, 231, 241, 242, 244–246, 249–251, 258, 296, 303, 311, 317, 329, 330, 339, 340, 372, 393
 ISI and, 116, 124, 126, 208, 211
 jihad in, 114, 116, 126, 207
 bin Laden, Osama, 207, 262
 Pakistan and, 55, 64, 79, 83, 84, 86, 88, 97–99, 102, 107, 109, 111–117, 122, 123, 125–127, 161, 167, 207–211, 254–256, 258, 261–264, 267, 270, 271, 273, 274, 280, 281, 329
 refugees from, 107, 111, 115, 126
 Soviet Union and, 75, 88, 102, 107, 109, 116, 149
 Taliban and, 126, 127, 207, 209–211, 241, 258, 262, 270, 274, 281, 317
 United States and, 125, 161, 250
 women's rights in, 251
Aguirre, Eduardo, 389
Ahmed, Mehmood, 208, 211
Aiyar, Mani Shankar, 101, 166
al Aqsa Mosque, 413
Ali, Syed Babar, 166
al Jazeera, 220, 227, 338
Allenby Bridge, 414, 415
al Qaeda, 282, 305, 338
 Abu Zubaydah and, 253
 Afghanistan and, 207, 209, 210, 219, 262, 263, 274, 280

© The Editor(s) (if applicable) and The Author(s) 2018
S. Tahir-Kheli, *Before the Age of Prejudice*,
https://doi.org/10.1007/978-981-10-8551-2

437

Iraq and, 218, 219
  bin Laden, Osama and, 207, 209, 262
  Pakistan and, 207–210, 253, 257, 258, 262, 263, 273, 274, 280, 281
  September 11 attacks and, 207
  Taliban and, 207, 209, 210, 262, 274, 280, 281
  US hunt for, 258
Ambassador Hildreth, 18
American Muslims, 206, 426, 427
  in government, 208
  impact of September 11 on, 426
  lives of, 404
  treatment of, 305
America the Beautiful, 23
Amtrak Train Collison, 421
Annan, Kofi, 220, 221, 242, 290, 291, 293
Arab-Kurd Relations, 298
Arab League, 325
Armitage, Richard, 90, 120, 128, 198, 208, 259
Assimilation of Muslims, 404, 427, 428
  alienation of, 239
  challenges of, 105
  in Europe, 240, 329, 427
  in the United States, 145, 206
Aznar, Prime Minister of Spain, 221, 224, 291, 390

B
Baker, James, 100, 132, 136, 138, 140, 150
BALUSA, 163–169, 174, 191, 198, 201, 408, 422–424
Bangalore, 105, 106, 255
Basrah Children's Hospital (BCH), 346, 347, 367–373, 375–385, 387–396

Bechtel and, 375, 381–384, 387
Bush, Laura and, 343
Project HOPE and, 381, 384
Rice, Condoleezza and, 343, 375, 383, 388, 394, 395
USAID and, 367, 368, 372, 378, 381, 382, 384, 387, 388
Bechtel, 375, 376, 381–384, 387, 396
  Basrah Children's Hospital and, 346, 347, 367–373, 375–385, 387–396
  Project HOPE and, 381, 384
  United States Agency for International Development and, 381, 382, 384, 387
Beg, Aslam, 123, 125
Bellinger, John, 295, 306
Bhutto, Benazir, 120, 121, 123, 125, 160, 261, 263, 265, 269–273, 276, 282
Bhutto, Zulfiqar Ali, 58
bin Laden, Osama, 207, 209, 262, 281, 426
  Afghanistan and, 207, 209, 262
  al Qaeda and, 207–209, 262, 305
  Pakistan and, 207–209, 262, 282, 426
  September 11 attacks and, 207, 426
  Taliban and, 207, 209, 262
  US search for, 207
Blair, Tony, 299, 340
Boldt, Cyrus, 420
Boldt, Gladia, 420
Boldt, Shehra, 58, 59, 65–68, 81, 82, 160, 192, 407, 420
Bolton, John, 129, 136, 234, 288, 300, 382
Bosworth, Steve, 86, 88, 90
Bowen, Stuart, 388
Brahimi, Lakhdar, 296
Bremer, Jerry, 90, 293, 361, 367
Brokaw, Tom, 335
Bush, Barbara, 90, 92, 93, 101, 106, 349, 418, 419

INDEX 439

Bush, George H.W., 88, 90, 93, 101, 109, 129, 138, 146, 152, 156, 197, 207, 214, 216, 217, 303, 324, 418
   Gandhi, Indira and, 92
   Gandhi, Rajiv and, 97, 98, 102, 109, 270
   India and, 88, 129, 216
   Iraq and, 214, 303
   Kuwait and, 152
   Musharraf, 270
   nuclear weapons and, 222
   Pakistan and, 88, 91, 92, 102, 119–121, 123, 129, 160, 161
   presidency and, 109
   Reagan, Ronald and, 92, 98, 102, 109, 157, 160, 161, 197, 216, 222, 303, 333
   Soviet Union and, 97, 102, 109, 152
   United Nations and, 129, 130, 135, 138, 146, 147, 150, 158, 197, 214
   vice presidency and, 109
   Zia-ul-Haq, Muhammad and, 270
Bush, George W., 197, 205, 207, 216–218, 226, 228, 234, 238, 248, 251, 254, 255, 262, 268, 273, 275, 276, 285, 287, 292, 293, 303, 329, 330, 340, 341, 375
   administration divide and, 234
   Afghanistan and, 224, 241, 250, 261–263, 303
   Bush, George H.W. comparisons and, 216, 303
   Cheney, Dick and, 222, 239, 241, 269, 287, 290, 292, 304, 333, 334, 336–339
   coalition of the willing and, 221, 293, 389, 390
   Dalai Lama and, 248
   democracy promotion and, 233
   Egypt and, 326–328
   freedom agenda and, 238, 239, 269, 273, 323, 326, 333
   Hussein, Saddam and, 214, 222, 226, 291
   Iraq and, 215, 218, 221–223, 226, 227, 230, 234, 239, 241, 242, 244, 245, 249, 250, 258, 286, 287, 290–293, 296–298, 303, 305, 317, 327, 329, 335–337, 339, 340, 343, 344, 347, 349, 375, 385, 389
   Islam and, 206, 326, 340
   Musharraf, Pervez and, 208, 209, 253, 254, 260–263, 268–272
   neocons and, 216, 217, 241, 286, 287, 290, 293, 333, 336–338
   Pakistan and, 197, 208, 209, 254, 255, 259–263, 265, 268–271, 273, 274, 281, 408
   presidency and, 147, 206, 218, 234, 238, 262, 337, 375
   Rice, Condoleezza and, 213, 218, 219, 233, 234, 250, 260, 269, 271, 273, 281, 286, 290, 292, 317, 326, 328, 337–339, 344, 390
   September 11 attacks and, 208, 233
   Singh, Manmohan and, 273
   United Nations and, 130, 138, 224, 241, 242, 287, 291, 296
   War on Terror and, 254, 317
Bush, Laura, 197, 245, 248, 342, 343, 349–351, 366–368, 370–373, 375, 376, 379, 382–385, 388, 390–392, 394, 397
   Basrah Children's Hospital and, 376
   Bush, George W. and, 197
   Howe, John and, 366, 379, 384, 392
   Rice, Condoleezza and, 350, 392

C

Callen, Herb, 32, 41, 46–48, 53, 58, 59
Camp Victory, 365
Carlisle Barracks, 66, 76, 421
Carlucci, Frank, 108
Carter, Jimmy, 75, 114
Casey, William, 115
Cheney, Dick, 221, 292
  Bush, George W. and, 226, 292, 329
  Hussein, Saddam and, 222, 226
  Iraq War and, 223
  Khalilzad, Zalmay and, 209
  neocons and, 220, 234
  Rice, Condoleezza and, 249, 250, 254, 343, 383
  United Nations and, 221, 290, 291
  War on Terror and, 223, 233, 315
  WMDs and, 222, 289
Cheney, Liz, 234, 245, 292, 368
China, 18, 19, 89, 135, 137, 152, 159, 201, 226, 240, 322, 350, 380, 423, 425
  communism in, 116, 237
  freedom in, 240, 322
  Pakistan and, 18, 19, 89, 165, 226, 423, 424
  United Nations and, 89, 136, 425
  United States and, 137
Cleveland, Robin, 347, 351, 369, 373, 382
Clinton, Bill, 192
Clinton, Hillary, 401
Coalition of the Willing, 293
  Iraq War and, 221, 389
  Spain and, 221, 389, 390
  United Nations and, 293
Coalition Provisional Authority (CPA), 246, 293, 295, 296, 351, 360–362, 367, 369, 372, 377

Cold War, 125, 152, 153, 161, 163, 250
Colorado State University, 23
Communism, 116, 237
Confidence Building Measures (CBMs), 88, 89, 102, 160, 255
Convent of Jesus and Mary Murree, 12, 13, 15, 94
Cooperative Monitoring Center, 165, 408
Cray XMP-14 Supercomputer. *See* Supercomputer
Crown Prince Hassan of Jordan, 165

D

Dalai Lama, 248
Day care for kids, 68
Delaware, Ohio, 24
Democracy, 97, 119, 120, 122, 127, 148, 213, 215, 219, 230, 232–235, 237–246, 249–251, 254, 257, 268, 273, 277, 279, 282, 285, 286, 290, 292, 293, 295, 300, 303, 304, 310, 313, 317, 318, 321, 323–331, 333, 334, 338–342, 364, 368, 373, 385, 424
  Afghanistan and, 122, 127, 241, 244–246, 250, 251, 303, 317
  building of, 219, 234, 240, 242, 243, 245, 249, 263, 271, 293, 310, 328, 333, 334, 368, 369
  Democracy Assistance Dialogue and, 321
  Egypt and, 323–328
  Iraq and, 148, 215, 219, 234, 239, 241–246, 250, 251, 285, 290, 292–295, 300, 303, 304, 310, 317, 323, 327–329, 334, 338, 339, 364, 368, 385

Pakistan and, 119–122, 126, 127, 193, 253, 254, 257, 258, 260–263, 265, 268, 271–273, 279, 281, 282
  promotion of, 230, 233–235, 241, 243–245, 251, 254, 285, 286, 290, 292, 325–327, 334, 338, 340
Diplomacy without Negotiation, 233
democracy promotion and, 233
Duelfer, Charles, 287, 289
Durrani, General Mahmud, 80, 166

E
Eagleburger, Larry, 84, 133
Egypt-Israel Peace Treaty, 327
El Baradei, Mohamed, 301
England. *See* United Kindgom
En-Lai, Chou, 18, 226
Enlightened Moderation, 260, 261, 264, 266, 267
  Musharraf, Pervez and, 260, 261, 264, 266
  Pakistan and, 260, 261, 266, 267
Estefan, Gloria, 153
Etpison, Ngiratkel, 143
Europe, 3–5, 17, 32, 55, 81, 82, 159, 192, 234, 240, 329, 331, 390, 410, 411, 420, 427
  Iraq War and, 240, 329, 389
  Muslims in, 240, 329, 427
  Organization for Security and Cooperation in Europe, 247
  United States relations with, 321, 329, 331, 427

F
Fahd, King of Saudi Arabia, 124
Foreign Policy Research Institute, 44, 52, 65, 165, 169

Fortier, Donald, 104
  India and, 99
  National Security Council and, 86, 87, 89, 95, 98
Forum for the Future, 292, 321
France, 4, 65, 293
  Iraq War, 135, 137
  Muslims in, 329, 427
  United Nations, 136, 137, 142
Freedom Agenda, 238, 239, 257, 269, 273, 323, 325–328, 330, 333
  Bush, George W. and, 239, 327, 329, 333
  in the Middle East, 239, 323, 326
  National Endowment for Democracy, 239
Freedom fighters, 115, 116
Fukuyama, Francis, 191, 341
Fulbright, 35–37, 230

G
Galbraith, Peter, 127, 130
Gales, Ruth, 67
Gandhi, Indira, 76, 88, 91, 92, 97, 98
  assassination of, 76, 97
  meeting with, 98
  relations with the United States, 77, 88, 97
Gandhi, Rajiv, 70, 97, 98, 100–102, 105–109, 111, 123, 166, 255, 270
  assassination of, 109
  Reagan, Ronald and, 88, 255
  Zia-ul-Haq, Muhammad and, 73
Gandhi, Sanjay, 92
Gandhi, Sonia, 101, 256
Geneva, 37, 52, 118, 149, 151, 152, 198, 199, 201, 306
Geneva Conventions, 305, 311–313, 316
  Guantanamo and, 305

Iraq and, 305, 311, 313
  United States and, 312
Gerber, Colonel Frederick, 394
Gere, Richard, 248
Germany, 3, 4, 247, 251, 293, 327, 329, 420, 421, 427
  Berlin Wall and, 327
  rebuilding Iraq and, 241, 242
Gorbachev, Mikhail, 116, 149
  Afghanistan and, 116, 149
  Berlin Wall and, 327, 328
  Geneva Agreement and, 149
  Reagan, Ronald and, 150
  Soviet Union and, 149
Gottesman, Blake, 246
Government Corruption
  in Afghanistan, 122, 127, 280
  Bhutto, Benazir and, 119
  in Pakistan, 120
  Sharif, Nawaz and, 120
Government of India (GOI), 8, 93
  Gandhi, Rajiv and, 102
  government of Pakistan and, 8, 11, 16, 58, 92, 102, 161, 164, 281, 424
  supercomputer and, 102, 108
  United States government and, 92, 95, 98, 161, 273
Government of Pakistan (GOP), 275. *See also* Islamabad
  Bhutto, Benazir and, 119–121, 125, 265
  government of India and, 7–9, 11, 58, 92, 95, 99, 102, 161, 163, 273, 281, 425
  nuclear weapons and, 124
  United States government and, 161
Graduate student, 406
  University of Pennsylvania, 406
Green Zone, 294, 295, 335, 336, 341, 360, 361, 364, 366–368

Brokaw, Tom and, 335
Iraq, 295, 336, 364, 366–368
Gregg, Donald, 88, 101, 216
  National Security Advisor and, 88–90, 101, 104, 216
Guantanamo (GTMO), 303, 305–308, 311, 317, 318, 370. *See also* Human rights; Torture
  prisoners in, 305, 306, 308
  tour of, 307
Guerra, Stella, 142–144
Gulf War, 125, 140, 141, 214, 219, 221–223, 299, 335, 348
  Iran and, 125
  Pakistan and, 125
  support for, 125, 219, 221

H
Hadley, Steve, 213, 216, 276, 309, 337
  Cheney, Dick and, 287, 337
  Office of the Vice President and, 216
  Rice, Condoleezza and, 255
Haj, 7, 171, 417
Hamas, 326, 341
  in Palestine, 326
Haram, 70, 74, 412, 417
Harnwell, Gaylord, 47
Harvard University, 27, 192, 420
Haynes, Jim W., 306
Heeger, Alan, 406
Heeger, Ruth, 155
Heiligenstein, Anne, 349, 351, 366, 370, 373
Hekmatyar, Gulbuddin, 116, 126
Hindu, 3, 7, 8, 405, 425
  divide with Muslims, 7
  in India, 3, 7, 8, 16, 217, 425
  partition and, 3, 8, 16, 405

Honeymoon, 37
Howe, John, 350, 351, 366, 368, 369, 372, 373, 376, 379, 384, 392, 393
  Basrah Children's Hospital and, 378
  Bush, Laura and, 350, 351, 366, 370, 376, 379, 384, 392
  Project HOPE and, 350, 372, 376, 379, 384, 393
  Zawawi, Omar and, 383
Hughes, Karen, 206, 230, 239, 329
  American Muslims and, 206
  Bush, George W. and, 238
  Iraq War and, 329
  Rice, Condoleezza and, 207
  September 11 and, 207
Human Rights, 136, 145, 151, 153, 155, 198–201, 213–215, 244, 247, 248, 251, 264, 269, 297, 304–308, 310–316, 318, 319, 326, 364
  activists for, 269
  commitment to, 201, 311, 314
  in Cuba, 145, 151, 199, 200, 307
  in Egypt, 326
  in Pakistan, 213, 264, 269
  United Nations and, 213, 214, 297
Humphrey, Gordon, 130, 131
Hussein, King of Jordan, 18
Hussein, Saddam, 126, 135, 137, 148, 214, 215, 218, 219, 221–223, 226, 229, 239, 241, 244, 251, 285, 287–292, 294, 297, 334, 340, 344, 360, 362, 364, 366, 397
  fall of, 226, 227, 239, 241, 292, 294, 344
  invasion of Kuwait, 135–137, 139
  Iraq and, 135, 139, 148, 149, 215, 218, 219, 221–224, 227, 229, 239, 241, 244, 251, 285, 287–292, 294, 297, 334, 340, 344, 346, 350, 363, 366, 379, 384
  Pakistan and, 127, 226, 365
  sons of, 294, 360
  United States and, 137, 285
  weapons of mass destruction and, 218–222, 241, 285–290, 334, 340
Hyderabad Deccan, 3, 71
  absorption of, 8
  childhood in, 3
  move from, 8
Hyderabad, Sind, 20, 37, 38

I

India, 3–5, 7–9, 11, 12, 15–17, 19, 21, 27, 34, 46, 55, 56, 58, 59, 65, 67, 71–73, 76, 83–100, 102, 103, 105–111, 118, 123–127, 129, 130, 133, 143, 152, 160, 161, 163–169, 174, 192–195, 197, 201, 209, 211, 216, 217, 225, 226, 228, 240, 254–256, 259, 260, 262–265, 270, 271, 273–276, 281, 282, 400, 403–405, 408, 410, 417, 422–426, 429
  Hindu-Muslim divide, 7
  Indian Diaspora, 100
  relations with Great Britain, 4, 59
  Taj Mahal, 93
  technology in, 98–100, 102, 105–108, 168, 255, 424
  See also Government of India (GOI); India–Pakistan relations; Indian–Soviet relations; Muslims in India; United States policy in India
India-Pakistan Relations, 7, 84–86, 88, 89, 94, 102, 109, 168, 174, 281, 255, 426

Hindu-Muslim divide, 7
government of India, 7
government of Pakistan normalization of, 84, 85, 88, 89, 94, 102, 109, 168, 281, 426
war, 89, 102, 174
See also Confidence Building Measures (CBMs); Partition
Indian–Soviet Relations, 88, 97, 98, 100–102, 109, 255
government of India, 97
Reagan, Ronald, 88, 92, 97, 98, 100–102, 109, 255
Soviet occupation of Afghanistan, 99, 102, 161
United States relations with India, 71
India–Pakistan Relations, 425. *See also* Confidence Building Measures (CBMs); Partition
government of India, 7–9, 11, 58
government of Pakistan normalization of, 84, 85, 89, 94, 102, 109, 124, 127, 163, 168, 271, 281
Hindu–Muslim divide, 7
war, 55, 58, 65, 89, 99, 102, 174, 209, 226, 264, 270, 425
International Atomic Energy Agency (IAEA), 31, 273, 288, 289, 300, 328
International Committees of the Red Cross (ICRC), 306, 307
Guantanamo and, 306–308
human rights and, 307
prisoners of war and, 306
International Republican Institute (IRI), 270, 276, 279, 282
Inter-Services Intelligence (ISI), 114–116, 122, 124–127, 208, 211, 257
in Afghanistan, 116, 124–126

Bhutto, Benazir and, 123
government of Pakistan and, 122
in Kashmir, 124, 126
religious extremism and, 126
Zia-ul-Haq, Muhammad and, 124
Iran, 64, 118, 123, 125, 172, 201, 288, 298, 324, 327, 328, 397
chemical weapons and, 222
relations with Pakistan, 123, 125
revolution, 75, 80
sanctions on, 288
Iran-Contra, 324, 421
Iranian revolution, 75, 80
Iran-Iraq War
Basrah Children's Hospital, 346, 397
Hussein, Saddam, 346, 397
Iraq, 18, 71, 135–140, 147–150, 152, 214, 215, 218–227, 229–231, 234, 239, 241–246, 249–251, 258, 285–301, 303–305, 310–313, 316, 317, 323, 326–331, 334–351, 359–370, 372, 373, 375–385, 387–397, 426. *See also* Iraq War
Basrah Children's Hospital, 343, 347, 367–369, 371, 372, 375, 378–382, 384, 387–392, 394, 395
democracy in, 215, 219, 234, 239, 241, 242, 244, 245, 250, 285, 286, 290, 292, 293, 300, 303, 304, 310, 323, 326–328, 334, 339, 364
government of, 231, 243, 286, 293, 296, 297, 328, 379, 389, 394
public health in, 348
rebuilding of, 241, 242
Iraq/Afghanistan Supplemental Appropriation Bill, 372
Iraq Coordination Group (ICG), 344, 347, 348

Rice, Condoleezza and, 344, 347
Iraqi Interim Government, 296, 297
Iraqi Ministry of Health (MOH), 379,
　381, 384, 387, 391, 394
　Basrah Children's Hospital and,
　　379, 381, 384, 394
　Project HOPE and, 380, 381, 384,
　　391, 394
Iraq Survey Group (ISG), 287, 289,
　300
　Bush, George W. and, 287
　Cheney, Dick and, 289
　Hussein, Saddam and, 287, 289
　Kay, David and, 287, 289
　weapons of mass destruction and,
　　287, 289
Iraq War, 218, 219, 221, 223, 299,
　305, 335, 336, 340, 342, 375
　Abu Ghraib, 258
　American invasion, 389
　Bush, George W., 218, 287
　Cheney, Dick, 221
　democracy promotion, 239,
　　241–246
　Hussein, Saddam, 135, 221
　neocons, 216, 218, 220, 299
　rebuilding, 241
　weapons of mass destruction, 218,
　　219, 221
Ishaq Khan, Ghulam, 120, 121, 123
　Bhutto, Benazir and, 120–123, 125
　Pakistan and, 120, 121, 125
Islam, 6, 7, 114, 115, 127, 128,
　172, 187, 206, 211, 215, 230,
　231, 241, 249, 258, 266, 326,
　329, 330, 340, 412, 417, 418,
　426. *See also* American Muslims,
　Assimilation of Muslims, Muslims
　in India
　Bismillah and, 6
　burqas and, 12
　Eid and, 7
　in Pakistan, 16, 58, 69, 70, 114,
　　115, 120, 121, 123, 125–127,
　　160, 172, 258, 266
　politicization of, 427
　Shariah and, 127
　Shia and, 123
　Sunni and, 293, 298, 363
　Wahhabi and, 114, 115, 271
　in the West, 231, 326
Islamabad, 54, 55, 69, 73, 94,
　120, 121, 127, 160, 161, 164,
　171, 173, 193, 194, 255, 260,
　262, 264–267, 270, 274, 275,
　280, 282, 408, 425. *See also*
　Government of Pakistan (GOP)
　New Delhi and, 161, 255
　Washington D.C., 94, 161, 255,
　　260, 262, 265, 270
Islamia College, 16
Ismail, Razali, 139
Isolationism, 159
Israel-Lebanon Relations, 388
Israel-Palestine Relations
　Hamas and, 326
　two state solution, 340
Ittar, 4

J
Jalal, Massaouda, 245
Jerusalem, 7, 346, 412–415
　Johns Hopkins trip to, 412
　religion in, 414
Jinnah, Mohammad Ali, 194
Johns Hopkins School of Advanced
　International Studies (SAIS), 191
Jordan, 18, 165, 167, 381, 382, 390,
　391, 414–416
　Basrah Children's Hospital and,
　　381, 390
　bridges in, 415
Junejo, Muhammad Khan, 112

Pakistan and, 97, 113
Reagan, Ronald and, 97, 98, 113, 114
Zia-al-Huq, Muhammad and, 115

K
Kabul, 55, 118, 126, 127, 207, 209, 249, 258
  Hekmatyar, Gulbuddin and, 126
  Taliban in, 126, 127, 207, 258
Karachi, 17, 20, 21, 31, 33–35, 37, 47, 53, 55, 70, 266
Kargil War, 198
Karzai, Hamid, 128, 270
Kashmir, 8, 58, 123–125, 161, 164, 166, 193, 195, 196, 261, 279, 424, 425, 429
  India in, 8, 59, 124–126, 164, 166, 193, 195, 425
  Pakistan in, 8, 58, 123, 125, 126, 164, 193, 195, 261, 424, 425
Kaul, Ambassador P.K., 167
Kay, David, 287, 289
Kemp, Geoffrey, 80, 90
Khalilzad, Zalmay, 132, 209
Khan, Abdul Jabbar, 72
Khan, Ayub, 35, 36, 55, 58
Khan, Khan Abdul Ghaffar, 72
Khan, Sardar Bahadur, 29, 72, 73
Khodai Khidmatgar, 72
Khyber Mail, 20
Khyber Pass, 14, 16, 19
King Hussein Bridge, 414–416
King Saud, 18
Kuwait, 126, 135–140, 147–150, 152, 214, 219, 223, 294, 359, 365, 390, 392, 393, 396
  Basrah Children's Hospital, 390, 391
  expulsion of Iraq from, 152
  Hussein, Saddam, 126, 135, 137, 148, 149, 219, 223, 365

Iraq invasion of, 135–137, 139
  oil resources and, 148
  Kuwait Ambassador Fundraiser, 392
Kuzai, Raja Habib, 245

L
Lahore, 8, 20, 53–56, 58, 168, 282
Laurent, Prime Minister of Canada, 18
Libby, Scooter, 215, 304, 306, 315, 342, 349
  Cheney, Dick and, 315
  National Security Advisor and, 349
Little Lulu Comics, 419
London, 5, 24, 27, 28, 30, 32, 41, 53, 70, 82, 128, 192, 211, 230, 328, 365, 412, 414, 415, 427
  Cambridge University and, 3, 16
  Oxford University and, 82
Los Angeles Times, 379, 385

M
Manhattan, 24, 26, 82, 133, 137, 146, 159, 401
Marriage to Raza, 33, 52, 65
McCormack, Sean, 269, 389, 392
McFarlane, Robert, 342
Mecca, 7, 124, 171, 412, 417, 418
  Islam and, 7, 171, 412
  Saudi Arabia and, 124, 417
Migration to the US, 105, 403
Moscow, 99, 100, 106, 108, 111, 116, 192. *See also* Soviet Union
  India and, 99, 100, 106, 108, 112
Mubarak, Gamal
  Egypt and, 327, 328
  Mubarak, Hosni and, 326, 330
Mubarak, Hosni, 323–328, 330
  Bush, George W. and, 326–328
  Egypt and, 323–325, 327
  Nour, Ayman and, 323, 324, 327, 328

Rice, Condoleezza and, 323, 328
United States and, 323
Mullahs, 122, 127, 172, 258, 261,
  266–268, 428
  extremism of, 258, 261, 266, 268
  Musharraf, Pervez and, 261, 266
  in Pakistan, 122, 127, 172, 258,
    261, 268, 428
Multinational Force (MNF), 296–299
Murphy, Daniel, 89, 101
Murphy, Richard, 90, 120, 128, 161,
  416
Murree, 12, 13, 16, 59, 94
Muscat, 5, 167, 169, 383
Musharraf, Pervez, 267, 274, 277
  Bhutto, Benazir and, 261, 265,
    269–272, 274
  Bush, George W. and, 209, 253,
    260, 261, 263, 268–271
  Clinton, Bill and, 195
  democracy and, 253, 254, 257, 258,
    261–263, 265, 271
  enlightened moderation and, 260,
    261, 264, 266, 267
  India and, 195, 209, 211, 262, 265,
    271, 282
  Kargil and, 195, 211
  Karzai, Hamid and, 270
  Pakistan and, 195, 208–211, 253,
    254, 256–258, 260, 261,
    264–268, 270–272, 274, 280,
    282
  Powell, Colin and, 259
  Rice, Condoleezza and, 260, 269,
    271, 273
  Sharif, Nawaz and, 265, 270–272,
    274
  United States and, 273
Muslim Brotherhood, 325
Muslim League, 16, 72, 73, 166, 265
  Pakistan and, 16, 73
  partition and, 72
Muslims in India, 424. *See also*
  Partition

Hindu–Muslim relations, 424

N
Nafisi, Azar, 191
Narcotics
  countering of, 373
  Pakistan and, 115, 280
National Assembly, 120, 249, 282. *See
  also* Government of Pakistan
National Endowment for Democracy
  (NED), 239, 244, 251, 323
National Security Advisor (NSA), 88,
  95, 107, 108, 192, 197, 198,
  213–217, 221, 227, 251, 254,
  304, 334, 338, 343, 344, 347,
  349, 351, 361, 367, 376, 379,
  383, 385
  Gregg, Donald and, 88, 101, 216
  Powell, Colin and, 107, 133, 197,
    334
  Rice, Condoleezza and, 197, 198,
    213–216, 221, 249, 254, 338,
    339, 347, 349, 379
Negroponte, John, 381
Nehru, Jawaharlal (Science Gold
  Medal), 11, 71, 91, 100
Neocons, 214, 216, 217, 220,
  234, 241, 286–288, 290, 293,
  299, 300, 313, 315, 333, 334,
  336–338, 344, 348, 351, 363,
  367–369, 377, 382
  Bush, George W. administration,
    234
  Cheney, Dick and, 220, 290, 293,
    299, 333, 334, 337
  hunt for weapons of mass destruc-
    tion, 220
  on National Security Council, 217,
    218, 333, 376
  in the Office of the Vice President,
    290, 299, 313, 315, 338
  United Nations, 214, 220, 234,
    287, 290, 293

448 INDEX

war in Iraq, 214, 290, 299
War on Terror, 315
New York, 24–26, 96, 118, 127, 128,
    133–136, 140, 142, 146, 147,
    149–152, 154, 155, 158, 159,
    165, 191, 192, 203, 211, 221,
    227, 228, 235, 251, 271, 274–
    277, 281, 295, 301, 318, 330,
    341, 342, 371, 373, 376, 397,
    399, 400, 405, 420, 423, 429
    September 11 and, 203
    United Nations in, 133, 135, 136,
        146, 147, 149–151, 154, 158,
        295, 371, 399, 400
New York Times, 127, 128, 155, 227,
    235, 275, 276, 282, 315, 331,
    341, 342, 396
Nixon Doctrine, 159
Nixon, Richard, 138, 159
Nizam, 1, 94
Non-proliferation, 263. *See also*
    Nuclear Weapons
    United States policy on, 125
North Atlantic Treaty Organization
    (NATO), 99, 105, 260
North West Frontier Province, 27, 72
Nour, Ayman, 322–324, 327, 328
    Egypt and, 322–325, 327
    imprisonment of, 328
    Mubarak, Hosni and, 323–325,
        327, 328
    Rice, Condoleezza and, 322, 324,
        325, 327
Nuclear Suppliers Group (NSG), 273
Nuclear Weapons, 79, 83, 85, 94, 102,
    111–113, 123–125, 127, 161,
    241, 263, 288, 289, 426. *See also*
    non-proliferation
    Bhutto, Benazir and, 125, 263
    Hussein, Saddam and, 241, 289
    Iraq program for, 287
    Pakistan program for, 79, 83, 94,
        112, 113, 426

threshold of, 112, 123

O
Oakley, Ambassador Robert, 121
    Bhutto, Benazir and, 121, 122
    Pakistan and, 95, 121, 123
Obama, Barak, 281
Ohio Wesleyan, 24–27, 31, 42, 43,
    46, 52, 406
Oman, 165, 167–169, 216, 382, 383,
    390, 393, 418
    Basrah Children's Hospital and,
        382, 390, 393
    public health in, 383, 393
    United States invasion of Iraq and,
        383
Organization for Security and
    Cooperation in Europe (OSCE),
    247
Othman, Narmeen, 245
Oxford University, 27, 60, 75, 82,
    118, 160, 420

P
Pakistan, 4, 5, 7–9, 11, 12, 14–21,
    23–27, 29–33, 35–38, 43, 49,
    52–56, 58–60, 64, 65, 67, 70–74,
    76, 77, 79, 80, 83–92, 95–100,
    102, 103, 105, 107, 109–129,
    133, 143, 160, 161, 163–169,
    171, 172, 174, 192–197, 201,
    207–213, 216, 224–226, 228,
    253–277, 279–282, 329, 365,
    403–405, 407, 408, 410, 418,
    422–426, 428
    Afghanistan and, 55, 64, 111, 113,
        117
    Afghan-Soviet War and, 84, 126, 209
    democracy in, 119, 121, 193, 253,
        257, 265, 268, 272, 273, 279,
        424

INDEX   449

education, 8, 14, 16, 19, 30, 60, 196, 210, 225
intelligence services in, 117, 122, 264
Islam in, 70, 210, 258
military of, 58, 84, 111, 115, 117, 125, 254, 256, 261, 268, 272, 274
nuclear weapons and, 79, 83, 94, 112, 113
Taliban in, 126, 127, 209, 267, 280, 282. *See also* Government of Pakistan; India–Pakistan relations; US policy in Pakistan
Pakistan Atomic Energy Commission, 32
Pakistan People's Party, 120, 166, 275
Bhutto, Benazir and, 120
Palau, 136, 141–144
Trusteeship Agreement and, 141
United Nations and, 136, 142, 144
Pandit, Vijaya Lakshmi, 71
Partition, 3, 4, 8, 16, 19, 72, 73, 163, 228, 256, 405
government of India, 7
government of Pakistan, 8
Hindu–Muslim divide, 7
move from India to Pakistan, 4. *See also* India–Pakistan Relations
Pathan, 14, 23, 34, 35, 405
Patterson, Anne, 297
Pentagon, 76, 77, 82, 105, 203, 204, 219, 225, 227, 242, 245, 254, 288, 292, 295, 300, 304, 337, 344, 346, 347
September 11, 203. *See also* United States Government
Persian Gulf, 75, 126, 134, 140, 168
Peshawar, 12, 14–17, 19–21, 23–25, 33, 34, 36, 48, 52, 55, 67, 115, 121, 260, 365, 405, 408, 419
education in, 16, 19, 23
move to, 16
Peshawar University, 17, 19, 23
Ph.D., 60, 65, 66, 404, 406. *See also* Graduate Student, University of Pennsylvania
Philadelphia, 41, 43, 47–49, 52, 59, 63–65, 67, 75–77, 80, 81, 131, 134, 155, 165, 169, 172–174, 213, 282, 345, 346, 395, 405–410, 412, 420, 421
move to, 76
universities of, 59
Pickering, Thomas, 129
Bolton, John and, 129, 136
Ismail, Razali and, 139
United Nations and, 129, 136, 140
Pierantozzi, Sandra, 143, 144
Pirzada, Hafeez, 73, 74
Powell, Colin, 107, 133, 197, 214, 259, 288, 316, 322, 334, 428
Bush, George W. and, 197, 248
Gandhi, Rajiv and, 107
Iraq War and, 219, 335
Musharraf, Pervez and, 208
Reagan administration and, 259
Princeton University, 160, 165, 235, 319
Cooperative Monitoring Center and, 165
Woodrow Wilson School and, 160
Project HOPE, 343, 346, 350, 351, 368, 370, 372, 376–382, 384, 385, 388, 391–396
Basrah Children's Hospital and, 343
Bush, Laura and, 350
Howe, John and, 350
Public Health, 348
Basrah Children's Hospital and, 362
in Iraq, 349
issues in, 349
support for, 361
United States Government and, 366

Public Service, 63, 121, 132, 158,
    159, 238, 404, 406
  career in, 63, 121, 404
  government and, 343
  women in, 251
Punjab, 13, 20, 30, 253
  Pathans, 16
Purdah, 15

Q
Qissa Qani Bazar, 12
Quran, 6, 171, 403

R
Rahman, Akhtar Abdur, 114
Ramadan, 6, 7, 206
Rao, Narisimha, 111
Raphel, Arnie, 106
Rawalpindi, 14, 55–57, 85, 208
Reagan, Nancy, 100
Reagan, Ronald, 83, 88, 150, 237,
    251, 255, 324
  administration of, 74, 109, 116
  Berlin Wall Speech and, 238
  Bush, George H.W. and, 98
  Gandhi, Rajiv and, 97, 98, 100
  India and, 98
  Junejo, Muhammad Khan and, 113
  Pakistan and, 87
  Soviet Union and, 97
  Zia-ul-Haq, Muhammad and, 83
Reagan-Gandhi Science and
    Technology Initiative, 108
Red Mosque, 266–268
Religious Extremism, 270, 272
  Inter-Services Intelligence and, 126
  Pakistan and, 270
  partition and, 405
Rice, 197, 198, 201, 207, 213–222,
    225, 227, 230, 231, 233–235,
    242, 245, 249–251, 254, 255,
    259–261, 263, 269, 271, 273,
    275, 276, 281, 282, 286, 290–
    292, 295, 299, 301, 304–306,
    309, 314, 317, 319, 322–327,
    329–331, 333, 334, 337–339,
    341–344, 346–351, 366–372,
    375, 376, 382–385, 388–392,
    394–397, 399–401
  Basrah Children's Hospital and, 343
  Bush, George W. and, 197
  Bush, Laura and, 197
  Cheney, Dick and, 221
  Condoleezza, 197, 207
  democracy promotion and, 213
  Iraq War and, 216
  Nour, Ayman and, 322
  Pakistan and, 197
  September 11 and, 207
  United Nations and, 198
  women's rights and, 317
Riza, Shaha, 234, 245, 292
Roosevelt, Eleanor, 18
Rove, Karl, 206, 227, 238, 335, 348,
    370, 375
  Cheney, Dick and, 239
  War on Terror and, 239
Rubinstein, Alvin Z., 64, 65, 79
Rumsfeld, Donald, 219, 287, 300,
    301, 340
  Cheney, Dick and, 338
  Guantanamo and, 305
  neocons and, 313
  Powell, Colin and, 335

S
Saint Xavier Presentation Convent, 16
Sanchez, General Ricardo, 361, 369
Sandia National Laboratories, 408
Sari, 5, 15, 42, 46, 50
Saudi Arabia, 18, 114, 124, 126, 127,
    172, 207, 216, 271, 276, 321,
    324, 327, 416–418, 426

INDEX   451

North Yemen and, 216, 418
Wahhabi Islam in, 114
Sayeeda, Idris, 15, 173
Schrieffer, Anna, 406
Schrieffer, Robert, 406
Sen, Ronen, 98, 106, 109
Senor, Dan, 335, 336
September 11, 156, 203, 205, 207, 208, 233, 261, 277, 305, 317, 426
    aftermath of, 208
    al Qaeda and, 305
    Bush, George W. and, 207
    terrorism and, 209
    War in Iraq, 234
    War on Terror, 233
Sexual violence, 400, 401
    prevention of, 400, 401. *See also* women's rights
Shariah, 127, 266, 268, 427
Sharif, Nawaz, 120, 126, 265, 270–272, 274
    Bhutto, Benazir and, 126
    Hussein, Saddam and, 126
    Musharraf, Pervez and, 265
Shultz, George, 80, 86, 90, 100, 104, 112, 119
Siachen Glacier, 102, 124
Sicherman, Harvey, 80, 84, 165, 412
Siddiqi, Khurshid, 403
Siddiqi, Raziuddin, 3, 187
Siddiqi, Toufiq, 5, 65, 164, 166, 169, 419, 420, 423
Sikh, 76, 98, 124, 405
    extremism and, 124
    Gandhi, Indira and, 98
Silberberg, Donald, 357
    Basrah Children's Hospital and, 343
    Rice, Condoleezza and, 405
    Project HOPE and, 346, 350, 357
Sind, 38, 49

Singh, Jaswant, 166, 167, 424
Singh, Zail, 92
South Asian Association for Regional Cooperation (SAARC), 425
Soviet-Afghan War
    Afghan Resistance Alliance, 114
    jihad, 114
    mujahideen, 131
    Pakistan involvement, 83
    Soviet invasion, 83, 86, 98, 101, 113
    United States involvement, 153
    withdrawal from, 99, 109, 111, 116, 122
Soviet Union, 71, 75, 88, 97, 102, 107, 109, 116, 135, 137, 149, 152, 163, 238, 338
    collapse of, 163
    Gorbachev, Mikhail and, 116, 149
    See also Indian-Soviet relations; Soviet-Afghan War
    United Nations and, 135–137
    United States relations with, 71
Spain, 71, 221, 224, 389–391, 396, 416, 420
    Basrah Children's Hospital and, 391
    coalition of the willing, 221
    rebuilding Iraq, 241, 242
    relationship with the United States, 389–391
Specter, Arlen, 67, 131
Sri Lanka, 97
Staudenmeier, Colonel William, 75
Strausz-Hupe, Robert, 44
Sukarno, President of Indonesia, 18
Sunni-Shia Relations
    Hussein, Saddam and, 363
    in Iraq, 298
Supercomputer, 102, 108, 255
    India and, 102, 255
Swat, 253

452 INDEX

Switzerland, 37, 38, 41, 199

T
Tahir-Kheli, Alexander, 422
Tahir-Kheli, Kazim, 420, 421
Tahir-Kheli, Raza, 30, 59
Tahir-Kheli, Taisiya, 422
Taliban, 126–128, 207, 209–211,
    241, 258, 262, 270, 272, 274,
    281, 282, 317
  al Qaeda and, 207, 208, 262
  eradication of, 210
  in Afghanistan, 127, 207, 211, 241
  in Kabul, 126, 127, 207
  Pakistan support for, 127
Temple University, 59, 68, 74, 75,
    155, 192
Torture, 258, 294, 305, 308–314,
    318, 319, 338
  See also Abu Ghraib; Guantanamo;
    Human rights
  Hussein, Saddam and, 305
  presidential statement against, 309,
    312
  Prisoner of War (POW), 316
Transnational Authority Law (TAL),
    297

U
United Arab Emirates, 127, 207
United Kingdom, 3, 135
  Cambridge University, 16
  United Nations and, 136
United Nations (UN), 48, 71, 89,
    102, 109, 116, 129–133, 135–
    141, 143–149, 151–153, 155,
    158–160, 165, 173, 197–199,
    201, 207, 213–215, 219–224,
    234, 241, 242, 274, 287–293,
    295–299, 309, 310, 376, 390,
    391, 399–401, 425
  1472, 291
  1483, 291
  1511, 291
  1546, 291
  G-8, 322
  P5, 137
  Reform of, 224
  Sanctions Committee, 149
  UN Iraq-Kuwait Observer Mission
    (UNIKOM), 149
  United National Special
    Commission (UNSCOM), 287
  United Nations Children's Fund
    (UNICEF), 381
  United Nations Commission on
    Human Rights (UNCHR), 200
  United Nations Development
    Program. United Nations
    Educational Scientific and
    Cultural Organization
    (UNESCO), 372
  United Nations General Assembly
    (UNGA), 140
  United Nations Security Council
    Resolutions 1441, 291
  United States relations with, 291
United States Government (USG),
    367, 368, 396
  Advisory Group on Public
    Diplomacy in the Arab and
    Muslim World, 229
  Department of Defense, 250
  Department of State, 79
  National Security Council, 130
  Office of Management and Budget
    (OMB), 347
  Office of the Vice President (OVP),
    242
  Policy Planning Staff, 79

United States Agency for
  International Development
  (USAID), 350
United States Army Corps of
  Engineers (USACE), 387
US Congress, 267
United States-India Science and
  Technology Initiative (STI US),
  108
United States-Israel Relations, 152
  United Nations and, 152
  United States support of, 146
United States Reputation, 258, 303
  Abu Ghraib and, 258
  impact of Iraq War, 135
  Pakistan opinion on, 258
United States' Policy in India, 123,
  160, 161
  Bush, George H.-W., 129
  Gandhi, Rajiv, 97
  normalization of India–Pakistan
    relations, 85
  nuclear agreement with, 273
  Reagan, Ronald *See also*
    Government of India, United
    States government
United States' Policy in Pakistan, 77,
  79, 127
  democracy promotion, 97
  normalization of India–Pakistan
    relations, 84
  nuclear agreement *See also* govern-
    ment of Pakistan
United States government, 79
University of Pennsylvania, 32, 41, 53,
  63, 65, 80, 155, 345, 406, 407,
  410
  doctoral program of, 63
  Van Pelt and, 46
Urdu, 12, 13, 70, 112, 113, 230, 307
  translation of, 113

V
Varma, Shamu, 70
Verveer, Melanne, 401
Veterans of Foreign Wars, 222, 300
Vienna, 31, 288, 399
Vietnam War, 159
Villa Serbelloni Bellagio, 165

W
WahhabI Islam, 114
Wall Street Journal, 251, 311, 376
War in Afghanistan, 112, 115, 254,
  262
  Taliban and, 262
  United States policy and, 115
War on Terror, 206, 212, 215, 223,
  233, 239, 241, 244, 254–256,
  262, 264, 270, 315–318
  Bush, George W. and, 255, 262
  Islam and, 206, 215
  Pakistan and, 256, 262, 264, 270
  response to, 233, 241
Washington D.C., 128, 196, 212,
  227, 251, 274–276, 282, 301,
  318, 319, 330, 331
Washington Post, 85, 95, 96, 275–277,
  305, 311, 318, 330, 375
Waziristan, 28, 253, 262
Weapons of Mass Destruction
  (WMD), 218–222, 229, 234,
  241, 242, 258, 263, 285–293,
  300, 322, 334, 339, 340, 348
  Hussein, Saddam and, 219
  Iraq War and, 219
Weems, Mar Ann, 410, 411
Weinberger, Caspar, 100, 105
  India and, Rajiv Gandhi and, 101
White House, 19, 78, 80, 82, 86–90,
  93, 95, 97, 100–103, 107–113,
  115–117, 120, 123, 129, 132,

136, 147, 149, 150, 157, 158, 160, 163, 165, 192, 194, 196–198, 200, 201, 203–206, 208, 213–229, 231, 239, 241, 242, 244–251, 255–257, 269, 270, 275, 286–291, 293–297, 299, 301, 303, 306, 308, 312–315, 317–319, 324, 326, 330, 331, 333, 335–338, 342, 344, 347–351, 359–361, 364, 367–373, 375, 376, 379, 384, 385, 389, 392, 404, 407, 408, 418, 420, 422, 423
Bush, George W. and, 197, 205, 208, 216, 218, 226, 248, 255, 303, 375
Bush George H.-W. and, 88, 93, 109, 214, 303, 418
events in, 107, 370
Reagan, Ronald and, 150, 255, 324
staff of, 78, 107, 116, 157, 192, 214, 216, 218, 219, 226, 238, 289, 290, 294, 299, 303, 314, 336–338, 350, 368, 369, 372, 392
working in, 107, 120, 160, 226, 336
Whiteside, Ruth, 86, 87, 314
Wiesel, Elie, 247
Wohlstetter, Albert, 86
Wolfowitz, Paul, 79, 80, 82, 86, 191, 197, 234, 245, 292, 294, 304, 314, 343, 347, 351, 382
Basrah Children's Hospital and, 343, 367, 368
Director of Policy Planning and, 79–81, 84, 86
Hopkins, Johns and, 191
neocons and, 234, 344, 363, 367, 368
Women's Empowerment, 171, 399–402

Rice, Condoleezza and, 399, 401, 402
Saundra Day O'Connor and, 399
Women and Justice Program, 317, 399
Women's Rights, 251
clothing and, 46
democracy and, 233, 249–251, 324
in the government, 249
in the work force, 103
World Bank, 234, 245, 292, 322, 357, 382
WW II, 17, 141, 144, 316

Y
Yaqub, Sahabzada, 80
Yemen, 135, 216, 321, 418
relations with Saudi Arabia, 216, 418
United Nations and, 140, 148, 158

Z
Zakat Ordinance, 196
Zardari, Asif Ali, 122, 274, 281
Zawawi, Dr. Omar, 165, 168, 383
Zein, Queen of Jordan, 18
Zia-ul-Haq, Muhammad, 73, 83, 110
Afghan-Soviet War and, 83
Bhutto, Benazir and, 73
Bush, George H.-W. and, 270
death of, 119, 121, 122
Gandhi, Rajiv and, 123
Inter-Services Intelligence and, 114, 115, 122
Junejo, Mohammad Khan and, 115
Pakistan and, 83
Reagan, Ronald and, 83
Zionism, 152, 155

CPSIA information can be obtained
at www.ICGtesting.com
Printed in the USA
LVHW06*1516070518
576146LV00002BA/3/P